TRANSNATIONAL ADMINISTRATIVE RULE-MAKING

In an age of globalisation, many regulatory problems lie beyond the reach of the nation state. Solutions have to be found which extend beyond territorial borders. Normally we would expect international law to be the appropriate forum for addressing these issues, but this assumes formal consensus amongst states, which is difficult to obtain. Therefore, a number of informal structures of pragmatic public governance have emerged as an alternative to formal law-making processes, operating within the transnational space between national and international law. These structures display a great variety—ranging from loose transboundary networks linking national administrative agencies and transnational expert committees, to networks involving administrative staff of international organisations. They work out their own agendas, and in some cases have emancipated themselves from formal national or international parent institutions. These network-like structures have become important building blocks of global governance, addressing today's regulatory issues in a more flexible way. At the same time their informality raises crucial questions of legitimacy.

The present volume shows how transnational administrative governance leads to a paradox: while it performs well in many areas, providing solutions that are not achievable by state and international law, its informality profoundly lacks legitimacy in a strict sense. This book explores, from a socio-legal perspective, a broad range of legitimation mechanisms of different types and quality and shows that there can be a fit between certain forms of legitimation and specific governance constellations. In doing so, the book adds an empirical layer to our understanding of transnational administrative governance.

Transnational Administrative Rule-Making

Performance, Legal Effects, and Legitimacy

Edited by
Olaf Dilling
Martin Herberg
and
Gerd Winter

•HART•
PUBLISHING
OXFORD AND PORTLAND, OREGON
2011

Published in the United Kingdom by Hart Publishing Ltd
16C Worcester Place, Oxford, OX1 2JW
Telephone: +44 (0)1865 517530
Fax: +44 (0)1865 510710
E-mail: mail@hartpub.co.uk
Website: http://www.hartpub.co.uk

Published in North America (US and Canada) by
Hart Publishing
c/o International Specialized Book Services
920 NE 58th Avenue, Suite 300
Portland, OR 97213-3786
USA
Tel: +1 503 287 3093 or toll-free: (1) 800 944 6190
Fax: +1 503 280 8832
E-mail: orders@isbs.com
Website: http://www.isbs.com

British Library Cataloguing in Publication Data
Data Available

ISBN: 978-1-84113-222-8

Typeset by Compuscript Ltd, Shannon
Printed and bound in Great Britain by
Lightning Source UK Ltd

Contents

List of Contributors

DIETER ARNOLD, Dr rer nat, is an expert in consumer health protection. He was director of the Federal Institute for Consumer Health Protection and Veterinary Medicine. He has many years experience in the field of risk analysis in both European and international bodies. He has been involved in the expert committees of the World Health Organisation and Food and Agriculture Organisation and works as an expert for the World Trade Organisation. Presently he serves as consultant assisting in the establishment of a food safety agency in Saudi-Arabia. He published widely on issues of toxicology and the organisation of food safety administration.

OLAF DILLING, Dr iur, is a senior research fellow at the Bremen Collaborative Research Centre on 'Transformations of the State'. He studied philosophy and law in Berlin and Frankfurt (Main). Recent publications include—co-edited with Martin Herberg and Gerd Winter —*Responsible Business—Self-Governance and Law in Transnational Business Transactions* (Oxford, Hart Publishing, 2008) and *Grenzüberschreitende Produktverantwortung—Zum prozeduralen Recht zwischenbetrieblicher Risikobewältigung* (Baden-Baden, Nomos, 2010).

JOYEETA GUPTA, Dr iur, is Professor on Climate Change Policy and Law at the Vrije Universiteit Amsterdam and on Water and Environmental Law and Policy at UNESCO IHE Institute for Water Education. She is editor in chief of International Environmental Agreements: Politics, Law and Economics, and recently co-edited *Mainstreaming Climate Change in Development Cooperation: Theory, Practice and Implications for the European Union* (Cambridge, Cambridge University Press, 2010) with Nicolien van der Grip; and *The Evolution of the Law and Politics of Water* (New York, Springer Verlag, 2009) with Joseph Dellapenna.

MARTIN HERBERG, Dipl Soz, Dr rer pol, is senior research fellow at the Bremen Collaborative Research Centre 597 'Transformations of the State'. Currently, he is preparing his post-doctoral thesis entitled 'Global Governance as Reflective Practice', which combines different case studies in the field of transnational environmental governance. Recent publications include: 'Bringing Professions back in: a Fresh Look on the Dynamics of Institution-Building in (World) Society' in C Joerges and J Falke (eds) *The Social Embeddedness of Transnational Markets* (Oxford, Hart Publishing, 2010 (forthcoming)).

ALEXIA HERWIG, Dr iur, is FWO post-doctoral research fellow at the Centre for Law and Cosmopolitan Values and lecturer in WTO law, both at the University of Antwerp, Belgium. Her research interests include WTO law and risk regulation, the liberalisation of trade in services and the constitutionalisation of international economic governance. Recent publications include 'Whither Science in WTO Dispute Settlement?' (2010) 21 *Leiden Journal of International Law*, 823–46.

BETTINA LANGE, Dr iur, is a University Lecturer in Law and Regulation at the Centre for Socio-Legal Studies, Oxford University. A graduate of Warwick University, UK, she currently works on a research project that examines the invocation of emotion discourses in European Union regulation of transgenic agriculture. Her recent book *Implementing EU Pollution Control: Law and Integration* (Cambridge, Cambridge University Press, 2008) explores from a discourse analytical perspective the contribution of environmental law in action' to EU integration.

ALEXANDRA LINDENTHAL, Dipl-Pol, Dr phil, is a senior research fellow at the Collaborative Research Centre 597 'Transformations of the State' at the University Bremen, Germany. Currently, her research focuses on norm-setting processes of private actors in the transnational sphere. Her PhD thesis about the leadership of the European Union in the international climate change regime was published in 2009 ('Leadership im Klimaschutz. Die Rolle der Europäischen Union in der internationalen Umweltpolitik', Frankfurt am Main, Campus).

KARSTEN NOWROT, Dr iur, is senior lecturer and researcher at the Transnational Economic Law Research Center (TELC) at the Faculty of Law, Economics and Business of the Martin Luther University Halle-Wittenberg, Germany. Among his current research interests are approaches to the dogmatic conceptualisation of governance structures in the international economic system with a particular focus on transnational steering networks. Recent publications include contributions on the Forest Stewardship Council, the Marine Stewardship Council and the Global Reporting Initiative, in C Tietje and A Brouder (eds) *Handbook of Transnational Economic Governance Regimes* (Leiden, Martinus Nijhoff, 2009).

STEFAN OETER, Dr iur, Professor of German and Comparative Public Law and Public International Law. Hamburg-University, Managing Director of the Institute of International Affairs, University of Hamburg Law School; Chairman of the Independent Committee of Experts of the European Charter for Regional or Minority Languages (Council of Europe); Member of the Scientific Advisory Board of the Federal Ministry of Transport; President of the Historical Commission, International Society for Military Law and the Laws of War; Member of the Permanent Court of Arbitration, The Hague. e-mail: stefan.oeter@jura.uni-hamburg.de.

MARIANA PEREIRA finished her MA studies at the University of Bremen, and is now a PhD candidate in the International Graduate Programme (IGP) of the Cluster of Excellence 'The Formation of Normative Orders' at the Goethe Universität Frankfurt am Main. She is a member of the research project on 'The Quest for a "New-Deal": Opposition and the Global Political Order'. Her present research is concerned with the democratisation of global governance and mechanisms of contestation.

JENS STEFFEK, Dr rer pol, is Professor of Transnational Governance at Technische Universität Darmstadt and Principal Investigator in the Cluster of Excellence 'The Formation of Normative Orders', His current research is focused on the legitimacy and accountability of global and European governance. He just published, with Kristina Hahn, an edited book on *Evaluating Transnational NGOs: Legitimacy, Accountability, Representation* (Basingstoke, Palgrave Macmillan, 2010).

CHRISTIAN TIETJE, Dr iur, LLM (Michigan), is Professor of Public Law, European Law and International Economic Law, Director of the Institute for Economic Law and Head of the Transnational Economic Law Research Center (TELC) at the Law School of Martin-Luther-University Halle-Wittenberg, Germany. His main areas of research are international administrative law, EU foreign trade law and international economic law. Recent publication: co-edited with Alan Brouder, *Handbook of Transnational Economic Governance Regimes* (Leiden, Martinus Nijhoff, 2009).

GERD WINTER, Dr iur, Lic rer soc, is Professor of Public Law and the Sociology of Law at the University of Bremen. He codirects the Center for European Environmental Law (FEU) and a section of the Collaborative Research Centre 597 'Transformations of the State' at the same university. His present research is concerned with the global architecture of climate governance. Recent publications include; 'The Climate is No Commodity: Taking Stock of the Emissions Trading System' (2010) 22 *Journal of Environmental Law* 1–25.

Introduction

Exploring Transnational Administrative Rule-Making

OLAF DILLING, MARTIN HERBERG, GERD WINTER

IN THE AGE of globalisation, many regulatory problems lie beyond the reach of the nation state. Therefore, solutions have to be found which extend beyond territorial borders. The appropriate forum for addressing these issues would be international law; but this requires formal consensus amongst states, which is difficult to obtain. A number of informal structures of pragmatic public governance have emerged as an alternative to formal law-making processes, which operate within the transnational space between national and international law. These structures display a great variety—ranging from loose transboundary networks that link national administrative agencies to transnational expert committees and networks involving administrative staff of international organisations. They work out their own agendas and problem-solving strategies, and to a certain extent emancipate themselves from their formal national or international parent institution. These network-like structures have become important building blocks of global governance, addressing today's regulatory issues in a more flexible way. At the same time, however, their informality raises crucial questions of legitimacy.

It is widely recognised that the emergence of such network-like mechanisms poses serious challenges for contemporary socio-legal research. This is evident with the vastly expanding literature on the subject.[1] The challenges arising in this new area can be structured as follows:

— Identifying the emerging phenomena of transnational administrative governance and framing them in proper terms.
— Studying cases empirically in order to understand their structures, procedures and performance, and developing typologies.

[1] A bibliography of Anglo-Saxon publications on global administrative law lists about 150 titles on the topic until 2006 (de Bellis 2006).

— Exploring relationships of formal national or international law to transnational soft law in order to understand how informal rules are made effective and thereby contribute to the exercise of power.
— Assessing the problem-solving capacity and procedural fairness of transnational arrangements to identify different ways of achieving legitimacy.

The present volume aims at contributing to all of these questions. Our overall message is that transnational administrative governance leads to a paradox: on the one hand, it performs well in many areas, providing solutions that are not achievable by state and international law; on the other, the very condition of its success, namely its informality, profoundly lacks legitimation in a strict sense. This notion of legitimation encompasses more than good output, and includes transparent and fair procedures. Alternative legitimation, which may supplement traditional formal international and national chains of legitimation, is one way of solving this paradox.

This book explores a broad range of legitimation mechanisms of different type and quality and shows that there can be a fit between certain forms of legitimation and specific governance constellations. For instance, the political character of many technical problems call for institutional arrangements which allow political judgments and expert opinions to be separated and assigned to different fora. Hereby it is avoided that technical and scientific issues are infiltrated by interests and power games. On the other hand, however, problems that require the settlement of fundamental conflicts of interests and cultural differences may best be handled, if the interests of all parties are effectively represented throughout the process.

To understand the different types of legitimation, it is necessary to explore the structures and the performance of the various transnational arrangements. Examples are taken from selected fields of transnational governance, such as technical standard setting, toxicology, chemicals management and regulation of food additives.

I. DEFINING THE OBJECT OF RESEARCH AND EXCAVATING A DISCRETE STRATA OF GLOBAL NORMS

A large number of definitions have been put forward to describe the phenomena under investigation. A widely used denominator is the term 'transnational'. A broad definition of the term takes credit from Philip Jessup, who defined transnational law as comprising 'all law which regulates actions or events that transcend national frontiers' (Jessup 1956). While this includes formal as well as informal law beyond the state, the informal nature of transnational law is better grasped by Robert Keohane and Joseph Nye who describe the emerging phenomena as 'contacts, coalitions, and interactions across state boundaries that are not controlled by the central foreign policy organs of governments' (Keohane and Nye 1971: 331). It might be added that the difference between these two approaches also corresponds with two different meanings of the Latin prefix *trans*. Whereas the classical 'beyond, over' (as in 'transcendence') is used to denote any regime beyond the state, the medieval 'through' (as in 'transparency') characterises activities that pierce state sovereignty. The second use of the term has the advantage in shedding light on the ubiquity of transnational norms inside the domestic sphere, as well as the erosion of territorial confines. This has also been pointed out in several recent studies (Slaughter 2004; Cassese et al 2008; Kingsbury, Krisch, Stewart 2005), emphasising that the emergence of transnational phenomena blurs the boundaries between the internal affairs and foreign policy.

Nevertheless, transnational private governance may be distinguished from public governance in terms of the predominant actors who take part in the process. While private governance involves mainly business representatives, public governance is mainly carried out by public officials. Overlaps in these spheres lead to a hybrid private/public governance-constellation.

A common question is whether these emerging arrangements can adequately be understood as administrative. Once again, reflection on the Latin origin of terms is illuminating in this respect. *Administrare* can be derived from the Latin word *manus* (hand) (Weinhart 1821: 442), which refers to the practical 'hand-ling' of matters, as in *manum agere* (to act by hand) or management.[2] In modern political and legal discourse, the term has often been used to emphasise the difference between matters of (high) politics, on the one hand, and technical or pragmatic issues, on the other. Thus, 'transnational administration' points to more pragmatic problem-solving mechanisms at the global level. Other than the legal statutes and international treaties as made by political actors and heads of state, these administrative settings are mainly concerned with producing norms and standards of a more technical and issue-specific character.

Taking this into account, the *first goal of this volume* is to prove the heuristic value of the confined and thus discrete conception of transnational administrative governance.

II. VARIETIES OF TRANSNATIONAL ADMINISTRATIVE CONSTELLATIONS

Transnational administrative governance takes many forms. This calls for the development of an adequate typology. Most prominent is the threefold

[2] Some etymologists also derive *administrare* from *minor*, referring to the subordinate character of the executive branch (Skeat 2005).

categorisation of (1) transboundary networks of national agencies emerging more or less spontaneously outside the realm of international organisations, (2) networks of national agencies acting with the symbolic and secretarial assistance of international organisations, and (3) expert and administrative staff implementing the objectives of international organisations (Slaughter 2003; Slaughter 2004). In all of these constellations, network actors can acquire a large amount of discretion and considerable manoeuvring room by emancipating themselves from their parent institutions. In some ways, the typology might be extended to include a fourth category: (4) arrangements in which actors from civil society play a significant role and which often lead to a hybridisation of public and private governance.

However, this typology is still very rough, as it fails to capture the core characteristics and issues concerning transnational administrative arrangements. The literature on this topic is highly productive in terms of developing concepts and evaluations, but often the empirical basis is rather anecdotal (see however Leuze, Martens, and Rusconi 2007; Dingwerth 2007). Only the empirical reconstruction of selected cases can reveal the wide range of issues, organisational structures, procedures, and problem-solving capacity of transnational administrative structures.

Therefore, the *second aim of this volume* is to enrich the empirical knowledge in this area in order to gain an insight into the different types of legitimate governance. A number of case studies are presented in order to learn more about the governance arrangements under research:

— What problems are at stake: can the main regulatory issues be addressed on a scientific basis or do the latter require political negotiation and compromise?
— How are governance systems organised: are there loose networks or dense committee systems? Is there a division of labour or a mixing of functions?
— Who is involved: experts, administrative staff, business representatives, non-governmental organisations (NGOs)?
— What procedures are established: publication and comment, reason-giving, access to information?
— What kind of output is produced: is sufficient consideration given to relevant scientific expertise? Are conflicting interests balanced? Are the relevant problems solved? What level of care for legally protected goods can be achieved?

III. FROM SOFT LAW TO HARD LAW: THE MANIFOLD SOURCES OF PUBLIC AUTHORITY

Although it is often observed that transnational norms enter the internal sphere of states in various ways, this statement deserves a more detailed analysis. Legal statutes may refer to transnational administrative standards in a number of different ways (for seminal examples see Tietje 2001 and Warning 2009). Such analysis can reveal how transnational law is made effective or even binding on administrative as well as private actors. Although from a more formalistic view, transnational actors are not authorised to make legally binding decisions, it is important to note that these rules and norms are still effective in practice. Likewise, the widespread belief is that transnational administrative bodies serve mainly an advisory function to the existing national institutions. In actual fact, however, the norms and rules created by these bodies are rarely critically assessed or revised at the national level. This situation calls for a fresh look on issues of public authority, power and domination (Bogdandy and Goldmann 2008 and Bogdandy, Dann, and Goldmann 2008). Often, the influence exerted by transnational administrative networks is based on additional informal or diffuse sources of authority. These differ significantly from the classical hierarchical model of modern statehood—a phenomenon which also calls for more detailed empirical inquiries.

It is important to note that transnational informal norms not only influence the internal formal law of states, but also the international formal law of state interactions. For instance, informal standards established by bureaucracies or expert networks operating under the umbrella of international organisations may change the agenda as officially defined by the Member States (see Lindenthal and Oeter, in chapters seven and eight respectively). Furthermore, informal standards can obtain a quasi-binding status in the framework of international treaties. The World Trade Organisation (WTO) Agreements on Sanitary and Phytosanitary Measures and on Technical Barriers to Trade are important examples of the latter. Such standards provide a basis for the justification of trade restrictions, and thus impact indirectly on the internal legal order of states (see Herwig, in chapter six).

Apart from developing a typology of governance arrangements, the *third goal of this volume* is to explore how state-based law—on the national and international level—refers to soft law and how transnational norms are thereby strengthened. These interrelations between state-based law and transnational norms take on a variety of forms, including:

- the blanket incorporation of transnational norms without detailed control;
- specific references to individual transnational norms by legal statutes;
- reference to transnational norms in general terms or as legal principles (such as best available techniques, good practice rules of business sectors, etc);
- clauses providing that formal decisions shall be based on (but are not determined by) transnational norms;

— the application of transnational norms as guidance for administrative discretion; and
— the direct application of transnational norms in the transactions of private actors.

While these are examples of a passive reception of transnational norms, national and international law can, as some of our cases show, also actively instigate or support the formation and performance of transnational arrangements.

IV. ELEMENTS AND ORIGINS OF LEGITIMATION

The considerable power-asymmetries implied in the creation and application of transnational norms calls for specific efforts of legitimation (Bogdandy and Goldmann 2008). Rather than postulating normative criteria of legitimation in a deductive way, the challenge is to pay due regard to the regulatory problems and institutional achievements of the transnational sphere.

Continental European authors, especially those from Germany, tend to borrow their criteria from constitutional law. According to this view, transnational administrative governance is only legitimate if it is authorised by the national legal system, and thus formally controlled by the democratic mechanisms of the nation state (see as a comprehensive study Dederer 2004). By contrast, Anglo-American scholars have proposed to apply principles of national administrative law to the transnational sphere. This has been discussed under the new approach of Global Administrative Law, which mainly focuses on rather general and procedural principles such as transparency, participation, impartiality, reason giving and court review (see Stewart 2005, with further references).

In addition to the normative approaches discussed so far, it should be emphasised that in some regards transnational arrangements are phenomena in their own right, and cannot be easily evaluated in terms of state-based concepts. In fact, given the wide range of issues, constellations of interests, organisational settings, working procedures and problem-solving capacities, transnational arrangements may produce their own specific brand of acceptability. Taken from this view, any assessment—although it may be informed by state-based concepts—should take this potential of self-legitimation into account.

State-centred conceptions of legitimacy are formalistic in nature, and thus lack the analytic and reformatory potential with regard to non-hierarchical coordination processes. In the emerging governance networks there are many different types of actors at different policy levels, which runs counter to the hierarchical control structures implied by traditional conceptions of legitimacy (see Kingsbury, Krisch and Stewart 2005). Despite its problematic constitutional status, transnational rule-making is often regarded as inevitable. While transnational governance mechanisms suffer from a rather obvious democracy deficit, their ability to perform does often provide a high degree of output legitimation (as defined by Scharpf 2001: 13). In an age of globalisation and privatisation, states often seek to retain their influence by participating in transnational rule-making, rather than simply resigning to the obstacles of international diplomacy and treaty-making.[3]

Even though performance is an important aspect of legitimation, procedural legitimation is also required, both as a value in itself and as a precondition for broad acceptability in a pluralistic society. To achieve this, more specific criteria should be developed that take account of the diversity of transnational rule-making structures.

The detailed exploration of the norms and practices of transnational governance brings to light a number of characteristics, which can serve as supplementary or even alternative sources and elements of legitimation, as opposed to the classical delegation model of the constitutional state. For example, a deliberative mode of decision-making, as often observable in scientific discourse and expert communities, can considerably increase the quality as well as the acceptability of the results, in particular where this comes with specific duties of reason-giving within a climate of mutual critique (see Cohen and Sabel 2006 and Joerges 2009; see also Herberg in chapter three and Lange, in chapter two). Paradoxically, even a mode of 'muddling through' (Lindblom 1959) can help to tackle the existing regulatory problems, especially if this goes along with a mixture of deliberation, negotiation and experimentalism (see Winter in chapter four). Furthermore, different initiatives from civil society can amount to new forms of democratic governance and participation on the global level (Dingwerth 2009 and Steffek and Gomes-Pereira, in chapter 10). In the long run this may eventually lead to the development of proto-federal and proto-parliamentary representation even in the absence of a world government (see Nowrot, in chapter nine).

In practice, these different modes of legitimation often complement each other in complex arrangements. In the Codex Alimentarius Commission, for example, more technical aspects of risk assessment are often worked out in scientific expert committees and distinguished from value-laden aspects of risk management. These are dealt with in political commissions,

[3] Abram Chayes and Antonia Handler Chayes write that '(i)n today's setting, the only way most states can realize and express their sovereignty is through participation in the various regimes that regulate and order the international system.' (*cf* Chayes and Chayes 1995: 27).

which require participatory elements and a higher degree of transparency (see Arnold and Herwig, in chapters five and six respectively). Nonetheless, while in some cases the different modes of legitimation can be reconciled and combined, they are mutually exclusive in others. For instance, where clear accountability structures still exist, the introduction of additional elements can blur responsibility.

In any case, these new modes of legitimation will not necessarily lead to a sufficient degree of democratic governance, to the protection of substantive human rights and procedural safeguards, which could be an adequate substitute for the existing international and national structures. In particular, the interests of less developed states are under-represented in many transnational networks—maybe even more so than in formal international law, where states can rely on the principle of sovereign equality (see Gupta, in chapter 11). Public participation is often lacking where it should be present (see Steffek and Gomes Pereira, in chapter 10); technical, economic, political and cultural differences are so intricately intertwined that transnational networks have difficulty in providing appropriate structures and procedures (see Winter, in chapter four). Besides, international organisations may be decoupled from the will of the Member States, if their staff become entangled in transnational bureaucracy networks (Lindenthal and Oeter, in chapters seven and eight repectively). As a result, state-related constitutional requirements still have a role to play in ensuring legitimation. For instance, in the *Kadi v Council of the European Union*[4] case, the European Court of Justice indirectly extended its jurisdiction to global norms by using its competence for judicial review of the Community acts, by which these norms were transposed into European law.

The fourth and main purpose of this book is to contribute to an understanding of legitimation as a plurality of possible approaches. This involves a close examination of the genuine innovations of the transnational sphere. Besides, the traditional solutions of state-based law (such as principles of administrative procedure and fundamental rights) should be developed further in order to meet the present demands. Such inquiry reveals that:

- expert discourse often provides suitable legitimation, but may tend to ignore the political or ethical dimension of the issue at stake;
- where it is obvious that political or normative issues are at stake, participatory modes of legitimation may play a more decisive role;
- there may be trade-offs between different modes of legitimation, such as participation and transparency on the one hand and problem-solving capacity on the other;

[4] Case C-402/05 P *Kadi v Council of the European Union* [2008] ECR I-6351.

- new principles must be developed, such as rules on negotiation mandates, inclusion and exclusion of participants, declaration of interest, separation between the determination of facts and evaluation, etc; and
- by accepting only transnational standards that have been developed with respect for certain procedural standards, national law may still retain some indirect influence on transnational rule-making.

V. OUTLINE OF THE CONTRIBUTIONS

This book shall add to the understanding of transnational administrative governance from a socio-legal perspective by addressing questions of legitimation on an empirical basis. Legitimation in the transnational sphere can only be understood and advanced by envisaging a plurality of concepts—a plurality which rests on a broad base of problem constellations, organisational settings, membership, procedures and problem-solving capacity. This plurality shall be shown by a number of case studies and theoretical essays.

The sequence of the contributions to this volume is as follows: after a description of some historical precursors to transnational administration (Tietje in chapter one), different modern types of administrative arrangements will be discussed. The empirical part of the book starts with a specific form of administrative settings, namely, networks, where experts possess a great degree of autonomy, and where the deliberative rationality of the expert discourse is brought to bear in a most favourable way. This becomes visible in initiatives such as the Sevilla process (Lange in chapter two) and the Organisation for Economic Co-operation and Development (OECD) test guidelines (Herberg in chapter three). By contrast, in some administrative arrangements it is hardly possible to settle conflicts on the basis of technical rationality alone. Therefore, different elements of interest representation come into play, as in the case of the Globally Harmonized System for the Classification of Chemicals (Winter in chapter four) and the Codex Alimentarius Commission (Arnold and Herwig in chapters five and six respectively). The next step is a close examination of international organisations. Apparently, administrative staff have the capacity to alter the organisational agenda by adopting public expectations (Lindenthal in chapter seven). Still, it is argued that Member States should retain control over rule-making processes, if these have considerable political implications (Oeter in chapter eight). Finally, arrangements will be addressed, in which actors from civil society play a significant role. In the absence of a world government, these democratic elements can only be of a provisional character, but they may in the future amount to a new model of interest representation on the global level (Nowrot in chapter nine and Steffek and Gomes-Pereira in chapter 10). However, the participation of, mostly Western, civil society actors can also have the consequence that countries of the South are increasingly pushed to the edge (Gupta in chapter 11).

As for the historical dimension, in chapter one, Christian Tietje shows that—contrary to a general perception in the literature on global governance—transnational administrative governance is not at all a new phenomenon. He explains why, under the influence of positivism, the older literature has been forgotten over the decades. To a large extent, such forms of governance had already developed during the nineteenth century, both in the form of enduring administrative unions and through spontaneous meetings and networks. Their importance and appearance in different legal and factual frameworks had already attracted significant attention from socio-legal scholars during the nineteenth century. For instance, the German political scientist and legal scholar Robert von Mohl had suggested that, apart from the approach taken under classical international law, there is a space of day to day administration that is characterised by more flexible transboundary interactions between state administrations. However, such notions, which focused on the question of power and legitimation, were superseded by the emergence of legal positivism in the second half of the nineteenth century which by focussing on formal law disregarded the existence of informal law. It was only almost a century later that transnational administrative governance was rediscovered as a subject for socio-legal inquiry—with this new wave of scholars being unaware of the efforts of their predecessors.

For the early historical stages of administrative standard-setting, Tietje observed that technical expertise plays an essential role in transnational standard-setting. This is even more so the case in the present knowledge-based society. In fact, most Western countries have adopted specialised agencies with scientific experts (such as toxicologists or food chemists) as an integral part of their public administration. These specialised agencies are important driving forces of transboundary administrative cooperation. Accordingly, the book starts by discussing the function of experts as actors of transnational governance.

Bettina Lange's contribution in chapter two draws on a conception of 'legitimacy in action'. She examines the procedures of three transnational networks of environmental governance, as well as the type of legitimacy that is fleshed out in these arrangements. One of these studies is concerned with the Sevilla process, which aims at harmonising best available technology reference standards (BREFs) under the European Community Directive on Integrated Pollution Prevention and Control.[5] Officially,

[5] Directive 2008/1/EC of the European Parliament and of the Council of 15 January 2008, [2008] OJ L24/8.

these standards serve only as recommendations, yet indirectly they have binding effects. This raises the question whether these standards develop a limited degree of self-legitimation. As Lange concludes, the procedures for setting BREFs give rise to a legitimacy that is local, embedded and fragmented. The chapter then analyses whether this link between procedure and legitimacy also applies in the context of two other initiatives: the European Union network for the enforcement of environmental law (IMPEL) and the 'Common Implementation System' under the EU Water Framework Directive (CIS).[6] On the basis of this comparative analysis, Lange shows how a variety of procedures and legitimation modes emerge in the transnational sphere depending upon the given circumstances. This conclusion stands in opposition to formalistic notions of 'legitimacy in the books'.

In chapter three, Martin Herberg addresses expert networks in the field of global chemicals regulation, showing the role that scientific deliberation has in the legitimation process. The paper combines a theoretical discussion with an empirical reconstruction of one single case, namely, the elaboration of the OECD Chemicals Test Guidelines for the Testing of Chemicals. An important feature of expert networks is their self-regulatory capacity: often, cooperation goes hand in hand with the creation of trust-based relationships, which are sustained by self-created rules and procedural standards. In the case under research, Herberg's core observation is that the proceedings inside the network can be characterised by a logic of falsification, ie the rational scrutiny under which proposals for new test methods are discussed and tested. Falsification of this kind ensures procedural legitimacy as long as all relevant experts are allowed to participate. Under such conditions, legitimation can be achieved on the basis of expertise. The success of expert networks can be explained in part by the degree of autonomy, particularly with regard to economic or political interests.

As Lange and Herberg show in their chapters, expert discourses have the potential to protect themselves against external interests, and at the same time make explicit the issues, which cannot be resolved on the basis of the scientific discourse. Thereby, both forms of encroachments can be avoided, namely the technocratic 'colonialisation' of the political sphere, as well as the political infiltration of the expert discourse. However, such self-restraint is not always guaranteed, as will be pointed out in the second section of case studies. In fact, some settings seem to oscillate between different rationalities and incompatible models of legitimation.

[6] Directive 2000/60/EC of the European Parliament and of the Council of 23 October 2000 establishing a framework for Community action in the field of water policy, [2000] OJ L327/1.

This becomes apparent in the case study presented by Gerd Winter, in chapter four, where the expert discourse turns out to be highly politicised. Winter starts by identifying the realm of transnational public administration. He then reconstructs the organisation, proceedings and effects of transnational administrative rule-making with regard to the case, dealing with the elaboration of the Globally Harmonized System of classification and labelling of dangerous substances (GHS). His major finding is that the elaboration of rules in the transnational sphere is a kind of negotiated deliberation—a mixture of discourse, bargaining and power play. In spite of non-discursive elements, the negotiated outcome results in rules of a considerable quality, which have incorporated wholesale into national legal orders without the substantive assessment resulting from parliamentary scrutiny. The indirect power resulting from negotiated deliberation raises the question of whether this transnational arrangement has a capacity for self-legitimation. Winter argues that although the arrangement does display some kind of second level self-control, it still bears shortcomings, which require further constitutionalisation with the help of both national and international law. Appropriate principles have yet to be developed, because the traditional forms of administrative law are hardly suited to provide expediency and legitimation for horizontal transnational structures. The setting could be characterised as one where an acceptable output has been achieved, but where the procedure itself still needs improvement. In short, this second-best output legitimation is still in need of better input legitimation.

This section is complemented by Dieter Arnold and Alexia Herwig, in chapters five and six respectively, who examine the work of the Codex Alimentarius Commission (CAC). The CAC has functioned as the principal organ of the Joint Food and Agriculture Organisation of the United Nations (FAO)/World Health Organization (WHO) Programme on Food Standards for the past 45 years. While Arnold describes the organisation and working procedures of the CAC system, Herwig assesses it in terms of its powers and legitimation. Both authors see legitimation emerging from the separation of scientific risk assessment and the political weighting of risk management options. While Arnold affirms the rationality of this approach, Herwig concludes that serious flaws still remain in this legitimation process.

Dieter Arnold describes the statutes and rules of procedure in the area of international food legislation, which have regularly been updated and adapted to new situations. Within this sphere, codex standards are known as 'gold standards' under the WTO agreements. Where health and safety matters are concerned, the elaboration of standards is based on a risk analysis paradigm, which is supported by sound science and other legitimating factors. This requires communication between experts working in the field of risk assessment and risk managers. Many health and safety standards are primarily based on scientific and technical considerations. Risk assessment is functionally separated from management issues. Nevertheless, expert bodies are sometimes given policy instruction on risk assessment by competent managers. Arnold concludes that such arrangements produce procedures which are favourable to consensus building. However, the standard-setting process itself is still relatively slow.

Alexia Herwig builds on Arnold's account of the CAC system. She analyses how the WTO Agreements on Sanitary and Phytosanitary Measures (SPS) and on Technical Barriers to Trade (TBT) refer to standards resulting from the CAC process. Hereby transnational soft law becomes a special brand of hard law, which restricts state sovereignty. This exertion of public authority through CAC standards raises the question of legitimation. Herwig assesses the organisational and procedural design of the CAC in terms of the criteria developed under the Global Administrative Law approach, which includes concepts of legality, due process and rationality. She concludes that, stripped of their domestic context, most administrative law principles display specific shortcomings at the global level. In particular, these concepts fall short of providing procedures for more effective third world participation and addressing environmental concerns in addition to human health issues. According to Herwig, this problem cannot be cured simply by combining a number of different modes of legitimation. In a nutshell, the CAC system might be characterised as legitimation through the institutional separation of science and politics. However, this approach has fundamental shortcomings in terms of participation and substantive scope.

As the case studies in the first sections of the book demonstrate, transnational administrative actors possess considerable scope of action and thus cannot be adequately described along the lines of a 'command and control' model. This finding is also highly consequential regarding the debate on international organisations and their status in the global governance architecture. Since the administrative staff have the capacity to alter the original agenda incrementally, international organisations can develop their own institutional dynamisms. Accordingly, specific additional sources of legitimation seem to be necessary as a supplement to the official legitimation on the basis of traditional international law.

In chapter seven, Alexandra Lindenthal studies the integration of environmental concerns into the World Bank's decision-making process and thereby contributes a notable case study for analysing the relationship between the international and national level. She shows that the World Bank's administrative bodies have detached themselves from Member State control. Drawing on the political science concept of principal-agent and sociological approaches of organisational behaviour, she discusses a number of theoretical perspectives, which explain her findings. The principal-agent concept corresponds with the classical model of legitimation as known from International Law. The chain of political accountability can be extended to cover relationships between states and international organisations. While Lindenthal observes that international bureaucracies possess enormous room for manoeuvre, she insists that international organisations must remain accountable to the Member States.

In contrast to Lindenthal's focus on international bureaucracies, in chapter eight Stefan Oeter deals with informal networks guided by international organisations. His chapter looks at how international organisations develop informal settings and procedures to create rule-making systems that produce quicker results, are more efficient at problem-solving, and are more flexible and adaptable to changing circumstances than formal treaty and rule-making. Although the rules resulting from such informal procedures are usually not legally binding, this 'soft law' is nevertheless applied in practice because the actors who generate these rules are often identical to those who use the rules in administrative adjudication on the national level. However, there is a price to be paid for such flexibility: if public rule-making completely dissociates from traditional treaty-making with its formalised parliamentary processes, these arrangements fail to guarantee a degree of public discourse and lack democratic legitimacy—rendering the rule-making process a rather technocratic affair. In highly technical fields, this may make sense. However, Oeter warns that there is a need to intensively police the boundary between the kinds of rule-making that might be sensibly conducted in a 'transnational' way, and rule-making processes interspersed with political issues which require public scrutiny and parliamentary discourse.

Despite the various procedural safeguards found in the discussed arrangements, the danger remains that the decisions are taken one-sidedly based on particularistic interests—be it societal interests or the collective selfishness of the experts themselves. An important corrective against such tendencies are elements of civil-society participation or even attempts at equal representation in transnational governance arrangements. In fact, in many cases various forms of dialogue and public hearings have been installed. Since this is often of a rather ritualistic character, it seems advisable to explore stronger and more reliable forms of participation and interest representation, which shall be accomplished in the subsequent section of the book. In this context, it is also important to consider power asymmetries between social groups as well as between countries of the North and of the South.

In chapter nine, Karsten Nowrot studies state-like institutions as a blue-print for the legitimation of transnational administrative networks. Summarising a number of representative cases, he points to the emergence of proto-federalist structures of transnational administrative governance, as well as proto-parliamentary representation. He argues that transferring features of this kind from the domestic sphere to the transnational realm is not simply a matter of institutional mimicry, but instead constitute a search for more effective decision-making processes within governance networks and a way to increase output legitimacy. Through the mutual reinforcement of effectiveness and legitimacy, the problem-solving capacity of these networks can ultimately be improved. This mirrors the rationale underlying the emergence of regionalised and representative institutional structures in larger and more formalised regimes. From a constitutional law perspective, Nowrot's findings reveal that the notion of open statehood (*'offene Staatlichkeit'*) can also serve as a normative 'guiding vision' for the emergence of a model of the 'open administrative network'. While this notion was originally applied with respect to international regimes, it may also serve as a paradigm for describing transgovernmental relations.

Jens Steffek and Mariana Gomes Pereira address the problem in chapter 10 of legitimation in terms of civil society participation. Their chapter discusses four variables, which call into question the democratic quality of transnational networks: the composition of networks, their mode of operation, their accountability to the wider public, and the possibility of contesting their choices and decisions. The network composition determines whose voices are heard and whose interests should be taken into account. Problems in this respect concern the exclusion of relevant societal groups, and asymmetries in power, resources, or information among participants. With regard to the mode of operation of networks, it is often insinuated that networks are prone to deliberation rather than bargaining, and to cooperative problem-solving rather than adversarial polarisation. This is desirable from a normative point of view; however, the authors see little empirical evidence to support this supposed advantage of transnational governance networks. Yet there is hope that with appropriate institutional engineering, specifically the empowerment of marginalised groups, network governance might approach reasonable standards of inclusiveness and deliberation. Nevertheless, even if networks are inclusive and allow for adequate deliberation, Steffek and Gomes Pereira argue that they cannot truly qualify as democratic unless they are accountable to the transnational public. In a similar vein, the question of contestation and revision of choices made by networks is a pressing, yet unresolved issue.

The book closes with a chapter by Joyeeta Gupta, who puts transnational administration into the broader context of the North-South divide. She contends that the accountability of the emerging transnational constellations is often rather one-sidedly framed with a view to their Northern constituencies. She forcefully argues that the perspective of developing countries must be taken into account in order to understand how the changing rules of governance produce new inequities. Gupta starts by identifying four features of transnational governance—administrative networks, legal pluralism, multi-level governance, and the merger of public and private governance. The changing 'rules of the game' are not the outcome of negotiations and open discussions between all parties, but the result of non-transparent processes where the most powerful set the tone. While within the classic case of interstate negotiation, developing countries struggle to participate effectively, their limited role in informal networks is even more concerning. Gupta shows how complicated negotiations have become in areas that touch upon a variety of disciplines. Often, multiple meetings are held simultaneously and sometimes even displace decision-making in formal sessions. This has led to the disenfranchisement of developing countries and it demonstrates that participatory and deliberative arrangements do not always lead to a more balanced representation of interests.

VI. CONCLUSION

As many authors have emphasised, in transnational governance arrangements the law tends to become marginalised or even replaced by technical standards and informal administrative settings (Guehenno 2000). At the same time, however, the present situation could also turn out to be an interim stage on a trajectory leading to constellations, where aspects of effectiveness and legitimation are fruitfully combined. As the socio-legal assessment of the cases in this volume shows, new procedures and institutional mechanisms do evolve from administrative practice and expert discourses. Although these procedures and meta-norms are a possible basis of legitimacy, they are rarely taken into account by the legal system.

As for the future developments in this field, there are various options to draw on these institutional achievements: to codify normative expectations towards transnational administrative actors in the form of an international convention might be a viable way. Besides, as authors from the Global Administrative Law approach have pointed out, these meta-norms have become a new strata of norms apart from traditional international law on a customary basis. Furthermore, nation states and regions such as the European Union could formulate principles of their constitutional law requiring fair procedures and minimum substantial quality that neither deny nor glorify but acknowledge and mould the potential of legitimation in the transnational sphere (see Winter in chapter four).

Irrespective of the specific form of juridification, there remains a considerable need for empirical socio-legal research. In the absence of a one-size-fits-all solution, the field is characterised by a huge variety of institutional structures, which correspond to the broad spectrum of regulatory problems, interest constellations and cultural backgrounds.

According to this state of affairs, a style of investigation seems to be appropriate, which studies the governance arrangements in action and in a most context-sensitive way—in opposition to a deductive application of predefined criteria, which are often taken from national legal traditions. The context-sensitivity of the approach does not preclude searching for a stock of generally applicable normative criteria, which could successively be developed from further research and could help to differentiate legitimate arrangements from the non-legitimate ones.

In the course of globalisation, the law-making monopoly of the nation state is contested, as numerous sources of quasi-binding norms with their own sources of validity are flourishing beyond state-based law. This results in legal fragmentation and colliding social rationalities. As a remedy, some authors have coined the term 'interlegality' in order to sensitise for a productive interplay between the different normative orders (Amstutz 2005 and Sousa Santos 2002: 437). With regards to the administrative realm, and acknowledging the self-legitimising potential of the transnational sphere, it might be fruitful to apply a model of 'interlegitimacy'. The plurality of elements and models of legitimation does not necessarily lead to instability, ambivalence or unsettled regimes, which suffer under incommensurable components: instead of conflicting with each other, the different models of legitimation may also synergetically interact.

The development of distinctive sets of context-sensitive criteria of legitimation opens up a wide range of possibilities to bring the state—and state-based international law—back in. If endorsement and legal effects of transnational standards will be conditioned on compliance with these criteria, nation states and international organisations could adopt the role of 'interface managers', ensuring the legitimacy and harmonious 'orchestration' (Abbott and Snydal 2009) of transnational administrative rule-making.

REFERENCES

Abbott, KW and Snydal, D (2009) 'Strengthening International Regulation Through Transnational New Governance: Overcoming the Orchestration Deficit' 42 *Vanderbilt Journal of Transnational Law* 501.

Amstutz, M (2005) 'In-Between Worlds: Marleasing and the Emergence of Interlegality in Legal Reasoning' 11 *European Law Journal* 766.

Bernstein, L (2001) 'Private Commercial Law in the Cotton Industry: Creating Cooperation through Rules, Norms and Institutions' 99 *Michigan Law Review* 1724.

Bogdandy, A v and Goldmann, M (2008) 'The Exercise of International Public Authority through National Policy Assessment' 5 *International Organizations Law Review* 241.

Bogdandy A v, Dann, P and Goldmann, M (2008) 'Developing the Publicness of Public International Law: Towards a Legal Framework for Global Governance Activities' 9 *German Law Journal* 1375.

Brunsson N and Jacobsson, B (2000) *A World of Standards* (Oxford, Oxford University Press).

Callies, GP (2009) 'Transnational Civil Regimes: Economic Globalisation and the Evolution of Commercial Law' in V Gessner (ed), *Contractual Certainty in International Trade. Empirical Studies and Theoretical Debates on Institutional Support for Global Economic Exchanges* (Oxford, Hart Publishing) 215–38.

Cassese, S, Carotti, B, Casini, L, Macchia, M, MacDonald, E and Savino, M (eds) (2008) *Global Administrative Law—Cases, Materials, Issues*, 2nd edn www.iilj.org/GAL/documents/GALCasebook2008.pdf.

Chayes, A and Handler Chayes, A (1995) *The New Sovereignty—Compliance with International Regulatory Agreements* (Cambridge, MA, Harvard University Press).

Cohen, J and Sabel, C (2005) 'Global Democracy?' 37 *NYU Journal of International Law and Politics* 763.

Cutler, A (2003) *Private Power and Global Authority: Transnational Merchant Law in the Global Political Economy* (Cambridge, Cambridge University Press).

De Bellis, M (2006) *Global Administrative Law: Bibliographical Resources* www.iilj.org/GAL/documents/GALBibliographyMDeBellisJune2006.pdf.

Dederer, HG (2004) *Korporative Staatsgewalt: Integration privat organisierter Interessen in die Ausübung von Staatsfunktionen; zugleich eine Rekonstruktion der Legitimationsdogmatik* (Tübingen, Mohr Siebeck).

Dezalay, Y and Garth, B (1996) *Dealing in Virtue* (Chicago, University of Chicago Press).

Dilling, O, Herberg, M, and Winter G (eds) (2008) *Responsible Business—Self-Governance and Law in Transnational Economic Transactions* (Oxford, Hart Publishing).

Dingwerth, K (2007) *The New Transnationalism: Transnational Governance and Democratic Legitimacy* (Basingstoke, Palgrave Macmillan).

Gessner, V (ed) (2009) *Contractual Certainty in International Trade. Empirical Studies and Theoretical Debates on Institutional Support for Global Economic Exchanges* (Oxford, Hart Publishing).

Guehenno, J-M (2000) *The End of the Nation State* (Minneapolis, University of Minnesota Press).

Hanschmann, F (2008) ‚Theorie transnationaler Rechtsprozesse' in S Buckel, Christensen, R and Fischer-Lescano, A (eds), *Neue Theorien des Rechts*, 2nd edn (Stuttgart, Lucius und Lucius) 375–99.

Haufler, V (2001) *A Public Role for the Private Sector—Industry Self-Regulation in a Global Economy* (Washington, Carnegy Endowment of International Peace).

Jessup, P (1956) *Transnational Law* (New Haven, Yale University Press).

Joerges, C, Sand, I-J and Teubner, G (eds) (2004) *Transnational Governance and Constitutionalism* (Oxford, Hart Publishing).

Keohane, R and Nye, J (1971) 'Transnational Relations and World Politics'25 *International Organisation* 329.

Kingsbury, B, Krisch, N and Stewart, R (2005) 'The Emergence of Global Administrative Law' 68 *Law and Contemporary Problems* 15.

Leuze, K, Martens, K and Rusconi, A (2007) (eds) *New Arenas of Education Governance—The Impact of International Organisations and Markets on Educational Policymaking* (Houndmills, Palgrave).
Meidinger, E (2008) 'Competitive Supra-Governmental Regulation: How Could It Be Democratic?' 8 *Chicago Journal of International Law* 513.
Renner, M (2009) 'Towards a Hierarchy of Norms in Transnational Law'26 *Journal of International Arbitration* 533.
Santos, B De Sousa (2002) *Towards a New Legal Common Sense: Law, Globalization, and Emancipation* (London, Butterworths).
Scharpf, F (2005) 'Legitimationskonzepte jenseits des Nationalstaats' in Gunnar Folke Schuppert, Ingolf Pernice, and Ulrich Haltern (eds), *Europawissenschaft* (Baden-Baden, Nomos) 705–41.
Skeat, WW (2005) *A Concise Etymological Dictionary of the English Language* (New York, Cosimo).
Slaughter, A-M (2004) *A New World Order* (Princeton, Princeton University Press).
—— (2003) 'Global Government Networks, Global Information Agencies, and Disaggregated Democracy' 24 *Michigan Journal of International Law* 1041.
Stewart, RB (2005) 'US Administrative Law: a Model for Global Administrative Law? 68 *Law & Contemporary Problems* 63–108.
Tietje, C (2001) *Internationalisiertes Verwaltungshandeln* (Berlin, Duncker und Humblot).
Weinhart, L (1821) *Die Verwandtschaft der Sprachen, insbesondere der französischen und deutschen* (Landshut, Philipp Krüll).

Part I

Setting the Stage—Early Origins of Transnationalisation

1

History of Transnational Administrative Networks

CHRISTIAN TIETJE

I. INTRODUCTION

TRANSNATIONAL ADMINISTRATIVE NETWORKS have increasingly become an area of attention for law and political science scholars over the past few years. One of the most significant scholarly works in this field is *A New World Order* by Anne-Marie Slaughter (Slaughter 2004). The central argument of this highly influential book ('[t]he mantra of this book') is 'that the state is not disappearing; it is disaggregating' (Slaughter 2004). In order to support this argument, Professor Slaughter presents a comprehensive study on global governance through complex and far-reaching government networks, among them global administrative (executive) networks.

Reading *A New World Order* and other scholarly studies on global governance and global administrative law (eg Kingsbury, Kirsch and Stewart 2005; Cassese et al 2008)[1] gives one the impression that we are actually dealing with an, at least in large part, entirely new phenomenon. Even the comprehensive study by Professor Slaughter does not provide for an historical analysis in order to assess how *new* government networks actually are. Typically, the only reference of a historical nature is that of the famous article 'Transgovernmental Relations and International Organizations' by Keohane and Nye, published in 1974 (Keohane and Nye 1974). It thus seems that the current debate on global governance structures of public governance networks is, to a certain degree, of a non-historical dimension, for example exclusively focusing on a given phenomenon without inquiring into its historical development and background.

The main proposition of this chapter is that transnational administrative networks are not at all a new phenomenon. On the contrary, important developments in public international law over the last 200 years are closely

[1] For a comprehensive overview, see Global Administrative Law: Bibliographical Resources, www.iilj.org/GAL/documents/GALBibliographyMDeBellisJune2006.pdf.

connected to the emergence of transnational administrative networks, particularly when one notes the developments of the nineteenth century. This, however, does not mean that nothing is new about the current debate. As will become clear in the course of this contribution, legal developments and academic writing in the nineteenth and beginning of the twentieth century were concerned with transnational administrative networks as such, but not with any implications on questions of legitimacy. It was clear at that time that legitimacy of any authority could be exclusively with the sovereign/state.

This chapter is structured as follows—in the first section, a general overview on the historical development of international or transnational cooperation concerning administrative issues is given. This is followed in the second section by an outline of specific forms of cooperation within the framework of so-called administrative unions. Based on these initial sections, the third part of the chapter will broaden the perspective even further by giving an overview on numerous forms of administrative networks of the nineteenth century outside formally institutionalised forums of cooperation. Finally, in the fourth section, it will be analysed how and in which way scholars in the nineteenth century developed early ideas, which are very similar to contemporary concepts of public governance networks. The chapter will then conclude with some brief remarks.

II. GENERAL OVERVIEW ON THE HISTORICAL DEVELOPMENT OF INTERNATIONAL OR TRANSNATIONAL COOPERATION CONCERNING ADMINISTRATIVE ISSUES

The history of modern public international law in the sense of law regulating the coexistence and cooperation of states begins with the Westphalian Peace Treaty (1648) which, for the first time in history, linked state power, people and borders and thus created the state as it is known today.[2] Even though numerous treaties between the sovereign emperors of Europe had been concluded after 1648, occurring in tandem with the increasingly sophisticated techniques of treaty-drafting that emerged in the seventeenth and eighteenth centuries (Ziegler 2007: 186; Grewe 2000: 360), a certain restriction on the content of those treaties must be noted. The vast majority of treaties concluded after 1648 regulated reciprocal, quid pro quo, issues, such as peace, determination of frontiers or transfer of territories. The possibility for non-reciprocal, or in other words, the modern 'law-making' function of treaties[3] was virtually unknown. Treaties stipulating principles or rules on abstract future conduct, as known today, for example, in the

[2] For details see de Zayas 2000: 1465.
[3] For the concept of law-making treaties see Dahm, Delbrück and Wolfrum 2002: 520.

environmental, economic or social field, did not exist.[4] Overall, the period following the Westphalian Peace Treaty can be characterised as a productive time of treaty-making with, however, a limited scope on political issues of a reciprocal nature. In 1758, the German scholar von Ompteda summarised that 'the treaties among nations ... usually concern peace agreements and treaties regulating war and peace' (Ompteda 1758: 58).[5] A similar assessment was made in 1874 by Ernst Meier. After a careful analysis of available treaty collections, he pointed out that the overall majority of treaties up to the end of the eighteenth century concerned military questions in a broad sense (Meier 1874: 583).[6] Public international law of that time was thus law dealing with issues of what contemporary political scientists refer to as 'high politics'. In legal terms, international treaties of that time were, in the words of Wilhelm Grewe in his famous 'Epochs of International Law', 'principally legal transactions, regulating a specific dispute and aiming at performance and counter-performance [...] Treaties with exclusively law-making character, establishing only general abstract norms of future behaviour, were almost unknown' (Grewe 2000: 360).

It is evident that the administration did not play a significant role in such a legal framework. The respective treaties of that time regulated the behaviour of sovereigns in a specific given situation, but did not leave any room for the administration of future behaviour of different branches of government based on abstract norms.

The abovementioned character of early international legal cooperation being exclusively devoted to legal transactions of a 'high politics' nature only changed in the time following the Vienna Congress of 1814/15. This is due to the fact that the Vienna Congress established the so-called 'Concert of Europe' as a 'political equilibrium' which ensured peace and stability in the region for practically the entire period until the First World War.[7] It was mainly due to the long-lasting peace period following the Congress of Vienna that the socio-economic structure of Europe of the nineteenth century developed in a way that had hitherto been unknown, in a period that would later come to be known as 'industrialisation' and 'internationalisation'. The driving forces in this regard have been important technological innovations such as the invention of the mechanical loom in 1769; the steam engine in 1766; new technology for iron in 1784

[4] See the comprehensive analysis from Grewe 2000: 360.

[5] 'Die Verträge der Völker bestehen gewöhnlich in Friedensschlüssen und solchen Tractaten, welche sich auf Krieg und Frieden beziehen.'

[6] 'Noch zu Ende des vorigen Jahrhunderts bezog sich die grosse Mehrzahl der Staatsverträge auf den Abschluss und die Erneuerung von Allianzen, auf Subsidien und Hülfstruppen, auf Durchmärsche, Besatzungen und Einquartierungen, auf die Behandlung von Deserteuren, die Ranzonirung von Gefangenen, endlich auf Waffenstillstände und Frieden.'

[7] For details see Grewe 2000: 429.

and subsequently, in 1855, for steel production. It was due to these and other innovations that the first rail journey was made in England in 1825 and in Germany 10 years later, in 1835. While there had only been 188 km of railway tracks in Europe in 1830, this had grown to 168,983 km by 1880 (Baumgart 1999: 26). A similar development occurred in the area of steam navigation. The European net-tonnage in steamboats expanded from 11,500 in 1821 to five million in 1881 (Baumgart 1999: 29). Over and above this, important developments also occurred in the communication sector after the invention of the Morse Code, the telegraph and the installation of the first transatlantic cable in 1858/1866 (for a comprehensive assessment, see Baumgart 1999: 33). All these technological developments were the basis for a dramatic increase in international trade at that time. The total volume of world trade in 1830 was £407 million, which increased to £3033 million in 1880 (Baumgart 1999: 38). These developments also caused a dramatic growth of the European population from approximately 180 million in 1800 to 225 million in 1830 and 332 million in 1880 (Baumgart 1999: 5).

The sum of the aforementioned socio-economic developments undoubtedly illustrates the intensity of internationalisation in Europe in the nineteenth century.[8] As a result of this, European governments faced new regulatory challenges because of the need to increasingly coordinate cross-border transactions in the areas of, for example, trade, communication and the prevention of diseases and epidemics being spread. It was thus a matter of practical necessity to concentrate on technical-administrative issues as a concern of international legal relations based on treaties stipulating abstract norms of future behaviour. Treaties concerning health, postal, telegraphic and railway communication, extradition, monetary matters, fishing, copyrights and patents, trade and numerous other 'administrative' issues were thus concluded among European and other states in order to fulfil needs of societies being involved more and more in transborder international activities. It is estimated that between 1815 and 1924 about 16,000 treaties were concluded, and approximately 10,000 treaties were in force in 1917.[9] Most of them dealt with technical-administrative issues. Moreover, during this time not only the content of international treaties changed from a political to an administrative character, but also the form in which the treaties were concluded developed. Whereas treaties until 1814/1815 were characterised by long introductory parts emphasising the mutual respect between sovereigns as contracting parties, this tradition as well as the usage of French as the exclusive treaty language in former times was increasingly supplanted during the nineteenth century. Treaties

[8] For historical details see also the contributions in Geyer and Paulmann 2001.
[9] For details, see Tietje 1999: 26.

were now frequently drafted in a pragmatic way without long introductory parts and the use of English as a treaty language became more and more prevalent.[10]

In sum, both the socio-economic development and the changing structure of international treaty law-making in the nineteenth century demonstrate a fundamental shift in public international law. Whereas international law until the Vienna Congress of 1814/1815 constituted law binding upon sovereigns rather than states/nations and their different branches of government (Grewe 2000: 514) and more or less exclusively dealt with issues of 'high politics', in the nineteenth century international law became increasingly concerned with technical-administrative issues, ie low politics, being of interest for the entire society, the people, and also for branches of government rather than exclusively the sovereign. International law also thus became of interest for the administration.

III. THE DEVELOPMENT OF ADMINISTRATIVE UNIONS

Similar to the described developments in international treaty law-making, the nineteenth century is characterised by the emergence of different forms of institutionalised international cooperation, namely within the framework of so-called administrative unions.

The first organisation which approximated to an institutionalised form of cooperation was established with the Rhine-Shipping Octroi of 15 August 1804, which granted its Directorate-General the right to collect shipping fees (Scheuner 1960: 117). The first so-called administrative union—the nineteenth century legal term for what is today known as international organisation[11]—was established in 1831 on the basis of the final document of the Vienna Conference of 1815 with the inauguration of the 'Central Commission for the Rhine-Shipment'. The organisation had significant powers with regard to quasi-legislative and administrative issues concerning the navigation of the river Rhine.[12] A similar administrative union was created for the river Danube with the Peace Treaty of Paris in 1856. The Danube Commission possessed legislative and enforcement competencies that were quite similar to what one would identify with a modern day supranational organisation (Köck and Fischer 1981: 86; Seidl-Hohenveldern 1992: 934). Thus, for the first time in the history of international law, the Danube Commission gave rise to a treaty regime

[10] For details, see Nussbaum 1960: 217.
[11] On the origin of the term 'international organisation', see Potter 1945: 803.
[12] For details see Meißner 2000: 237.

that was authorised by the contracting parties to pursue its own legal life in terms of authoritative legislative and administrative powers.

Moreover, a development in international law towards the creation of an increasing number of international organisations was initiated by the experience with the abovementioned river regimes. Due to the rapid development in the technology and its accompanying new possibilities for cross-border communication, international organisations were created to administer the emerging problems. The International Telegraphic Union (ITU) was established in 1865 which, after several changes in its treaty-based constitution, continues to operate today.[13] The Universal Postal Union (UPU) followed in 1874.[14] International unions not only came into existence in the field of communication, but also in other areas of administrative concern,[15] eg the International Union of Railway Freight Transportation (1893), the International Maritime Committee which have held annual conferences since 1897, the Metric Union (the International Bureau of Weights and Measures) established in 1875 in Paris, the Unions for the Berne and Paris Convention which merged in 1892 and is now known as the World Intellectual Property Organisation (WIPO), the Union for the Publication of Customs Tariffs of 1890 and the Permanent Commission for the Sugar Convention established in 1902.[16]

With regard to the topic of this chapter, it is interesting to see how those administrative unions were structured and what their main functions were. As it is not possible to analyse this with regard to all administrative unions established at that time, a closer look at the ITU will serve as a succinct case-in-point for the purposes of this chapter.[17] The legal setting of the ITU in itself demonstrates its administrative character: the legal basis of the ITU is twofold, the basic act establishing the Union is called Convention; the administrative details of the work of the ITU are laid down in the so-called *règlement*. The structure of the ITU has not changed since its establishment, even though the ITU itself has undergone major reforms since 1865. With regard to the functions of the ITU at the time of its establishment, it is worth recalling that 'it constitutes the first important attempt to arrange for permanent co-operation between sovereign states in administrative matters' (Reinsch 1907: 583). This general description of the functions of the ITU is reflected in the concrete tasks assigned to the

[13] For details on the ITU, see Noll 1995: 1379 and Tegge 1994.

[14] For details on the Universal Postal Union, see Weber 1995: 1235.

[15] For historical aspects on this development, see Bindschedler 1995: 1289 and Weber 1983.

[16] For details see Reinsch 1907: 579. For a detailed empirical assessment on all international organisations established between 1815 and 1964 see Wallace and Singer 1970: 239.

[17] For details on the similar structure and functions of the administrative unions of that time, see Reinsch 1907: 579, 582.

Union at the time of its establishment. In the words of Paul S Reinsch in his important article on 'International Unions and Their Administration' in the first volume of the *American Journal of International Law* of 1907, the *règlement* adopted in 1864

> provides that the various telegraphic administrations shall keep each other informed through the intermediary of the bureau of all changes and improvements of their service and of interruptions in communication. They shall also furnish to the bureau all statistical account of the international telegraphic services' (Reinsch 1907: 585).

This description of the main functions of the ITU may be applied to most of the administrative unions of the nineteenth century. Their primary task was to collect and distribute information provided for by the national administrations of the Member States. The unions thus served as an intermediary for national administrations; they provided, using more contemporary terminology, the institutional framework for international administrative networks. However, certain administrative unions were even empowered with the right to control Member States' actions and with, limited, legislative powers.[18]

Thus, two main functions characterise administrative unions of the nineteenth century—first, providing an international forum for the cooperation of national administrations being responsible for specific social and governmental needs and, second, pursuing certain autonomous tasks in the interest of the Member States. It is obvious that these functions and tasks of international administrative unions as new actors in the international system provoked the question of their legal status under public international law. The predominant legal view of that time was that only states are subjects of international law. The recognition of the independent legal status of international organisations only became accepted in academic writing in the 1920s and in state practice only with the advisory opinion of the International Court of Justice (ICJ) in the case *Reparation for Injuries Suffered in the Service of the United Nations* in 1949. Up until that point, international organisations had mostly only been categorised as administrative unions without the benefit of legal personality in public international law. However, as it was already obvious in the nineteenth century that the administrative unions of that time did in fact carry out autonomist functions and practiced decision-making, complicated legal constructions were developed in order to explain their status. The predominant view of that time was that the administrative unions did not have any legal relevance as such, but that only their organs were of interest. The organs of the administrative unions, however, were not considered independent;

[18] For details see Vec 2006: 132.

rather they were merely considered as organs of their constituent Member States. Thus, from a strictly legal point of view, there were always as many organs of a respective administrative union as there were Member States. The problem of this approach is of course obvious—it is necessary to argue that with regard to any decision-making or other expression of a will of the administrative union, a pre-existing decision concerning the respective matter by all Member States individually was necessary.[19]

It was only with the establishment of the League of Nations that a new concept evolved. The League was considered by the majority of scholars to be a confederation and as such, by prevailing legal definition of that time, a subject of law. The other possible option to grant the League independent legal personality without the need to classify it as a confederation was put forward only by a few scholars. This legal opinion was only recognised with the advisory opinion of the ICJ in the *Reparation for Injuries* case of 11 April 1949 (ICJ Reports 1949: 174).

IV. FORMS OF ADMINISTRATIVE NETWORKS IN THE NINETEENTH CENTURY OUTSIDE FORMALLY INSTITUTIONALISED FORUMS OF COOPERATION

The nineteenth century was not only the age of (administrative) treaty law-making and the emergence of administrative unions as new actors in the international system, but also the century of international conferences and congresses. It became increasingly obvious at that time that international cooperation is not and cannot exclusively be a task for diplomats dealing with issues of 'high politics'. Instead, also because of improved means of communication and transportation, national specialists in specific subject areas such as science, technology, health, medicine, religion, arts, literature and sports increasingly met and exchanged views. The number of international conferences and congresses increased dramatically during the nineteenth century and up until the First World War.[20] The increase was evidence of the fact that interaction on the international level was no longer an exclusive domain of diplomats. Paul Reinsch, in his famous book *Public International Unions*, summarised this development in 1911 in the words that while no state possessed 'a monopoly of the best scientific and administrative processes', nations were forced 'to seek opportunities for the interchange of experience such as are afforded by congresses of experts in various fields of public activity' (Reinsch 1911: 14).[21] The administration, of course, played an important part in the increasingly

[19] For details see Fassbender 1986: 17, 19.
[20] For details see Vec 2006: 75.
[21] Quoted after Herren 2001: 121.

complex international interaction of experts. In this regard, it is interesting to see that the Prussian Foreign Ministry was already reorganised in 1810 in a manner that established a separate department for dealing with issues not relating to high politics (Tietje 2001: 119). Moreover, in the second half of the nineteenth century, the increasing practice of international congresses and conferences dealing with administrative rather than political issues caused a long-lasting dispute between the US President and the US Congress. The decisive question of this dispute was whether the President could decide, without congressional approval, to send administrative staff to international congresses and conferences. In his State of the Union Address of December 1882, President Chester A Arthur (1830–86) thus suggested that '[t]he Executive be invested by Congress with discretionary powers to send delegates to such conventions, and that provision be made to defray the expenses incident thereto'.[22]

With regard to international congresses and conferences in the nineteenth century, it is also worth noting that, at least from the perspective of some international lawyers of that time, a distinction had to be made between the two different forms of informal, non-institutionalised international cooperation. They suggested that congresses had more of a political character, whereas conferences were devoted to technical-administrative matters (Vec 2006: 90). Thus, in order to make a distinction between congresses and conferences, it was proposed that the presence of a sovereign was the decisive characteristic of a congress. This distinction, however, was disputed by other authors who argued from a more functional perspective. At the beginning of the twentieth century, it was thus more or less accepted that both conferences and congresses dealt and could deal with technical-administrative matters. The former distinction based on classical ideas of a predominant role of the sovereign in international affairs was thus abolished. The idea of 'technical internationalism' prevailed.[23]

Moreover, by the end of the nineteenth century it also became increasingly evident that there was no possibility for a clear-cut distinction between non-institutionalised international cooperation of the 'private' and the 'public' sector. The factual rather than legal cooperation that took place in the form of international congresses and conferences was rather characterised by what today would be called public-private-partnership. In 1909, Walther Schücking even proposed that historical development showed that 'the private internationalism in all areas eventually leads to official public internationalism'[24] (Schücking 1909: 62).

[22] See the entire debate and the sources Herren 2001: 137.

[23] For details on the development, see Vec 2006: 89 with further references.

[24] 'dass der private Internationalismus sich auf allen Gebieten in den offiziellen staatlichen umzusetzen pflegt'.

In sum, international administrative cooperation in the form of administrative networks started to develop in the nineteenth century, even outside of institutionalised frameworks such as administrative unions. In the nineteenth century, international conferences and congresses dealing with 'public' and 'private' issues became an important factor in international life. In fact, if one took the emergence and growth of administrative unions and the phenomenon of international congresses and conferences together, typical characteristics of global administrative governance as discussed today are clearly present.

V. 'THE INTERNATIONAL COMMUNITY' AND 'INTERNATIONAL ADMINISTRATIVE LAW'

The described developments of an increased importance of transnational administrative networks gained significant attention from legal scholars in the nineteenth and the beginning of the twentieth century. Without going too much into detail, two principally important concepts developed by legal scholars in the nineteenth century shall be mentioned: the concept of the international community as a legal category and the theory of an international administrative law.

The legal notion of an international community has been developed namely by the German scholar and politician Robert von Mohl (1799–1875). Robert von Mohl was inspired by the book *Kritik des Völkerrechts* published in 1847 and written by the then Assistant Professor for Public International Law at the University of Halle, Carl Baron Kaltenborn von Stachau.[25] In his book, Kaltenborn developed a comprehensive concept of the international legal order ('eine internationale Ordnung des Rechts') (Kaltenborn 1847: 261). Robert von Mohl adopted these ideas and published in 1860 a comprehensive analysis on the 'maintenance of the international community as a task of public international law'[26] (Mohl 1860: 579-636). In this contribution, he essentially argued that it is not sufficient to look at public international law exclusively from the perspective of state sovereignty. Instead, von Mohl argues that it is necessary to look at structures that comprehensively fulfil human purposes. Thus, following liberal ideas, he saw states as representatives of individuals and societies. It was thus necessary for him to look at the international cooperation of states from this specific perspective of individuals and society. However, as those interests were much broader than reflected by the then notion of state sovereignty, von Mohl identified several areas of administration and

[25] For details see Tietje 2001: 47; see also Koskenniemi 2001: 24.
[26] 'Die Pflege der internationalen Gemeinschaft als Aufgabe des Völkerrechts'.

administrative law, which a state by itself could not deal with without international cooperation. Robert von Mohl thus presented for the first time ever a comprehensive theory of international cooperation in administrative issues, of an internationalised administrative law.[27]

The idea of an international administrative law was further elaborated upon some years later and comprehensively presented by Lorenz von Stein (1815–90). Even though von Stein did not make explicit reference to Robert von Mohl, his ideas are in line with the earlier writings of von Mohl. Lorenz von Stein, in his article 'Remarks on international administrative law', published in 1882 (Stein 1882: 395–442), followed a functional approach and did not make a differentiation between national and international sources of law. Instead, the only differentiation made by him concerning national and international legal matters is one based on the question of whether the relevant subject matter in question exclusively deals with national issues, or whether it has transnational implications. This approach comes close to the idea of transnational law as formulated by Philip C Jessup in 1956 (Jessup 1956).[28]

Based on his functional approach and also on an empirical study of the international system of his time, von Stein proposed a differentiation between inter-state law ('Staatenrecht') or 'pure' public international law ('reines Völkerrecht') on the one side, and international administrative law on the other. Whereas, in von Stein's concept, 'pure' public international law deals with issues affecting the sovereignty of states, international administrative law is both—international law and national law of states dealing with the daily cross-border interaction of states, societies and individuals. It is, in von Stein's terms, the place where abstract law comes to life (Stein 1882: 439) and includes, for example, alien law, health protection, education, economic law, financial and monetary law, and labour law.

The idea of an international administrative law as a broad area of law covering the different legal and factual cooperation between states and administrations in administrative matters gained significant attention from other scholars in Germany and other countries in the second half of the nineteenth century.[29] Paul S Reinsch, in his article 'International Administrative Law and National Sovereignty', published in the *American Journal of International Law* in 1909, summarised the idea of international administrative law in the following words:

> The body of law which is thus being created by the action of the authoritative organs of public international unions, and by cooperation among governments, is distinguished from general international law in that it not merely regulates

[27] See comprehensively Tietje 2001: 50.
[28] For a comprehensive assessment see Tietje, Brouder and Nowrot 2006.
[29] For details see comprehensively Tietje 2001: 67.

> the relations between national states, but undertakes to establish positive norms for universal action. We may tentatively apply to it the designation of international administrative law, defining it as that body of laws and regulations created by the action of international conferences or commissions which regulates the relations and activities of national and international agencies with respect to those material and intellectual interests which have received an authoritative universal organization (Reinsch 1909: 1, 5).

However, the visionary and, from today's perspective, very modern idea of international administrative law as described by von Stein, Reinsch and others, did not survive. With the ideas of legal positivism that emerged during the second half of the nineteenth century came also the concept of dualism, which is the strict separation between national and international law. Most famous and influential in this regard is the book *Völkerrecht und Landesrecht* ('Public International Law and National Law') by Heinrich Triepel, published in 1899. Based on the concept of dualism, Triepel argued in strong words against any 'international' law, such as international administrative law, that has its roots both in the national and the international legal system. For him there was only public international law dealing exclusively with the coordination of interests of sovereign states on the one hand, and national law dealing with the relationship of the state and individuals on the other. There was obviously no place in this concept for any transnational, in modern terminology, network-oriented character of law and administrative cooperation.[30] It was thus consequent that as a follow-up to Triepels work, 'international administrative law' was exclusively characterised as the national law of a state dealing with conflict of law and choice of law in national administrative issue.[31] With few exceptions (Menzel 1969: 1–24; Delbrück 1987: 386–403), it took almost a century before the notion of administrative structures in international treaty regimes, international organisations and governance networks witnessed a renaissance among international lawyers.[32]

VI. CONCLUSION

Transnational administrative networks are not at all a new phenomenon. They had already, to a large extent, developed during the nineteenth century. Moreover, their importance and different appearance in different legal and factual frameworks had already attracted intensive attention from legal scholars during the nineteenth century. However, most of these

[30] For details on Triepel's concept see Tietje, 2001: 90.
[31] For details on the development see Tietje, 2001: 94.
[32] See eg Pan, 1997: 503-35; comprehensively Tietje, 2001; Möllers, Voßkuhle, and Walter, 2007; Schmidt-Aßmann, 2006: 315; Classen and Biaggini, 2008: 365, 413.

earlier developments failed to be noted by the international scientific community in the twentieth century. It is thus important and fruitful to have this historical background borne in mind during our current discussion on transnational administrative networks, even though the factual and legal challenges of today are admittedly different to those of the nineteenth century. In this regard it is very interesting to see that questions of legitimacy in the sense of the current academic discussion have not been of any concern for a long time. Legitimacy became only an issue once it became clear that the disaggregated state leads to new authority.

REFERENCES

Baumgart, W (1999) *Europäisches Konzert und nationale Bewegung—Internationale Beziehungen* 1830-78 (Paderborn/München/Wien/Zürich, Schöningh).

Bindschedler, RL (1995) 'International Organizations, General Aspects' in R Bernhardt (ed), *Encyclopedia of Public International Law* (Amsterdam/London, North-Holland) vol 2.

Cassese, S, Carotti, B, Casini, L, Macchia, M, MacDonald, E and Savino, M (eds) (2008) *Global Administrative Law—Cases, Materials, Issues,* 2nd edn www.iilj.org/GAL/documents/GALCasebook2008.pdf.

Classen, CD and Biaggini, G (2008) 'Die Entwicklung eines Internationalen Verwaltungsrechts als Aufgabe der Rechtswissenschaft' 67 *Veröffentlichungen der Vereinigung der Deutschen Staatsrechtslehrer* 365 and 413.

Dahm, G, Delbrück, J and Wolfrum, R (2002) *Völkerrecht,* 2nd edn (Berlin, De Gruyter) vol I/3.

Delbrück, J (1987) 'Internationale und nationale Verwaltung—Inhaltliche und institutionelle Aspekte' in K Jeserich, H Pohl and GC von Unruh (eds), *Deutsche Verwaltungsgeschichte* (Stuttgart, Deutsche Verlags-Anstalt) vol 5.

Fassbender (1986) 'Die Völkerrechtssubjektivität internationaler Organisationen' 37 *Österreichische Zeitschrift für Öffentliches Recht und Völkerrecht* 17.

Geyer, MH and Paulmann, J (eds) (2001) *The Mechanics of Internationalism—Culture, Society from the 1840s to the First World War* (Oxford, Oxford University Press).

Global Administrative Law: Bibliographical Resources www.iilj.org/GAL/documents/GALBibliographyMDeBellisJune2006.pdf.

Grewe, WG (2000) *The Epochs of International Law* (Berlin, New York, De Gruyter).

Herren, M (2001) 'Governmental Internationalism and the Beginning of the New World Order in the Late Nineteenth Century' in H Geyer and J Paulmann (eds), *The Mechanics of Internationalism—Culture, Society, and Politics from the 1840s to the First World War* (Oxford, Oxford University Press).

International Court of Justice (ICJ) (1949) Reparation for Injuries Suffered in the Service of the United Nations, Advisory Opinion of 11 April 1949 in *ICJ Reports* 174.

Jessup, PC (1956) *Transnational Law* (New Haven, Elliots Books).

Kaltenborn, C (1847) *Kritik des Völkerrechts* (Leipzig, Mayer).

Köck, H and Fischer, P (1981) *Grundzüge des Rechtes der Internationalen Organisationen* (Eisenstadt, Prugg).

Keohane, RO and Nye, JS (1974) 'Transgovernmental Relations and International Organizations' 27 *World Politics* 39.
Kingsbury, B, Krisch, N and Stewart, R (2005) 'The Emergence of Global Administrative Law' 68 *Law and Contemporary Problems* 15.
Koskenniemi, M (2001) *The Gentle Civilizer of Nations—The Rise and Fall of International Law 1870-1960* (Cambridge, Cambridge University Press).
Meier, E (1874) *Über den Abschluss von Staatsverträgen* (Leipzig, Duncker & Humblot).
Meißner, F (2000) 'Rhine River' in R Bernhardt (ed), *Encyclopedia of Public International Law* (Amsterdam/London, North-Holland) vol 4.
Menzel, (1969) 'Nationale und internationale Verwaltung—Vom Wandel des Verhältnisses zwischen nationaler und internationaler Regelungszuständigkeit' 22 *Die öffentliche Verwaltung* 1.
Möllers, C, Voßkuhle, A and Walter, C (eds) (2007) *Internationales Verwaltungsrecht* (Tübingen, Mohr-Siebeck).
Mohl, R (1860) 'Die Pflege der international Gemeinschaft als Aufgabe des Völkerrechts' in R Mohl (ed), *Staatsrecht, Völkerrecht und Politik* (Tübingen, Laupp).
Noll, A (1995) 'International Telecommunication Union' in R Bernhardt (ed), *Encyclopedia of Public International Law* (Amsterdam/London, North-Holland) vol 2.
Nussbaum, A (1960) *Geschichte des Völkerrechts* (München, Beck).
Ompteda, DHL von (1785) *Literatur des Völkerrechts* (Regensburg, Montag).
Pan, EJ (1997) 'Authoritative Interpretation of Agreements: Developing more Responsive International Administrative Regimes' 38 *Harvard International Law Journal* 503.
Potter, PB (1945) 'Origin of the Term International Organization' 39 *American Journal of International Law* 803.
Reinsch, PS (1907) 'International Unions and their Administration' *American Journal of International Law* 579.
—— (1909) 'International Administrative Law and National Sovereignty' 3 *American Journal of International Law* 1.
—— (1911) *Public International Unions, their Work and Organization: A Study in International Administrative Law* (Boston, World Peace Foundation).
Scheuner, U (1962) 'Rhein' in K Strupp and H-J Schlochauer (eds), *Wörterbuch des Völkerrechts* (Berlin, De Gruyter) vol 3, 2nd edn.
Schmidt-Aßmann, E (2006) 'Die Herausforderung der Verwaltungsrechtswisse nschaft durch die Internationalisierung der Verwaltungsbeziehungen' 45 *Der Staat* 315.
Schücking, W (1909) *Die Organisation der Welt* (Leipzig, Kröner).
Seidl-Hohenveldern, I (1992) 'Danube River' in R Bernhardt (ed), *Encyclopedia of Public International Law* (Amsterdam/London, North-Holland) vol 1.
Slaughter, A (2004) *New World Order* (Princeton and Oxford, Princeton University Press).
Stein, L v (1882) 'Einige Bemerkungen über das internationale Verwaltungsrecht' *Jahrbuch für Gesetzgebung, Verwaltung und Volkswirtschaft im Deutschen Reich* 5.
Tegge, A (1994) *Die Internationale Telekommunikations-Union* (Baden-Baden, Nomos).

Tietje, C (1999) 'The Changing Legal Structure of International Treaties as an Aspect of an Emerging Global Governance Architecture' 42 *German Yearbook of International Law* 26.
—— (2001) *Internationalisiertes Verwaltungshandeln* (Berlin, Duncker & Humblot).
Tietje, C, Brouder, A and Nowrot K (eds) (2006) *Philip C. Jessup's Transnational Law Revisited—On the Occasion of the 50th Anniversary of its Publication* (Halle) www.jura.uni-halle.de/telc/publikationen.html.
Vec, M (2006) *Recht und Normierung in der Industriellen Revolution—Neue Strukturen der Normsetzung in Völkerrecht, staatlicher Gesetzgebung und gesellschaftlicher Selbstnormierung* (Frankfurt aM, Vittorio Klostermann).
Wallace, M and Singer, JD (1970) 'Intergovernmental Organizations in the Global System, 1815-1964' 24 *International Organization* 239.
Weber, A (1983) *Geschichte der internationalen Wirtschaftsorganisationen* (Wiesbaden, F Steiner).
Weber, E (1995) 'Universal Postal Union' in R Bernhardt (ed), *Encyclopedia of Public International Law* (Amsterdam/London, North-Holland) vol 2.
Zayas, A de (2000) 'Westphalia, Peace of 1648' in R Bernhardt (ed), *Encyclopedia of Public International Law* (Amsterdam/London, North-Holland) vol 4.
Ziegler, KH (2007) *Völkerrechtsgeschichte*, 2nd edn (München, CH Beck).

Part II

Emerging Procedures in Expert Committees

2

Procedure and Legitimacy in Environmental Networks

BETTINA LANGE

ABSTRACT

THIS CHAPTER SEEKS to develop an empirical, analytical conception of 'legitimacy in action'. It examines what procedures actually operate in three transnational environmental governance networks and what type of legitimacy they give rise to. The chapter argues that in the transnational governance network under article 17 (2) of the Directive 2008/1/EC of the European Parliament and of the Council of 15 January 2008 concerning integrated pollution prevention and control (the IPPC Directive)[1] procedures are decentred, inductive and unsettled, giving rise to legitimacy that is local, embedded and fragmented because it is specific to the various legitimacy communities associated with the network. The chapter then examines whether specific types of procedures and forms of legitimacy are linked in similar ways in the context of two other transnational governance networks, the EU network for the enforcement of environmental law (IMPEL) and the 'Common Implementation Strategy' (CIS) under Directive 2000/60/EC of the European Parliament and of the Council establishing a framework for the Community action in the field of water policy (the Water Framework Directive (WFD)).[2] In both of these networks, procedures still seem to be evolving and thus unsettled, but in the CIS they are more formalised and thus less decentred and inductive than in the IPPC network. Legitimacy 'in action' is thus less local and embedded here than in the IPPC network.

[1] OJ L 24/8, 29.1.2008.
[2] OJ L 327/1, 22.12.2000.

I. ASKING QUESTIONS ABOUT THE RELATIONSHIP BETWEEN PROCEDURE AND LEGITIMACY

This chapter reflects upon the relationship between legitimacy and procedure in three transnational governance networks. Debates in the literature often start from a normative perspective and conceptualise legitimacy as a pre-given standard with which the exercise of public powers should comply (see, for example, Steffek in chapter 10). How procedures can help to promote the legitimate exercise of public powers is the key question here (see, for example, Oeter and Nowrot in chapters eight and nine respectively). This perspective also draws support from various classical and contemporary social theorists. Procedures are seen here as one answer to legitimacy 'problems'. For instance, for Max Weber, legal domination in the modern state involves the exercise of public powers in accordance with procedures and legal rules. Legal rationality is manifested in the rule of law, which establishes legitimacy for public power. In legal domination, procedures become increasingly rational and can also involve the exercise of public powers through bureaucratic administration. The power that officials wield through public administration is curtailed by impersonal legal rules and procedures, such as the requirement that administrative acts have to be conducted in writing in order to be valid (Bendix 1977: 294). However, according to Weber, this notion of *formal* legal rationality, also found in judicial formalism, must be complemented by *substantive* legal rationality, which encompasses standards of fair and morally right decisions, in order to fully legitimate the exercise of public powers:

> No degree of formalization can entirely eradicate *beliefs* in the legitimacy of the legal order that transcend the actual law and its instrumental values, and no concern with *substantive justice* can entirely subvert the orientation of the legal profession toward the formal properties of the law' (emphasis added, Bendix 1977: 438).

However, not just Max Weber's classical social theory considers procedures as important for achieving legitimacy. The idea of legitimation through procedure is also developed in the contemporary social theory of Niklas Luhmann (Luhmann 1983: 27, 31). In contrast to Max Weber's idea of citizens' *beliefs* in the legitimacy of the exercise of public powers, Luhmann's systems-theoretical perspective suggests that perceptions do not impinge on the acceptance of decisions. Instead, he argues that in modern industrial societies the public administration deals with many complex issues. It becomes therefore impossible for citizens to form individual convictions about the legitimacy and rightness of all of these decisions. Decisions of the public administration are thus accepted in general, outline terms (ibid: 32). Legitimacy is 'the generalized tendency to accept decisions which are still indeterminate as far as their contents is concerned, within a particular margin of tolerance' (ibid: 27). Procedures, such as the right to be heard or the duty of public authorities to give reasons for their decisions, institutionalise the acceptance of decisions and hence dispense with the requirement for any personal, individual acceptance. Procedure helps to manage citizens' expectations and disappointment of those who are disadvantaged by the decisions of the public administration. Procedures also help to reduce conflict in the exercise of public powers and can neutralise opposition to the final decision being taken (ibid: 4). Luhmann moves beyond the classical, liberal perspective in which procedures *restrain* the exercise of public powers and help to determine the 'truth' in relation to the matter under decision (ibid: 23). He suggests that procedures can also facilitate the exercise of public powers by reducing complexity in the decision-making process (ibid: 26). By prefiguring selective steps in decision-making procedures limit uncertainty in the exercise of public powers. They also reduce complexity by programming the premises upon which decisions are made into decision-making (ibid: 243). Moreover, often the outcome of one procedure becomes the starting point for another (ibid: 245). Finally, a straightforward means-purpose, as well as cause and effect relationship between procedure and legitimacy is questioned in Luhmann's analysis since social contexts can also influence whether an administrative decision becomes accepted as legitimate (ibid: 223, 231).

This chapter seeks to further develop an understanding of procedures and how they link to legitimacy in the context of transnational governance networks. It develops a particular perspective. It asks what notion of legitimacy is constructed if particular procedures for exercising public powers are adopted in a specific setting. The chapter argues that decentred, inductive and unsettled procedures frame the exercise of public powers by three EU environmental governance networks, giving rise to a form of legitimacy that is local, fragmented and embedded in the work of the networks themselves. Hence, the chapter's argument is not normative but empirical. It is based on an analysis of how social actors actually construct, in real life, procedures and thus particular meanings of legitimacy. However, the research findings may also contribute to normative debates about the relationship between procedure and legitimacy because empirical analysis can provide conceptual foundations for abstract, normative debates (Black 2008: 1).

The chapter develops its argument through four sections. In the first, I discuss how transnational governance networks transform the exercise of public powers and why they raise particular challenges for the legitimacy of their activities. In the second section, I develop the theoretical framework for this chapter by critically examining some of the assumptions that underpin various contributions to the policy network literature. I argue that a discourse analytical perspective can further develop the idea that the construction of meaning is central to understanding the exercise of public powers through policy networks. The third and main section examines how in practice legitimacy is constructed through the development of procedures by participants in a transnational governance network which produces guidance documents that outline 'best available techniques, standards under the IPPC Directive. The fourth section critically examines this analysis in the context of two other EU environmental governance networks, the 'Common Implementation Strategy' under the Water Framework Directive and the EU Network for the Implementation and Enforcement of Environmental Law (IMPEL).

II. HOW DO TRANSNATIONAL GOVERNANCE NETWORKS TRANSFORM THE EXERCISE OF PUBLIC POWERS?

While transnational governance networks are not an entirely new phenomenon (see Tietje in chapter one), they are increasingly important for deploying public powers (Castells 2000: 338–90). Where public powers are increasingly exercised in new ways, questions about the legitimacy of governance become particularly salient (Haines, Reichman and Scott 2008). Traditional modes of legitimating public power may no longer be applicable or appropriate. National representative democracy and the constitutional as well as the administrative law of liberal Western nation states may no longer provide the main reference point for thinking about legitimacy. Globalisation and regional integration in the EU have limited the significance of nation states[3] and their people in governance (Rhodes 1997: 18). Transnational governance networks project their own constitutional vision of an international order. However, what legitimacy for public policy-making do they provide?

I use the term 'transnational governance network' in order to refer to a specific type of policy network. A transnational governance network draws together public and private actors who are involved in the exercise of public powers across nation state boundaries (Kasim 1994). A policy network is 'a complex of organizations connected to each other by resource dependencies and distinguished from other clusters or complexes by breaks in the structure of resource dependencies' (Benson 1982: 148).

I depart from this definition for the purposes of this chapter by also including policy networks which consist of individual social actors (see also Biermann and Siebenhüner 2007: 27). Policy networks are characterised by

[3] A nation state can be understood as 'a complex set of institutional arrangements for rule, operating through continuous and regulated activities of individuals acting as occupants of offices' (Nordlinger 1981: 9, referred to in Rhodes 1997: 11). Moreover, nation states have a legitimate monopoly of coercive power.

reciprocal, heterarchical relationships between participants which endure over time. In contrast to formal organisations, they involve less systematic rule formation and enforcement. Solutions to problems can be worked out locally, for instance by adapting rules or negotiating new ones directly at the point of interaction (Machado and Burns 1998: 378).

Policy networks capture three new ways in which public powers can be exercised. First, they recognise a new role for nation states in public policy-making and implementation. While transnational governance networks are often seen as an aspect of 'governing or governance without government' (Rhodes 1998: 266; Rosenau 1992: 266), nation states are not becoming obsolete (Bogason and Toonen 1998: 224; Picciotto 1996–97: 1015). In fact, transnational governance networks may even enhance the power of nation states, in particularly where they are composed entirely of state actors and where they can help to address governance problems, such as pollution or foreign relations which nation states by themselves cannot resolve (Slaughter 2000: 232).[4] In the EU, Member States may enhance their power through transnational governance networks, particularly where they assume a pivotal role in constructing and managing the network, for instance by choosing their partners and by determining which issues need co-operation (Kohler-Koch 1996: 197).

Second, policy networks capture new forms of interest intermediation between the state and civil society (Schmitter and Lehmbruch 1979). In the German literature particularly, they are considered as a form of governance which is different from hierarchy and markets (Boerzel 1998: 253). Markets usually involve impersonal and distant forms of organisation and interest intermediation. Economic exchange relationships become co-ordinated through the 'invisible hand' of the market, the abstract laws of demand and supply. Hierarchy steers behaviour through authority relationships and 'command and control' law. In contrast to this, networks rely on high degrees of personal or professional mutual trust and commitment in order to facilitate transactions (Machado and Burns 1998: 362). It is clear that there are overlaps between markets, hierarchy and networks, for instance when economic transactions in markets are governed by commercial producer-supplier chains or when power imbalances in policy networks establish hierarchies. However, interest intermediation through networks is distinct because it is different from pluralist and neo-corporatist relationships between state and

[4] In the EU this point may apply to transnational governance networks such as comitology committees which constitute a delegation of powers of the Member States back to the European Commission in order to implement the details of EU legislation agreed in the Council. The Council, however, delegates this power to the Commission upon the condition that Member States' representatives participate in comitology committees.

civil society (Rhodes 1997: 29).[5] From a pluralist perspective private civil society interests bargain directly and freely, often bilaterally, with, for instance, government departments in the public policy-making process. However, from a policy network perspective relationships between the state and civil society are not necessarily free. Governments may become dependent on private actors outside their hierarchical control because the latter possess financial or informational resources necessary for developing or implementing a public policy (Bogason and Toonen 1998: 224). Moreover, in contrast to pluralist bargaining arrangements, policy networks usually exist over longer periods of time and thus provide a structural framework for ongoing interest intermediation activities. In addition, policy networks capture interest intermediation in a variety of policy fields and thus are not restricted to neo-corporatist intermediations between labour, capital and the state in economic, industrial and employment matters.

Third, policy networks highlight both de- and recentralising tendencies in the exercise of public powers. For some policy networks are an expression of the 'centreless society' (Luhmann 1982: xv, 253–55). Policy communities, a particular type of policy network, proliferate because they assemble specialist expertise and thus can help to develop and implement public policies. They reflect the functional differentiation of contemporary societies into partly autonomous societal sub-systems. However, policy networks can also recentre the exercise of public powers by drawing various public policy actors together who would otherwise be dispersed in disparate policy communities (Dowding 1995: 157; Wilks and Wright 1987). In the EU, transnational governance networks can help to address co-ordination problems caused by attempts to achieve convergence among the public policies of 27 different Member States (Peters 1992: 77). Having outlined various ways in which the exercise of public powers is being transformed through policy networks, the question arises as to what legitimacy challenges are generated by this?

A. What Legitimacy Challenges Arise?

Legitimacy addresses the justification and acceptance of the exercise of public power (DeBurca 1996: 349). More specifically, it is 'a generalized perception or assumption that the actions of an entity are desirable, proper, or appropriate within some socially constructed system of norms, values, beliefs and definitions' (Suchman 1995: 574). Although transnational governance networks do not fit easily into conventional legitimacy

[5] For Rhodes 1997, however, corporatism is a sub-type of policy networks: 'a tight policy community composed of the state and the interest groups representing capital and labour'.

structures, it has been argued that transnational governance networks nevertheless should exercise public powers in a legitimate way. One of the reasons for this is that Western liberal democracies in particular have contributed to the proliferation of such transnational governance networks, for instance in the context of EU and North-American regional integration (Slaughter 2000). However, transnational governance networks raise several legitimacy challenges.

First, transnational governance networks do not usually directly involve EU citizens and hence there is limited democratic control over them (Benz 1995; Scharpf 1993). This is especially the case where the purpose of the network is to provide expert advice, for instance to the European Commission or national implementing agencies. However, it is open to debate whether expertise really detracts from legitimacy. Specialist knowledge provides its own type of justification for decisions that are taken in the course of public policy-making and implementation. Moreover, decisions which are well grounded in expert knowledge and which may therefore be effective may benefit from 'output legitimacy' (Scharpf 2003: 3). In addition, the involvement of economic and professional interests directly affected by a public policy can facilitate its acceptance and thus its successful implementation, again contributing to its 'output legitimacy'. For instance, the article 17 (2) network under the IPPC Directive includes stakeholders most directly affected by its decisions, such as environmental regulatory authorities, regulated industries and, to a limited extent, environmental non-governmental organisations (NGOs). The delegates for these stakeholders represent a significant section of the demos in the decision-making process. However, the link between involvement of stakeholders in a network and successful implementation of a policy is complex and subject to a number of intervening variables. For instance, it is a narrow range of representatives of national public authorities and regulated sectors that are involved in the article 17 (2) network. Research commissioned by the European Commission shows that uptake of the technical guidance produced by the network has been limited. National regulators and industry sectors have disagreed with EU guidance and in several Member States actual conditions imposed in IPPC licences deviate from the emission levels associated with the best available techniques (BAT) in the network's guidance documents (EU Commission 2005). Second, it is more difficult to identify in a network which is a dominant actor and thus controls public policy-making, since transnational governance networks usually involve a large number of participants. Who can and should account for the public policy and render it legitimate (Rhodes 1997: 21)? This becomes even more of an issue where the policy network is only loosely integrated (Heclo 1978: 102). Third, transnational governance networks can render public policy-making simply less visible, not just less transparent, and thus raise legitimacy challenges (Rhodes 1997: 54). This argument applies with particular force in the EU context where networks often have a multi-level governance dimension. EU wide networks usually do not just operate on the EU level, but frequently also involve actors from the Member States, such as civil servants from national ministries, regulatory agencies and national representatives of economic and other civil society interests, as well as regional and local actors, such as devolved administrations and representatives for local government. Such complex webs of influence in policy networks that straddle EU, national, regional and local levels provide for low visibility of actual decision-takers. Distributed responsibility for decisions in a network sits uneasily with a traditional conception of legitimacy which requires that the source of authority is identified first in order to restrain it through procedures and thus confer legitimacy upon it. But how should these legitimacy challenges be addressed? The following section sets out the perspective through which this chapter seeks to address, in particular the role that procedures play in thinking about legitimacy. It critically examines some assumptions of the policy network literature and outlines the contribution of a discourse analytical perspective for understanding relationships between procedure and legitimacy.

III. HOW TO OPEN UP THE 'BLACK BOX' OF POLICY NETWORKS?

There are different lenses through which dynamics of power within networks and their control through procedures can be analysed. Some contributions to the policy network literature consider power as a commodity which social actors and institutions either already possess or seek to obtain and employ for the realisation of their interests. Power is considered to flow from participants' specific resources in policy networks, such as specialist knowledge, information, reputation, as well as legal or financial means (Dowding 1995: 146).[6] This conception of power is, in fact, the reason for the very existence of policy networks. It is because policy actors possess different resources that they come together in a network. For instance, public actors receive information in exchange for private interest groups having the opportunity to influence the content of the policy. However, where public actors retain control over access to policy-making processes and agenda-setting, they may still retain significant influence. In that case the idea that policy networks eradicate distinctions between public and private power may be questioned (Kasim 1994: 23). The idea

[6] In Daugbjerg's terminology (Daugbjerg 1998: 285–86; referring to Smith 1990: 39) the invocation of such resources in a particular situation is an indicator of non-structural power, whereas structural power refers to 'rules, procedures and beliefs supporting the interests of the powerful without the powerful having to decide on every occasion what should be allowed on the agenda'.

of power as a commodity underpins, for instance, accounts which suggest that different networks can be classified according to their internal 'balance of power' which may be uneven because some actors in the network possess more of it than others (van Waarden 1992).

This perspective on power as a commodity is sometimes associated with a second assumption. Members are perceived as rational actors who seek to realise their interests through the network (Dowding 1995: 146). The German policy network literature particularly analyses the role of actors on the basis of rational choice and institutionalist assumptions. Rational actors seek to maximise their preferences within the framework of institutions that provide opportunities and constraints (Mayntz and Scharpf 1995). Individual actors are considered to engage in self-interested opportunistic behaviour and hence the function of institutions is to overcome these dynamics in order to enable collective action (Boerzel 1998: 263). Here, the exercise of power in policy networks becomes visible through competition between individual actors over their specific interests.

However, some contributions to the policy network literature do not share these assumptions. Instead they emphasise the importance of policy *ideas* for understanding public policy-making and implementation in networks (Dowding 1995: 147; Haas 1992). Ernst Haas' (1992) work on epistemic communities[7] suggests that values and ideas are important in shaping how policy networks develop public policies. In fact, shared beliefs and values may generate such a strong sense of community that policy networks become homogeneous. Also, the idea of the advocacy coalition illustrates that public policies are belief systems and result from shared perceptions (Sabatier 1988). From this perspective, public policies developed in transnational governance networks are not the result of power-bargaining between self-interested nation states, but evolve from a much more subtle merging of perceptions and ideas. Hence, in some contributions to the policy network literature the construction of meaning is central for understanding power dynamics and how they may be circumscribed.

This chapter seeks to develop this perspective further through a discourse analytical approach, in particular in relation to the example of the IPPC network. It focuses on the communicative aspects of interactions in policy networks and traces the contribution that language makes to the construction of agency, interests and power. That communication is key to how the technical guidance documents are written by the IPPC network and is also illustrated by the following quote from a former head of the IPPC Bureau, which organises the work of this network. It suggests that through

[7] Epistemic communities are defined as 'a network of professionals with recognised expertise and competence in a particular domain and an authoritative claim to policy relevant knowledge within that domain or issue area' (Haas 1992: 3).

a process of communication, more specifically through particular claims advanced by network members in a discussion process, procedures for writing the technical guidance documents are established. The particular discussion concerned what role the economic viability of techniques should play for determining 'the best available techniques (BAT)':

> He stressed that the detailed assessment of economic viability for determining BAT in a sector was expected to be carried out *in case of apparent conflict by the parties claiming that a technique is too expensive to be BAT*' (emphasis added, official minutes of the 14th IEF meeting).

Here, a claim by a network member that a technique would be 'too expensive', if judged to be controversial, would trigger a wider examination of the economic feasibility of a technique. Analysing processes of communication seems therefore central to understanding what is otherwise a lacuna in some contributions to the policy network literature—the inner dynamics of policy networks seem difficult to grasp because 'Their flexibility and decentralization means that it is very difficult to establish precisely who is acting and when. Influence is subtle and hard to track, important decisions may be made in very informal settings' (Rhodes 1997).

At the core of policy networks seems to be a 'black box'. Interactions between participants are described in terms which invoke intangible, ephemeral aspects of social life. 'Trust', 'we-feeling', 'co-operation' and 'commitment' are referred to in order to capture dynamics at the heart of policy networks (Slaughter 2000: 224; Rhodes 1997: 52; Boerzel 1998: 263; Machado and Burns 1998: 362). Even 'the rules of the game' for policy networks have been considered as fluid (Rhodes 1997: 39). Hence, not just material aspects of the social world, such as institutional frameworks, and the incentives and restraints they create, matter for understanding power dynamics in policy networks, but also less material aspects, such as the construction of meaning in communicative processes.

Discourses are central to the construction of meaning because discourse is 'a complex communicative act, a structure of spoken or written language' (Machado and Burns 1998: 374). In contrast to an interpretivist perspective, discourse analysis starts from the idea that there is no identifiable, real world referent to which language connects to (Gergen 1986: 143). Hence, discourse analysis enables to examine *competition for meaning* as a central aspect of the construction of the social world (Fox and Miller 1995). Moreover, meaning flows not just from statements but from exchanges between participants in a communicative situation in which broader interpretative schemes, world views, contexts and belief systems are also constructed. Discourses establish in Foucault's terms 'regimes of truth' (Foucault 1972: 131). By constructing meaning they also contribute to the production of social order (Machado and Burns 1998: 374). Discourses help to establish common realities and thereby also have the potential to exclude some perspectives while reinforcing others. Discourses construct topics and generate objects of knowledge. They regulate what can and cannot be said about an issue (Hall 2002: 72). An analysis of discourses therefore allows us to trace the 'micro-physics of power' in a policy network (Foucault 1989). Foucault's concept of power refers to discourses and knowledge. Discourses embody historically contingent knowledge about a subject (Hall 2002: 72). Knowledge is also a form of power, but power relationships can also shape what knowledge becomes applied or not (ibid: 76). In addition, from a discourse analytical perspective power is not clearly delineated. It is not a property or resource that social actors possess, but circulates through society. Both the powerless and powerful can be caught up in its circulation (Foucault 1980: 119). Hence, power does not emanate from one place or source (Hall 2002: 77). Consequently, a Foucaultian perspective enables us to understand how power is working in different locations, including 'on the ground' and 'from the bottom-up'. In addition, it does not just regulate social life but is also productive and constitutive. Power produces discourses, knowledge and 'subjects' as agents. The following section, which is based on a qualitative empirical case study,[8] starts to apply this perspective to the transnational governance network set up under article 17 (2) of the IPPC Directive. It traces how power is manifested in, not just restrained by the discursive construction of procedures and what type of legitimacy these procedures generate.

IV. RELATIONSHIPS BETWEEN PROCEDURE AND LEGITIMACY IN THE TRANSNATIONAL GOVERNANCE NETWORK UNDER ARTICLE 17(2) OF THE IPPC DIRECTIVE

A. The Article 17(2) Network

Article 17(2) states:

> The Commission shall organize an exchange of information between Member States and the industries concerned on best available techniques, associated

[8] The case study involved the collection of qualitative empirical data through semi-structured interviews with all eight best available techniques (BAT) reference documents (BREF) writers present in the European IPPC Bureau in 2000. This Bureau co-ordinates, on a day-to-day basis, the output of the transnational governance network. The data was collected in 2000 at the initial phase of the IPPC Bureau which had started its work in 1997. Six more interviews, again with all the BREF writers present at the time, were conducted in April 2008 in order to update the original data and capture the second phase of BREF writing which involved the revision of the original BREF documents. The researcher spent two months in 2000 and one week in 2008 in the European IPPC Bureau. During this time documents relating to the BREF writing process were also collected. For further empirical case material and detailed discussion of interview material, see Lange 2008.

monitoring, and developments in them. Every three years the Commission shall publish the results of the exchanges of information.

Under this article 17(2), the Commission has set up a transnational governance network that produces technical guidance documents, so-called 'best available techniques' (BAT) reference documents (BREFs). These guidance documents advise local permitters about how to define the legal obligation—to employ 'the best available techniques' that operators of a specific range of industrial and intensive agricultural installations have to employ. Environmental regulatory authorities shall take into account these BREF documents, but are not bound by them when licensing individual installations (Annex IV No 12 of the IPPC Directive).

Why is this network one of the three case studies? First, the drafting of the BREF documents represents an important change in the exercise of public powers. Article 18(1) of the IPPC Directive empowers the Commission to put forward a proposal to the Council setting out binding emission limit values for IPPC installations, covering the pollutants identified in Annex III to the Directive. According to article 18(2), the information exchange under article 17(2) can help to identify a need for such emission limit values. In practice, the Directorate General (DG) Environment in the Commission decided right from the beginning of the implementation of the IPPC Directive that it would not propose binding emission limit values. Instead it would only provide specification of the general 'best available techniques' standard[9] through the technical guidance documents written by the transnational governance network (Interview No 9). Hence, the IPPC network's advice to local permitters replaces the exercise of public law powers by the EU through the traditional community method, legislation containing specific environmental standards.[10]

[9] Laid down in art 2 of the IPPC Directive 2008/1.

[10] Moreover, the art 17(2) network is an important case because its format is being extended to other EU environmental policies. It will be applied to the assessment of environmental technologies. This European Environmental Technology Verification system will evaluate the potential of new technologies to achieve pollution control in various industrial sectors. DG Environment also seeks to apply the art 17 (2) network approach to the production of technical guidance relating to best agricultural practices for managing the co-existence of genetically modified, organic and conventional agriculture in the EU. Moreover, there are discussions within the Commission to apply the art 17(2) IPPC network model to the European Environmental Management System (EMAS), set up under Regulation (EC) 761/2001 of the European Parliament and of the Council of 19 March 2001 allowing voluntary participation by organizations in a community eco-management and audit scheme (EMAS—OJ L 114/1, 24.4.2001). Best environmental management practices would be defined by technical guidance documents written by a transnational network. There are also considerations to extend the 'bureau approach' of the art 17 (2) IPPC network to the EU's eco-labelling scheme.

Second, and most importantly, questions about the relationship between procedure and legitimacy will become even more important if the current proposal for a revised IPPC Directive is accepted.[11] The proposed changes will turn the BREF documents into '*the* reference for setting the permit conditions' (new article 15(3)).[12] The documents will also be more central to the definition of the legal obligation to employ BAT because the proposed new article 17(2) requires national permitting authorities to set emission limits 'that do not exceed the emission levels associated with BAT *as described in the BREFs*' (emphasis added). Moreover, BREF documents will also be more important because they will now be the main reference point for defining BAT through generally binding rules. Some Member States[13] have chosen to define BAT in national law through generally binding rules. This reduces discretion for permitters when they define BAT for individual installations. Article 18 of the proposed new IPPC Directive states that standards defined in Member States' generally binding rules must not exceed emission levels associated with BAT that are set out in the BREFs. Hence, the article 17(2) network is a key example of new ways of exercising public powers, here setting EU environmental standards. It also creates specific legitimacy challenges.

B. Legitimacy Challenges for the Article 17(2) Network

Legitimacy matters to the network participants.[14] Various challenges arise. First, technical working groups (TWG) set up in this network can be large and there is thus limited visibility of decision-taking. The TWG for the horizontal[15] BREF on energy efficiency measures for IPPC installations, for instance, comprises 90 members. The information submitted by the TWG is collated and evaluated—in discussion with the

[11] Commission (EC), 'Proposal for a Directive of the European Parliament and of the Council on Industrial Emissions (Integrated Pollution Prevention and Control) (Recast)' COM (07) 843 final, 21 December 2007.

[12] This is slightly modified through a point in the legally non-binding preamble ten to the proposal for a revised IPPC Directive which states that permitting authorities in the Member States can supplement the BREF documents with other sources of technical guidance.

[13] For example Germany through the Technical Instruction Air (TA Luft) and the Water Discharge Regulation (*Abwasserverordnung*).

[14] See, for example, the following statement during one of the network meetings: 'Austria expressed concern over the level of transparency in the future work' (extract from the official minutes of the fourteenth meeting of the Information Exchange Forum (IEF)).

[15] The majority of BREFs are so-called vertical BREFs which provide guidance on what constitute the 'best available techniques' for the specific sectors covered by the IPPC Directive. Horizontal BREFs cover cross-sector issues, such as storage, energy efficiency and cooling.

TWG—by a single person, the writer of the BREF document.[16] Hence, there is limited visibility of decisions in relation to what information is accepted or rejected and what techniques should be considered as BAT. Over the 11 years during which the BREF writing process has evolved, the transparency of information handling, however, has improved. BREF writers now usually construct Excel spreadsheets which log all the comments which are provided on draft BREFs by TWG members. On average about 1967 comments are submitted in relation to the various drafts through which a BREF develops (European IPPC Bureau communication).[17] BREF writers have also enhanced the transparency of the BREF writing process by rating comments for their significance to finding a BAT conclusion and noting reasons in the spreadsheet for the acceptance, partial acceptance or rejection of comments. This spreadsheet is made available to all members of the TWG before the second and final TWG meeting. It mimics an administrative law requirement to give reasons for decisions in order to ensure fairness in public administrative decision-making.

Second, legitimacy challenges arise from the fact that the article 17(2) network often engages in new and complex tasks. Ways of doing the work—or procedures—emerge as new tasks are carried out. Rendering the work legitimate by giving reasons for why it was carried out in a particular way is difficult when the procedures are only gradually developed in the first place.[18] For instance, the costs of a technique for an industrial sector are one criterion, which should be considered when the 'best available techniques' are defined (article 2 number 11 of the IPPC Directive). However, the text of the Directive does not provide a methodology for calculating such costs:

> Of course, data is the problem but also the way of calculating. The assumptions that you put when you are estimating. And also, the final, the comparison. How to compare the costs, associated to a specific measure and the benefit that you have when you introduce that measure. I think that is a mystery, a problem. (extract from Interview No 3).

So, what procedures have been developed for BREF writing and determining BAT?

[16] BREF writers usually work for two to four years in the European IPPC Bureau in order to co-ordinate the writing of the specific BREFs. Most of them are detached national experts who are seconded from environmental permitting work in their Member State. Some are Commission functionaries.

[17] The number of comments for different BREFs ranges from 900 to 7244 per BREF (European IPPC Bureau communication).

[18] Black 2008 defines legitimacy as the acceptance of an organisation and its activities by others, such as the regulated and third parties, and more specifically the reasons that are given for such acceptance.

C. Procedures for Writing BREFs and Determining BAT

While there is a 'General Outline for writing BREFs' and the 'Generic Schedule for Revising BREFs', the detail of *how* BREFs are written usually emerges during the process of actually carrying out the work and through negotiation between the BREF writer and members of the TWGs. Hence, procedures in the context of the article 17(2) network are often not an externally imposed, pre-specified restraint on the activities of the network participants. Instead, they are gradually developed as the activities of the TWGs progress. Developing and, in particular, agreeing on procedures within the TWGs can be even difficult. Hence, procedures governing the work of the IPPC transnational governance network are inductive, unsettled and fragmented. The inductive nature of procedures flows from the fact that normative aspects, 'this is the right way to do this task', become blurred with description, 'this is how the task is actually being carried out'. Context matters for inductively generated procedures. For instance, restraints on time can shape procedure. Significant information relevant to BAT conclusions has to be submitted, not during, but *before* the second and final TWG meeting. Hence, only information that reaches the BREF writer and the TWG 'in time' will be evaluated and discussed by the TWG and thus can form the basis for a BAT conclusion. Also other contextual factors, such as restraints on information, can frame the procedure for writing BREFs. For example, the 'Generic Schedule for the Revision of the BREFs' suggests that a 'wish list' should be established which contains the key points which will be addressed in the updating of the original BREF for a specific sector. According to one BREF writer it is essential to recognise that only those issues can and should be included in the 'wish list' for which information is actually available (Interview No 6). Practical time and information constraints can shape procedures, also because they establish criteria for evaluating BREF writing. As one BREF writer suggested, 'it is better to be 100 per cent accurate and 80 per cent complete, than 100 per cent complete and 80 per cent accurate' (slide from presentation for the final TWG meeting for the Energy Efficiency BREF). Hence, by responding to various contextual factors the procedure for BREF writing is inductively generated. However, the procedure for writing BREFs is not only inductive, it is also decentred.

BREFs are written in many places, not just at the EU level.[19] BREF writing includes national and regional level actors. National working groups have been set up that support the work of Member State and

[19] Sometimes proposals for BAT conclusions from national or regional groups, if accepted by the TWG, are cut and pasted directly into the BREF from the document submitted by these groups.

national industry representatives in the EU TWGs and thereby prepare BREF writing.[20] Hence, proposals for what should be considered as BAT are developed in a number of different locations, and the work in each of these fora is guided by different procedures. There are various procedures, not one central, single, unified procedure for arriving at BAT conclusions. Hence, procedures for BREF writing are decentred. Finally, not only is the procedure for BREF writing decentred it also keeps evolving and is thus unsettled.

The IPPC Directive itself does not spell out a procedure for the exercise of public powers in relation to BREF writing through the transnational governance network under article 17(2). Hence, procedures have evolved over 11 years during the writing of the BREFs. The basic procedural framework for BREF writing, the 'BREF outline and Guide', has been revised five times. In addition to this the procedure for writing BREFs has evolved from the first original round of writing BREFs to the second round of revising and updating the original BREFs. The procedure for updating is shorter than the original procedure for writing BREFs. There is only one plenary TWG meeting after the first TWG kick-off meeting. For writing the first round of BREFs, two full plenary TWG meetings were held. Moreover, not only does this formal external procedural framework for BREF writing keep evolving, but the very question of how BAT should be determined and thus the way in which BREFs are written is frequently raised and reopened in discussions in the TWGs. For instance, some representatives for EU industry associations argued that only broad ranges for emission limits associated with a particular technology should be included in BREF documents. It was up to local permitters to narrow down emission ranges in the individual permit granted to an installation. Moreover, the procedure for writing BREFs is unsettled because there were attempts to open up BAT conclusions through an appeals procedure. Sometimes, TWG members would seek to turn the Information Exchange Forum (IEF) into a forum where BAT conclusions with which they disagreed could be reopened. The official task of the IEF is, however, only to consider complete draft BREFs and to approve them. Having argued that procedures for BREF writing are inductive, unsettled and decentred, the next question that needs to be addressed is how these procedures are discursively constructed.

Various discourses developed during BREF writing provide key arguments about how BREFs should be written. They also signpost specific criteria that should be taken into account when BAT is determined for

[20] For instance, the German Federal Environment Agency (*Umweltbundesamt*) has set up national working groups which collate information and provide recommendations about BAT in order to support the work of the EU TWGs in BREF writing.

an industry sector. They thereby generate procedure for the writing of BREFs. Three main discourses can be identified: a political, technical and economic discourse. There is some overlap between them and specific discursive strategies help to manage overlaps and blurred boundaries between various discourses.

According to a technical discourse, the task of determining BAT is essentially a technical one. It draws on 'objective', 'validated' and 'accurate' information.[21] Differences of view about what constitutes BAT are decided in the TWG through technical discussion among peers and with reference to specialist knowledge. BREF writing is based on 'iterative expert judgement' and BAT determinations in BREFs are achieved by consensus not voting (European IPPC Bureau communication). Time and resource constraints introduce a pragmatic element into a technical discourse, which is distinguished from scientific assessments of BAT that draw on elaborate methodologies.

A technical discourse on BREF writing can be distinguished from a political discourse. The latter recognises the intrusion of 'mere opinions' and interest-based positions into BREF writing. For instance, sometimes Member States seek to preserve their national approach towards pollution control when different interpretations of BAT are discussed.[22] Similarly, Member States in the Information Exchange Group[23] collectively rejected DG Environment's idea that the IMPEL[24] network of environmental regulators in the EU should provide guidance on BAT determinations for national regulators. A political discourse also includes the expression of industry interests, such as minimising the impact of BREFs on the activities of an industrial sector in order to reduce costs or simply to preserve flexibility in industrial operations (Interview No 5). In a political discourse on BREF writing, the limits of defining BAT through technical consensus are rendered explicit. Split views, ie dissenting opinions about what constitutes BAT for a sector, are recognised and recorded in BREFs.

In an economic discourse, BREFs are 'products' (European IPPC Bureau communication) and the costs of the BREF writing procedure itself become relevant for how BREFs are written. BREF writers were financed in various ways and this can impact on how BREFs are produced. The majority of BREF writers are 'detached national experts' who work in

[21] These terms are used by BREF writers and TWG members.

[22] For instance, Germany initially favoured emission *limit values* to be specified in the BREFs. It was then agreed that BREFs would only *report emission levels* which are associated with particular techniques documented in the BREFs. Emission limit values would be imposed by local permitters in licences for specific installations.

[23] This is a body composed of Member States only which discusses issues of BAT determination under the IPPC Directive 2008/1. It is chaired by the Commission.

[24] IMPEL is an informal network of the environmental authorities of the Member States, acceding and candidate countries of the European Union and Norway.

national environmental, usually permitting, authorities and who are seconded for two to three years to the European IPPC Bureau in Seville, Spain. Some BREF writers are Commission functionaries, who have worked in DG Research before and temporarily move into the European IPPC Bureau. The latter have a more generalist perspective rather than specific knowledge in the particular area in which the BREF is written. However, specialist knowledge is considered to enhance a BREF writer's capacity to steer a TWG (Interview No 7).

Tensions between economic, political and technical discourses are managed through discursive strategies. At the heart of the BREF writing procedure is the management of potentially problematic overlaps between a technical and a political discourse. The European IPPC Bureau and its BREF writers seek to render a technical discourse central to the determination of BAT. However, political discourses may infiltrate BREF writing as the following statement from the 'BREF outline and Guide' suggests: 'a BREF should remain a fundamentally technical document [...] Similarly, political opinions and views should not be introduced into a BREF.' Reference by members of the TWG and BREF writers to the 'applicability' of techniques is one of the discursive strategies which helps to deal with potential tensions between a technical and a political discourse. To discuss the 'applicability' of a technique involves spelling out the conditions under which the technique could be considered as BAT and thus to *qualify* its *general* applicability. When discussing 'applicability', different considerations—technical but also interest-based ones—can be accommodated. For instance, technical issues can be addressed such as whether there is sufficient space in an existing installation to fit the technique. However, wider considerations can also be taken into account, such as whether the technique is process specific and hence cannot be necessarily considered as BAT for a whole industrial sector in which different processes are employed (Waste Incineration BREF 2006: 206). A section on 'applicability' is contained in chapter four of each BREF which lists the techniques to consider in the determination of BAT. Chapter five which lists the BAT conclusions sometimes also contains a paragraph on 'applicability' which states that the technique cannot be considered as BAT for a sector in general and unqualified terms. For instance, whether a technique can be applied in a particular waste incineration installation can depend on the characteristics of the waste incinerated (Waste Incineration BREF 2006: 444). Hence, discussions of 'applicability' are a discursive strategy that generates further procedure by facilitating compromises that qualify the selection of a particular technique as BAT. To summarise, technical, political and economic discourse generates procedures for BREF writing. Participants in BREF writing identified, as a potentially problematic overlap, the relationship between a political and a technical discourse. Such overlaps are managed through specific discursive strategies, such as references to the 'applicability' of techniques. But what forms of legitimacy are constructed through the application of these procedures to the work of the article 17(2) transnational governance network?

D. From a Decentred, Inductive and Unsettled Procedure to Local, Embedded and Fragmented Legitimacy

The decentred, inductive and unsettled procedures for writing BREFs generate local, embedded and fragmented legitimacy for the actions of the article 17(2) network. Legitimacy is local and embedded because it flows from the particular procedures which are constructed in a specific setting. It is fragmented because there is no one overarching European demos, which confers legitimacy on the actions of the article 17(2) network. Instead there are various, partly overlapping legitimacy communities which evaluate the BREF writing process (see also Black 2008: 148). Legitimacy communities are groups of social actors who question and hold to account the exercise of public powers by their peers or by individuals or groups of social actors operating at a distance from them.[25] There are legitimacy communities within, but also outside transnational governance networks. In the context of BREF writing, various legitimacy communities matter. First, there are the national people of the different Member States. Member State representatives in the TWGs, IEF and IEG (the Information Exchange Group)[26]—when drawn from environmental ministries—are part of national governments. They can claim some, though limited legitimacy for their input into BREF writing from the national democratic processes that lead to the formation of their Member State's government. Second, the BREF writing process itself creates its own legitimacy communities, such as the TWG and the IEF. BREF writers have to discuss with and justify their actions to the TWG and finally the IEF. TWGs can therefore confer 'credibility'—the term most frequently used by BREF writers—in order to legitimise their actions. 'Credibility' captures a form of legitimacy that is conferred by a group of fellow professionals with specialist expertise in industrial production and pollution control. By overseeing, evaluating and finally approving the work carried out by the TWGs, the IEF bestows legitimacy upon their activities.

[25] A legitimacy community can give rise to forms of legitimacy different from legal validity of the exercise of public powers (Black 2008: 147). Legitimacy can be conferred by those over whom powers are exercised, by those on whose behalf the powers are exercised and by those involved in the exercise of public powers.

[26] This is an advisory group for DG Environment that discusses legal issues associated with the implementation of the IPPC Directive in Member States.

It provides legitimacy, however, through reactive and potentially limited forms of accountability[27] since the IEF is convened only once or twice a year in response to issues which call for strategic consideration.

V. LINKING PROCEDURE AND LEGITIMACY IN THE TRANSNATIONAL GOVERNANCE NETWORK OF 'THE COMMON IMPLEMENTATION STRATEGY' UNDER THE EU WATER FRAMEWORK DIRECTIVE

The question arises whether the argument that decentred, inductive and unsettled procedures give rise to local, embedded and fragmented legitimacy applies beyond the specific context of the article 17(2) IPPC transnational governance network. Hence, this section examines what procedures and forms of legitimacy are generated through the 'Common Implementation Strategy' (CIS), a transnational governance network under the EU Water Framework Directive. It was chosen as the second case study because this network also signifies a transformation in the exercise of public powers. Key authority in relation to the definition of legal standards is—not by national state environmental authorities—but a transnational governance network that involves civil servants and scientific experts. Moreover, the powers exercised by the transnational governance network are significant, because the WFD has a very wide scope. It sets legally binding targets for both water quantity and quality in relation to a whole range of water courses: inland surface, transitional, coastal and ground water for all 27 EU Member States. The WFD also plays a central role in EU water pollution control because it implements a number of other EU water directives. Finally, while the WFD is concerned with the exercise of public powers in the specific field of water pollution, it integrates water pollution control with a range of other policy fields, in particular agriculture, fisheries, energy, tourism, regional policy, navigation and transport which all influence water quality and quantity. Moreover, how public powers are exercised by CIS and whether this is 'legitimate' matters because CIS' reach is extended through its links with other networks, similar to IMPEL discussed in section VI below. CIS links with the European Environmental Information and Observation Network (EIONET). EIONET, in turn, connects with the European Environment Agency (EEA) which also supports Member States' implementation of EU environmental law.

[27] Accountability and legitimacy can be distinguished. Accountability mechanisms are the means that can be deployed by legitimacy communities in order to ensure that their claims for legitimacy are met (Black 2008: 150).

A. Key Elements of the CIS

The transnational governance network of the CIS, which was set up by the Commission in 2001, is key to the implementation of the WFD. It helps to define the WFD's key legal obligation which is phrased in broad and general terms: Member States have to achieve 'good' surface and ground water status by the end of 2015. The network collates information and benchmarks best practices in the implementation of the WFD. The CIS shares characteristics with both the article 17(2) and the EU network for IMPEL, discussed below, but it is also different. Like the article 17(2) network, the CIS involves both political actors and technical expertise (Scott and Holder 2006: 227). Like the IMPEL network, the CIS draws on social learning in order to implement legal obligations. As in the case of the IMPEL network, participation in CIS is voluntary. Its results are not binding upon the Member States. However, the organisational structure of the CIS is more complex than the IPPC or IMPEL networks. It consists at the EU level of various interlinked networks and a comitology committee (article 21):[28]

('Supporting the Implementation of the First River Basin Plans' Workprogramme 2010–12 2009: 3).

Moreover, the organisational structure of CIS is in flux and thus unsettled. For instance, Working Groups E and F which deal with priority substances and the implementation of Directive 2007/60/EC of the European

CIS Organisation 2010–2012

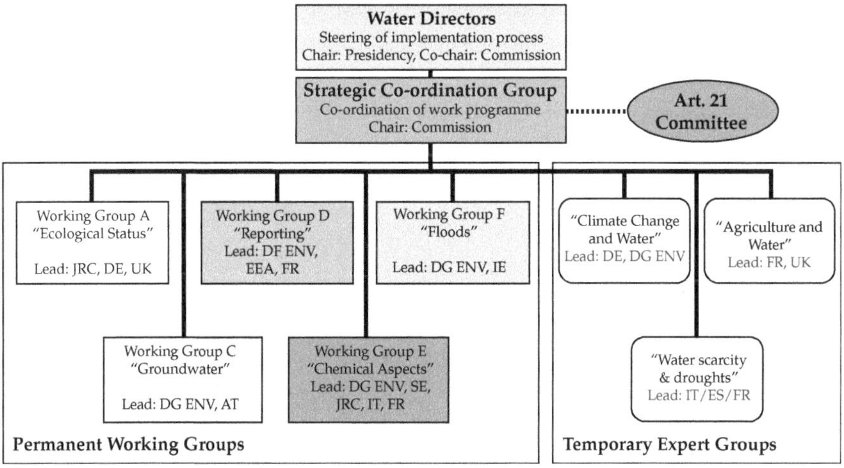

[28] This Comitology Committee assists the Commission in the revision of the technical annexes to the WFD 2000/60 and in the development of guidelines that help to implement the technical annexes.

Parliament and of the Council of 23 October 2007 on the assessment and management of flood risks[29] were only added at a later stage. A further activity on climate change and water has now been integrated ('Improving the Comparability and Quality of the WFD Implementation' 2006: 5).[30] CIS is managed by the Water Directors, who are high level members of national environmental ministries with particular responsibilities for water regulation. They are the final decision-making forum tasked with developing water policy. The Water Directors meet informally with the Commission twice a year. Like the article 17(2) IPPC network, CIS also comprises working groups which prepare technical, non-binding guidance documents. Similar to the article 17(2) network and different from IMPEL, CIS also involves private actors, such as the Union of Water Supply Associations (EUREAU) and the European Crop Protection Industry (ECPA). It seeks to include 'stakeholders, NGOs, like the European Environmental Bureau and the World Wildlife Fund for Nature, as well as civil society' (Scott and Holder 2006: 228). What legitimacy challenges does this network raise?

B. Legitimacy Challenges Raised by the CIS

The CIS seems to raise an interesting paradox in relation to legitimacy challenges. On the one hand, it seeks to enhance Member State accountability in the implementation of the WFD (Scott and Holder 2006: 230). Member States are required under CIS soft law to regularly submit reports to the Commission, such as copies of river basin management plans and interim progress reports about planned measures to achieve compliance with the WFD (ibid: 231).[31] The Commission then prepares its own reports on Member States' progress in implementing the Directive. The CIS also develops benchmarks for measuring Member States' performance in implementing the WFD. Member States can therefore be compared to each other and against a best practice standard (see, for example, 'Supporting the Implementation of the First River Basin Management Plans' 2009: 29). On the other hand, however, the proliferation of organisational fora associated with the CIS reduces transparency and thus ultimately accountability for its activities. The working groups which draft guidance documents

[29] OJ L 288, 27; 6.11.2007.

[30] Moreover, Working Group B 'Integrated River Basin Management' was discontinued. Issues discussed in this group are now dealt with by other groups or tackled through ad-hoc workshops or information exchange activities. Also, a new Stakeholder Forum and an Expert Network on Water Scarcity and Droughts has been set up ('Improving the comparability and quality of the WFD implementation' 2006: 8).

[31] There is no legal requirement for Member States under the WFD to comply with the format of reporting suggested by the CIS and the guidance documents produced by the CIS are legally not binding, Howarth 2009: 393.

have set up a number of additional groups, such as steering, drafting and expert groups (Scott and Holder 2006: 232; Howarth 2006: 21). If it is not clear who carries out what work and who has contributed to what extent to a final decision, accounting for this work and ensuring that it is carried out to relevant standards becomes difficult. Moreover, output legitimacy is an issue for the CIS. Some Member States do not use the guidance documents produced by the working groups. Also, according to the preliminary analysis of the reports submitted under articles 3 and 5 of the WFD, there is significant diversity in the implementation of the WFD ('Improving the Comparability and Quality of the Water Framework Directive Implementation' 2006: 2). There is the danger that the CIS may just be 'another meeting machinery created by the Brussels bureaucracy' (ibid: 1). Hence, it is by no means certain that the CIS actually enhances accountability and ultimately legitimacy assessed with reference to an abstract, normative conception of legitimacy. So, what procedures actually frame the work of the CIS and what 'legitimacy in action' do they construct?

C. Procedures Governing the Work of the CIS

The procedures governing the work of the CIS are unsettled but seem to be less decentred and inductive than those of the article 17(2) IPPC network. CIS exercises various powers that are not expressly conferred to it by the text of the WFD, but were simply assumed and are being expanded as the CIS is developing. Thus, procedures guiding the network are not pre-specified and pre-given through general administrative law. The fourth strategy document spells out specific procedures for some but not all CIS activities (ibid). Procedures are developed out of a managerial administrative culture, drawing on new public management techniques, such as benchmarking with reference to best practices. This is different from classic, bureaucratic public administration that is restrained by procedures enshrined in formal administrative law.[32] Hence, CIS procedures are in flux, evolving as the activities of the network develop. They are closely associated with and mirror the characteristics of the various tasks carried out by the CIS.

Procedures governing the work of the CIS are unsettled in various ways. First, the whole structure of the CIS was reviewed and adjusted

[32] This does not mean, however, that EU administrative law provisions do not apply to the exercise of some powers by the network. For a discussion of the administrative law provisions guiding comitology committees, a particular form of EU transnational governance network, see Craig 2006: ch 4.

in 2003, 2005 and 2009, with the most recent work programme 2010–12 seeking to simplify the previous programmes (Scott and Holder 2006: 227; 'Supporting the Implementation of the First River Basin Management Plans' 2009: 1). Also, the purpose of the first review—similar to the revision of the IMPEL network discussed below—was to streamline the procedural framework for the CIS. Two of the three expert advisory fora were shifted to working groups and the total number of working groups was reduced from 11 to five (Scott and Holder 2006: 231). Second, the formal organisational elements that frame the work and procedures of the CIS are in flux. For instance, Working Group E which supports the implementation of the Directive on Priority Substances was first an expert advisory forum but then metamorphosed into a working group. Similarly the activities on 'hydromorphology' and 'agriculture' will be organised as a continuation of the existing strategic steering groups but will become more of an expert network which works mainly through an information exchange. It is currently being discussed whether a new expert group for work on biodiversity and water shall be established ('Supporting the Implementation of the First River Basin Management Plans' 2009: 2).

Procedures governing the work of the CIS are not just unsettled, but also decentred at the EU level because there is not one specific, uniform central procedure. Instead, procedures vary between different work activities according to who participates and who leads. For instance, Working Group A is lead jointly by two research institutions and two Member States.[33] In contrast to this, DG Environment leads Working Group E in which Member States are merely rapporteurs ('Improving the Comparability and Quality of the WFD Implementation' 2006: 36). A sub-group of Working Group E is assisted by Commission consultants ('Supporting the Implementation of the First River Basin Management Plans' 2009: 27). The involvement of private actors is decided on a case by case basis depending on the task tackled by the CIS ('Strategic Document' 2001: 13). Procedures vary between the different activities. For instance, for Working Group C it is specified that the work will be carried out in some cases through co-ordinated exchanges of emails under the leadership of 'volunteered WG C members' ('Improving the Comparability and Quality of the WFD Implementation' 2006: 24). In order to report on progress, reports have to be submitted to the plenary working group twice a year in meetings organised by the successive EU presidencies. Other working groups follow different procedures.

However, not only are procedures governing the work of CIS decentred at the EU level, they are also inductively developed. They are established

[33] They are the EC Joint Research Centre (JRC), the Institute for Environment and Sustainability (IES), as well the UK and Germany.

in close connection and often contemporaneously with the development of CIS activities, 'Unanticipated solutions have emerged to meet practical need, and have received formal endorsement at a later stage' (Scott and Holder 2006: 233).

The CIS is involved in six heterogeneous tasks, information sharing, the development of technical guidance documents, information and data management, as well as application, testing and validation, policy development, and the integration of the WFD into other policy areas ('Improving the Comparability and Quality of the WFD Implementation' 2006). Mandates for some but not all of these six activities have been agreed so far (ibid: 6). Procedures are inductively generated in response to the requirements of particular work tasks. There are three types of activities, guided by different procedures. Type one activities consist of work mandated by the WFD itself, such as support for the article 21 comitology committee. The procedures framing these activities include an advance specification of 'clear deliverables and timetables', as well as 'regular progress reports to the Strategic Coordination Group' (ibid: 1). In contrast, two other activities consist of work in which Member States have merely a strong interest to co-operate. These activities are not required by the WFD. The main procedures here are information exchanges and the more informal sharing of experiences and practices. However, these procedures are more formalised than those governing the work of the article 17(2) IPPC network and they are therefore less inductive. The latest strategy document 'Supporting the Implementation of the First River Basin Management Plans' specifies 'mandates' which consist of 'objectives', 'tasks', 'deliverables'[34] and 'timelines' for all five working groups and the three temporary expert groups. These 'mandates' entail authoritative instructions for the various groups. While they vary in their detail, for some groups they are very specific and thus frame quite tightly and in formal terms what issues can be tackled in what way. For instance, the mandate for the drafting group on environmental objectives and exemptions lists very specific questions to be addressed in relation to proportionality assessments that should be carried out when determining the range of permissible exemptions under article 4 of the WFD.[35] Moreover, for some of the working groups, organisational structures are pinned down through

[34] 'Deliverables' can comprise various outputs, ranging from formal guidance documents to reports, handbooks, informal discussion papers and guides, the development of indicators, as well as research and case studies ('Supporting the Implementation of the First River Basin Management Plans' 2009: 36).

[35] These include 'Which categories of costs and benefits to consider?', 'How to embed non-monetised costs and benefits in the analysis?', 'How to embed taxes and subsidies in the assessment?', 'Where does disproportionality start?', 'How do the distribution effects of the costs and the benefits influence the assessment?' (affordability/ economic viability of a particular group or sector) and 'How to take into account past expenditures?'.

organigrams. In addition, in contrast to the technical working groups of the article 17(2) IPPC network, CIS working groups are permanent and have a stable membership ('Supporting the Implementation of the First River Basin Management Plans' 2009: 3). So, what forms of legitimacy do unsettled, decentred and, though in comparison to the article 17(2) IPPC network, less inductive procedures framing CIS work give rise to?

D. Local, Embedded and Fragmented Legitimacy for Powers Exercised under the CIS?

There seems to be primarily local legitimacy bestowed upon the powers exercised through the CIS. Legitimacy turns inward, away from the demos in the various Member States. The Water Directors are members of national environmental ministries, which in turn form part of national executives accountable to their people through parliamentary processes. However, these are fairly remote, loose and thus weak chains of legitimacy. Accountability, a means by which to achieve legitimacy, is established in the network through a hierarchy. The Water Directors, at the apex of this hierarchy, steer the CIS. The working groups report on progress with the drafting of technical guidance documents to the Strategic Coordination Group. Thus, the CIS seeks to render accountable its technical to its political branch (Scott and Holder 2006: 233). Its procedures generate local and embedded legitimacy which appears, however, to be less embedded than legitimacy for the article 17(2) IPPC network. Procedures framing the work of the IPPC network operate in a more shadowy, informal realm, whereas the basic procedural framework for the CIS is fairly formalised. Moreover, the task allocation between the technical working groups and the IEF in the article 17(2) IPPC network is not completely fixed but responsive to requests by participants. CIS procedures are also more formalised than article 17(2) network procedures because the CIS technical working groups are in the process of drawing up clear mandates and terms of reference for the new additional steering, drafting and expert groups which assist them (Scott and Holder 2006: 233). Inside the network, legitimacy is generated by a peer group of international scientists, in particular when work involves significant chemical expertise, such as the definition of priority substances and ecological status. The co-existence of internal accountability mechanisms within the CIS network and weak external legitimacy derived from national parliamentary processes creates an appearance of fragmented legitimacy. However, in comparison to the IPPC network, the CIS is more focused on EU level working groups and involves a clear central steer through the Water Directors. This is different from the very significant input of various local, regional and national working groups into the activities of the technical working groups in the

IPPC network. Hence, legitimacy seems to be less fragmented in the CIS than in the IPPC network.

VI. LINKING PROCEDURE AND LEGITIMACY IN THE TRANSNATIONAL GOVERNANCE NETWORK FOR THE ENFORCEMENT OF EU ENVIRONMENTAL LAW (IMPEL)[36]

Are procedures in the context of the IMPEL network also inductive and unsettled and hence give rise to local, embedded and fragmented legitimacy? IMPEL is an informal network of the environmental authorities of EU Member States, acceding and candidate countries, as well as Norway. It was set up in 1992 and since December 1993 also includes the European Commission which co-chairs its meetings (Hedemann-Robinson 2007: 461). Its sphere of influence is also significant because it links with various other environmental networks.[37]

IMPEL shares some features with the article 17(2) IPPC network but is also different. Like the IPPC network, IMPEL addresses both technical and political issues, here in the implementation of EU environmental law. IMPEL is an experts' network which draws on the regulatory and technical expertise of inspectors permitting installations and enforcing EU environmental law. However, IMPEL also becomes involved in politics when it gives advice to the Commission on proposals for new EU legislation, advising also on its enforceability. Moreover, it evaluates existing EU and national environmental legislation with reference to the EU's 'better regulation' agenda. In addition, it gives advice on the revision of existing EU environmental legislation, as it has done in relation to the IPPC Directive

[36] The analysis of this IMPEL case study is based on official EU documents and secondary literature, not on empirical data.

[37] An IMPEL network for accession countries was established in January 1998 (AC-IMPEL) which merged in 2003 with IMPEL. There is also now an Environmental Compliance and Enforcement Network for Accession (ECENA), which includes new pre-accession Member States in the Balkans. IMPEL is also a member of the executive planning committee of the International Network for Environmental Compliance and Enforcement (INECE). This comprises over 2500 enforcement practitioners from governmental agencies, NGOs and international organisations. IMPEL also shares results from its projects with the REPIN (Regulatory Environmental Programme Implementation Network) network which is part of an Organisation for Economic Co-operation and Development (OECD)/Environmental Action Programme (EAP) taskforce and operates in Eastern Europe, Caucasus and Central Asia since 1999. In addition, IMPEL has links with the Greenforce network which started in 2006 with a particular emphasis on the enforcement of Council Directive 92/43/EEC of 21 May 1992 on the conservation of natural and of wild fauna and flora (OJ L 114, 1, 24.4.2001) and the Birds Directive 2009/147/EC of the European Parliament and of the Council of 30 November 2009 on the conservation of wild birds (OJ L 20,7; 26.1.2010) and the setting up of the NATURA 2000 sites. Moreover, IMPEL has connections with the Network of Heads of the European Environment Protection Agencies.

review. It also contributes to the development of EU environmental *soft* law, such as the legally non-binding Recommendation (EC) 2001/331 on Minimum Criteria for Environmental Inspections, which were adopted by the European Parliament (EP) and Council [2001] OJ L118/41; Brochure about the IMPEL network: 7).[38] Hence, Member States have secured for themselves through the IMPEL network a new informal channel for influencing Commission legislation (Hedemann-Robinson 2007: 464).

However, IMPEL is also different from the IPPC network and thus provides an important third case study for examining links between procedure and legitimacy. First, IMPEL is more 'public' than the IPPC network both in terms of its membership and funding. Only staff from national environmental ministries and enforcement authorities belong to it. Industry representatives and environmental NGOs merely participate in some of its conferences (IMPEL anniversary newsletter 2007: 14). IMPEL is mainly financed by the EU, while Member States and industry contribute significantly to the funding of the IPPC network. Second, IMPEL's reach is wide because it deals with the enforcement of all EU environmental law in contrast to the article 17(2) network which drafts guidance documents for a technology standard under just one EU directive.[39]

IMPEL's work clearly raises questions of procedure and legitimacy. For instance, what procedures should govern the organisation of joint inspections in Member States? How can IMPEL's activities be legitimate, for example when it regulates national public authorities by benchmarking their enforcement activity through the development of performance indicators for inspections? (ibid: 8). Hence it is important to examine what procedures actually guide IMPEL's work and what type of 'legitimacy in action' they construct.

The procedures governing IMPEL's work are unsettled. The basic procedure governing IMPEL's work has evolved over the last 15 years. It is contested and subject to ongoing negotiation. The initial procedural framework for IMPEL included plenary meetings, an 'enlarged troika', clusters and working groups. *Plenary meetings* provided the organisational framework for its main strategic discussions. They were also held twice a year in order to approve the detailed work programme and final reports for specific projects. These plenary meetings were assisted by an *'enlarged troika'* which included representatives for the Commission and five Member States (with three old Member States 'enlarged' by two

[38] The IMPEL network has also contributed to the implementation of the IPPC Directive through its contribution to horizontal BREFs, such as on monitoring emissions.

[39] The IMPEL network also includes a focus on a particular directive. Cluster two of IMPEL contributes to the control of transboundary waste movements under article 50 of Regulation 1013/2006 of the European Parliament and of the Council of 14 June 2006 on shipments of waste (OJ L 190, 1; 12.7.2006).

new Member States). This troika prepared the agenda for the plenary meetings and was the forum through which IMPEL communicated with the outside world, including Members of the European Parliament and NGOs. Finally, IMPEL also works through *clusters*, informal fora that discuss new and review existing projects. Three clusters were set up on 'improving permitting, inspection and enforcement', on 'the transfrontier shipment of waste' and on 'better legislation'. For each specific project a *working group* was set up. Furthermore, IMPEL's work was supported by a secretariat—located in DG Environment—which liaised between IMPEL's national co-ordinators and the Commission.

This procedure changed over time. In 1997 a plenary meeting decided that a more flexible structure of project groups would replace the four technical working groups. Two standing committees were set up in order to oversee the work of these project groups and to dissolve them once projects were completed. However, in 1999, the two standing committees were disbanded in order to further reduce bureaucracy. Initially the plenary meeting took on the task of supervising the work of the project groups. However, this proved to be too onerous and hence three clusters took over this task (IMPEL anniversary newsletter 2007: 2).

The most significant and recent change in procedure is the transformation of IMPEL—a 'light, informal and voluntary' network—(letter from Commissioner Stavros Dimas) into a formal organisation recognised by law. Since 1 January 2009, IMPEL is a not-for-profit international organisation under Belgium law. This also enables the network to apply for EU funding under the Life+ Regulation.[40] There are now statutes that formalise and reform existing IMPEL working procedures. The General Assembly decides on policy and IMPEL's internal rules, as well as its budget and the Annual Work Programme. The Board deals with the day-to-day management of IMPEL and implements the decisions of the General Assembly. Most of the work is carried out through a project structure and clusters address more strategic issues.

This evolving, and thus unsettled procedure provides a basic framework for IMPEL's activities. Particular work projects are governed by a variety of more specific and inductively generated procedures. Hence, there is not one single, unified central procedure governing the activities of IMPEL, but procedures are generated at the EU level in relation to various work activities that are carried out in different organisational fora. Procedures are inductive because they are often closely related to the actual task to be tackled. IMPEL is engaged in a wide range of heterogeneous

[40] Regulation (EC) No. 614/2007 of the European Parliament and of the Council of 23 May 2007 concerning the Financial Instrument for the Environment (Life +) (OJ L 149,1; 9.6.2007).

tasks, ranging from organising exchange programmes for inspectors,[41] to developing training seminars on accidents in plants, to writing reports on various topics.[42] Procedures to carry out these tasks vary. A comparison of three reports of IMPEL projects illustrates the point.

IMPEL's work reforming the Recommendation Establishing Minimum Criteria for Environmental Inspections (RMCEI) involved a survey of Member States soliciting information about whether and how the criteria should be changed. The survey results were discussed in working groups during two workshops. On the basis of this, a final draft report with proposals for the amendment of the RMCEI was drawn up. The work was organised by a team of 13 Member State representatives and lead by a member of staff from DG Environment (Report 2007).

However, a workshop on the benchmarking of quality parameters for environmental inspectorates adopted a different procedure. First, the explicit purpose of this procedure was to move towards some convergence among the quality management systems in the different Member States. Three sub-groups, formed during a workshop, were asked to follow in their discussions a common, fairly detailed template consisting of six questions which connected goals to be achieved through inspections to suitable performance indicators ('Benchmarking of Quality Parameters for Environmental Inspectorates Report' 2005: 6). Second, the procedure adopted in this case—in contrast to the reform of the minimum inspection criteria—did not seek the *views* of different Member States on a particular issue, but simply collated information about the state of existing quality management procedures for environmental inspections. Workshop participants presented a one page description of existing and planned quality management systems for environmental inspections in their Member States.

Yet another procedure guided a project on IMPEL review initiatives. These initiatives offer advice to a host Member State on inspection procedures and the structure of its inspectorates. The procedure for reviewing these initiatives was a basic social science evaluation. The first phase of the project involved the design of a review mechanism. During the second phase this review procedure was trialled in Denmark. Phase three broadened the trial review to six volunteer Member States. Phase four concluded the review with an examination of the lessons learnt and the drafting of recommendations for future IMPEL review initiatives (Report 2007: 6).

[41] This includes a distance learning programme on environmental inspections.

[42] There are, for instance, reports on complaint procedures and access to justice for citizens and NGOs in the field of the environment within the EU (May 2000), a report on the inter-relationship between the IPPC, EIA and SEVESO Directives and EMAS Regulation (Dec 1998), as well as a report of a workshop on licensing and enforcement practices in a cement plant using alternative fuel (Dec 1998).

To summarise, the unsettled and inductive procedures governing the work of IMPEL embed legitimacy in the particular activities of the network. 'Legitimacy in action' for the powers exercised by the IMPEL network is not grounded in a pre-specified, abstract and highly normative conception of legitimacy rooted in support from a European demos. Instead, it arises from specific procedures that are negotiated, sometimes on an ad-hoc basis by the participants in various tasks. Several actors construct and bestow legitimacy, not just one demos and hence legitimacy is fragmented. There are both external and internal legitimacy communities that can justify IMPEL activities and thus fragmented legitimacy. One external legitimacy community involves Member States' Parliaments, which in turn represent national peoples. In comparison to the two other networks, national Parliaments have more significance for the IMPEL network. The Dutch Parliament and ultimately the Dutch people provide some legitimacy for the foundation of the IMPEL network. IMPEL was established in response to a recommendation from a report into the implementation of EU environmental law commissioned by the Dutch Council presidency in 1991. This suggested that a network of EU enforcement inspectors should be set up. Hence, the Dutch Parliament and ultimately the Dutch people indirectly bestowed legitimacy upon the Dutch Government that started the formation of the IMPEL network. But national parliaments and the people they represent also bestow some legitimacy upon the activities of the representatives of Member States in the various IMPEL working groups. About half of IMPEL members[43] are staff from national environmental ministries. These ministries are part of a national elected executive and hence derive some legitimacy from national democratic processes, with the executive being accountable to a national Parliament. Another external legitimacy community for IMPEL work is the European Parliament (EP). While IMPEL is not formally accountable to the EP, its co-operation with it, evidenced in three meetings with the EP's environment sub-committee, bestow some democratic legitimacy upon IMPEL. However, as in the IPPC network, there are also legitimacy communities internal to the IMPEL network. Acceptance of work activities within the network by a critical peer group of environmental inspectors themselves can also confer technical credibility, and thus legitimacy upon IMPEL's work.

VII. CONCLUSION

This chapter started with a critical review of some of the literature that charts a shift in the exercise of public powers away from nation states to

[43] The other half of IMPEL network members are staff from environmental regulatory authorities in Member States, such as the Environment Agency in the UK.

transnational governance networks that can also include private actors. Such a change in the exercise of public powers raises questions about what procedures should govern the activities of networks in order to bestow legitimacy upon them. Procedures have been considered as key in both classical and contemporary social theory, as well as administrative law for achieving legitimacy in the deployment of public powers. This link between procedure and legitimacy has usually been approached from an abstract, normative angle where particular understandings of 'legitimacy in the books'—informed by classical democratic theory—are assumed. Procedures, often more specific expressions of the rule of law, then flow from this conception of legitimacy. They are meant to curb the exercise of powers, for instance by imposing a duty to provide reasons for decisions taken or by requiring proportionate and consistent decisions that respect the legitimate expectations of those being regulated. This chapter has developed a different, empirical and analytical perspective for understanding the link between procedure and legitimacy. It has suggested that pre-established conceptions both of procedure and legitimacy 'in the books' developed in the context of liberal Western nation states, do not fully capture new forms of legitimacy 'in action' that are relevant to the work of transnational governance networks. The chapter has argued that in order to understand such new forms of 'legitimacy in action', it is necessary to analyse what procedures actually govern 'on the ground' the exercise of powers by transnational governance networks. It is these procedures that enable and thereby construct particular conceptions of 'legitimacy in action'. In developing this perspective the chapter has built upon those contributions to the policy network literature that emphasise the importance of communication in the working of networks. It has sought to develop these further by drawing on the Foucauldian idea of discourse and micro dynamics of power in order to understand how procedure and legitimacy work in transnational governance networks.

The chapter argued that unsettled, inductive and decentred procedures give rise to local, embedded and fragmented legitimacy for the article 17(2) IPPC network. A similar link between particular types of procedures and forms of legitimacy can also be observed in the context of the IMPEL and CIS networks.

The chapter's analysis brackets two important issues. First, the normative question whether fragmentation weakens the very concept of legitimacy needs separate and further analysis that is grounded in empirical data of how members of transnational governance networks actually give meaning to the idea of legitimacy (see DeBurca 1996: 349). Second, the analysis has focused on EU environmental governance networks, which illustrate a particular type of transnationality. It is informed by the experiences of elite bureaucrats and field inspectors whose ideas of procedure and legitimacy have been shaped by the public administrations of advanced and industrialised Western liberal nation states and states which seek to conform to this model after their transition from socialist to liberal democratic systems. Moreover, the networks examined operate in a specific policy field in which procedures have to grapple with a particular issue, how to reconcile technical expertise and political interests in the exercise of public powers. Further qualitative empirical research into other networks may also uncover the crystallisation of work routines into settled, deductive and centralised procedures that question the idea of local, embedded and fragmented legitimacy advanced here.

REFERENCES

'Benchmarking of Quality Parameters for Environmental Inspectorates' (IMPEL workshop, Copenhagen 8–9 September, Report 2005) http://impel.eu/projects/benchmarking-on-quality-parameters-for-environmental-inspectorates.

Bendix, R (1977) *Max Weber: An Intellectual Portrait* (Berkeley and Los Angeles, University of California Press).

Benson, JK (1982) 'A Framework for Policy Analysis' in D Rogers, D Whitten and Associates, *Interorganizational Co-Ordination* (Ames, Iowa State University Press).

Benz, A (1995) 'Politiknetzwerke in der horizontalen Politikverflechtung' in D Jansen and K Schubert (eds), *Netzwerke und Politikproduktion, Konzepte, Methoden, Perspektiven* (Marburg, Schüren) 185–204.

Biermann, F and Siebenhüner, B (2007) 'Managers of Global Change: Core Findings from the Manus Project' (Amsterdam, Global Governance Working Paper No 25).

Black, J (2008) 'Constructing and Contesting Legitimacy and Accountability in Polycentric Regulatory Regimes' 2 *Regulation and Governance* 137–64.

Börzel, T (1998) 'Organizing Babylon – On the Different Conceptions of Policy Networks' 76 *Public Administration* 253–73.

Bogason, P and Toonen, TAJ (1998) 'Introduction: Networks in Public Administration' 76 *Public Administration* 205–27.

Brochure about the IMPEL network, 'Cluster 1: Permitting, Inspection and Enforcement' http://impel.eu/cluster-1.

Castells, M (2000) *End of Millennium*, 2nd edn (Oxford, Blackwell Publishers).

Craig, P (2006) *EU Administrative Law* (Oxford, Oxford University Press).

Daugbjerg, C (1998) 'Linking Policy Networks and Environmental Policies: Nitrate Policy-Making in Denmark and Sweden 1970–1995' 76 *Public Administration* 275–94.

DeBurca, G (1996) 'The Quest for Legitimacy in the EU' 59 *Modern Law Review* 349–56.

Dowding, K (1995) 'Model or Metaphor? A Critical Review of the Policy Network Approach' 43 *Political Studies* 136–58.

EU Commission (2005) 'First Report on the Implementation of the IPPC Directive' COM (2005) 540 final, 3 November 2005 http://ec.europa.eu/environment/air/pollutants/stationary/ippc/ippc_report.htm.

Fox, CJ and Miller, HT (1995) *Postmodern Public Administration; Towards Discourse* (London, Sage Publications).
Foucault, M (1972) *The Archaeology of Knowledge* (London, Tavistock).
—— (1980) 'Power/Knowledge: Selected Interviews and other Writings' in C Gordon (ed), *Power/Knowledge: Selected Interviews and other Writings* (Harlow: Longman and Pearson Education).
—— (1989) 'The Order of Things: An Archaeology of the Human Sciences' (Abingdon, Routledge).
Gergen, KJ (1986) 'Correspondence versus Autonomy in the Language of Understanding Human Action' in DW Fiske and RA Shweder (eds), *Metatheory in Social Science: Pluralisms and Subjectivities* (Chicago, Chicago University Press).
Hall, S (2002) 'Foucault: Power, Knowledge and Discourse' in M Wetherell, S Taylor and SJ Yates, *Discourse Theory and Practice: A Reader* (London, Sage Publications) 72–81.
Haas, P (1992) 'Introduction: Epistemic Communities and International Policy Co-Ordination' in 46 *International Organization* 1–35.
Haines, F, Reichman, N, and Scott, C (2008) 'Problematizing Legitimacy and Authority in Law and Policy' in 30 *Law and Policy* 1–11.
Heclo, H (1978) 'Issue Networks and the Executive Establishment' in A King (ed), *The New American Political System* (Washington DC, American Enterprise Institute) 87–124.
Hedemann-Robinson, M (2007) *Enforcement of European Union Environmental Law* (London, Routledge Cavendish).
Howarth, W (2006) 'The Progression towards Ecological Quality Standards'18 *Journal of Environmental Law* 3–35.
—— (2009) 'Aspirations and Realities under the Water Framework Directive: Proceduralisations, Participation and Practicalities' 21 *Journal of Environmental Law* 391–417.
'Improving the Comparability and Quality of the Water Framework Directive Implementation' *Progress and Work Programme for 2007–2009'* (2006), as agreed by the Water Directors, 30 November/1 December 2006, fourth Strategy Document http://ec.europa.eu/environment/water/water-framework/objectives/pdf/strategy4.pdf.
IMPEL anniversary newsletter (2007) Newsletter 15th Anniversary IMPEL 1992–2007 http://impel.eu/about/organisation.
Kasim, H (1994) 'Policy Networks, Networks and EU Policy-Making: A Sceptical View' 17 *West European Politics* 15–27.
Kohler-Koch, B (1996) 'The Strength of Weakness: the Transformation of Governance in the EU' in S Gustavsson and L Lewin (eds), *The Future of the Nation State: Essays on Cultural Pluralism and Political Integration* (London, Routledge).
Lange, B (2008) *Implementing EU Pollution Control: Law and Integration* (Cambridge, Cambridge University Press).
Letter from Commissioner Stavros Dimas (nd) http://ec.europa.eu/environment/impel/pdf/dimasletter.pdf.
Luhmann, N (1982) *The Differentiation of Society* (New York, Columbia University Press).

Luhmann, N (1983) *Legitimation durch Verfahren* (Frankfurt aM, Suhrkamp).
Machado, N and Burns, TR (1998) 'Complex Social Organization: Multiple Organizing Modes, Structural Incongruence and Mechanisms of Integration' 76 *Public Administration* 355–86.
Mayntz, R and Scharpf, FW (1995) 'Der Ansatz des akteurszentrierten Institutionalismus' in R Mayntz and et al (eds), *Societal Change between Market and Organization* (Aldershot, Avebury) 39–72.
Peters, G (1992) 'Bureaucratic Politics and the Institutions of the European Community' in S Sbragia (ed), *Euro-Politics: Institutions and Policy Making in the 'New' European Community* (Washington, the Brookings Institution).
Picciotto, S (1996–7) 'Networks in International Economic Integration: Fragmented States and the Dilemmas of Neo-Liberalism' 17 *Northwestern Journal of International Law and Business* 1014–56.
Report (2007) 'IMPEL Input for the Further Development of the Recommendation on Minimum Criteria for Environmental Inspections (RMCEI)' http://impel.eu/wp-content/uploads/2010/02/2007-07-input-tmcei-FINAL-REPORT.pdf.
Rhodes, RAW (1997) *Understanding Governance: Policy Networks, Governance, Reflexivity and Accountability* (Buckingham and Philadelphia, Open University Press).
Rosenau, J (1992) 'Governance, Order and Change in World Politics' in JN Rosenau and EO Czempiel (eds), *Governance without Government: Order and Change in World Politics* (Cambridge, Cambridge University Press) 1–29.
Sabatier, PA (1988) 'The Advocacy Coalition Framework: Revisions and Relevance for Europe' 5 *Journal of European Public Policy* 98–130.
Scharpf, F (1993) ‚Positive und Negative Koordination in Verhandlungssystemen' in A Héritier (ed), *Policy-Analyse, Kritik und Neuorientierung*, PVS Sonderheft 24 (Opladen, Westdeutscher Verlag).
—— (2003) 'Problem-Solving Effectiveness and Democratic Accountability in the EU' in *Max-Planck Institut für Gesellschaftsforschung Working Paper 03/1*, February 2003 www.mpifg.de/pu/workpap/wp03-1/wp03-1.html.
Schmitter, PC and Lehmbruch, G (eds) (1979) *Trends Towards Corporatist Intermediation* (BeverlyHill, London, Sage).
Scott, J and Holder, J (2006) 'Law and New Environmental Governance in the European Union' in G DeBurca and J Scott (eds), *Law and New Governance in the EU and the US* (Oxford, Hart Publishing) 211–42.
Slaughter, A (2000) 'Government Networks: the Heart of the Liberal Democratic Order' in GH Fox and BR Roth (eds), *Democratic Governance and International Law* (Cambridge, Cambridge University Press) 199–235.
Strategic Document (2001) as agreed by the Water Directors under the Swedish Presidency http://ec.europa.eu/environment/water/water-framework/objectives/pdf/strategy.pdf.
Suchman, M (1995) 'Managing Legitimacy: Strategic and Institutional Approaches' in 20 *Academy of Management Review* 571.
'Supporting the Implementation of the First River Basin Plans' Workprogramme 2010-12, November 2009, http://circa.europa.eu/Public/irc/env/wfd/library?l=/framework_directive/implementation_documents/final_2010-2012/_EN_1.0_&a=d.

Waarden, F van (1992) 'Dimensions and Types of Policy Networks' in G Jordan and K Schubert (eds), Policy networks, in Special Issue No 21 *European Journal of Political Research* 29–52.
Waste Incineration BREF (2006) http://eippcb.jrc.es.reference/wi.html.
Wilks, S and Wright, M (eds) (1987) *Comparative Government-Industry Relations: Western Europe, the United States and Japan* (Oxford, Clarendon Press).

3

Global Governance Networks in Action: The Development of Toxicological Test Methods at the OECD[1]

MARTIN HERBERG

I. INTRODUCTION: THE SHIFT FROM WORLD POLITICS TO GLOBAL STANDARD-SETTING

GLOBAL GOVERNANCE INCREASINGLY takes the form of standard setting by transnational expert systems and transgovernmental policy networks. Working alongside international organisations and international diplomacy, various sub-units of national governments are engaged in intense cooperation with their foreign counterparts to harmonise technical standards (*cf* Bermann 1993; Ladeur 2004; Slaughter 2005). While international treaties are normally negotiated by either the heads of states or foreign ministers, the rise of horizontal governance networks brings administrative actors and mid-level practitioners up to the stage. Often, their interactions are not strictly controlled by the policies of cabinets or chief executives of domestic governments (see Keohane and Nye 1977: 43), which allows them enormous discretion and room for manoeuvre.

In a world where 'problems and contexts are changing faster than centralized authorities could ever respond to' (Slaughter, 2005: 188), global administrative networks and expert committees are an indispensable governance tool. At the same time, the functional superiority of such governance arrangements raises enormous challenges in terms of legitimacy.

[1] The following considerations are part of research project A 3 'Transnational Governance' at the Collaborative Research Center 597 of the University of Bremen. Originally, the study was planned as a comparative analysis of two different initiatives, namely, the 'OECD Test Guidelines Programme for the Testing of Chemicals', and the GHS 'Global Harmonized System for the Classification and Labelling of Chemicals'. For the purpose of this volume, it was decided to present the data as two separate case studies. For a detailed discussion of the GHS, see Winter 2010, in this volume.

This chapter discusses the advantages and potential disadvantages of the emerging network-like governance arrangements in the light of current sociological and juridical debate. An important reference point for the study is the self-regulatory capacity of networks as described by Sabel (1993). The paper combines a theoretical discussion of the relevant literature with an empirical reconstruction of one concrete initiative, where this self-regulatory potential comes to light in an almost paradigmatic way.

As an analytical background for the case study, section II starts with a discussion of the network concept. Until recently, networks used to be characterised primarily by their flexibility and innovation potential, as opposed to the classical ideal type of hierarchical organisation. However, since analysts have begun to perceive networks as 'constitutional orders' (Sabel 1993: 70), many other aspects have come into play, such as their social embeddedness and the evolution of an elaborated role structure and a system of checks and balances within networks. This constitutionalist approach displays many interconnections with current debates on an emerging Global Administrative Law (see Kingsbury, Krisch, and Stewart 2005). Many of the classical principles of administrative law, such as transparency, impartiality and reasoned decision-making, are also highly relevant to regulatory initiatives that take place in the transnational sphere. However, most of these principles are rather vague, guiding our attention to the emergence of more concrete procedures on the practical level.

The empirical considerations in sections III and IV apply these concepts to a concrete standard-setting initiative, namely, the Test Guidelines Programme of the Organisation for Economic Cooperation and Development (OECD). The initiative is one of the oldest governance mechanisms in the field of global chemicals regulation, dating back to the late 1970s. Mid-level officials from all OECD countries, working for specialised national authorities like the German *Federal Environmental Agency*, are coming together in regular intervals to harmonise toxicological methods, ie methods to determine the carcinogenic, mutagenic and ecotoxic potential of chemicals. The extent to which the OECD test methods are legally binding is determined by the OECD Council's Decision on the Mutual Acceptance of Data from 1981 (*cf* Warning 2009: 120). By providing a stock of harmonised test methods, the initiative aims at minimising trade barriers and avoiding duplicative testing, as well as the rapid diffusion of new developments in this area.

In the case under research, aspects of legitimation are tightly interconnected with criteria of scientific validity. The envisaged test methods must be tightly tailored to the regulatory needs of modern societies, and, furthermore, they must reflect the risks of different chemical substances in an objective and unbiased way. To achieve this, the Test Guidelines Programme integrates a broad range of proposals for new test methods, while at the same time binding these proposals on the criterion of their empirical testifiability. In this requirement, the overall rationality of the initiative becomes manifest; a rationality which might adequately be called a fallibilist logic or a logic of falsification. Many institutional features of the OECD Test Guidelines Programme draw their specific meaning from this falsificationist logic, and at the same time, they are an important step towards the institutionalisation of general principles like fairness, consistency, impartiality and transparency.

Section V summarises the results of the study, extrapolating the findings to more general questions of the future of governance and statehood under the conditions of globalisation. Admittedly, the case is only representative of a limited number of constellations, where aspects of legitimacy are broadly congruent with criteria of scientific validity. In fact, this convergence might be much weaker in other initiatives, especially where experts have to build their judgement on estimates or political preferences. However, as a general rule, if an issue can be addressed on a falsificationist basis, this potential should be used as far as possible, instead of anchoring policy in 'soft' factors such as the personal experience or reputation of individual experts, or shifting the responsibility onto actors from civil society.

II. GLOBALISATION, NEW MODES OF GOVERNANCE, AND THE QUEST FOR LEGITIMACY

A. Making Sense of the Network Concept

Network-like forms of decision-making on all levels of governance are not of recent origin. More than 30 years ago, political scientists addressing the national level started to discuss different forms of 'cooperative statehood' (Ritter 1979), 'multi-organisational policy implementation' (O'Toole 1993), 'horizontal self-coordination' (Scharpf 1993: 137) and many other arrangements that cut across ministerial departments and administrative sections or divisions. As the network concept indicates, these inter-organisational interactions imply much more than conventional forms of consultation between one agency and another in cases where activities of the former might affect the jurisdiction of the latter ('negative coordination', see Scharpf 1993: 143). Instead, actors of different provenance define certain issues as a common goal, and try to achieve these goals through intense cooperation. As with many other phenomena of informal administrative action, network-like arrangements are an important response to the shortcomings of bureaucratic organisation, and often, they emerge in response to functional needs and practical necessities.

In many cases, however, identifying the need for joint action is not the same as achieving it. To some extent, these coordination problems are caused by opportunistic behaviour: participants might falsely pretend to invest in the cooperation, while pursuing a 'wait and see' strategy; they may give promises without seriously intending to keep them; and, since collective decision-making often involves joint fact-finding, they may use false information or hide important facts from each other in order to push their own interest through (on the problem of opportunism in general *cf* Williamson 1975). Besides, cooperation in multi-actor settings can be affected by a variety of cognitive factors, such as disagreement about the nature of the problem and differences in practitioners' methodological and epistemological backgrounds. In the literature on networks, the growing awareness for issues like these has led to several approaches of a more interpretative, deliberative and argumentative conceptualisation, which sensitise us to the fact that what seems to be a conflict of interests at first glance, may very well turn out to be a clash of different patterns of interpretation or views of reality (*cf* Hajer and Wagenaar 2003).

However, even if networks can overcome such conflicts and cognitive blockades, there is a severe caveat: the formation of a common goal among the participants of a network is not necessarily the same as an orientation towards the common good—participants' behaviour might just as well be guided by what Scharpf has called the 'collective selfishness' (Scharpf 1993: 157) of multi-actor arrangements. Although personal relationships and trust can serve as an important medium to overcome the dilemmas of collective action, the same factors can also seal off the expert discourse from the broader public and third party interests. For example, a climate of mutual trust can be an important precondition to admit possible knowledge gaps or uncertainties, but, while inside the expert group existing uncertainties might be discussed frankly, the same uncertainties may be kept secret from the public. Furthermore, an overeager approach towards maintaining trust may also affect the argumentative climate inside the expert group, especially in cases where there is a fear that points of criticism will weaken the achieved consensus.[2]

On the national level, many of these dangers are mitigated by the embeddedness of policy networks in an overarching institutional structure. In an era of informal interagency coordination, many of the traditional forms of vertical control are executed in a much looser, steering

[2] Obviously, the social phenomenon called trust is of a double-edged character here. Analytically, the problem requires a somewhat higher degree of differentiation—besides trust based on personal relationships, there is also trust based on rules and institutions, and besides unconditional trust, one should take into account possible forms of 'deliberate trust' (Sabel 1993: 90), which help to reconcile loyalty towards each other with a climate of mutual criticism.

at-arm's-length manner. If everything that is currently accomplished by mid-level officials at the intersection of different agencies was shifted upwards, the ministers and high-policy level officials would certainly have an overfull agenda. However, loosening control is not losing it. Even under today's conditions, superiors still exert considerable influence, eg by allocating resources to specific actors and by demanding information and imposing sanctions in cases of dissatisfactory conduct. Thus, at the national level, interagency negotiations across functional boundaries should rather be seen as a supplement, not a substitute to vertical integration, and research on governance in the European Community reveals a similar picture (see Schilleman 2008).

It is against this background that transnational governance displays its particular complications. Whereas on the national level, one finds different forms of 'meta-governance' (Soerensen and Torfing 2005: 202) with the capacity to enhance the legitimacy of network governance, the absence of strong supranational institutions in the transnational sphere makes it more difficult to define and implement standards of legitimate action and accountability. As international organisations have enormous problems to impose constraints on transnational governance networks, so too have domestic governments. To be sure, finding the right balance between formal procedures and informal practices is one of the most characteristic features of modern statehood. However, through the process of transnationalisation, this balance becomes ever harder to achieve. In an ideal-typical way, three dimensions can be distinguished where these problems come to light most clearly:

1. First, the emergence of transnational governance networks can lead to the loss of clear-cut responsibilities (see Herberg 2007). In purely national contexts (to the extent that these still exist at all), the participants of interagency networks are formally appointed as representatives of the involved agencies, and normally, their designation also includes the definition of specific rights and duties. By contrast, the composition of networks operating on the transnational level often takes a more unstable and contingent character. This makes it more difficult to achieve accountability in the sense that the central decision-makers can be identified and held responsible for a certain policy outcome. Instead of waiting for a formal appointment from 'above', network actors often seem to recruit themselves. While in the national context, the power struggles inside networks can be mitigated by monitoring and supervision, these games can take a more dramatic form on the transnational level, resulting in the marginalisation of weaker actors.
2. Another threat to legitimacy is the danger of a continuous privatisation of political decisions. It is often emphasised that the integration

of private actors might help to overcome several knowledge gaps and other shortcomings of more traditional forms of governance (*cf* Streck 2002). However, in cases where a few powerful actors dominate a network, there is the danger that they will usurp or monopolise the policy process. Due to their extensive experience with corporatist self-regulation, most nation states have developed institutional safeguards to mitigate these risks. At the same time, the institutional achievements of the cooperative state are not easily transferable to the transnational sphere, and this situation is clearly mirrored in the structure of international law: until now, international law represents a normative order where rules for actors other than states are vastly missing (*cf* Zumbansen 2001).

3. The third aspect relates to the often-cited disaggregation of the nation state (see Slaughter 2005: 48). At the national level, each agency has its own (sub-)sectoral interests and viewpoints, and the permanent confrontation between different agencies helps to aggregate the multitude of dispersed interests into a generalised picture of the common will (*cf* Bohne 1981; Mayntz 1979). Thus, rather than threatening democracy, the administrative fabric of interagency negotiations seems to stabilise the constitutional state. However, as soon as the administration gets involved in transnational governance networks, this arrangement tends to become destabilised. By switching back and forth between the national and the transnational level, mid-level officials can considerably increase their room for manoeuvre—by presenting their own sectoral view as their country's national interest, they can acquire enormous influence on the global level, and by withholding relevant information from their national counterparts, they may emancipate themselves from the domestic framework of mutual checks and constraints.

To sum up, a number of developments, such as the loss of clear-cut responsibilities, the privatisation of (world) politics, and the emancipation of mid-level officials from their national context pose serious threats to legitimacy. Under certain circumstances, the existing problems might be recognised by network members themselves, which often leads to the installation of adequate forms of meta-governance inside the networks. While principles such as fairness, honesty or equality are certainly an important driving force of the self-constitutionalisation of networks and expert systems, the daily operations of the latter call for more detailed rules and procedural standards. For example, in order to allow for frictionless, discoursive and argumentative processes, there must be commonly shared criteria which help to distinguish strong arguments from weak ones, and by applying these rules in a diligent and impartial way, general principles such as fairness and equality are brought to bear in an operational and practical manner.

B. The Debate on an Emerging Global Administrative Law

Many characteristics of contemporary administrative law go hand in hand with increasing discretion on the part of the executive branch. This constellation calls for specific safeguards in order to prevent possible abuses of regulatory power and/ or administrative solo actions. In the absence of the 'one best way' or the one and only solution for individual cases, courts normally grant administrators a great deal of discretion, restricting themselves to control whether the decision contains major mistakes. At the same time, courts seek to promote a 'dialogic rationality' (Stewart 2005: 16), by asking whether the decision was made on a well-informed basis, and whether the given reasons and justifications are convincing. Furthermore, with view to administrative standard-setting, authorities are normally obliged to publish the proposed rules and to accept comments. The functions of these participatory elements in administrative law are: first, to make the best use of practical knowledge that is widely distributed throughout society; and second, to guard against violations of citizens' rights as a result of administrative error or negligence.

Over the last decades, issues of citizen participation have attracted much attention in the literature on administrative law. However, many other, more conventional, elements are still of utmost relevance. One of these issues is the existence of pre-defined rules that clarify the powers and competencies of each organisational unit or individual agency. In fact, clear organisational settings and the assignment of specific tasks to different authorities are a necessary condition of administrative efficiency and public participation. Clearly arranged organisational structures help to avoid different forms of adhocracy, and furthermore, they serve as a necessary precondition to hold agencies responsible for their conduct. A related aspect is the principle of written documentation, emphasised by Max Weber almost 100 years ago (Weber 1978 [1922]: 957), which remains just as important under today's conditions. On the basis of proper documentation, public officials can self-critically evaluate their own conduct, and in addition, these records are an indispensible prerequisite for public participation and judicial review.

As the overview shows, the accountability relations of administrative actors are manifold. In addition to vertical relations as emphasised by the old, hierarchical view, the architecture of modern administrative law serves to integrate the individual agency into a dense web of horizontal interconnections with civil society actors and other agencies which are concerned with adjacent or conflicting tasks. For a more detailed picture, the broad spectrum of more concrete norms which govern administrative activities would deserve more attention, among them different requirements of record-keeping, the full range of information-gathering techniques, and the design of adequate channels for inter-agency coordination.

At the national level, the arrangement as established by procedural administrative law has considerably contributed to the legitimacy of the modern nation state, and many of the seemingly bureaucratic and formalistic elements of administrative law have rightly resisted recent trends of administrative reform, of deregulation and de-bureaucratisation (*cf* Olsen 2006).

An open question is whether these legal tools can be transposed to the field of global regulatory governance. Inquiries into this area have given rise to a specific branch of literature, namely, the Global Administrative Law discourse (see Kingsbury, Krisch and Stewart 2005). There are two reasons why the norms and standards generated by global governance networks can be perceived as administrative in character. First, many of these norms resemble in their scope and substantive content the norms and standards that were traditionally the product of national administrative rule-making. Second, most of these norms are created without following the procedures, such as ratification, required for international treaty-making. Instead, these norms often gain practical relevance without any formal transmission from the international to the domestic level. At the same time, the legal systems of most countries provide the executive branch with great latitude in shaping their cross-border relations. As a consequence, global standard-setting tends to bypass the procedural safeguards of domestic administrative law.

As a remedy, authors from the Global Administrative Law literature are advocating for the globalisation of administrative procedural law, either 'bottom up', by an extension of domestic safeguards, or 'top down', by establishing these safeguards directly on the global level (ibid: 54). A bottom up approach aims to strengthen national law as a tool to control the decisions of global agencies. This can take various forms, which all come with specific problems. For example, as Stewart has pointed out (Stewart 2005: 18), existing national procedural standards might be extended to the conduct of national officials in international negotiations. However, if each country defines its own requirements, this might result in a highly fragmented constellation which endangers the very possibility of transnational decision-making.

By contrast, procedural safeguards against possible abuses of public power might also emerge directly at the global level. While the general principles of good governance remain broadly the same here, questions of legitimacy cannot be addressed by simply replicating the structures of domestic administrative law. Often, adequate forms of participation and institutional mechanisms emerge from processes of experimentalism inside global governance networks, and in several cases, the emerging mechanisms are even more ambitious than those in use domestically. It is due to the plurality of such procedural achievements that authors from the Global Administrative Law literature advocate for an increased empirical effort. In a relatively unexplored field of research like this one, case studies on individual governance arrangements appear to be the most appropriate research strategy.

C. Methodological Remarks: A Case Study Approach to Global Governance Networks

In the early stages of a case study, one has to think about appropriate data. One possible source of data are audio-recordings of everyday interactions, as used by authors from the tradition of Conversation Analysis (see Drew and Heritage 1992 and Lange in chapter two). Such data allow for the detailed examination of the patterns, through which interactions in the concerned context are made orderly and consistent. At the same time, however, generating such data requires much effort, often combined with long-term participation in the field. Alternatively, many institutional settings can also be accessed through pre-existing documents. In order to avoid errors in interpretation, however, one has to be aware that many routines which govern the decision-making process are not necessarily mirrored in the documents. Finally, the reconstruction of network-like settings can also be based on interviews with participants. While delivering pieces of information that are missing in the official documents, survey data poses its own methodological challenges, such as the difficulty to differentiate between the level of personal views, and the level of the network as the actual unit of analysis.

Whichever data one uses, interpretation always requires the utmost openness for the structural characteristics of the material (see Glaser and Strauss 1960). With regard to global governance networks, it is mainly two dimensions in which important discoveries can be made; namely, the level of possible institutional achievements, and the dimension of the underlying problems and threats to legitimacy. As for the achievements, many innovations will only come to light if the analyst keeps his own normative expectations at a distance. Sometimes, these structural aspects are stated quite clearly in the official documents, and in some cases, they are still in their infancy, demanding extensive inquiry on the practical ground. Likewise, the underlying problems may also be of different shape, size and visibility.

For many authors, interactions in multi-actor settings are mainly a matter of negotiation and compromise, characterised by 'principles of sovereign respect, live and let live, and reciprocity' (Slaughter 2005: 201). By signalising their readiness to be persuaded themselves, members increase their chance of persuading others (ibid: 207). Put simply, deliberation in global governance arrangements is often portrayed as something weak and fluid, in contrast to rather hierarchical or interest-oriented settings.

Here again, reconstructive research can help to overcome some of the simplifications in current theorising. Whereas qualitative researchers' obsession with the fluid and processual features of daily life has often been criticised, this approach is certainly no end in itself. To the contrary, it is structures and structural mechanisms that one tries to reveal through such microscopic events as turns at talk or single episodes in an interview. In fact, deliberation in networks can take many different forms, and in some cases, specific mechanisms of internal monitoring can play a constitutive role for the deliberative processes taking place. Thus, for an adequate reconstruction of global governance networks, it seems indispensible to remain aware of aspects of a rather firm and lasting character.

That global governance networks can take on a 'life of their own', by developing their specific and individual structural patterns, is the methodological precondition to make them the object of a case study. Thus, analysing a given network should not be confused with aggregating the different aspects of its appearance in order to arrive at an exhaustive description (the latter being an illusionary goal in itself). Instead, the aim should be to discover the underlying pattern, logic or 'grammar' through a broad variety of different activities and manifestations upon which the network has left its mark. Put differently, the aim is to detect what authors from Conversation Analysis have called the 'unique "fingerprint"' of a given institutional setting (Drew and Heritage 1992: 26). Admittedly, the degree of autonomy that a given network will reach might vary, and often, the processes inside a network might be characterised by a considerable amount of instability; yet taking this as the normal case would heavily militate against the necessary openness of the analysis.[3]

As a concrete case for the empirical reconstruction, the OECD Test Guidelines Programme for the Testing of Chemicals was selected. Many factors speak for this choice. As the name of the initiative indicates, global standard-setting is conducted under the umbrella of an international organisation in this case. However, at the same time, key actors are almost exclusively recruited from national agencies. In addition, the initiative is of an enormous age and degree of development, and to some extent, its procedural achievements can be regarded as an institutional prototype for a series of other initiatives in the field of global risk regulation. Toxicological test methods as developed by the OECD Programme are an indispensible tool in assessing the risks and dangers of chemical

[3] In qualitative sociological research, this search for an underlying pattern or 'grammar' is also known as the 'documentary method of interpretation', a term which was originally introduced by K Mannheim und further developed by H Garfinkel (1972), the founding father of Ethnomethodology (as for the application of these methods in current socio-legal research, see Herberg 2009).

substances, and, thus, the initiative is located in a field of powerful and partially competing interests. As will be shown, the ability to keep a distance from such external interests is one of the most important achievements of the Test Guidelines Programme.

As for the choice of adequate empirical data, a broad variety of official documents is available, among them descriptions of test methods as developed thus far, different protocols of meetings, as well as a number of guidance documents concerning the procedural framework of the initiative. The latter serve as the organisational blueprint of the initiative and are a promising point of departure for the analysis. Having described the findings from the guidance documents, the chapter will proceed to look at the empirical insights from different expert interviews with the members of the Test Guidelines Programme. As purposefully generated data, interviews do certainly not possess the same degree of authenticity as other, naturalistic data. However, as long as one manages to stimulate narrations and descriptions on the basis of personal experiences, it is possible to gain a realistic picture of how the existing rules are applied on a practical level.[4]

The methodological concepts described thus far all point towards the same direction: in the current stage of theoretical debate on global governance networks, it seems necessary to take a fresh look at these phenomena. By keeping a distance from pre-defined concepts, case studies may help to enrich the ongoing discussion. In fact, even a sociological concept such as that of 'experts' should not be taken for granted, as authors from Ethnomethodology and Conversation Analysis postulate (*cf* Samra-Fredericks 2005: 221)—which concrete rules or requirements one has to comply with in order to be taken serious as an expert in the institutional setting concerned is an empirical question, and it is surely an indicator for institutional failure if the mere reputation of a scientist enables the scientist to establish his or her opinion as valid.

III. SCIENCE IN THE AGE OF UNCERTAINTY: THE INSTITUTIONAL DESIGN OF THE OECD TEST GUIDELINES PROGRAMME

The OECD Test Guidelines Programme was initiated in the late 1970s with the aim to develop and harmonise a stock of standard methods for the testing of chemicals. The result is an ever-increasing collection of detailed specifications, which cover the sections physico-chemical properties; effects on biotic systems; environmental fate (like degradation

[4] Three of the interviews were conducted with national officials, in order to explore their problem-solving strategies. In addition, two interviews were conducted with OECD members, in order to gain further information on issues of network governance and internal coordination.

and bioaccumulation); and health effects. Test methods are used by professionals in governments, in the industry, and in academic institutions in order to generate risk-related information on existing or new chemicals. For an effective management of chemical risks, the development of scientifically sound methodologies is an indispensible prerequisite. In fact, the administrative procedure of chemicals registration and notification at the national level, as required by the law in most countries, would be unthinkable without standardised test methods, and the same is true for most other regulatory measures in this field.

Due to the variety of species that might be affected by a chemical, and due to the complex vulnerabilities of the human body, today's large-scale production of chemicals creates a high level of uncertainty. Test methods developed by the OECD Programme are an indispensible instrument to reduce this complexity, but, at the same time, toxicological testing is also subject to many sources of uncertainty itself. Short of a 'holistic' approach, which could integrate the manifold interactions between species in nature, most toxicological studies are restricted to a single species strategy: from the estimated 10 to 100 million species of the world, only a handful are used for laboratory purposes (*cf* Leeuwen and Vermeine 2007: 282). An additional difficulty relates to the measurement of chronic toxicity. Due to the cost and effort required for long-term toxicity testing, such tests are normally limited to species with a relatively short life cycle. Furthermore, since laboratory studies on humans are the exception in modern toxicology, human risk assessment is largely dependent on animal testing, which poses several problems concerning the transferability of results.

However, as recent developments in the science of toxicology illustrate, the problems just mentioned are not necessarily leading to an attitude of relativism. Instead, the attempt to overcome uncertainty in its various forms is an important driving force of methodological innovations. For example, where toxicology is cultivating an intense exchange with biologists, chemists, experts from toxicokinetics, statistics, epidemiology and medicine, the substantive content of experiments with a single species can considerably be strengthened. In addition, classical *in vivo* tests can partially be replaced by innovative *in vitro* testing, which often leads to more precise results than the former. Another source of innovation is the systematic comparison of existing test methods. Even if all available methods on a certain issue or endpoint have their specific limitations, distinguishing between weaker and stronger tests might still be possible. It is this orientation towards scientific progress on the basis of deliberate self-criticism that lies at the heart of the OECD Programme, as the following passage from one of the Guidance Documents indicates:

> Test method validation is a process based on scientifically sound principles by which the reliability and relevance of a particular test (...) are established for a

> specific purpose. Reliability is defined as the extent of reproducibility of results from a test within and among laboratories over time, when performed using the same standardized protocol. The relevance of a test method describes the relationship between the test and the effect in the target species and whether the test method is meaningful and useful for a defined purpose with the limitations identified (OECD 2005: 13).

The quotation is from Guidance Document No 34 entitled 'Guidance Document on the Validation and International Acceptance of New or Updated Test Methods for Hazard Assessment'. The high priority given to the principles as defined here is also evidenced by the relatively early position of the just-quoted passage in the document, coming directly after some preliminary remarks on the aim of the text. As a closer look at the passage reveals, a paragraph like this one with its rather prosaic definitions could just as well be found in a toxicology introduction book. Within the context of an international standard-setting initiative, however, the emphasis on such quality standards is highly consequential under institutional aspects. The orientation towards validity gives distinction to the overall procedural design of the initiative, determining, amongst others, the way in which negotiations and discussions inside the expert network should be conducted.

Having explained reliability and related quality standards, the Guidance Document proceeds to describe the process of test method validation. Even if the test-developing laboratory has taken much effort to ensure the accuracy of the proposed test method, formal adoption by the OECD is not possible without independent peer review. This requires a number of inter-laboratory studies. In contrast to normal toxicological testing, where the test is taken as given, validation studies are conducted in order to assess the performance of a test method. As long as the method stands up to the test, it is accepted; if it does not, it is rejected—a logic well known from the writings of Karl Popper (see, for example, Popper 2002: 72). As becomes obvious here, an integral part of this falsificationist approach is an element of impartiality: according to its performance in the validation process, the test method will be accepted or rejected, irrespective of by whom it was invented. As might be added here, this finding provides a striking counterpoint to the above-mentioned literature on persuasion and compromise.

In the early stage of the validation process, it is necessary to appoint a validation manager or management team, which oversee the whole process. Their responsibility is to define the standards against which the results will be evaluated, including the tolerable degree of empirical variance in the results from different laboratories. Then, the number of participating laboratories has to be determined, and in advance, laboratories are selected, considering their expertise. Furthermore, appropriate reference chemicals must be chosen, which are representative of the substances that the method is designed to address. Normally, one uses chemicals whose properties are already known and well-documented. In order to optimise the objectivity of the validation study, the identity of reference chemicals is concealed from the participating laboratories (see OECD 2005: 38). In other words, substances must be handed over to the laboratories in an anonymised form in order to prevent possible sources of bias. From an outsider's perspective, one would hardly have expected this to be a problem; and yet, the prescription to mask chemicals shows the enormous intelligence of the expert system, ie its capacity to minimise possible sources of bias on the basis of self-created rules.[5]

In sum, the process of test method validation, as described in Guidance Document 34, appears to be tailored to the maintenance and advancement of toxicological professionalism, and herein lies an important precondition for both the effectiveness and legitimacy of the initiative: even in the absence of a global *demos*, toxicological professionalism proves to work towards preventing certain forms of malpractice, of error and negligence, the avoidance of which is in the best interest of society as a whole (on the issue of professionalism in general, see Herberg 2010).

In the overall architecture of the OECD Test Guidelines Programme, however, processing proposals for new or updated test methods is a relatively complex affair, and it is in a relatively late stage of the process that validation studies can be conducted. In the earlier stages, the principles of falsification and testifiability are supplemented by other, more policy-related criteria, such as the regulatory need of the proposed test method. These aspects are described in Guidance Document No 1, which defines 'the process of Test Guidelines development, including the structure of the Test Guidelines Programme (TGP) and the responsibilities of those involved' (OECD 2006: 10). In brief, the process of Test Guidelines development can be portrayed as a sequence of six working steps (see figure below). To start with, member countries send their proposal for new or updated test methods to the Secretariat, which, after a preliminary assessment, circulates the draft to all of the other countries. On the basis of the comments received from the member countries, an adequate design for validation studies is developed, and then, these studies are conducted by independent laboratories. The results of these studies are then passed around for comment, and then, if possible, the test method is ratified by an expert group called the 'Working Group of National Coordinators', as well as several other higher-policy bodies of the OECD, such as the Council.

[5] The mechanisms leading to such bias are not explicated in the document. However, it is most likely that toxicologists, who are familiar with the substances that are used as reference chemicals, might unconsciously tend to compensate for possible shortcomings of the test procedure, thereby interfering with the objectivity of the whole validation procedure.

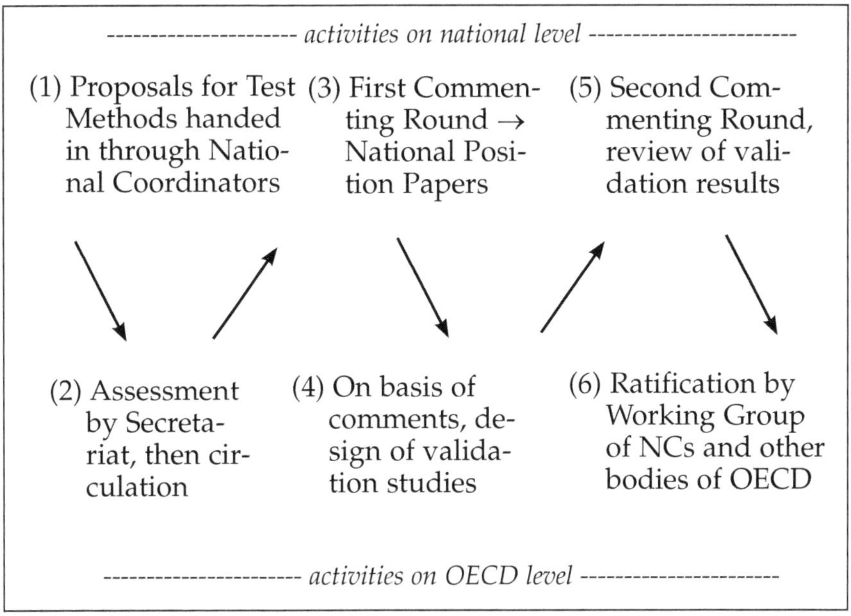

The key actors of the initiative are national representatives, working for national authorities such as the German Federal Environmental Agency, or the US-American Environmental Protection Agency. By appointing only one (or, in some cases, two delegates from each member country) and by charging these persons with the relevant tasks in a long-term way, a clear allocation of competencies is established. The delegates hold the title of 'National Coordinator of the Test Guidelines Programme', and are members of the so-called 'Working Group of National Coordinators of the Test Guidelines Programme'. Put shortly, they fulfil the function to intermediate between the national and the transnational context, coordinating the multiplicity of ideas and interests on the national level and synchronising this plurality with the discussions inside the OECD:

> The National Coordinators (NCs) from the respective OECD member countries (...) have a central position in the Test Guidelines Programme. They submit national proposals for new or revised Guidelines and provide comments agreed on at the national level on proposals circulated by the Secretariat. In order to be most efficient, NCs provide a national focus point to gather input from a network of experts and thus are required to be aware of developments related to test methods in their own country (OECD, 2006: 13).

In a very condensed way, the passage describes a cycle of idea-gathering and repeated review. Proposals for new Test Guidelines may be preliminary, and yet, they must contain sufficient information to allow for rational debate. Within the context of the OECD Programme, this requirement is clearly mirrored in the provision of a so-called 'Standard Project Submission Form' for new proposals (see OECD 2006: 14), which advises the submitter to give reasons on aspects such as the regulatory need of the method and its validation status. For the analysis of the OECD initiative as a 'constitutional order' (Sabel 1993: 105), this *qualified openness* for proposals from outside is of utmost importance. In fact, the institutional design of the initiative is such that it allows for both, the necessary degree of responsiveness to the knowledge spread throughout society and the maintenance of professional autonomy. At the same time, it is here that a particularly egalitarian element of the initiative becomes visible: in principle, even laboratories with low reputation can feed their proposals into the system, as long as they are able to underpin their suggestions with relevant information and fact-based justifications.

Theoretically, if one compares this arrangement with other initiatives that are described in the network literature, the OECD Programme could just as well have been shaped in a way that would allow actors from academia, private institutions and different parts of the administration to address their project submissions directly to the Secretariat. There are various reasons why this option was not chosen. One possible reason lies in the attempt to organise the initiative as a 'network of networks' by drawing on existing forms of interorganisational and intersectoral communication at the national level. In fact, by creating the position of a National Coordinator, the initiative manages to build on the fabric of intra-state coordination, which already existed prior to the process of transnationalisation.

After the submission via one of the National Coordinators, the proposal will undergo critical appraisal by the OECD, and then, depending on its suitability for the Test Guidelines Programme, it will be included in the official work plan. In this early stage of the process, project submissions are normally evaluated in a rather cursory fashion, assessing them against the information requirements specified in the Standard Submission Form. As soon as a proposal is included in the work plan, the Secretariat circulates the draft to the National Coordinators of the Member States, who then are expected to distribute the documents to all relevant experts in their country for critical comment.

Here again, similar to their function at the proposal-making stage, National Coordinators serve as an important transmission belt between the Secretariat and the various actors from academia, from private institutions and administrative bodies. The National Coordinators' duty is to identify relevant national experts and to diligently manage these contacts. As for the comments collected at this stage, critical objections to a proposal can significantly vary in form and character. Some of the objections may refer to methodological problems, such as missing variables. Often, possible shortcomings of a proposal will come to light only from the perspective of another discipline; and partly, it is the experience with specific regional characteristics such as a country's flora and fauna, which leads to critical objections against a proposed test method. It is the National Coordinator's responsibility to collect these comments and compile them in the so-called National Position Paper, which is subsequently sent to the Secretariat. This paper must, at least to some extent, reflect the diversity of perspectives in the country:

> The National Position Paper should preferably contain a national view on each issue raised in the document under review, but could also be a compilation of alternative views when no scientific agreement on certain issues was possible within a member country. In order to allow the views of individual experts to be seen by the WNT, National Coordinators should attach comments (...), either in their original form or as summarized by the National Coordinator. The professional affiliation of the consulted experts may be indicated so that the Secretariat and other member countries can obtain an insight into how broadly the scientific community has been consulted (OECD, 2006: 22).

As the quotation shows, the trustworthiness of National Coordinators is not taken for granted. Instead, what can be observed here is the phenomenon of 'deliberate trust', as described by Sabel (Sabel 1993: 80). It is the National Coordinator's responsibility to include in the discourse all agencies engaged with chemicals, as well as all private institutions and academic actors who might be able to contribute relevant information. However, if the National Position Paper handed in by the National Coordinator does not represent a broad spectrum of opinion, this may very well lead to critical reactions by the Secretariat or the Working Group of National Coordinators, although such measures are not defined in the document. However, the mere establishment of a duty to give account of the agencies included in the process helps to avoid an overly selective pattern of participation on the national level (for further information on this aspect, see section IV. C).

In contrast to international treaty-making and classical international regimes, where each country generally speaks with one voice, the major challenge for an initiative such as the OECD Test Guidelines Programme is to cope with pluralism. Rather than acting as representatives of an aggregated will, participants work as careful *intermediaries* between the national and the transnational context. It is here that one finds the solution to the problem of an increased disaggregation of the nation state (see, section II. A)—the danger of administrative solo actions can very well be anticipated by network members themselves, and by creating appropriate rules, global governance networks allow for both, strengthening pluralistic communication between states as well as inside the nation state.

IV. INSTITUTIONAL CRISES AND INSTITUTIONAL LEARNING: FURTHER INSIGHTS FROM THE EXPERT INTERVIEWS

'Traditional conceptions of global governance tend to simplify governance (...) along a vertical axis of "multi-level" governance. They tend to de-emphasize transnational mechanisms of horizontally allocated authorities among and between states' (Nicolaidis and Shaffer 2005: 277). The quotation accentuates one of the most important insights from the literature on Global Administrative Law, namely, the growing awareness for the limitations of the old, state-centric model of international relations. This is also highly visible in the OECD Test Guidelines Programme, which goes far beyond the classical model of global governance and indicates a transgovernmental rather than an intergovernmental style of governance. Most importantly, the official ratification procedure at the end of the decision-making process—which might be seen as the basis of political legitimation—is of a rather marginal character in practice. As an alternative, legitimation is achieved on the basis of professional rationality and certain procedural rules, which are built into the decision-making process from the outset. Furthermore, national delegates do not act as representatives of a pre-defined national will within the context of the OECD initiative, and, since Member States are discharged from the duty to speak with one voice, a high degree of pluralism is achieved.

Since the Guidance Documents were developed by practitioners themselves (ie the Working Group of National Coordinators), there is a high probability that their work is broadly congruent with the official requirements in the documents. However, it seems advisable to complement these findings with results from the expert interviews. The purpose of the latter is twofold: first, interview data help to gain a more detailed picture of existing routines and problem-solving strategies inside the network; and, second, the interviews contain information on the transformation of the network at different stages of its development. Whereas a complete historiography of the system is not intended here, the analysis focuses on some critical stages in the development of the programme, which significantly have influenced its current shape.

The results are divided into three sections, each of which is arranged around a specific problem that the OECD Programme has seen itself confronted with in the past. One of these problems is to intermediate between different national (and sub-national) views. This issue leads us back to the formation phase of the Programme, where the global applicability of Western toxicology was seriously called into question (see the next section). The subsequent section addresses tendencies towards the 'privatization' of the decision-making process. As the interviews show, members of the OECD Test Guidelines Programme have learned to domesticate the interests of non-state actors, and to include them into the initiative in a favourable way (section IV. B). The chapter concludes with some thoughts on the tension between the rather decentralised character of the initiative and the existing demand for internal monitoring and network governance (section IV. C).

A. Transnational Standard Setting and 'Glocalisation': Dealing with Diversity, Avoiding Fragmentation

In the interviews conducted with national mid-level officials, different structures of different origin become manifest; among them the structures of the OECD Programme, but also administrative cultures that already existed prior to the process of transnationalisation. In general, specialised authorities, such as the German Federal Environmental Agency, enjoy a high degree of autonomy, due to their expertise and the scientific skills of their members. By providing commonly shared methods and epistemologies, such skills are an important catalyst for the emergence of cross-border interactions between national agencies. However, even in an era of globalisation, local knowledge still plays an important role. Administrative actors must keep in touch with different groups of actors in their country or region to observe relevant developments, and often enough, it is individual actors at the periphery, who initiate innovations:

> Many processes are triggered by new regulatory needs. An example is veterinary medicals. Some time ago, at a conference, some Professor, I think he was a zoologist, was showing pictures of areas which were totally karstified. In these areas, which were used for intensive mass animal farming, the cows were treated with medicals against parasites. And the substance had a toxic effect on the dung flies, and so, the cow dung was not decomposed, instead, it sealed the soil. It is in our interest that dung flies or other species are not wiped out by chemicals, and thus, we need adequate test methods (Interview 15 December 2004).

As the last sentence of the passage shows, the relevancy of regulatory interests is surely not cast into doubt by the interview partner. However, as a closer look reveals, these interests are no trigger of innovations themselves. Rather, it is the discovery of new hazards which keep the system moving. This picture matches very well with an aspect often highlighted in the network literature—political actors are often not able to stay in touch with relevant stocks of knowledge. Instead, a good portion of today's regulatory innovations come from specialised agencies. In the example given, it seems that the zoologist who discovered the effect did not try to get into contact with the agency on his own. Instead, it is members of the agency who try to catch up with relevant information, and this surely represents an indispensible element of their professional role and competence. In the context of the interview, the example serves to demonstrate how important these skills are, and at the same time, it becomes clear how inadequate it would be to shift these competencies upwards or replace them with a global 'superstructure'. Thus, what can be observed here is a specific division of labour between both levels, where many information-gathering functions rest at the national level.

Looking at this division of competencies more closely, it is often at the local level that the risks and dangers of modern technologies emerge most clearly, be it hazards which vary from context to context, or hazards which are global in character, but which have not been identified as such yet. Later on in the interview, the respondent touches upon one of the most famous examples of this, the so-called 'TBT story'. In this case, it was the observed degeneration of marine snails in the North Sea and the Baltic Sea in the early 1980s which led to the discovery of the endocrinic effects of TBT (tributylin) and other chemicals, as well as to the emergence of endocrinology as an ever increasing field of research. In fact, up to this time, the ecotoxicological importance of endocrinically active substances had been strongly underestimated, and it was by accident that field biologists discovered the masculinisation of female snails in coastal waters (*cf* Bateson 2001). Sociologically, such cases are a good illustration for the concept of 'glocalisation', as developed by Robertson (1995), which sensitises us to the fact that most aspects of global change are not directly recognisable, but only through the prism of local processes.

While the OECD Programme in its current form is designed to cope with the existing diversity of local contexts, it was not until an international crisis that this diversity was taken seriously. In fact, it was this crisis that gave rise to the OECD Programme in the late 1970s. At that time, many countries had just instituted their own national chemicals legislation, which included specific requirements on the registration, notification and restricttion of chemicals. However, what caused international conflict was not the legal provisions themselves, but instead the technical standards on a non-legislative level. In particular, standards for the testing of chemical substances were regarded as highly incommensurable, which posed a serious problem for the global tradeability of chemicals. The conflict led to the announcement by the Japanese Government that none of the then existing European or US-American test methods would be accepted anymore, which means that for each substance additional testing would have been required (for this debate, see Schneider 1988: 53). With the Mutual Acceptance Decision of the OECD Council in 1981, this conflict has, at least on a political level, been brought to an end. In the context of the OECD Test Guidelines Programme, however, the confrontation between different national and regional views still plays an important role, albeit in an institutionalised and disciplined form, and this is what provides the system with its specific dynamics.[6]

The results of the interviews indicate that, in addition to diverging national views, the programme must also be tailored to deal with a broad variety of diverging sub-national views. Consequently, the discussion of proposals for new or updated test methods is organised in an utmost open and inclusive manner. For example, the German Coordinator as located at the German Federal Environmental Agency routinely includes a number of bodies in the process, among them the Federal Institute for Materials Research and Testing, the Federal Institute for Occupational Safety and Health, the Federal Institute for Risk Assessment, as well as different private associations such as the Society for Chemical Engineering and Biotechnology and the German Animal Welfare Organisation. Often enough, even experts from the same institution hold different standpoints, and this makes compiling and synthesising these opinions in the form of the abovementioned National Position Paper a highly challenging task:

> Having received the comments, it is my task to write a summary, which is then sent to the Secretariat. Writing this is not trivial at all. Sometimes, one receives a mishmash of contradictory ideas. Here, one has to find a way through this chaos. What I try to avoid is sending lots of contradictory opinions there. This is what our colleagues in the USA are doing. They are real champions of transparency. In their papers, one finds in detail what US Commentator One, Two or Three were thinking. We don't need this. If it is done properly, the key issues will be documented in the text. And the less important issues—well, we all have enough work, nobody here is an amateur (Interview 15 December 2004).

Apparently, the task to compile the received comments into a concise text implies a twofold challenge—on the one hand, National Coordinators are expected not to suppress the existing diversity of opinions, while, on the other hand, they must take care that the process is not overwhelmed by a flood of details or rather marginal aspects. Normally, National Coordinators strive to keep the National Position Paper as narrow as possible, and for this purpose, they actively try to settle minor controversies on their own. The passage shows that the fashion in which the paper is written may vary from country to country. National Coordinators from the United States tend to describe the range of opinions in broad length,

[6] In the interviews, questions on the formation phase of the Programme were rather fruitless, since none of the participants could answer them on the basis of their own experiences. Yet, to the extent that this period can be reconstructed in the literature, one gets the impression that the conflict was a clash of different perspectives rather than one of pre-defined national interests. Once again, this confirms the importance of a more deliberative and interpretative paradigm in modern governance theory, as pointed out in section II. A.

and this is sometimes perceived as disproportionate by actors in other member countries.

Yet focussing on the essentials, as postulated by the interview partner here, does not exclude giving due regard to different opinions. Thus, the slight anger or irritation that is expressed in this quote should not be taken as resentment against pluralism; rather, it shows how seriously the task is taken. As emphasised above (*cf* section II. B), one of the most important functions of modern administrative law is to make the best use of the knowledge spread throughout society, and this goal also gives shape to many of the procedural standards of the OECD Test Guidelines Programme. In order to guarantee the necessary degree of openness for impulses from society, key actors of the Test Guidelines Programme must show a specific attitude of neutrality and impartiality.

B. Power Asymmetries, External Interests, and the Struggle for Autonomy

As stated in Guidance Document No 34, 'the most obvious reason for the development of a new test method is to address an area of toxicological concern for which tests do not yet exist' (OECD 2005: 21). While the previous section concentrated on proposals for new test methods, another type of proposal also deserves attention, namely, proposals which are intended to replace an existing test. For the programme to remain up-to-date, the continuous revision of existing Test Guidelines is just as important as the elaboration of new test methods. This twofold goal is often emphasised in the official documents. Partly, the reason for the revision lies in the discovery of more precise test methods, and partly, the revision is due to the fact that the revised test method allows for a reduced number of test animals, or that the same test results can be achieved using cheaper or more basic technical equipment.

Before a new test can be incorporated into the official stock of OECD Test Guidelines, the proposed replacement test method must prove to be as accurate as the previous one. At the same time, the criteria of validity, of testability and falsification must be supplemented by other, additional criteria such as the regulatory usefulness of a test method. In fact, since the validation of new or revised test methods takes much effort, the revision of test methods should lead to significant improvements, either by improving toxicological accuracy or through cost savings. If the initiative were to integrate all proposals which come from outside, irrespective of their added value, this would surely lead to a blockage in the system, since proposals with only minor advantages would absorb many of the resources required for more innovative developments. As the following passage shows, it is exactly this situation which the initiative saw itself confronted with some years ago:

> It was decided, when the Programme was refocused, that only National Coordinators could submit proposals, and this had to do with the decision to focus on the regulatory use of Test Guidelines. And because of this focus, it was considered that only countries should submit the proposals. So if industry wants to be involved, it should contact one of the National Coordinators, usually in the country where they are. It was also, I think, to avoid pressure from industry. Because Test Guidelines, you know, it means a lot of money, a lot of interest behind. And so it was decided to do it like that (Interview 13 September 2007).

The picture as drawn by the interview partner here matches very well with popular ideas on the 'privatisation' of world politics. In the case under research, however, the wording 'pressure from industry' should not be taken at face value. On the one hand, the search for cheaper and more user-friendly test methods is officially regarded as a legitimate interest in the context of the OECD initiative. On the other hand, an exorbitant number of proposals of this type may lead to a specific form of bias, although this can hardly be blamed on actors from industry who make these proposals. Instead, the quantitative mismatch between efficiency-oriented proposals and proposals of a more innovative character brings to light the asymmetric allocation of resources between industrial actors and other actors in society. Notwithstanding this, the just mentioned problem must be taken seriously as a threat to the effectiveness as well as the legitimacy of the initiative. Apparently, in the formation phase of the initiative, this problem has not been sufficiently anticipated, and thus, it was in the later stages in the development of the initiative that it came to light.

The counter-measures taken against such forms of bias have already been mentioned (see above, section III), and it is here that the relevant passages of the documents reveal their full significance. In order to get included into the official work plan of the OECD initiative, proposals for new or updated test methods must be submitted via the National Coordinators of the member countries. It is the National Coordinators' function to preselect the proposals and identify those projects that might lead to significant improvements in toxicological accuracy or cost efficiency. Furthermore, as stated in the 'Standard Project Submission Form', proposal-makers are required to give detailed information on the usefulness of the proposed method and its advantages over existing methods. It is notable that criteria such as the usefulness of a method do not compete with the broader aims of testability, validity and falsification. Rather, they serve as an additional filter, in order to protect the initiative against proposals whose added value over existing methods seems marginal.[7]

Just like many other global standard-setting initiatives, the OECD Programme is located in a field of powerful and competing interests, among them national and transnational health and environmental concerns, interests in animal welfare, as well as industry's interest in minimal testing effort. In general, these interests are an important driving force of methodological innovations, but, at the same time, they might also turn out to be a source of bias. In order to avoid this, proposals for new test methods must take a specific form, namely, the form of detailed and testifiable proposals, whose substantive content is then evaluated. As discussions inside the network are conducted in a fact-oriented and de-politicised way, extensive inquiries into actors' motives and interests become unnecessary here—other than in many other initiatives of global standard-setting, where such political and/ or personal aspects often play an important role (as an example of a highly contrasting case in this regard, see the empirical findings on the GHS 'Globally Harmonized System for the Classification and Labelling of Chemicals' as presented by Winter 2010, in chapter four). At the same time, it is quite obvious that those responsible for the initiative have a clear view of actors' interests and possible sources of bias resulting from them:

> We don't know exactly why a country proposes something. They propose something, when they think it is useful. (…) Sometimes, we have the impression that there is research in this domain and that, if it is included as an OECD project, it would help to get money. We have sometimes this impression. But I can't… it's just an impression (Interview 13 September 2007).

As in the quotation above, the constellation described here comes with its own problems and pitfalls. Apart from the industry's interest in reducing testing effort, the initiative sees itself confronted with what might be termed the selfishness of scientific actors, ie their orientation towards reputation and fund-raising. Here again, the initiative is faced with the danger of being overwhelmed by a number of proposals of limited practical applicability and usefulness. In principle, the strong appeal exerted by the OECD Programme on actors from academia and private research institutes can be interpreted as an indicator of its success: placing one's ideas in the context of the initiative has become an effective way to

[7] It might be added that the large discretion which National Coordinators enjoy in preselecting proposals is partly counterbalanced by a mechanism called the 'informal channel': if a proposal is rejected, the test-developing institution still has the possibility of addressing its project directly to the Secretariat. Such proposals are not included in the official work plan of the OECD, and yet, if the proposed test method seems to bear considerable advantages over existing methods, the Secretariat can get in contact with the respective Coordinator, inquiring about the reasons for the rejection.

give prominence to them. However, since scientific sophistication is not necessarily the same as practical usefulness, the success of the OECD Programme can easily result in failure, for example, if a significant number of the proposals address risks that are unlikely to occur in the real world. Once again, this demonstrates the vulnerability of the initiative, as well as the significance of the safeguards and protective measures that have been taken.

From a Global Administrative Law perspective, what can be observed here is the emergence of rules and procedural standards that regulate the conduct of non-state actors. Such rules are mainly absent in classical international law, given its orientation towards the conduct of states and international organisations. As highlighted by concepts such as the self-constitutionalisation of networks, the various governance networks of the transnational realm may reach a considerable degree of autonomy *vis á vis* private actors—but this autonomy must be re-established again and again.

C. Implementing Soft Law, Monitoring Autonomy: The Role of the Secretariat

Although the fundamental norms of the initiative are codified in the form of specific guidance documents, these rules are more informal than international treaty norms or other forms of 'hard law'. Thus, the enforceability of the network-internal rules deserves further examination given their paralegal status. In order to evaluate the self-regulatory capacity of the network, one must also look for internal monitoring and sanctioning mechanisms in cases where a violation has occurred. To a certain extent, control is an integral part of the expert discourse; at the same time, however, the effectiveness of such horizontal forms of control is rather limited. Accordingly, the self-constitutionalisation of networks is unthinkable without the emergence of specialised organs that exert specific meta-governance functions: 'Constitutional orders consist of constituent units and a superintendent' (Sabel 1993: 73).

In the case under research, this position is held by the Secretariat. In contrast to official statements such as 'we only do what the countries want us to do' (Interview 13 September 2007), it would be a mistake to reduce the Secretariat's position to a purely assisting role. In fact, many functions that appear as mere service-delivery at first glance prove to be of enormous regulatory potential in reality. Surprisingly, as the following passage shows, this even holds true for a rather 'harmless' activity such as hosting a conference:

> I: The example you mentioned, when you were surprised to receive so few comments, what was that?

S: It was a Test Guideline on bees. You know, in country x, there were suspicions of some pesticides killing bees, and also in country y, it was a big issue. So, when this test was developed, and country x was the lead country for this, and we received so few comments from country y, I said, I am quite surprised, because they had made lots of tests.
I: Didn't they have enough time or?
S: To do it? Yes. We even had a meeting here with country y and country x, we had a meeting and they came, yes. It was sure that they didn't know about the project (Interview 13 September 2007).

Obviously, the procedural standards of the initiative are not immune to possible breaches. In the example given, the focus is on the National Coordinators' task to include a broad spectrum of experts in the discourse. As the last sentence shows ('it was sure that they didn't know about the project'), important national experts had not been informed at all. This surely represents a severe breach of duty. The members of the Secretariat had already suspected this due to the papers they had received, and therefore, they gave particular attention to this case. In the context of the interview, this episode is characterised as an exception. Normally, as is often emphasised by the members of the Secretariat, National Coordinators fulfil their tasks satisfactorily, and consequently, the Secretariat has no reason to become engaged more intensively. In the case reported here, however, the affair seemed so dubious that the Secretariat judged it necessary to deviate from the existing routine.

According to the functions laid out in Guidance Document No 1, the Secretariat 'assists member countries in the steps necessary for developing or revising Test Guidelines, including the organization of workshops and meetings' (OECD 2006: 14). Obviously, such meetings can be an important tool for information exchange; and other purposes, such as the need to raise awareness or agenda- setting, would also be conceivable. However, in the episode reported here, the influence exerted by holding a meeting goes much further—in fact, the activity of the Secretariat serves to work against the restrictive pattern of participation as caused by the National Coordinators. Even though the Secretariat seeks to avoid any affront to the members of the initiative, the meeting (as described in the passage above) is still a mechanism for correction and repair.

In contrast to institutions of a supranational character, where the supervisory organs pursue their own policy goals, it is the rules and standards created by the members of the OECD initiative themselves which are implemented by the Secretariat, and which are used as the yardstick for monitoring. In this way, the Secretariat serves as a safeguard against possible obstructions by individual actors. The following passage further elaborates on this point. The episode concerns the later stages in the process of Test Guidelines development, namely, the moment when the WNT Working Group of National Coordinators comes together for a final meeting in order to adopt the validated draft method. Since the decision requires consent, individual actors can significantly disturb the process:

> In some cases, I say, if there is no agreement, I will go to the Joint Meeting. For example, we have a Test Guideline on the Uterotrophic Bioassay, which was there for at least ten years. And it was submitted for approval at the last WNT meeting. And it was only for few things, it was linked to the number of animals, and country z didn't agree. And I said, if we don't agree at this meeting, I will take all this to the Joint Meeting. And it helped a little bit. At the Joint Meeting, people think twice, before they continue to block (Interview 13 September 2007).

In some regard, the passage leads us back to the more conventional elements of the OECD Programme. In order to officially come into force, the final product of the expert discourse must be ratified by higher policy actors and heads of state. In the case of the OECD, these actors are mainly represented in the OECD Council. Below the Council, one finds several other organs where members of national ministries are represented: the Environment Policy Committee (EPOC), the Chemicals Committee, and the Working Party on Chemicals, Pesticides and Biotechnology. The latter two bodies form the Joint Meeting, which represents the immediate superior of the WNT Working Group of National Coordinators. Before a toxicological test is incorporated into the OECD Test Guidelines, it must pass all these levels. Yet, in the history of the Test Guidelines Programme, none of these organs has ever rejected a draft Guideline that had been approved by the Working Group of National Coordinators. Accordingly, the whole procedure seems rather formalistic.[8]

Nevertheless, as the example shows, the higher-policy organs of the OECD can considerably contribute to the coordination of the process. In some cases, recourse to the Joint Meeting appears to be an effective way to increase the pressure on dissenting members: face to face with heads of state and members of ministries, the dissenting voter will have enormous problems in explaining whether his or her idea is important enough to sacrifice the work of many years, and why the voter failed to make his or her objection in an earlier stage of the process.

[8] As stated in one of the interviews, members of these higher-level organs are 'more policy-oriented people, who know nothing about this, or (*laughter*), they don't know much about it' (Interview 1 October 2007). The self-correction in this utterance shows the speaker's good will, and yet, he has enormous difficulties in making any sense of the complicated procedure. From the view of most participants, the initiative would function just as well without its multi-level superstructure.

V. CONCLUDING REMARKS: LESSONS LEARNED FROM THE OECD TEST GUIDELINES PROGRAMME

In the field of global chemicals regulation, the OECD Test Guidelines Programme represents one of the oldest and most effective standard-setting mechanisms. By now, 148 test methods have been adopted, covering the sections physical-chemical properties, effects on biotic systems, degradation and accumulation and health effects (see Leeuwen and Vermeire 2007: 625). The initiative is an important step towards the creation of worldwide, standardised test methods, and yet, it goes far beyond harmonisation in the classical sense. In addition to coordinating standards at the national level, the initiative has triggered many new developments and innovations. At the same time, the success of the initiative is mirrored by the fact that over the years, several older test methods were replaced by more advanced ones, ie standards which come with a higher level of accuracy, a reduced number of test animals and less cost and effort. An important precondition for this is the elaborated institutional design of the initiative, which guarantees the legitimacy of the process and its results. The analysis shows that aspects of legitimacy are not an additional element of the initiative, but instead should be seen as an inherent aspect of effective decision-making.

In general, many of the aspects discussed in the literature on global governance networks can also be found in the case under research, such as the influential position of mid-level practitioners and their wide discretion. As the case study shows, the range of advantages and disadvantages of network governance, as described by Slaughter in 2005, can be a useful point of departure for the analysis, although from the view of reconstructive sociological research, these concepts should be applied in a heuristic way rather than taking them as pre-defined categories. The potential disadvantages of governance networks include possible threats to their effectiveness and legitimacy. Many authors tend to be too fixated on a more interest-based approach, focussing on opportunistic strategies of those participating. Empirically, however, many of the problems related to transnational governance networks seem to be of a more cognitive character, such as the danger that a proposal made by an expert may be judged too optimistically due to the expert's reputation or the risk of underestimating the diversity of local conditions in different countries.

At the same time, network members themselves can anticipate these problems, a notion which supports the constitutionalist approach in network theory, as proposed by Sabel (1993). Analytically, it proves to be advantageous to combine this constitutionalist approach with the current debate on an emerging Global Administrative Law: due to the increasing degree of discretion on the part of administrative actors, it seems of utmost importance to look out for mechanisms of legitimation which go beyond the classical conception of international law. However, in many cases, network-internal safeguards against possible distortions are just as subtle and hard to detect as the impending problems. Even where an initiative has developed its own guidance documents, the existing problem-solving strategies are represented only partly in these texts, and thus, much reconstruction work must be undertaken on a more practical level.

In this regard, the empirical case reveals three important institutional developments, which should be interpreted as important building blocks of an emerging Global Administrative Law:

— First, by establishing a specific obligation to give reasons, the initiative manages to decouple the discourse from all person-related aspects. In the case of the OECD Programme, due to its evidence-based approach and its falsificationist logic, this becomes visible in an almost paradigmatic form, but, at the same time, similar techniques to disentangle *Geltung* from *Genesis* may also be observed in most other initiatives and standard-setting networks. Furthermore, by dividing the discourse into separate phases or stages—such as assessing the testability of a proposal before testing it in more detail—the initiative manages to organise the decision-making process in an utmost rational and revisable way, thereby avoiding premature decisions.

— Another important dimension of meta-governance in transnational policy networks is the installation of specific safeguards against a possible capture or blockage of the process by non-state actors. Since the exclusion of non-state actors is not a viable option under today's conditions, the solution lies in specific provisions which provide the network with the above mentioned *qualified openness* for external input. Once again, it is by imposing specific obligations to give reasons which helps to disentangle the discourse from the actors and their interests. The way in which this is handled in the context of the OECD initiative may be recognised as exemplary, and in some regards, the institutional structures are a refreshing alternative to the popular idea that the domestication of industry actors could best be accomplished by installing other actors from civil society as a 'counterweight'.

— In addition, meta-governance in networks calls for an effective and transparent allocation of competencies and the assignment of specific actors with separable tasks and duties. As often stated in the literature, governance beyond the nation state poses the problem that individual agencies might emancipate themselves from the fabric of interagency coordination at the national level, resulting in an increased fragmentation of the nation state (see Slaughter 2005: 254). In this regard, too, the OECD initiative can be seen as highly innovative: by creating the role of National Coordinators, the OECD Programme helps to strengthen interagency coordination at the national level. Besides several other tasks, National Coordinators are obliged to include all relevant actors and agencies from their country into the discourse, and to some extent, this is supported and monitored by the Secretariat.

In sum, the spread of transnational administrative networks and cross-border expert systems should be regarded as one of the most challenging tasks for modern governance research, forcing us to overcome many of the traditional patterns of political and juridical thought. While many of today's controversies still adhere to traditional dualisms, such as the dichotomy of supranationalism and intergovernmentalism, an increasing number of highly innovative initiatives follow a third path, namely, the path of transgovernmentalism. In general, each network invents its own norms and procedures, and sometimes, relevant procedures and organisational blueprints are also imported from different institutional contexts. At the same time, it is important to see that these elements must be contested in practice. Often, it is critical events and processes of institutional learning by which the procedural design of an initiative is shaped and re-shaped. In order to detect such elements of meta-governance in the sphere of transnational administrative networks, one has to emancipate oneself from all associations and analogies with international diplomacy, as well as from the traditional model of international governance with its overemphasis on the well-integrated, sovereign nation state that speaks with one voice.

REFERENCES

Bateson, P (2001) *Endocrine Disrupting Chemicals (EDCs)* (London, Working Papers of the Royal Society).

Beck, U (2002) *Macht und Gegenmacht im globalen Zeitalter.* Neue weltpolitische Ökonomie (Frankfurt aM, Suhrkamp).

Bermann, G (1993) 'Regulatory Cooperation with Counterpart Agencies Abroad. The FAA's Aircraft Certification Experience' 24 *Law and Policy of International Business* 669–89.

Bohne, E (1981) *Der informale Rechtsstaat.* Eine empirische und rechtliche Untersuchung zum Gesetzesvollzug unter besonderer Berücksichtigung des Immissionsschutzes (Berlin, Duncker & Humblot).

Brunsson, N and Jacobsson, B (2000) *A World of Standards* (Oxford, Oxford University Press).

Drew, P and Heritage, J (1992) *Talk at Work: Interaction in Institutional Settings* (Cambridge, Cambridge University Press).

Garfinkel, H (1972) 'Common Sense Knowledge of Social Structures: The Documentary Method of Interpretation' in J Manis and B Meltzer (eds), *Symbolic Interaction: A Reader in Social Psychology* (Boston, Allyn and Bacon).

Glaser, B and Strauss, A (1960) *The Discovery of Grounded Theory. Strategies for Qualitative Research* (Chicago, Aldine Publishing Company).

Hajer, M and Wagenaar, H (2003) *Deliberative Policy Analysis: Understanding Governance in the Network Society* (Cambridge, Cambridge University Press).

Herberg, M (2007) 'From Diffusion to Interplay. Rethinking the Constitutional State in the Age of Global Legal Pluralism' in A Hurrelmann, S Leibfried, K Martens, and P Mayer (eds), *Transforming the Golden Age Nation State* (Basingstoke, Palgrave MacMillan) 63–82.

—— (2009) 'Innenansichten des Weltrechts. Methodologische Überlegungen zur aktuellen Rechtspluralismusdebatte' in G-P Callies, A Fischer-Lescano, D Wilsch and P Zumbansen (eds), *Soziologische Jurisprudenz. Festschrift für Gunther Teubner zum 65. Geburtstag* (Berlin, De Gruyter) 739–52.

—— (2010) 'Bringing Professions back in. A Fresh Look at the Dynamics of Institution-Building in (World) Society' in C Joerges and J Falke (eds), *The Social Embeddedness of Transnational Markets* (Oxford, Hart) (forthcoming).

Jessup, PH (1956) *Transnational Law* (New Haven, Yale University Press).

Keohane, R and Nye, JS Jr (1977) 'Transgovernmental Relations and International Organizations' 27 *World Politics* 39–59.

Kingsbury, B, Krisch, N and Stewart, RB (2005) 'The Emergence of Global Administrative Law' 68 *Law and Contemporary Problems* 15–42.

Ladeur, K-H (2004) 'Globalization and Public Governance–A Contradiction?' in K-H Ladeur (ed), *Public Governance in the Age of Globalization* (Aldershot, Asgate) 1–24.

Leeuwen, C and Vermeine, TH (2007) *Risk Assessment of Chemicals. An Introduction* (Dordrecht, Springer).

Mac Cormick, N (2002) *Questioning Sovereignty: Law, State, and Nation in the European Commonwealth* (Oxford, Oxford University Press).

Mayntz, R (1979) 'Public Bureaucracies and Policy Implementation' 31, Nr 4 *International Social Science Journal* 633–45.

Nicolaidis, K and Shaffer, G (2005) 'Transnational Mutual Recognition Regimes: Governance Without Global Government'68:2 *Law and Contemporary Problems* 267–322.

OECD (2005) 'Guidance Document on the Validation and International Acceptance of New or Updated Test Methods for Hazard Assessment' http://appli1.oecd.org/oli2005doc.

—— (2006) 'Guidance Document for the Development of OECD Guidelines for the Testing of Chemicals' www.Oecd.org/dataoecd/2/24/40472761.pdf.

O'Toole, L (1993) 'Multiorganizational Policy Implementation: Some Limitations and Possibilities for Rational-Choice Contributions' in FW Scharpf (ed), *Games in Hierarchies and Networks. Analytical and Empirical Approaches to the Study of Governance Institutions* (Frankfurt aM, Campus) 27–64.

Popper, K (2002) *Conjectures and Refutations. The Growth of Scientific Knowledge* (London and New York, Routledge).

Robertson, R (1995) 'Glocalisation: Time-Space and Homogeneity-Heterogeneity' in M Featherstone, S Lash and R Robertson (eds), *Global Modernities* (London, Sage) 25–45.

Samra-Fredericks, D (2005) 'Talk-in-Interaction/ Conversation Analysis' in C Cassell and G Symon (eds), *Essential Guide to Qualitative Methods in Organizational Research* (London & Thousand Oaks, Sage Publications) 214–27.

Scharpf, FW (1993) 'Coordination in Hierarchies and Networks' in FW Scharpf (ed), *Games in Hierarchies and Networks. Analytical and Empirical Approaches to the Study of Governance Institutions* (Frankfurt/ Main Campus) 125–66.
Schilleman, TH (2008) 'Accountability in the Shadow of Hierarchy: The Horizontal Accountability of Agencies' 8 *Public Organization Review* 175–94.
Schneider, V (1988) *Politiknetzwerke der Chemikalienkontrolle. Eine Analyse einer transnationalen Politikentwicklung* (Berlin/ New York, De Gruyter).
Shapiro, M (2005) '"Deliberative", "Independent" Technocracy v. Democratic Politics: Will the Globe Echo the EU?' 68 *Law and Contemporary Problems* 341–56.
Sabel, CH (1993) 'Constitutional Ordering in Historical Context' in FW Scharpf (ed), *Games in Hierarchies and Networks. Analytical and Empirical Approaches to the Study of Governance Institutions* (Frankfurt aM, Campus) 65–124.
Slaughter, A-M (2005) *A New World Order* (Princeton, Princeton University Press).
Soerensen, E and Torfing, J (2005) 'The Democratic Anchorage of Governance Networks' 28 *Scandinavian Political Studies* 195–218.
Stewart, RB (2005) 'U.S. Administrative Law: A Model For Global Administrative Law?' 68 *Law and Contemporary Problems* 63–108.
Streck, CH (2002) 'Global Public Policy Networks as Coalitions for Change' in D Esty and M Ivanova (eds), *Global Environmental Governance, Options and Opportunities* (New Haven, Yale School of Forestry) 121–40.
Warning, M (2009) *The Legitimacy of Transnational Bureaucracy Networks* (Basingstoke, Palgrave MacMillan).
Weber, M (1978) [1922] *Economy and Society: An Outline of Interpretive Sociology* edited by G Roth and C Wittich (Berkeley/ Los Angeles/ London, University of California Press).
Williamson, OE (1975) *Markets and Hierarchies: Analysis and Anti-Trust Implications* (New York, Free Press).
Zumbansen, P (2001) 'Die vergangene Zukunft des Völkerrechts' 34 *Kritische Justiz* 46–68.

Part III

Negotiation and Deliberation in Regulatory Committees

4

Transnational Administrative Comitology: The Global Harmonisation of Chemicals Classification and Labelling

GERD WINTER

ABSTRACT

THE CHAPTER[1] STARTS by identifying the realm of transnational public administration. It then studies as a case the development of a globally harmonised system of classification and labelling of dangerous substances (GHS). The transnational administrative rulemaking is reconstructed in terms of its organisation, proceedings and outcome. Its organisational substructure is made up of a relatively stable and differentiated system of committees and working groups connecting civil servants from national and international technical administrations. The proceedings were characterised by a combination of rational discourse with bargaining and power play. Material and procedural meta-rules were established to guide the proceedings. These provided a modest level of self-legitimation, which still requires bolstering. Principles of domestic administrative law may be drawn on for this purpose. However, given their liberal roots in checking centralised public power, these principles will need to be modified to accord with the diffuse polyarchy of transnational public administration. Furthermore, the self-legitimation process cannot undercut national constitutional yardsticks controlling the entry of informal transnational rules into the national spheres of formal law. In addition, international law may develop juridifying informal rules of the transnational sphere.

[1] I wish to thank Olaf Dilling and Martin Herberg for helpful comments and Anna-Maria Hubert for skilful language editing.

I. THE PHENOMENON OF TRANSNATIONAL PUBLIC ADMINISTRATION

National civil servants have interacted with colleagues from other states since the rise of the nation state (Tietje 2010). With the overall globalisation of societies, economies and states, the areas where this happens and the frequency of interaction have, however, substantially increased. A growing number of networks, working groups, committees, organisations and other structures have evolved, fixing these interactions on a more permanent and organised basis.

Transnational (as opposed to 'international' or 'inter-governmental') are these transboundary arrangements inasmuch as they connect actors from the working level of national administrations thus bypassing their ministers and the diplomatic relations practised between heads of government.[2] The forms and levels of the institutionalisation of transnational interactions are diverse. Looser, less-developed forms are characterised by a low frequency of interactions, unstable membership, unstructured work programmes and lack of centralised guidance. More established committees are more likely to exhibit features such as a long-standing membership, a well-determined work programme and perhaps a system of committees with assigned competences.[3]

What makes a structure administrative? One possible answer is that administrative arrangements are made up of public officials. However, this would reverse the logic that applies to the formation of administrative structures. Normally (but not always[4]), a problem arises and structures emerge to solve it. What it is that calls national public officials to a task, can only be explained by looking at the nature of the task itself. What then makes a task administrative? Some suggest that administrative matters are those that are neither political nor judicial in character (*cf* Kingsbury, Krisch and Stewart 2005). This approach of defining by subtraction is hardly seminal. We could define it positively as a task concerned with the practical management of technical problems, and not the formation of political will.[5] This definition is supported by reference

[2] Keohane and Nye 1974: 43 defined this level as 'direct interactions among sub-units of different governments that are not controlled or closely guided by the policies of the cabinets or chief executives of those governments'. They contrast this with the 'club model' of networks of cabinet ministers from a small group of leading states which tend to elaborate their agreements secretly and impose them on the less powerful governments.

[3] An elaborate example of this type is the Codex Alimentarius Commission. See the contributions by Arnold and Herwig in chapters five and six respectively.

[4] Once structures have been created and after having solved the problem they tend to search for new tasks, but even those will be 'administrative'.

[5] For the German tradition, see Lorenz v Stein (1869: 60), who defined *Verwaltung* as the activity of the state that subjects the real conditions of life (*wirkliche Lebensverhältnisse*) to the will of the state.

to the latin roots of the term, *administrare* and *manum agere*, which mean 'lending a hand', or by looking at the German word for administration, *Verwaltung*, with its connotation of 'mastering things'.[6]

Practical and technical matters of this sort should be distinguished from matters of high politics and fundamental policy orientation. High politics are handled by different fora and in a different way than by administrations.[7] Frequently, administrators 'execute'[8] a political will, but often act on their own initiative, and as a consequence, implicitly answer any political questions that may be involved.[9]

This state-bound characterisation of administration can also be applied to the transnational sphere, if it is taken into account that cases involving the execution of political will are much rarer in the transnational than in the national realm. In the transnational sphere, it is more typical that the 'policy' of management is incrementally elaborated in the administrative process, rather than hard-won from battles in a separate political arena. If the political will was formed through a process of transnational administrative cooperation, it is generally not conclusive, but is rather vague and more symbolic in nature.[10] Thus, transnational administration could be understood as the management of technical matters of a transnational character, including the political implications of the technical.

The case studied in this chapter concerns the global harmonisation of chemicals standards. In organisational terms, it is an example for established committee systems that are more stable than loose networks. The task that the transnational arrangement took upon itself—the definition and labelling of chemicals hazard categories—was a technical/scientific one which involved, however, intricate political questions. How this was reflected in the proceedings of rule-elaboration will be explored further.

[6] The term *walten* means to perform, to master, to deal with something. The prefix 'ver' marks intensity (or a negation like in *Verbot*). *Verwaltung* is then the committed mastering of something. See Deutsches Wörterbuch 2004, Articles 'Ver' and 'Walten'.

[7] Unfortunately, the US notion of administration ('the Clinton, the Bush administration') is often used precisely to denote such fundamental orientation. In the German tradition, this would be called *Regierung* (government). See again Stein who defines *Regierung* as the formation of a general will and deed representing the entirety of the state, whilst *Verwaltung* adapts the general will and deed to the given facts and life conditions (Stein 1869: 60 and 134).

[8] From *exsequi* meaning to follow-up.

[9] While Max Weber's (Weber 1964: 1047–62) ideal type of bureaucracy stresses the instrumental role of administrative bodies, more recent literature emphasises trends towards a self-programming of the administration (Mayntz 1978: 61–81). Based on Eisenstadt 1963, Mayntz proposes three types of self-programming: administration using its expertise in the public interest, administration pursuing selfish goals (eg maximal remuneration, defence of powerful positions), and administration advocating a specific interest (eg of a specific class or stratum). The first type is of most interest in the present context. It was already identified by Weber himself when he opposed the experienced bureaucracy with the dilettantism of politicians (Weber 1964: 730; *cf* Mayntz 1978: 63).

[10] See, as an example, the role of the International Forum of Chemical Safety (IFCS) within the fabric of international chemicals regulation (Warning 2009; Nowrot 2010).

Did they follow a style of rational discourse,[11] or were they instead characterised by negotiation and power play? Did meta-rules emerge to establish at least second-best insurance of rationality? In the absence of such self-control, can and if so, how is formal state-based law to be brought in to tame creeping transnational power?

II. THE CASE

A. The Issue

Trade restrictions have come under close scrutiny with the growing world market of products, tariffary and non-tariffary. The classification of hazardous chemicals and associated regulations is one of those non-tariffary restrictions. Categories of hazards include bio-accumulation, persistence, and toxicity to human health, environmental toxicity, explosiveness, mutagenicity, and cancerogenicity. Obligations are tied to this classification such as that the chemical must be safely packaged, warnings and safety recommendations must be printed on packages, safety data sheets must be provided to downstream users, specific precautions must be taken at the workplace, and, for some categories, sales to end consumers may even be prohibited. The classification and regulation of such products may have the effect of restricting cross-border trade. This is particularly true where classification systems and laws differ among states. A producer will have to reclassify the same chemical as toxic, highly toxic or not toxic depending on the legal requirements in the country of importation. A common classification scheme would eliminate these obstacles, allowing a product to have a single classification on any national market. Under a unified system, the producer would still face different sanctions under national law. However, a common approach to classification is indispensable for harmonisation. A similar problem arises in relation to the labelling of products (ie printing symbols and additional consumer information about the substance on packaging). Different labelling systems are a barrier to transnational trade, because products would have to be labelled differently depending on the country of importation.

The harmonisation of classification and labelling schemes is not merely a matter of establishing common categories and labels. The legal consequences tied to the hazard categories impact upon sales and thus the profitability of the product. The regulatory framework also channels the product through the market to end consumers, ensuring its proper use and preventing it from being released into the environment. For instance, a non-toxic product that is classified as toxic will be held back, frustrating

[11] For a case of this kind see M Herberg, chapter 3 in this volume.

economic expectations. Conversely, a toxic product that is classified as non-toxic will enter the market without restriction, endangering human health and the environment.

Cross-cutting the classical conflict between economic interests and health and the environment is a third interest: developing countries. Developing countries are in a paradoxical situation. They have reasons to oppose strict chemicals regulation, such as in the area of pesticides, to protect their agricultural production and to remain attractive for investment in the chemicals production sector. On the other hand, they have an interest in protecting the health of workers and consumers, as well as the environment. The result is that they have often hesitated to adopt any chemicals regulation at all.

A further concern relates to how national legal systems view the particular approach of another country. There is a significant divergence between the way the United States and European Union regulates chemicals, respectively referred to as the risk approach and hazard approach (Pallemaerts 2003). The EU hazard approach identifies the inherent characteristics of a substance or preparation, and classifies and labels them independently of the question of 'end-points' exposure (ie whether the chemical will come into contact with humans or the environment). By contrast, the US risk approach takes into account the chemicals end-points from the outset, with the consequence that certain substances may not be classified at all, or that labelling is not required. For instance, a substance normally used in closed systems would not have to be classified as toxic, or bear the symbol for toxicity. The European Union assumes that the properties of a substance must be determined and communicated regardless of its normal use by the end consumer. The European approach is precautionary, and assumes that by not providing specific information, the substance will ultimately end up in the environment. The US approach is more pragmatic, standing by until there is evidence of potential damage.

There are also ideological differences to take into account. This is a consideration with regard to the symbols used for the labelling of packages. The St Andrew's cross, a diagonal cross or X,[12] was traditionally used in Europe to mark the toxicity of a substance. Its allusion to death may be misunderstood in the non-Christian world.

In conclusion, in contrast to matters of 'high' transnational politics, such as the establishment of rules concerning global trade or the fight against terrorism, the classification and labelling of hazardous chemicals is certainly a technical matter. Nevertheless, the interests and traditions at stake show that significant policy questions are also involved.

[12] The Apostle Andrew, when martyred, requested out of modesty that a different type of cross should be used than that used for Jesus Christ. See www.en.wikipedia.org/wiki/St._Andrew.

B. The Run Up[13]

Plans to harmonise the classification and labelling of chemicals at the international level have long been part of more comprehensive initiatives to manage the risks of hazardous chemicals. These include the harmonisation of test guidelines, the registration of chemicals, prior information provided to the importing state about risks of chemicals, and the restriction of production and trade of chemicals. These initiatives have different origins. The Organisation for Economic Cooperation and Development (OECD) became involved at an early stage. In 1971, the OECD Council adopted an Environment, Health and Safety Programme and established the Environment Policy Committee (EPOC), which then set up a Working Party on Chemicals, Pesticides, and Biotechnology. In 1987, the OECD Council established the Chemicals Committee, which set up the 'Joint Meeting' with EPOC. Around the same time, a number of other international organisations took an interest in the problem of hazardous chemicals, including the International Labour Organisation (ILO), the World Health Organisation (WHO), and the United Nations Environmental Programme (UNEP). Each organisation looked at the problem from its own sectoral perspective—occupational health (ILO), human health (WHO) and environmental pollution (UNEP).

In 1980, the ILO, WHO and UNEP concluded a Memorandum of Understanding to set up the International Programme on Chemical Safety (IPCS). Thirty six countries have agreed to participate in the programme activities. Participation has been based on memoranda of understanding between IPCS and each individual country and has involved certain financial contribution. After years of slow progress, chemicals regulation—including the harmonisation of classification and labelling—gathered new momentum as part of Agenda 21, which was concluded at the Rio Conference in 1992.[14] In 1995, the Inter-Organisation Programme for the Sound Management of Chemicals (IOMC) was established by a Memorandum of Understanding between UNEP, ILO, the Food and Agriculture Organisation of the United Nations (FAO), the United Nations Industrial Development Organisation (UNIDO), OECD, and was later joined by other international organisations. While IOMC has strategically coordinated the activities of different international organisations, IPCS has operated on a working level developing risk assessment rules and elaborating assessments of individual substances.

The most important practical step in the global harmonisation of chemicals classification and labelling was the creation of the Coordination

[13] See, for a more detailed description, Warning 2009.

[14] Agenda 21 ch 19 no 19.24 to 19.32 detail the agenda for the classification and labelling of chemicals.

Group for the Harmonisation of Chemicals Classification Systems (CG/HCCS) in 1995. This was based on a Memorandum of Understanding concluded under the auspices of the IOMC. The Coordination Group was conceived as part of the IPCS and supported logistically by the ILO Secretariat. Its task was to elaborate the rules of the GHS. While the right to vote in the CG was restricted to government representatives, non-governmental organisations (NGOs) representing the interests of industry and the public were admitted as observers.

In 2001, the CG completed its work. To enhance its acceptance by states, the CG sought the endorsement of the UN Economic and Social Council

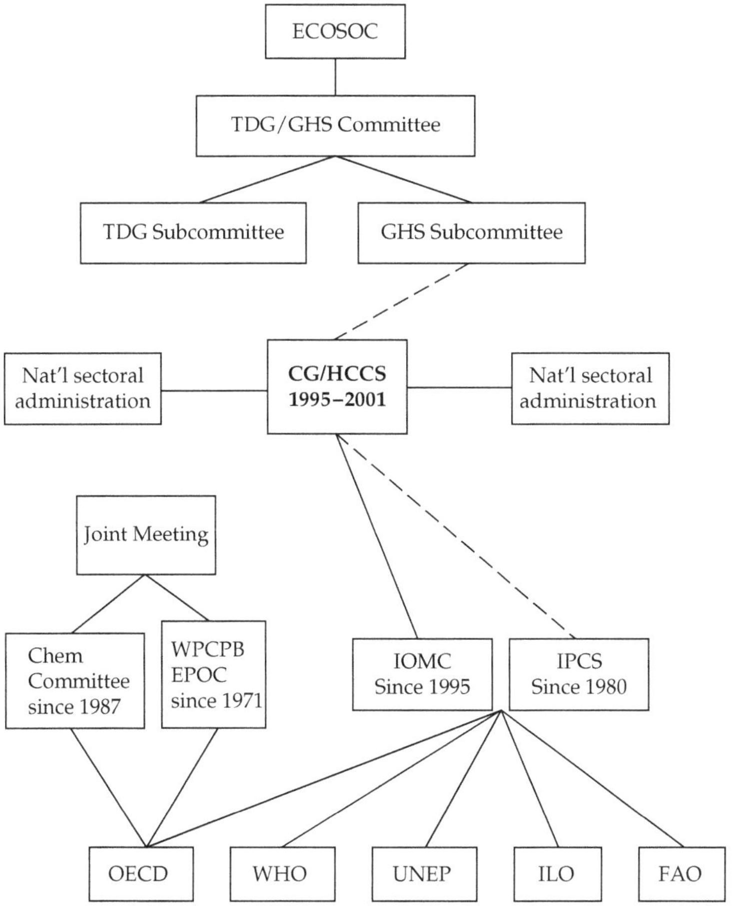

Figure 1: Organisations, programmes and committees participating in the development of the GHS; dotted line = working relationship; straight line = constituting relationship.

(ECOSOC), which could provide the necessary authority to crosscut the views of participating sectoral organisations (ILO, WHO, UNEP) and the OECD, a regional organisation. Accordingly, the work document was handed over to the United Nations. For many years, ECOSOC had been engaged in classification and labelling issues through its Committee of Experts on the Transport of Dangerous Goods (TDG Committee). This sectoral focus on transport was too narrow to encompass the broad scope of the GHS, and, as a result, ECOSOC enlarged the mandate of the TGD Committee by reconfiguring it into a joint Committee of experts on TGD and GHS (TDG&GHS Committee). At the same time, two sub-committees were formed: one on the Transport of Dangerous Goods (TDG Sub-Committee) and the other on the Globally Harmonized System (GHS Sub-Committee). In 2001, the GHS Sub-Committee took note of the GHS as developed by the Coordination Group, and endorsed it. In 2002, ECOSOC approved the GHS in a resolution expressing its 'deep appreciation' for this work, and 'inviting all governments' to implement it. The GHS Sub-Committee was also charged with further developing and promoting the implementation of the GHS. It was to report to ECOSOC through the TDG/GHS Committee.

C. The Proceedings[15]

i. The Organisational Fabric

The organisational fabric of the GHS committee system may suggest that all activities occur within the formal structures of international organisations. However, almost everyone acting within this complex structure were employees of participating states. Hence, the working level was very

[15] Most of the following observations rely on four interviews with experts who have for many years participated in the elaboration of the GHS. Interviews I and II were conducted in 2004 and 2007 with public officials from the Federal Institute for Occupational Safety and Health (*Bundesanstalt für Arbeitsschutz und Arbeitsmedizin*), Interview III in 2007 with a public official of the Federal Institute for Materials Research and Testing (*Bundesinstitut für Materialforschung and -prüfung*), and Interview IV in 2005 with a public official of the IPCS. The interviews were conducted by my collaborators, Martin Herberg and Michael Warning. I am very thankful that they allowed me to make use of their material. As I am not trained in qualitative sociological methods, my observations can only achieve plausibility, not full reliability. I carefully read the interviews, tried to understand from them the reality of proceedings, reorganised the most significant passages around characteristic aspects, and abstracted summary observations from them. I present the results of my study by first giving the summary observations and then illustrating them by citing core passages from the interviews. Of course, for reasons of space not every single conclusion can be fully proven; a measure of trust in the objectivity of the researcher is requested. May this be furthered by my acknowledgement that my 'null-hypotheses' about the observed discourses were fundamentally different from what I learned from the material. I expected scientific deliberations but learned about a complex mixture of rationalities.

much determined by transnationalism in the meaning explained above. International organisations contributed two additional functions: they participated in agenda-setting by making strategic recommendations and concluding interorganisational memoranda of understanding; and they furthered the practical progress of negotiations by providing secretarial assistance.

The whole setting was structured according to working groups and 'official' committees, such as the global CG and the OECD 'Joint Meeting' in the initial phase, and later the TDG/GHS Committee and its sub-committees. While the bulk of deliberation and drafting was done in numerous informal working groups, the committees served as clearing houses for controversial issues, coordinators setting terms for working groups, and ratifyers of texts submitted by working groups. Here is one account of the relationship between working groups and committees:

> In the UN sub-committee it is true that they do have discussions there, but they do not treat the technical details. This is done in the working groups, for instance, those dealing with chemically instable gases, sensitives, explosives. Or, regularly, at every July session the working group on explosives meets, which then, for instance, discusses such and such footnote and at the end recommends that it shall be adopted and then the subcommittee decides whether to follow the recommendation or not.[16]

The OECD as a special organisation, which comprises the developed world (and in fact most of the chemical-producing countries), had similar groups working in parallel with the CG and its working groups which operated at the global level. These groups provided assistance and heavily influenced the global process.

ii. Participating Members

Committees and working groups were made up of public officials from sectoral (not foreign) ministries and the expert administrative bodies of participating states. Even the chairpersons were national officials. Only very few appointees from international organisations attended, providing either secretarial assistance or as observers. Membership in working groups, sub-committees and committees overlapped to a certain extent, simply because many states did not have sufficient personnel to staff so many bodies. Industry members were also admitted as observers, and frequently made use of this opportunity. However, they were not allowed to vote. Public interest NGOs were also admitted, but were present less frequently, and were therefore less active. Even though the acting bodies

[16] Interview III.

operated within the framework of global international organisations (IOs), developing states were underrepresented. This is due to the fact that developing countries could not normally afford the costs of travel and preparation for sessions.

iii. Principles of Procedure and Policy

The IOMC functioned as the umbrella programme that coordinated chemicals regulation within the framework of sectoral international organisations. The IOMC's acting body, the Inter-Organisation Coordinating Committee (IOCC), had set out certain organisational and procedural rules for coordination groups operating under its auspices. According to these rules

> the coordination groups must obtain IOCC approval of their tasks, membership, and observers (which they are basically free to determine themselves);
>
> industry, labour and public interest NGOs are responsible for coordinating representation and membership within and among their respective nongovernmental organization groupings;
>
> the coordination groups are to 'operate on the basis of consensus';
>
> members and observers must bear their own costs.[17]

There is no rule regarding procedural transparency in the interest of the general public.

These principles were also binding for the Coordination Group for the GHS. However, the Coordination Group amended these by adding a number of more specific rules on policy and procedure. These concerned the level of health and environmental protection, as well as the involvement of and communication with stakeholders. Some of them read as follows:

> the level of protection offered to workers, consumers, the general public and the environment should not be reduced as a result of harmonising the classification and labelling systems;
>
> the involvement of concerned international organizations of employers, workers, consumers, and other relevant organizations in the process of harmonization should be ensured;
>
> in relation to chemical hazard communication the safety and health of workers, consumers and the public in general, as well as the protection of

[17] See IOMC Co-ordinating Groups Standard Operating Procedures. See www.who.int/iomc/groups/standard_operating_procedures.pdf (last visited 2 November 2008).

> the environment, should be ensured while protecting confidential business information, as prescribed by the competent authorities.[18]

The principles once again do not address the question of transparency for the general public. De facto, however, the CG/HCCS did make some documents available on the internet; this was not an invitation for public comment, but instead done with the intention to inform the public about what had been achieved.[19]

iv. The Discourse

Much of the discourse in the working groups and official committees centred on technical expertise. For instance, one discussion concerned whether, based on an LD_{50}-Test[20] of rats, it is appropriate to classify a substance as toxic. Even though scientists may have different views in this regard (for example, some may argue that tests of a different animal are more applicable to issues of human health), this kind of discussion involves largely a scientific question. Based on this, one may expect that the deliberations were of the type of Habermasian rational discourse. Such discourse would presuppose an 'ideal speech situation': in which participants argue on point (*sachhaltig*), without bias (*vorurteilsfrei*), and are uncompelled (*herrschaftsfrei*) (Habermas 1992). Nevertheless, such discourse remains embedded in social structures of opportunity, interest and power. If the issue is highly technical and other conditions are favourable, the structural setting may be 'rationalised', ie fully transformed by arguments and deliberations. However, often the nature of the issue and context are such that rational discourse is severely limited, and the negotiations are instead characterised by bargaining, tactical behaviour, and even obstruction or demonstrations of power. Ultimately, it was this style that characterised the GHS proceedings.

a. Status Quo, Vested Interests and Blocking

Major obstacles to achieving scientific consensus are arguments in defence of the status quo and the protection of vested interests by those who fear the uncertainty or costs brought about by new rules. Anxiety about changes to the status quo is often present and disrupts open discourse,

[18] Coordination Group for the Harmonization of Chemical Classification Systems, Revised terms of reference and work programme Genevy 1996 No 8. Available at www.ilo.org/public/english/protection/safework/ghs/ghsdocs/index.htm (last visited 2 November 2008).

[19] See overview of available documents at www.ilo.org/public/english/protection/safework/ghs/cghccs.htm (last visited 2 November 2008).

[20] LD means lethal dose (LD), and LD_{50} that dose of a tested substance which causes the death of 50% of a sample of test organisms exposed to the substance.

if the participants at meetings are higher administrative officials or non-expert industry representatives:

> Well, the first point is that the structures and the behaviour of acting persons are very formal. This is even more common in the UN Committee than at the OECD level. The second point is that, at the UN level, normally or often persons participate at meetings, or at least partially is that so, who I may say represent the higher levels, but do not understand the technical details, ie who act more politically than technically, substantially. A further point is, that even at the OECD level in the expert groups representatives of certain interest groups can be found, I mean also of industry, who partly have insufficient technical expertise and act for the industrial interest. This of course renders negotiations very, very difficult (laughing). Our German industry can well keep pace her, that if there is a fear that new burdens may result and the issue is not well understood the industry is not in a position to clarify the matter for them but blocks the further proceeding for the single reason that there might be a burdensome result.[21]

> In the UN Subcommittee, I must say, of course, sit experts. You can certainly come in with technical arguments. Sometimes however our impression is that technical arguments do not help. When certain countries are against, it is hard to get through.[22]

However, according to one interviewee, perseverance in advancing scientific argument can break new ground:

> Every change is burdensome and therefore normally participants act so that nobody—really nobody—is committed to discuss with a view to improve things. Well, this is about what I realise, I am here—and this is also the position of my [agency]: we allow ourselves the luxury in the technical bodies to argue technically. We argue like we find it appropriate in technical terms and, well, I am not a politician and sit in these bodies and always struggle for something. I rather repeat things once and again, even when I know that this is bound to fail from the outset. But it is important for me to make clear what makes sense technically, and to do this again and again.[23]

Interviewee II reports a case where—after long and exhausting debates—a particular industry that had blocked further progress gave in when its members finally discovered that the new rule was also in its own best interest.

b. Policy Questions

Ideally, interests can be transformed into policy arguments instead of being pursued by obstruction. This can be achieved by separating

[21] Interview II.
[22] Interview III.
[23] Interview I.

scientific from socio-economic aspects, for example by distinguishing between risk assessment and risk management. Many expert participants in the proceedings draw a distinction between technical and policy questions and try to refer the latter to bodies other than just the technical working groups:

> During the negotiations experts are closer to one another than the negotiation chairpersons in relation to their countries, I would say, because the technical problems are always comparable. But there is always a superstructure (*Überbau*).[24]

However, not all experts make this distinction, instead choosing to blur expertise and policy questions:

> My experience from my activities is that the representatives from sectoral authorities in the EU discuss partly openly as experts while partly the policy background smears [*verschmiert*] a bit, I should say. Well, we in Germany always try, and this is in principle also supported by our ministries, to say clearly this is our expert assessment, and if we shall include socio-economic concerns, then this may well lead to another assessment. Yet, it is very important to so to speak clearly distinguish the technical assessment from the political. And unfortunately this is not the case in the EU and the international sphere, and especially it is not so with the North-Americans.[25]

c. Interest and Power

In transnational negotiations, where there is a need for consensus and technical rather than political matters are at stake, there appears to be little room for power in Max Weber's sense of the possibility of executing one's will even against resistance (Weber 1972: 28). Still, power exists in more subtle or indirect ways, such as by refusing to put a theme on the agenda or by stubbornly maintaining certain discordant positions or vetoing of other proposals. Some of this behaviour was observed in the GHS proceedings, particularly in matters concerning the gap between European and US basic approaches to chemicals regulation:

> I believe, well my impression of negotiations by agency officials [of the US, GW], is that they are purely political. This means they in fact are not free at all. Well, I am (laughs), when one in popular saying speaks of the country of unlimited possibilities and one actually realizes how concreted these experts of the US administration are, that is how narrowly they proceed. Ah, that is frightening, I find this utterly frightening—this is my impression. But there are of course nuances, but the proceeding and the intellectual and technical freedom and the utterance of technical positions is very, very restricted.

[24] Ibid.
[25] Interview II.

> And the self-understanding, the American, this is my impression, is us first and then the rest of the world. No, I mean, you can see this in the general US politics and this is also mirrored in the more modest contexts. And when such things come up, then there is first of all an attitude of blocking and, ah, that is more or less intended, not to let the process run too fast. At least, I believe this. And then it is also intended that for the work in the committees they accept only a sort of persons who act very formally (laughs), I would say who react in a way that one can only take very small steps.[26]

While on the rules on classification and labelling of substances, some kind of agreement or compromise could nevertheless be reached after prolonged negotiations; this has been much more difficult in relation to actual decisions on the restrictions of trade in substances. For instance, specific negotiations conducted within the framework of the Rotterdam Convention concerned whether Crysotile Asbestos should be prohibited, but agreement among technical experts was stymied by those advancing certain interests:

> I was in the expert group. In the expert group, there was unanimity, but this did not go through, because Canada said we manufacture asbestos, we like it, and they were so clever to say our [internal, GW] decision-making process has not yet been completed. The Russians also said we manufacture it, and Zimbabwe too said we produce it and we do not want the prohibition. Full stop![27]

d. Input from Industry

Industry representatives are quite influential in spite of their mere observer status. Influence comes from feeding documents and proposals into the process. The lack of formal status can be made good by approaching national representatives who have voting rights to support the industry position:

> Yes, well, they can take a very active role even in the subcommittee, like, for instance, CEFIC, the European association of chemicals industry. There was, until shortly [name], who is now retired. He played a very active role. As also non-governmental organisations and observers can submit documents, they can make applications, they only do not have a voting right. But in principle they can file applications as they wish, they also do this, for instance, together with a delegation. There can be, for instance, a German association I say I just arrange something with the German delegation.[28]

As one interviewee states, industry representatives have contributed to the formal quality of the GHS process by condensing and structuring the

[26] Interview II.
[27] Ibid.
[28] Interview III.

often chaotic draft texts. However, they have also sometimes refused the reasonable position and blocked further consensus:

> The point is that even on the OECD level you can find in the expert groups, let me say, representatives of certain interest groups, ie, also of the industry, who sometimes have insufficient expertise and defend the industry position. This, of course, makes technical negotiations often very, very difficult (laughing). And this is the case with industry—I do not only experience this on the OECD level, our German industry can very well keep up with others here—that if there are fears that aggravations may come up, and it is not at all understood what the matter is, if the industry is actually not in a position to clarify the problem for itself, what the real problems are, but alone for fear that there may be an aggravation they block things.[29]

e. Individuals and Institutions

Committed individuals are of major importance to the whole process. Often they initiate harmonisation projects and keep them moving by putting issues on the agenda, providing relevant information and building consensus. Although they are national civil servants, it would be a misunderstanding to speak of lead countries: rather, it is certain lead individuals who often work towards winning the support of their country for their own initiatives. These individuals often strive to become chairpersons, because this position allows them to exert influence over procedure and substance. If they do not succeed in their bid for chairperson, such individuals will often try more indirect ways to push their views through:[30]

> Well, okay, as soon as you have a working group, you need someone who is responsible and in a way coordinates and pushes things forward, and for that you need somebody, whether you call this lead country or chair, or whatever, someone who is simply active and also committed. Well, these are normally specific interests, where specific interests stand behind. Or, if you wish to forward a matter, it of course makes sense that you take the lead position. Then you push things forward. Or, on the other hand, sometimes the US take the lead, so that, ah, then you have only the possibility to—ah—act more modulating, so that things do not go into a direction you do not wish.[31]

The statement shows that active individuals often represent special interests, rather than working towards overarching interests. It also sheds light

[29] Interview II.

[30] Ibid.

[31] The distinction between a motivation in the 'matter itself' and specific interests may not be 100% clear from this passage but is fortified by earlier passages. Of course, it could be questioned in theoretical terms whether the interest in the 'matter itself' is not also a specific interest. The repeated 'ah(s)' and hesitating phrasing can be interpreted as insecurity of the speaker regarding how far to go in blaming other persons.

on the role of chairpersons, suggesting that there is no practice, nor even an expectation, that the chair must be neutral; most chairpersons have a specific result in mind that they are working towards:

> Question: I should like to ask what rules or measures there are or if there are discussions about measures in order to ensure something like the impartiality of the chair.
>
> Answer: no, that does not exist, does not exist! They also act politically, …[32]

f. Bargaining and Consensus Strategies

Since the entire process is based on consensus, consensus building is of utmost importance. One way to achieve this is through negotiations in small informal circles, outside of the more formal working sessions.

> Well, I could say, if I exaggerate–but that is, I mean, I do not have so much experience in committees that so to speak what happens during the break or what happens in small groups, ah, has a very, very high importance. Thus, I do not want to say a higher …, but that actually these agreements, ah, the lobbying and the building of accordance, or that, if you want to effectively bring something through, that one must, of course, do that with much political skill. Or if one wants to block things that this is not treated by open discussion in the session but that is then achieved in other ways.[33]

Unassuming and perhaps a bit hesitant, the interviewee seems to struggle when addressing this apparently elusive issue. In addition to more informal discussions outside of the regular meetings, chairpersons can build consensus by intentionally proposing equivocal formulations that leave further clarification to later stages of negotiation or implementation. However, such tactics are risky, because of the potential that ambiguous formulations will be given an unintended meaning:

> Sometimes it was indeed so that in the technical negotiations I intentionally left matters unclear. And the lawyers made it clear later on. And out of this came results which we did not want, and since then Mr. S [the lawyer] and I have always precisely arranged the terms that this and that should remain unclear (provided it is also legally undetermined), for this cannot at all be solved in the committee, but we can then proceed, even though this is left open—but that was really a thrill when all of a sudden things were on the table which nobody had intended.[34]

[32] Interview II. The signs of hesitation and consideration show that the interviewee feels as though the issue is of a sensitive nature.

[33] Ibid. The hesitant mode of speaking again indicates the issue is somewhat sensitive in nature.

[34] Ibid. The passage is related to negotiations in the framework of the Rotterdam Convention, not of the GHS.

g. Ties with Home States

National officials often have an ambiguous relationship with their home state. To participate in transnational proceedings, they require the approval of their state, normally from the relevant government ministry. However, the home authority does not provide close direction, allowing national officials significant room for manoeuvre. If they are committed to the process and possess tactical skills, national representatives can have significant influence over the overall direction of the proceedings. The German example shows that individual character can be more important than institutional affiliation. For example, the coordinator of the German delegation was a civil servant of a regulatory agency which belonged to the Ministry of Economy and Labour. This ministry was not primarily responsible for chemicals regulation. The competent ministry, the Ministry for the Environment, accepted this because this individual had many years of accumulated experience, as well as recognition and important connections within the transnational field. The trust he enjoyed from the competent ministry was so firm that he could not imagine ever receiving precise and binding instructions:

> This would be totally exciting, if I got an instruction. I would be at odds how to handle that. I do act on a mandate from the BMU [Ministry for the Environment], that is the construction, but I belong to the Ministry for Economy and Labour. Therefore, should they [the BMU] give me an instruction—that would be interesting, I am going to wait for that. And there is now even a working group on the issue in the BMU. The BMU is lead agency. But in principle I can act because I have a good standing. Theoretically, this should be done by someone from the BMU departments.[35]

Before travelling to the meetings of transnational working groups and committees, German officials usually come together or have telephone conversations in order to coordinate the German position among colleagues from the different national authorities affected by the issue at stake. This is particularly the case for non-technical matters with policy implications:

> Well, we arrange for a national coordination of positions beforehand and this is so not only for GHS–often in the framework of a so-called consultants circle (*Beraterkreis*). That has been practised at some point in the process. Apart from that, there exists a large e-mail distribution list where of course also representatives of stakeholders are involved. And normally we have for each UN session a meeting where we coordinate ourselves on those topics that are on the agenda of the UN session. Within the OECD it is normally so that because there are continuous telephone conversations we believe, I believe, that there is not always a duty to provide information and to coordinate ourselves, because we discuss a technical question.[36]

[35] Interview I.
[36] Ibid.

However, the coordination process is not always conclusive. The national representative may then decide to remain silent, but also dare to fill the void by taking action:

> We speak with each other beforehand. And at the end normally we agree on something. And this is then what we represent. But if we do not reach an agreement, things become difficult. Then there are two possibilities: either we do not say anything [in the transnational meeting, GW], or I say something taking the risk that I get my ears torn off. When we agree on something I note this in the minutes. This is then distributed, all know this, and when someone does not like it, he can always go to the ministry and ask for an instruction.[37]

h. Input from Developing States

A serious problem is the under-representation of newly industrialised states, states of transition and developing states. The problem is based on the simple fact that funds for travel are scarce and that many of these states lack expertise and personnel within the given technical area (ie chemical regulation in this case). Even though some support for capacity building is offered (for example by the United Nations Institute for Training and Research (UNITAR)), these few individuals are often heavily overloaded with work:

> Developing countries [...] when we look how they operate in intergovernmental meetings and in negotiating meetings, lack, in my view, the real skills to negotiate their vested interest. There is very few of them that have that kind of background or...or expertise. They need [...] to go for a long time through the UNITAR training school for diplomats, you know, the [training on] chemicals management. I fully agree with a person who said there are too many meetings. And I can tell you why. If you look at the countries in economic transition, at developing countries, if, for example, you look at Senegal, the Ministry of Environment, you have two or three professionals that are doing Basel, Stockholm, Rotterdam, climate change, you know, forest...deforestation, everything. They spend their whole time going to international meetings, not doing any work at home. And that's the problem. It's a major, major problem, okay?[38]

Even within the OECD the work is not evenly distributed. This is mainly due to differences in person-power, providing an advantage to the larger and highly industrialised countries:

> Germany is large so that competences are widespread and tasks are more frequently distributed. [...] The workload—especially for the small member states—is very much heavier because they must do everything with a handful of people. [...] I know from colleagues from Finland, for example, that they

[37] Ibid.
[38] Interview IV.

> have to prioritise. One must say for some issues, I don't do anything about it, one only takes those issues that are regarded as absolutely important.[39]

As a consequence, third world perspectives are under-represented in GHS discourse:

> What astonished me when I stepped into the process (I have negotiated a few conventions) was that the developing countries did not play any role. Zero! ... When we set up the committee I told the EU this cannot be true, that the developing countries are not taken into account. They had already fiddled with each other on the chairs and so on, one American and one European, and I said we must now have a third for the developing countries, and now we have a Brazilian in the chair group... Presently there are about 8 or 9 developing countries involved, Brazil, China, South Africa, Senegal, Chile, maybe eight, nine, ten. But 25 [of the participating states] are OECD countries. And that is a serious problem. The outcome resulting from the process is as I always say 'from the white man for the white man', and then the rest of the world shall take this up and the rest of the world asks itself: why should we and how can I influence it?[40]

Greater participation by other world regions could, for instance, have led to a differentiation of hazard categories reflecting differences in dose-response ratios depending on climate, ecological, health and working conditions. Differences in language, culture and technical expertise could have been reflected in greater variation in labels, precautionary sentences and safety data sheets.

While greater opportunity for representation of developing states is provided in the meetings of the International Programme for Chemical Safety (IPCS), even their shortcomings have been noticed. For example, safety warnings on pesticides are often not read or understood by users of chemicals, or are not respected because of climatic conditions or financial restrictions:

> The pesticides industries' standard statement is, that if you follow our use rules, the pesticides can be used safely. The problem is developing countries in the tropics. There, you can't put on the [safety, GW] suits.
>
> And language across borders. For instance, Cambodia. You have green borders there. Everything's in Thai. All the pesticides are going across there. No one can read the label. Nobody knows, what they say. Yet Bayer said 'That's not our problem. It's the problem of the border control.' Can Cambodia control the border? You see you get into these kinds of ethical issues where I say industry can do better.
>
> And pesticides have an entirely different character than other chemicals in relation to the whole development infrastructure, in particular, because in

[39] Ibid.
[40] Interview II.

> developing countries the bulk of the economy is usually based on agriculture. [The practice of using pesticides is:] More is better, you know, and that is a different way. When we dealt with acutely toxic pesticides this raised issues of [voluntary, GW] commitments, not obligations. Nevertheless, it was the first time that the pesticide industry said that they were willing to withdraw a pesticide from the market—if it was proven it could not be used safely. You would never have gotten them to make that statement in the Rotterdam or Stockholm Convention. Still, whether they live up to it and honour it remains to be seen.[41]

A further problem, often disregarded in GHS discussions due to third world underrepresentation, is the increasing relocation of chemical production to developing countries that lack the personnel and technical infrastructure to ensure tight surveillance:

> If you look at the OECD Outlook that predicted what's gonna happen in the chemicals future, you now, I think it's by 2010 most of the what you call generic chemicals, HPV chemicals, that is high-production-volume chemicals, are gonna be manufactured in developing countries, whereas in the OECD countries, you will have the designer chemicals. So where is the infrastructure going to be to ensure the quality and the control of this, you know. These are all recognized problems, but how pressure builds up to…to act on this, I don't know. You know, it's not…you'd never would have the blame game. At IFCS or anywhere else, no. It would be counterproductive. It has to be win-win for everybody who comes to the table.[42]

v. The Result

The product of the described transnational organisational processes was a comprehensive and precise text of 443 pages.[43] It sets out new hazard categories pertaining to physical, health and environmental risks and also establishes new hazard symbols (as a means of communicating the nature of the hazard) and formats for safety data sheets. Chemicals are classified according to hazard type (eg, explosiveness, toxicity to humans, and environmental toxicity) and subtype (eg, human toxicity categories one to five). The text specifies which tests are required and establishes the applicable threshold values for each hazard category. For instance, toxicity for humans is defined as lethality for 50 per cent (LD_{50}) of rats exposed to a dose of up to 50 mg/kg body weight for 48 hours. For mixtures containing hazardous substances, alternative methods of determining the hazard of the entire mixture are set out. The new symbols are pictograms, which alert consumers and users to the inherent dangers of a substance. For

[41] Interview IV.
[42] Ibid.
[43] The 2003 version is available at www.unece.org/trans/danger/publi/ghs/ghs_rev00/00files_e.html (last visited 1 November 08).

instance, a skull with crossed bones means danger to human health due to acute toxicity. Safety data sheets contain information for professional users of substances regarding the hazards of substances and mixtures and precautionary measures.

Discussions and negotiations achieved compromises on the differences in approach between the major players: the European Union and the United States. Sometimes this required the European Union to lower its standards. For instance, in the European Union, the strictest category for acute toxicity used to range up until $LD_{50} < 25$ mg/kg body weight of the exposed rat. Adopting the American approach, the GHS reduced this to $LD_{50} < 5$ mg/kg.[44] This means that those restrictions that are triggered by the highest toxicity class will now apply to a significantly smaller number of substances.

> Yes, it is the smallest common denominator. It is now as we start with the global harmonisation actually that what is acceptable for all. This is the smallest common denominator and certainly not much.[45]

On the other hand, the GHS 'building block' approach produces built-in flexibility, allowing states to set their own standards as long as a minimum threshold is met. For instance, the GHS has five classes of acute toxicity. States are obliged to use the first four classes (Categories one to four ranging from higher to lower toxicity), but are free not to apply the fifth:

> Of course you would like to have a worldwide, harmonised system, but I do not achieve a worldwide harmonised system through a very rigid system, a sink or swim, either you take or you leave it. Then the opposition will be too strong. This is the reason for the building block approach contained in the UN-GHS. It shall facilitate implementation on the national level.[46]

The process did not end with the adoption of the 2002 text. The work continued and improvements were added, and a new consolidated version was adopted in 2007.[47] The major amendment concerns the codification of hazard and precautionary statements.[48] Two TGD and GHS subcommittees of the ECOSOC TDG/GHS Committee are continually working on further improvements.

[44] See a draft comparison of the EU and GHS criteria by the EU Commission, DG ENTR G1 REACH, 2005, available at http://home.hetnet.nl/~MSDS.SAFETYDOCS/downloads/eughscomparisonclassifications.pdf (last visited 1 November 2008).

[45] Interview II.

[46] Interview I.

[47] Available at www.unece.org/trans/danger/publi/ghs/ghs_rev02/English/00e_intro.pdf (last visited 1 November 2008).

[48] Laid down in Annex III of the GHS version 2007.

While the GHS aims at harmonising the rules of classification and labelling, it has not gone further and harmonised the classification and labelling of individual substances. The European Union proposed this as a next step, but the United States opposed this proposition:

> The next step the EU took was to say, okay, we have harmonised the rules how everybody must classify and label but because different people produce different test results we must also harmonise the actual classification, and the EU has set up a list of classified substances. There is therefore a substance list in the EC on which the administrative bodies work meticulously, and they then say substance A is flammable, carcinogen, category 1 or 2. This costs much, much work. This is intentionally left out of the GHS, because the Americans did not want it. That is a European invention. ... But if I was a developing country—and I tell this them all—I would ask for such a list.[49]

vi. Implementation

Many states have worked on transposing the GHS into national law. A 2007 OECD study shows that the OECD countries were at different stages of implementation.[50] Most of them planned to adopt GHS in all of the four main sectors: transport, industrial/workplace, consumer products and agriculture/pesticides. Several countries indicated that they did not plan to implement the GHS in certain sectors, or hazard classes and categories, taking the building block approach as provided under the GHS.

The EU Commission submitted a proposal for an implementing regulation in June 2007.[51] It was (in record time for a document of not less than 1355 Official Journal pages) adopted by co-decision of the Council and European Parliament as Regulation (EC) 1272/2008.[52] The Regulation is directly binding in the Member States. Almost all of the hazard classes, labels, hazard and precautionary statements and safety data sheet requirements of the GHS were adopted. However, the European Union made use of the building block approach, for instance, introducing more hazard categories than provided under the GHS. For some categories the level of health and environmental protection is lowered. Heavy costs for industry and public administration are expected from the changing from the old to the new classification and labelling system. These were

[49] Interview I.

[50] OECD 2007.

[51] Commission (EC), 'Proposal for a Regulation of the European Parliament and of the Council on classification, labelling and packaging of substances and mixtures, and amending Directive 67/548/EEC and Regulation (EC) 1907/2006' COM (2007) 355.

[52] Regulation (EC) 1272/2008 of 16 December 2008 on classification, labelling and packaging of substances and mixtures, amending and repealing Directives 67/548/EEC and 1999/45/EC, and amending Regulation (EC) No 1907/2006 [2008] OJ L353/1.

considered to be worth the advantage of worldwide standardisation. Overall, the legislative bodies felt that they had no choice than to adopt GHS in full, retaining regional particularities only insofar as the GHS provided for this. As the EU Economic and Social Committee (EESC) stated in its comment on the Commission proposal:[53]

> The EESC also notes the views expressed by the Commission in its Legislative Financial Statement that 'the legislative proposal relates to the implementation of an international agreement. Even a negative ex-ante evaluation would not result in the Commission not putting forward a legislative proposal since other policy options do not exist. A negative ex-post evaluation would not induce the Commission to withdraw from its commitment to implement the internationally agreed system of Classification and Labelling.' Simply put, the Commission believes it had no choice but to put forward the proposal, whatever the calculated or actual balance of costs and eventual benefits.

III. THEORISING ON THE CASE

A. Summary of Characteristics

The characteristic features of the case study can be summarised as follows:

- Differences between states in the classification and labelling of chemicals are perceived to hinder free transnational trade. Many states do not operate any classification and labelling system.
- Plans to harmonise and adapt national systems appear on the international agenda.
- Soft law resolutions and memoranda of understanding of international organisations, often initiated by committed individuals, prepare the ground for further negotiations.
- Networks of national experts emerge who act for their home states, but enjoy significant room for manoeuvre. They develop into a complex set of transnational committees, subcomittees and working groups. International organisations provide these structures with symbolic backing and secretarial support.
- A few states (or rather their civil servants) take a lead position. Representatives from developing, transitional and newly industrialised states have very little impact.

[53] Opinion of the European Economic and Social Committee on the Proposal for a Regulation of the European Parliament and of the Council on classification, labelling and packaging of substances and mixtures, and amending Directive 67/548/EEC and Regulation (EC) No 1907/2006 COM (2007) 355 final [2008] OJ C204/47.

— Industry representatives are very active, feeding information and assessments into the process, but also sometimes obstructing it. They do not have a right to formal vote.
— NGO representatives acting for the public interest are invited to participate, but are largely absent.
— Documents are made publicly available online, but only with the intent to inform about the results achieved and not to solicit comments from the public at large.
— Ongoing discourse is based on scientific argumentation, but is also characterised by policy disputes centering on the balancing of interests between industry and health/environmental protection, as well as between divergent regulatory philosophies in the United States and the European Union.
— In addition to scientific and moral discourse, the proceedings are characterised by bargaining and power play.
— The outcome is a comprehensive text, which harmonises standards sometimes at a low common denominator and provides some limited discretionary margins of state implementation. For many states, the outcome is a higher level of protection, but for others, such as the European Union, standards will in certain respects be lowered.
— Due to underrepresentation of developing interests some fundamental issues have received little attention, such as a differentiation of standards according to differences in climatic, ecological, cultural and technical conditions.
— While the transnational structures have produced proposals for regulation of classification they have not ventured into the classification of individual substances. This would have been helpful, especially for developing states, which lack the technical infrastructure to generate data and carry out risk assessments.
— The transnational network sought approval of the resulting text from ECOSOC, a global body that spans sectors and regions. ECOSOC endorsed the text, but did not make it binding. The text can therefore be regarded as a form of global soft law.
— This global soft law was later incorporated into the law of a growing number of states and regional communities, such as the European Union. The EU felt that they had no choice other than to adopt the scheme in full. There are deviations only to the extent allowed by the text.

B. Organisational Setting

The organisational setting that generated the resulting text could be characterised as a transnational network of national and international personnel and institutions. It is important to note, however, that the transnational arrangement was relatively developed and sophisticated. A number of layers consisting of formal bodies and informal working groups and contact systems were incorporated into the process. As a result, the setting was more stable than the notion of network would suggest. While loose networks may be found in other transnational structures, our case is better characterised as a transnational committee system. Alluding to a similar phenomenon in the European Union, I suggest speaking of a transnational comitology, although it must be kept in mind that the GHS committee system is more fluid and autopoietic than the legally pre-formed EU comitology (Falke and Winter, 1996; Joerges and Vos 1999; Savino 2006). In particular it is much less controlled by mandates from states and international organisations than EU comitology is in relation to Member States and the EU Commission. The transnational comitology of our case embraced:

— formal councils like ECOSOC;
— committees such as the coordination group established by ECOSOC;
— semi-formal committees like the committee of experts on GHS established by Memorandum of Understanding between the sectoral international organisations;
— a multitude of issue-specific working groups;
— parallel working groups of regional organisations like the OECD;
— parallel expert rounds within states;
— parallel working groups within transnational industry associations and single companies;
— parallel working groups within public interest NGOs;
— last but not least, networks of individuals cross-cutting all of these formal and informal structures.

C. Procedures

It is noteworthy that the ongoing proceedings involve a multifaceted reasoning characterised by scientific argumentation and policy deliberation, but also sometimes ill-founded assertions, a stubborn refusal to learn, bargaining, compromising, tactics, collusion, and even blockades. In more theoretical terms, a peculiar mélange of four styles can be identified in this case study: scientific argument, policy-oriented reasoning, bargaining and power play.

The concept of deliberation does not fit comfortably within this mélange. As a result, the case cannot be taken as an example of directly deliberative democracy or deliberative polyarchy as proposed by Joshua Cohen and Charles Sabel (Cohen and Sabel 2005). Deliberation emphasises the use of argument[54] and underrates the role of bargaining and power (Möllers 2005: 382). While the preconditions of deliberation—such as freedom from external and internal pressure—did to some extent materialise in this case, many other and less discursive behavioural patterns were also present.[55]

Another way of characterising our case study is to draw on what is called the Open Method of Coordination (OMC). OMC was introduced in the European Union as a means of coordinating Member State policies in areas where the European Commission only has a coordinating function, and no regulatory powers (eg, social, education and immigration policies) (European Commission 2001: 21; Devetzi and Platzer 2009). The same situation exists in many areas of transnational administration, including the harmonisation of chemicals regulation. In this respect, the GHS process is one example of OMC. However, the heuristic value of OMC is undermined by the fact that the OMC has failed to produce a concept of structures and processes that may be used as a blueprint for comparison.[56]

The concept of *negotiated order*, as proposed by Anselm Strauss, may also be consulted in the search for concepts that are less idealistic than the theory of deliberative democracy. This concept conceives of bargaining and power as core characteristics of interactions within organisations, in addition to technical and moral communication. Taking hospitals as their case, Strauss and his collaborators analyse conflict scenarios between doctors and staff to develop a complex picture of various styles of communicative and negotiative problem-solving (Strauss et al 1990: 189).

There are clear differences between Strauss's hospital study and our case, in particular because the treatment of patients is a service, not a

[54] See Cohen and Sabel 2005: 779: 'Deliberation subjects the exercise of collective power to reason's discipline, to what Habermas famously described as "the force of the better argument", not the advantage of the better situated. Questions are decided by argument about the best ways to address problems, not simply exertions of power, expressions of interest, or bargaining from power positions on the basis of interests.'

[55] Although it is not a prevalent idea in Western thought, the concept of *palaver* comes to mind as an alternative framework (for an exemplary anthropological case—the palaver of the Ndendeuli in Tansania—see Gulliver 1969). Stripping it of its pejorative meaning, handed down from 'developed' cultures, palaver has been a constructive approach to solving conflicts in traditional African societies. It is now being studied as a concept for modern societies in Africa and elsewhere, Hegenbarth 1980: 55–58; UNESCO 1979; Richard 2008. Its appeal consists in that it allows for and integrates different kinds of reasoning and conduct that tend to be dissected and rationalised in 'developed' rules of discourse. In contrast to the approach in 'developed' literature and practice, this style does not distinguish between moral, instrumental, scientific, bargaining and strategic rationality. All features are intermingled. It is not far-fetched to consider transnational rulemaking under the GHS as a case of palaver. However, even the more modern conceptions of palaver seem to be more suited to resolving conflicts that are deeply rooted in culture, ideology and tradition, such as religious, racial or ideological wars, Koudissa 2004.

[56] I leave out as EC-specific the quest of the Commission that it should play a guiding role, and that the European Parliament should be kept informed, European Commission 2001.

regulatory undertaking. Still, there are also significant similarities. In both cases bargains between economic interests and concerns of a general public (or patients) have to be struck besides scientific or technical expert deliberations. Expertise alone does not guarantee conclusive solutions. Therefore, it appears to me that the notion of bargaining should be systematically integrated into concepts of deliberative democracy. Blending the work of Cohen/Sabel and Strauss, one might speak of negotiative deliberation, or—stressing the transdiscursive element of trading positions even further—'bargaining deliberation'.

The product derived from these structures and processes can be termed negotiated or bargained consensus, reflecting the compromise that bridges the conflicting interests within societies and between states: in terms of health and environmental concerns, the result marks a relatively high level of protection; in terms of economic concerns, the costs of introducing the system are probably outweighed by the benefits of eased transnational trade; and in terms of national traditions, the marked difference between the US risk approach and the EU hazard approach was bridged. The achieved order leaves discretionary margins for implementing states and remains under permanent revision and improvement. There are also serious flaws due to the neglect of developing world interests. Nevertheless, the concept is broad enough to grasp such flaws, which resulted from the underrepresentation of developing world participants and their lack of bargaining power in the negotiations.

D. Implementation

In regards to implementation, it is noteworthy that the comprehensive GHS document was fully incorporated into EU law, without checking either the health and environmental impacts, or the economic costs of the system change. While the legislative procedure was correctly executed, the transnational product was not subjected to any democratic deliberation at the EU level. As the incorporating EU Regulation is directly applicable in Member States, there was no possibility of democratic control on the national level.

IV. THE QUESTION OF LEGITIMATION

A. Performance and Legitimation

The primary concern of much of the literature on global administrative regulation is legitimation (Möllers 2005; Kingsbury, Krisch and Stewart 2004/2005). This focus rests on the assumption that transnational governance is likely to usurp hidden power, ie to establish itself as 'techno-cracy', whose activities must be tamed (*cf* Dahl 1989: 252; Habermas 1992: 385). Indeed, there are examples of usurpation and technocracy in the transnational arena. The International Monetary Fund (IMF) has often been blamed for transgressing its original mandate of guaranteeing the stability of the international monetary system. Despite this, IMF bureaucrats have incrementally expanded their mission into conditionalities and local politics reform (Barnett and Finnemore 2005: 45–72, 155–73).[57] The World Bank has also been criticised for its neo-liberal approach to health policies (Aginam 2005). Further examples include the aspirations, and failure, of the Basel Committee on Banking Supervision to prevent the credit crunches (Balin 2009) and the ongoing clandestine negotiations for an Anti-Counterfeiting Trade Agreement (ACTA), which works toward strengthening the intellectual property regime (Latrive 2010).

There are also cases of a more benign technocracy in transnational administrative rulemaking. By and large our case belongs to them, notwithstanding the shortcomings of the system with respect to US-EU compromises and developing world disregard. Therefore, before following the common emphasis on legitimation, it should be acknowledged that something surprising has been achieved by the fragile fabric and negotiative deliberation of transnational administration: it brought about economic and environmental harmonisation. The case shows that soft structures, processes and norms have the potential to be more expedient than their formal international counterparts. Consensus of the sort achieved in the transnational field appears to be a powerful problem-solving tool.

Given that the world is always in need of this kind of negotiated consensus, case studies of different transnational administrations could provide an explanation of how such processes are facilitated (Keohane and Nye 2000: 26). Such studies may also reveal why some initiatives are helpful and others turn out to be detrimental or counterproductive. Favourable conditions include the following:

- — Conflicting interests pushing for harmonised rules (in casu: economic and environmental costs of diverse legal systems).
- — A public awareness of the problem within the transnational sphere (in casu: the campaign in the late 1980s alleging 'toxic ignorance' of hazardous chemicals[58]).
- — The symbolic backing by international institutions (in casu: the Rio Conference and its Agenda 21).

[57] Refuting this allegation in part, see Head 2005: 78. For more examples of such so-called mission creep, see Stewart 2005.

[58] The campaign was based on a report published by the US Environmental Defense Fund in 1998. For impacts on EU politics, see Winter 2000: 177.

— The support of a number of individuals to act as policy entrepreneurs (in casu: experts from national sectoral administrations).
— The broad participation of many states, with a small number of states taking the lead (in casu: the United States and European Union).
— The participation of international organisations that are willing to provide logistical support (in casu: ILO, WHO, and OECD).

Returning to the examples of the IMF, the World Bank, the Basel Committee and ACTA, their counterproductive result may be explained by the closed shop style of their proceedings.

The search for effectiveness and constructive output must not be confounded with the normative question of legitimation. A resulting rule may be helpful for the resolution of a problem and thus be factually 'accepted', but this alone does not make it legitimate, ie 'acceptable'. To make it acceptable, the rulemaking procedure must respect certain safeguards, providing input legitimation. The content of the rule must also respect certain substantive yardsticks that guarantee output legitimation. Normally, procedural and substantive legitimation ensures the effectiveness of procedures and quality of output. In our case, for example, the text of the GHS could have been much improved in these terms by looking more specifically at third world conditions of human and environmental exposition to chemicals had the third world representatives had a better presence. Fair procedures may cost additional time, and the need to find compromises sometimes leads to sub-optimal results. These are the costs of democracy and respect for fundamental rights in exchange for the social cohesion and long-term welfare they provide. In the following section, I concentrate on procedural legitimation, leaving aside questions of fundamental substantial rights.

B. Practices and Criteria of Legitimation

When examining procedural legitimation, we should first of all specify what phenomenon ought to be legitimated. Legitimation in the traditional sense presupposes power and provides means to domesticate it. In the transnational sphere, however, power is not evident. Three aspects are relevant here, as follows:

— 'Public authority' has been suggested as a common characteristic of transnational public administration (Bogdandy, Dann, and Goldmann 2008). This notion shall capture the transnational informal rulemaking by a legal concept that triggers questions of law, and in particular democratic constitutional principles which require the legitimation of any public authority. The authors' intention to contrast the 'external' view on law of politological concepts (eg, governance, networks, etc) with an 'internal' legal concept of authority is, I believe, highly commendable.

— The notion of public authority must, however, be well understood in order to fit our case and many other cases of transnational networks and comitology. It should not presuppose some kind of centre that represents authority and is separated from a constituency. International organisations may be centres of this sort. However, in the transnational arena, administrative structures are normally highly fragmented and held together by weak connections. The GHS process is an example of such complex setting. Thus, authority in transnational networks and comitology is decentred and diffused.

— Authority in the transnational sphere is often based on consent. In our case, individual and state participants in the GHS bargaining process reached a consensus—if only in the sense customary in international frameworks, ie that there is no expressed dissenting opinion. They did not have to accept the command of others without their agreement. Thus, if power means the possibility to induce certain behaviour in a person against that person's will (Weber 1972: 28), there is no power relationship, and thus no need for additional legitimation (Lepsius 2007: 356). However, not all affected and interested parties were able to participate, including developing states, the public at large and NGOs representing it.

Looking for criteria of legitimation of diffuse authority in the transnational sphere, it has been suggested that principles of national administrative law should be scaled up to the transnational sphere (cf Stewart 2005). Traditional administrative law requirements for domesticating power are referred to as the three rules of 'natural justice' in English common law or procedural due process in US law. These are the rules against bias of decision-makers, the right of affected persons to be heard, and the duty of decision-makers to give reasons.[59]

These rules are, however, not an exact fit because they are liberal concepts, presupposing identifiable sources of public authority, while transnational authority is diffuse and consent-based. While the duty to give reasons is also suitable for transnational arrangements the rule against bias is of questionable benefit, because there is no deciding body that is detached from conflicting parties. Chairpersons are certainly expected to ensure that the proceedings are fair, but they are not required to be unbiased and keep a distance from a substantive position. On the contrary, progress depends on them taking an active role; often they use their position to drive the process in a certain direction. Likewise, the right to be heard does not fit well. It is based on the notion that individuals are directly and legally affected by a decision. This was not the case due to the general and soft law character of the rules resulting from the transnational proceedings.

When looking for better-suited rules of procedure the very practice and meta-rules observed in the GHS can serve as a source of inspiration.

[59] Wade 1982: 413–20, 486. Sometimes, only the first two (*nemo iudex in re sua and audiatur et altera pars*) are counted as the core elements of natural justice, and the duty to give reasons as a later achievement, Wade 1982: 486.

Indeed, the process of 'bargaining deliberation' observed in the GHS case study did not advance without rules of procedure. The rules established by IOMC and the Coordination Group[60] indicate which procedural problems need to be addressed. According to the IOMC rules, committees must have a clear mandate, a defined number of members and observers, a chair and their own rules of procedure. They were also required to report to the IOMC body. Moreover, a practice—although imperfect–emerged to separate questions of science from questions of policy, and refer them to different bodies. These requirements and practices were a response to potential risk that consensus-building structures would become diffuse in terms of task, membership and procedure.

A number of rules were, however, missing from the GHS process that would be essential for fair proceedings. They may be drawn from what is called the second generation administrative law. While the first generation provides liberal rights in view of potential misuse of power, the new generation strives to democratise public administration, reacting to the fact that the bilateral relationship between authority and the individual has been replaced by multipolar constellations (Harlow 2006).

One issue to be taken care of is the limiting of powerful interests and the representation of weaker interests. Both the IOMC and Coordination Group neglected to establish any precise rules on the roles of participants in meetings. Although there was a rough distinction between observer and voting status, the rules did not specify where observation ends and voting begins. This is a question of crucial importance to prevent the capture of regulators by the regulated. Moreover, there were no rules to ensure that weaker interests are taken into account—either in the social dimension (health and environmental protection), or in the regional dimension (developing countries, countries in transition, newly industrialised countries).

Another issue is the bargaining and obstruction element in real world discourses: there were no rules for dealing with unbridgeable differences of interests that may lead to destructive tactics or bargaining. One minimum rule, somewhat domesticating such non-deliberative aspects of the proceedings, would be that the political question and achieved compromise should be laid open and explained.

Most significantly, there were no rules in place to ensure public transparency, such as access to information and notice and comment procedures. However, caution is appropriate as to the simple transfer to the transnational realm of national principles of second generation administrative law. The fragility of the transnational fabric should be taken into account: the proceedings were already so complex and information-loaded that to allow for more openness and to seek further input could jeopardise

[60] See above II. C. iii.

progress. After all, the consensus rule practised in the proceedings hardly precluded anyone from participating. Of course, candidates had to make an effort to enter the game.[61]

What then would be a concept of transparency reflecting the peculiarities of the transnational realm? Transnational administrative arrangements are often highly accessible via the internet. GHS negotiators have made numerous documents available online. However, acting committees, working groups and networks have complete discretion as to whether they will operate a website and what information will be posted. Instead, transnational administrative comitology should provide a right of access for all, and public participation should be facilitated. Given the concerns about information overload, this right can certainly not expose every move to public notice and comment. However, notice should be given and comments invited at strategic points, eg on draft terms of reference, draft membership, organisational and procedural rules, and major intermediate draft reports. In addition, exemption rules can be established denying access to state or trade secrets or privacy information.

In conclusion, we have seen that liberal conceptions of administrative law are incompatible with models of transnational proceedings that potentially include everybody, and operate by 'bargaining deliberation'. New rules of structures and procedures that aim to build consensus, and not majority decision-making, must be developed. The content of this new regime should include rules on determining membership, mandates, reporting, separation of technical and policy discourses, access to information, transparency of reasons and interests, public notice and comment at strategic and other stages.

C. A Role for the State?

How could these rules be elaborated, agreed upon and made binding? There are three strands of thought answering this question, one relying on informal self-regulation, the second on legal framing by state-based law, and the third on legal framing by international law.

i. Informal Self-Regulation

The first strand believes in a global law without the state (Teubner 1996, 2003; Fischer-Lescano and Teubner 2007). They trust that the transnational sphere will autopoietically develop its own means of self-control, through practice and—incrementally—informal meta-rules of procedure

[61] Lange in chapter two.

and substance. A very optimistic version of this thought can be seen in a statement by Cohen and Sabel (2005: 296):[62]

> Suppose, in particular, a deepening of global administration in a wide range of areas of human concern, including security, health, education, environment, and conditions of work and compensation. Suppose, too, that such global rulemaking is increasingly accountable: preceded by hearings, shaped by participation of affected parties, subject to review, and defended by reference to what are commonly cognized as reasons in an emerging public reason of global political society. And suppose that accountable administration, in its deliberative polyarchic form, has a substantial, constructive impact on human well-being. We should venture to design a new network-related model which links different public and private actors beyond and within the state in a productive way. [...] Couldn't this all be true? Even without a global state? And if so, is it plausible that dispersed peoples might come to share a new identity as common members of an organized global populace, and not only in the humanitarian sense that all are human beings cohabiting the same planet, or the spiritual sense that all are living from dust to dust, or the utilitarian sense that we are all mutually interdependent?

Likeable as this proposition appears, there are too many examples, and foremost the stranding of self-control in the recent credit crunch, that advise against full trust in the self-organisational potential of the transnational sphere. The potential does certainly exist and should not be disregarded, but it must be critically checked.

Therefore, according to the second and third school, formal law is necessary to push informal law-making ahead. The state appears to be the only institution able to do this. Even if permeated by manifold external interferences, it still possesses, as a potential and last resort, the power of filtering out what shall be law and what shall not.

While both 'formal' schools of thought rely on the law-making power of the state, they differ with regard to degrees of internationalisation, one proposing a concept of 'society of states' (*Staatengesellschaft*) and the other a concept of 'community of states' (*Staatengemeinschaft*) (*cf* Paulus 2001; Roeben 2005; Sanson 2008). While the first stresses the power of the state controlling the entry of norms into its internal sphere (Giegerich 2009), the other emphasises the possibilities of international lawmaking (Fischer-Lescano 2005).

ii. State-Based Entry Control

Those that advocate entry control inquire into how the state might provide legitimation for transnational administrative rulemaking at the point at which transnational rules are integrated into national law.

[62] Similarly dithyrambical, see also Ladeur 2004: 16.

a. Legislation

As yet, state-oriented scholars have not been very creative in designing models of how states could provide for fair procedures within the transnational realm. The orthodox approach is to channel inter- and transnational rules, once adopted, through national legislation to provide ex post facto legitimation. The constitutions of many states require that the legislature must, by law[63] or other decision,[64] consent to an international treaty before it can be ratified and become binding upon the state. In addition, for states belonging to the dualist tradition, a further legal act (which may be combined with the ratification law) is required to incorporate the international treaty into domestic law.[65]

However, such (dual) involvement of the legislature is concerned with binding international and subsequent binding national law. When the international level is not aiming at making binding international rules, a law for ratification is not needed. Moreover, as transnational soft law does not oblige states to incorporate it, states are constitutionally not obliged to introduce incorporation laws. Indeed, in the GHS case, the aim was not to conclude binding international obligations, as ECOSOC only took a resolution recommending the GHS for implementation by states.

Therefore, in principle, domestic administrative bodies are constitutionally allowed to apply soft law on their own initiative, albeit within the framework of existing laws. Administrative decisions can, however, trigger constitutional protection where they encroach upon the individual rights of citizens or are deemed otherwise essential (eg, where manufacturers are asked to observe GHS rules when selling chemicals, or consumer health is endangered from misclassification of chemicals). For such cases state constitutions sometimes contain a 'legislative reservation' requiring legislation as a basis for administrative action. This is a constitutional requirement both under German[66] and EU[67] law. In conclusion,

[63] In Germany, for instance, a parliamentary law is required. See art 59 para 2 sentence 1 of *Grundgesetz.*

[64] In the EU the Council is responsible in approving a treaty. The European Parliament must inter alia give its consent in those areas which belong to the realm of co-decision of the Council and the Parliament. See art 218 TFEU.

[65] Dualism is much relativised by constitutional practice. In Germany, for instance, although a parliamentary law is in principle required for this purpose, the task of incorporation can be simplified in the following ways: (a) The law may empower government to incorporate treaties of a certain category by regulation. (b) If the treaty is sufficiently precise it may even directly be applied (the so-called self-executing treaties); the ratification law is then interpreted to contain a command of incorporation besides allowing ratification of the treaty.

[66] Thus, the German constitutional legislative reservation (*Gesetzesvorbehalt*). See Ladeur 1996 on its design and origin.

[67] The European Court of Justice (ECJ) has developed a doctrine reserving 'essential elements' of a policy to the decision of the legislative institutions (the European Parliament and

while a law is neither required for the ratification of transnational soft law nor for its incorporation into national law, it may well be necessary, if implementing decisions interfere with individual rights.

This raises the question of how much legitimation is in fact provided by this mechanism. Concluded in the transnational sphere without direct state involvement, the GHS does not leave much room for states to decide. States can refuse to adopt the GHS rules altogether, but, given the level of harmonisation that has been achieved, it would be extremely unwise to refuse transposition or make amendments beyond the discretionary margins allowed under the text. Proponents of the view that the state is still the master of the game disregard this factual dimension. Therefore, given that national legislators are not free to reject or modify soft law standards, the legitimation provided by incorporating soft law standards into domestic law must be regarded as a fiction.

b. Scaling Up Procedural Standards

An alternative approach would be to formulate a national policy that aims at making transnational rulemaking more transparent and participative. This could be accomplished in three ways:

- States might ask their representatives to promote these principles when acting in the transnational sphere.
- States could introduce safeguards to ensure that their representatives publish information on important aspects of transnational negotiations and invite public comments before negotiating in the transnational sphere.[68]
- States could introduce a policy or legislative requirement that technical rules cannot be transposed into national law unless certain procedural safeguards have been met (Stewart 2005). Although this requirement could only be enforced at the transposition stage, it may have a prejudicial effect on the transnational negotiations, ensuring transparency and public involvement from the outset.

iii. International Lawmaking

State-based entry controls are problematic in that the transnational achievements may be wasted if states insist on copious control in order to

the Council), see for instance Case C-156/93 *European Parliament v Commission of the European Communities* [1995] ECR I-2019. *cf* Triantafyllo 1996. The principle was later codified in Art. 290 (2) TFEU.

[68] A legal provision in that direction was proposed by a German expert committee called the Risk Commission in a report of 2003 (www.bfs.de) saying that German positions in European and international rulemaking procedures of essential importance must be published beforehand. Along the same lines, see Stewart 2005.

accomplish de facto legitimation. It is therefore interesting to explore the possibility of making transnational rules of legitimation binding on the international level.

This process of juridification could be based on the self-organising potential of transnational structures. Our case shows that committees and transnational networks have themselves established certain procedural rules, for instance, subcommittees and working groups must have clear terms, they must regularly report on results, NGOs can participate but not vote, etc, although this potential is likely to be limited (Schmidt-Assmann 2008). In our case, a number of rules were lacking, such as rules on how to deal with conflicts of interests of participants, what documents shall be published, what documents shall be accessible to the public, what drafts shall be subjected to notice and comment procedures, what compensatory measures could be taken to ensure representation of disadvantaged, poor parties and NGOs. It is notable that transnational networks in other areas have generated more elaborate rules of procedure. For instance, technical committee members working under the Codex Alimentarius Commission framework are required to declare possible conflicts of interest.[69] On the whole, however, more ambitious rules must be developed.

Such achievements can be expected from horizontal transfers and the mutual learning of practices between different policy areas. Given the wide range of transnational administrative negotiations, binding international law might be developed to crosscut sectoral policy areas. Based on frequent practice and an emerging *opinio iuris*, and keeping in mind parallel developments within the national arena, international customary law or general principles of international law in the sense of article 38 lit b) and c) of the Statute of the International Court of Justice may emerge concerning a minimum set of procedural rules.[70]

More ambitious rules could be laid down in an international convention. Following the path of the Aarhus Convention, such an agreement could concentrate on specific policy areas (eg environmental policy) and later be extended to other fields. Alternatively, a general approach that crosscuts different policy areas could be adopted. Its frame of reference would be the Vienna Conventions on the Law of Treaties between States and International Organisations and on the Representation of States in their Relations with International Organizations of a Universal Character.[71] Of course, as these draft conventions create rules between states and international organisations, they are not applicable to more

[69] FAO/WHO Framework for the Provision of Scientific Advice on Food Safety and Nutrition, available at www.fao.org/ag/AGN/agns/files/Final_Draft_EnglishFramework.pdf 18–19. See Arnold and Herwig in chapters five and six respectively.

[70] The UN International Law Commission might be given a mandate to compile such a set.

[71] Drafted by the UN International Law Commission and not yet in force.

informal networks between sub-state units and transnational structures. However, they could serve as a starting point for further conventions that structure the transnational realm.

D. Conclusion

Although an analysis of the three theoretical strands—autopoiesis, state entry control and international law—help to understand differences in constructing transnational administrative law, all of them must be combined if a viable solution is to be found. This is somewhat disenchanting from a theoretical perspective, but is in a way typical for the handling of practical problems. In the real world of transnational administrative rule-making, self-evolution, state input and international law coexist. Thus, three things must come together to improve transnational comitology:

- first, as evolving rules in the transnational space, an emerging practice of procedural and substantive self-control,
- secondly, as requirements by states, the postulate that transnational regulatory output is only accepted if derived from fair proceedings and obeyance of minimal standards, and,
- thirdly, the gradual development of international principles and agreements on fair transnational procedures.

REFERENCES

Aginam, O (2005) *Global Health Governance. International Law and Public Health in a Divided World* (Toronto, University of Toronto Press).

Balin, BJ (nd) *Basel I, Basel II, and Emerging Markets: A Nontechnical Analysis*, unpublished article accessible at https://jscholarship.library.jhu.edu/handle/1774.2/32826 (Accessed 7 January 2009).

Barnett, M and Finnemore, M (2004) *Rules for the World. International Organizations in Global Politics* (Ithaca, Cornell University Press).

Bogdandy, A v, Dann, PH, Goldmann, M (2008) 'Developing the Publicness of Public International Law' 9 *German Law Journal* 1375–1400.

Cohen, J and Sabel, Ch (2005) 'Global Democracy?' 37 *NYU Journal of International Law and Politics* 763–97.

Dahl, RA (1989) *Democracy and its Critics*, 4th edn (New Haven, Yale University Press).

Devetzi, St and Platzer, HW (2009) (eds) *Offene Methode der Koordinierung und Europäisches Sozialmodell.* Interdisziplinäre Perspektiven (Stuttgart, ibidem-Verlag).

Dezalay, Y and Garth, B (1996) *Dealing in Virtue: International Commercial Arbitration and the Constitution of a Transnational Legal Order* (Chicago, University of Chicago Press).

Dilling, O (2008) 'Proactive Compliance? Repercussions of National Product Regulation in Standards of Transnational Business Networks' in O Dilling, M Herberg and G Winter (eds), *Responsible Business. Self-Governance and the Law in Transnational Economic Transactions* (Oxford, Hart Publishing) 89–122.

—— (2010) *Grenzüberschreitende Produktverantwortung. Zum prozeduralen Recht zwischenbetrieblicher Risikobewältigung* (Baden-Baden, Nomos).

Giegerich, Th (2009) 'The Is and The Ought of International Constitutionalism: how Far have we Come on Habermas's Road to a 'Well-Considered Constitutionalization of International Law?' 10/1 *German Law Journal* 31–62.

European Commission (2001) 'European Governance' (White Paper) COM (2001) 428 final.

Falke, J and Winter, G (1996) Management and Regulatory Committees in Executive Rule-making, in G Winter (ed) *Sources and Categories of European Union Law. A Comparative and Reform Perspective* (Baden-Baden: Nomos) 541–82

Fischer-Lescano, A (2005) *Globalverfassungen. Die Geltungsbegründung der Menschenrechte* (Weilerswist, Velbrück).

Fischer-Lescano, A and Teubner, G (2007) 'Fragmentierung des Weltrechts: Vernetzung globaler Regimes statt etatistischer Rechtseinheit' in M Albert and R Stichweh (eds), *Weltstaat und Weltstaatlichkeit. Beobachtungen globaler politischer Strukturbildung* (Wiesbaden, VS Verlag für Sozialwissenschaften).

Gessner, V (2009) *Contractual Certainty in International Trade. Empirical Studies and Theoretical Debates on Institutional Support for Global Economic Exchange* (Oxford, Hart Publishing).

Grimm, J and Grimm, W (2004) *Deutsches Wörterbuch Digital Edition*, (Frankfurt aM, Zweitausendeins).

Gulliver, PH (1969) 'Dispute Settlements without Courts: The Ndenedeuli of Southern Tansania' in L Nader (ed), *Law in Culture and Society* (Berkeley, University of California Press).

Habermas, J (1992) *Faktizität und Geltung. Beiträge zur Diskurstheorie des Rechts und des demokratischen Rechtsstaats* (Frankfurt aM, Suhrkamp).

Harlow, C (2006) *Global Administrative Law: the Quest for Principles and Values* 17 *European Journal of International Law* 187–214.

Haufler, V (2001) *A Public Role for the Private Sector: Industry Self-Regulation in a Global Economy* (Washington, Carnegie Endowment).

Head, JW (2005) *The Future of the Global Economic Organizations. An Evaluation of Criticisms Leveled at the IMF, the Multilateral Development Banks, and the WTO* (Ardsley, Transnational Publishers).

Joerges, Ch and Vos, E (eds) (1999) *EU Committees: Social Regulation, Law and Politics* (Oxford, Hart Publishing).

Keohane, R and Nye J (1971) 'Transnational Relations and World Politics' 25 *International Organisation* 329.

Keohane, RO and Nye, R (2000) 'Introduction' in JS Nye, JD Donahue (eds), *Governance in a Globalizing World* (Washington DC, Brookings Institution Press) 1–45.

Kingsbury, B, Krisch, N and Stewart, RB (2004–2005) 'The Emergence of Global Administrative Law' 68 *Law & Contemporary Problems* 15–62.

Koudissa, J (2004) ‚Palaver und Kultur der Versöhnung in Afrika' 52 *Communicate Worldwide* 13–16.

Ladeur, K-H (1996) 'Sources and Categories of Legal Acts—Germany' in G Winter (ed), *Sources and Categories of European Union Law* (Baden-Baden, Nomos) 235–72.
—— (2004) 'Globalization and Public Governance a Contradiction?' in Ladeur (ed), *Public Governance in the Age of Globalization* (Ashgate, Aldershot).
Latrive, F (2010) 'Das gebunkerte Wissen' *Monde Diplomatique March 2010,* 7.
Lepsius, O (2007) 'Standardsetzung und Legitimation' in Chr Möllers, A Vosskuhle, Chr Walter (eds), *Internationales Verwaltungsrecht* (Tübingen, Mohr Siebeck) 345–74.
Möllers, Chr (2005) 'Transnationale Behördenkooperation. Verfassungs- und völkerrechtliche Probleme transnationaler administrativer Standardsetzung' 65 *ZaöRV* 351–89.
OECD (2007) 'Report on Preparation of GHS Implementation by the OECD Countries', Environment Directorate, Environment, Health and Safety Publications Series on Testing and Assessment, No 70 (Paris, OECD).
Pallemaerts, M (2003) *Toxics and Transnational Law: International and European Regulation of Toxic Substances as Legal Symbolism* (Oxford, Hart).
Paulus, A (2001) *Die internationale Gemeinschaft im Völkerrecht. Eine Untersuchung zur Entwicklung des Völkerrechts im Zeitalter der Globalisierung* (München, Verlag CH Beck).
Richard, A (nd) *Das Palaver—ein afrikanisches Modell der Konfliktlösung?* www.africavenir.com/publications/student-papers/RichardPalaver.pdf.
Röben, V (2005) *Außenverfassungsrecht* (Tübingen, Mohr Siebeck).
Sanson, M (2008) *International Law and Global Governance* (London, Cameron May).
Savino, M (2006) 'The Role of Transnational Committees in the European and Global Orders' in 6/3 *Global Jurist Advances* 1–22
Scharpf, F (2005) 'Legitimationskonzepte jenseits des Nationalstaats' in GF Schuppert, I Pernice, U Haltern (eds), *Europawissenschaft* (Baden-Baden, Nomos) 705–33.
Schepel, H (2005) *The Constitution of Private Governance. Product Standards in the Regulation of Integrating Markets* (Oxford, Hart Publishing).
Schmidt-Aßmann, E (2008) 'The Internationalization of Administrative Relations as a Challenge for Administrative Law Scholarship' 52 *German Law Journal* 2061–79.
Slaughter, A-M (2004) 'Global Government Networks, Global Information Agencies, and Disaggregated Democracy' in K-H Ladeur (ed), *Public Governance in the Age of Globalization* (Ashgate, Aldershot) 121–55.
Stein, L v (1869) Die Verwaltungslehre Teil 1 Abt. 1: *Die Vollziehende Gewalt. Allg Teil. Das verfassungsmäßige Verwaltungsrecht,* 2. Neudruck (2004) (Aalen, Scientia Verlag).
Stewart, RB (2005) 'U.S Administrative Law: a Model for Global Administrative Law?' 68 *Law & Contemporary Problems* 63–108.
Strauss, A, Bucher, R, Ehrlich, D, Sabshin, M, Schatzman L (1990) 'Negotiated Order and the Coordination of Work' in A Strauss (ed), *Creating Social Awareness. Collective Images and Symbolic Representation* (New Brunswick, Transaction Publishers) 177–232.
Teubner, G (ed) (1996) *Global Law without a State* (Ashgate, Aldershot).
Tietje, Chr (2001) *Internationalisiertes Verwaltungshandeln* (Berlin, Duncker und Humblot).

Wade, HWR (1982) *Administrative Law* (Oxford, Clarendon press) 5th edn.
Warning, M (2009) *Transnational Law through Bureaucracy Networks. The Case of Hazardous Chemicals* (Basingstock, Palgrave).
Weber, M (1972) *Wirtschaft und Gesellschaft*, edited by J Winkelmann (Tübingen, JCB Mohr/Paul Siebeck).
Winter, G (2000) 'Redesigning Joint Responsibility of Industry and Government' in G Winter (ed), *Risk Assessment and Risk Management of Toxic Chemicals in the European Community. Experiences and Reform* (Baden-Baden, Nomos) 177–84.
Winter, G (2007) 'Dangerous Chemicals: a Global Problem on its Way to Global Governance' in M Führ, R Wahl, P v Wilmowsky (eds), *Umweltrecht und Umweltwissenschaft. Festschrift für Eckard Rehbinder* (Berlin, Erich Schmidt Verlag) 819–33.

5

The Codex Alimentarius Commission—A View from Practice

DIETER ARNOLD

ABSTRACT

The Codex Alimentarius Commission (CAC) has been the principal organ of the Joint Food and Agriculture Organisation of the United Nations (FAO)/ World Health Organisation (WHO) Programme on Food Standards for 45 years. It has a statute and rules of procedures which have regularly been updated and adapted to new situations in the field of international food legislation. Codex standards are the 'golden' standards under the WTO agreements. When health and safety matters are concerned, the elaboration of standards is based on the risk analysis paradigm, which draws its information from sound science and other legitimate factors. Therefore, the interaction of experts in the field of risk assessment and managers of risks is required. Many standards are primarily based on scientific and technical considerations. The assessment of risks is functionally separated from management issues; however, expert bodies are given risk assessment policy instructions elaborated by the competent managers. In general, the procedures are favourable for reaching consensus; still, many of the standard-setting processes are relatively slow.

I. BACKGROUND

THE CAC WAS established in 1963 as the principal organ of the Joint FAO/WHO Programme on Food Standards. Between full sessions of the CAC,[1] an 'Executive Committee' functions as an executive body.[2] A jointly funded 'Codex Secretariat' housed in the headquarters of the FAO technically supports the work of the CAC.

[1] The CAC shall in principle hold one regular session each year at the headquarters of either the FAO or WHO.

[2] The Executive Committee shall consist of the Chairperson and the Vice-Chairpersons of the Commission, and the (Regional) Coordinators (appointed on the basis of r IV) together

The FAO/WHO Conference on Food Standards held in Geneva in 1962 defined the purpose of the Codex Alimentarius as follows:

> The Codex Alimentarius is to be a collection of internationally adopted food standards presented in a unified form. These food standards aim at protecting consumers' health and ensuring fair practices in the food trade. Their publication is intended to promote the standardisation of foodstuffs in the world, to facilitate harmonisation of standards and in so doing to further the development of the international food trade.[3]

These basic principles have remained the same although the wording has slightly changed and some additions have been made.[4] The new wording reads:

> The Codex Alimentarius is a collection of internationally adopted food standards and related texts presented in a uniform manner. These food standards and related texts aim at protecting consumers' health and ensuring fair practices in the food trade. The publication of the Codex Alimentarius is intended to guide and promote the elaboration and establishment of definitions and requirements for foods to assist in their harmonisation and in doing so to facilitate international trade.

Codex standards are developed through subsidiary bodies comprising regional, commodity and general committees. Expert scientific advice is provided by ad hoc expert committees and joint meetings financed and administered independently from the Codex by the FAO and the WHO.

Thus, the FAO/WHO Joint Expert Committee on Food Additives (JECFA) started evaluating food additives in 1956. Today, its work also includes contaminants, naturally occurring toxicants and residues of veterinary drugs. Since 1963, the Joint Meeting of the FAO Panel of Experts on Pesticide Residues in Food and the Environment and the WHO Core Assessment Group on Pesticide Residues (JMPR) has been assessing pesticide residues. Since the year 2000, the Joint FAO/WHO Meetings on Microbiological Risk Assessments (JEMRA) have developed, promoted and carried out risk assessment in this area. Other expert consultations are set up from time to time as needed.

Procedures for the elaboration of Codex standards, guidelines for an efficient operation of the Codex committees and task forces, policy documents

with seven further members elected by the Commission at regular sessions from among the members of the Commission, one each coming from the following geographic locations: Africa, Asia, Europe, Latin America and the Caribbean, Near East, North America, South-West Pacific. For details, see CAC, *Procedural Manual*, 17th edn (WHO/FAO, 2008).

[3] CAC, 'Alinorm 62/8: Report of the Joint FAO/WHO Conference on Food Standards' (Rome, FAO, 1962). The URL under which Alinorm documents can be found is: www.codexalimentarius.net/web/archives.jsp?lang=en.

[4] See art 1 of the Statutes of the Codex Alimentarius Commission as published CAC, *Procedural Manual* (2008) and the paragraph entitled 'Purpose of the Codex Alimentarius' in the section on general principles of the Codex Alimentarius on page 29 of the 17th edn of the Procedural Manual.

on risk analysis, a list of subsidiary bodies and their terms of reference, and the members of the CAC are contained in the Procedural Manual of the CAC.[5] The seventeenth edition of the Manual lists 175 members and one member organisation, the European Union.[6] The Procedural Manual also determines the principles concerning the participation of international non-governmental organisations in the work of the CAC, defines organisations eligible for 'observer status', appoints procedures for obtaining this status, and describes the privileges and obligations of observers. Once it has been granted, the observer status can be reviewed and terminated.

II. PROCEDURES FOR THE ELABORATION OF CODEX STANDARDS AND RELATED TEXTS

Initially, the Elaboration Procedure consisted of 10 steps and included formal acceptance by the members. The standard was called 'provisional standard' until at Step 10 the CAC determined that a sufficient number of members had formally accepted it at the preceding ninth step.[7]

The elaboration procedure and the acceptance procedure were subsequently separated. For example, the ninth edition of the Procedural Manual published in 1996 describes a uniform procedure for the elaboration of Codex standards and texts consisting of eight steps and an accelerated uniform procedure. Under the accelerated procedure the Commission, the Executive Committee or any subsidiary body subject to the confirmation of the Commission or the Executive Committee, may decide that the urgency of elaborating a Codex Standard is so pressing that Steps six and seven can be omitted. The Elaboration Procedure has been significantly amended by the twenty-seventh session of the CAC.[8] The core of the elaboration procedure, which has been published, for instance, in the fourteenth edition of the Procedural Manual still consists both of the eight-step procedure and the accelerated procedure. However, the CAC shall now base its decision to elaborate a new standard on strategic planning encompassed by an ongoing critical review to ensure that proposals for new work and draft standards are being submitted to the Commission for adoption and continue to meet its strategic priorities. At the same time, the standards need to be developed within a reasonable

[5] CAC, *Procedural Manual* (n 2).

[6] Rule II of the Rules of Procedure of the CAC (ibid 6) lays down the principles governing such membership. A core principle is that a member organisation shall exercise membership rights on an alternative basis with its Member States. Whenever a member organisation exercises its right to vote, its Member States shall not exercise theirs, and conversely.

[7] See for example, Appendix IV to the report of the third session of the CAC (Alinorm 65/30), accessible at http://www.fao.org/docrep/meeting/005/31879e/31879e00.htm.

[8] CAC, 'Alinorm 04/27/41: Twenty-seventh Session' (Report) (Geneva, Switzerland, 28 June–3 July 2004) app II.

period of time, taking into account the requirements and availability of scientific expert advice. Both the strategic planning process and the critical review process are also laid down in the Procedural Manual.

The current principles of the eight-step procedure for the elaboration of a worldwide Codex Standard can be summarised in a condensed form[9] as follows:

Preparation of a proposed draft standard in Steps one, two and three:

— The Commission decides, taking into account the outcome of a critical review conducted by the Executive Committee, to elaborate a *Worldwide Codex Standard* and also determines which (subsidiary-) body should undertake the work.
— The Secretariat arranges for the preparation of a *proposed draft standard*. In the case of Maximum Limits for Residues of Pesticides or Veterinary Drugs, the Secretariat preferably obtains recommendations for maximum limits from the JMPR, or the JECFA.
— The *proposed draft standard* is sent to the Members of the Commission and interested international organisations for comments on all aspects, including possible implications of the *proposed draft standard* on economic interests.

Adoption of a *draft standard* in Steps four to eight:

— At Step four, the Secretariat sends the received comments to the subsidiary body (or other concerned bodies), which has the power to consider such comments and amend the *proposed draft standard*.
— The Secretariat then submits the *proposed draft standard* to the Commission with a view to its adoption as a *draft standard* at Step five. At this step, due consideration is both given to the outcome of the critical review and to any comments of the members with regard to the implications of the *draft standard* on their economic interests.
— The *draft standard* is sent to members and interested international organisations for comments on all aspects at Step six, including possible implications of the *draft standard* on their economic interests.
— The comments received are sent by the Secretariat to the subsidiary body (or other concerned bodies), which has the power to consider such comments and amend the *draft standard* at Step seven.
— At Step eight, the Secretariat passes the *draft standard*—along with written proposals by members and interested international organisations—on to the Executive Committee and Commission for critical review, for amendments and with a view to its adoption as a *Codex Standard*. At this step, the Commission will give due consideration to

[9] For the full text, see CAC, *Procedural Manual* (n 2) 23.

the outcome of the critical review and to any comments that have been submitted by any of its members with respect to the implications that the *draft standard* may have on their economic interests.

In case the Commission decides to amend or revise a standard, the un-revised standard will remain the applicable *codex standard* until the amendment to the standard or the revised standard has been adopted by the Commission.

Rule XII of the Rules of Procedures states:

> The Commission shall make every effort to reach agreement on the adoption or amendment of standards by consensus. Decisions to adopt or amend standards may be taken by voting only if such efforts to reach consensus have failed.[10]

An acceptance procedure no longer exists.

III. RELATIONSHIP OF THE CODEX ALIMENTARIUS COMMISSION WITH GATT/WTO

As early as the 1970s, when the *General Agreement on Tariffs and Trade* (GATT)—through its Agriculture Committee and on an exploratory basis—started working out solutions to the problem of non-tariff barriers to trade such as health and sanitary regulations, marketing standards, packaging and labelling regulations and a number of other measures which can affect international trade in agricultural products, the CAC developed a working relationship with GATT.

An early output of the GATT work was a draft 'Code of Conduct for Preventing Technical Barriers to Trade'. However, it had never been the intention of GATT to become involved in the standard setting procedures, but rather to strengthen international standard-setting bodies such as the CAC by obliging GATT signatories to actively participate in the establishment of internationally recognised standards and to adopt such international standards as far as possible.

The CAC was informed about this activity by two of its delegations at its ninth session, and asked the Secretariat to bring the work of the Codex to the attention of the GATT Secretariat so that all necessary steps could be taken to ensure that the Code did not in any way prejudice the work of the Commission in the elaboration of food standards. Additionally, it asked the Executive Committee to keep the matter under review.[11]

[10] Ibid 16.

[11] CAC, 'Alinorm 72/35: Report of the Ninth Session of the Joint FAO/WHO Codex Alimentarius Commission' (Rome, 6–17 November 1972).

The above Code was then discussed by the Executive Committee at its nineteenth and twentieth session.[12] An explanatory statement on scope and work progress of the CAC[13] was provided at the tenth session by a GATT representative.[14] It was concluded that the Codex Secretariat should maintain close liaison with the GATT in both directions as regards work of all the GATT activities that were having possible implications for the work of the Commission and, in addition, GATT should be made fully aware of the scope and nature of the work of the CAC. The discussion of the code was continued at subsequent sessions of both the Executive Committee and the CAC. The code itself developed into the 'Draft Agreement on Technical Barriers to Trade' which called for the use of already existing international standards rather than national standards.[15] This agreement, which was later revised during the Uruguay round of trade negotiations, came into force in 1980.

At this time a close cooperation between the GATT and Codex secretariats had already been in place. However, the thirty-fifth session of the Executive Committee felt the need to revitalise this cooperation since it had been informed of a proposal which had been made to the current round of GATT to eliminate potential trade barriers by urging all nations to accept Codex Alimentarius, International Plant Protection Convention (IPPC) and Office International des Epizooties (OIE) standards by the year of 2000.[16] A detailed discussion was then held at the eighteenth session of the CAC. The CAC was informed that a GATT Working Group on Sanitary and Phytosanitary Regulations and Barriers had been established to reduce the use of sanitary and phytosanitary regulations that were unnecessary barriers to trade. The CAC was also alerted to the fact that GATT had embarked on the harmonisation of national sanitary and phytosanitary regulations as a long-term goal. This programme consisted of seven objectives of which objective number two attempted to ensure that measures taken to protect human, animal or plant life or health are consistent with sound scientific evidence. Hence, GATT member countries were encouraged to use internationally accepted standards. The programme also

[12] CAC, 'Alinorm 74/3: Report of the Nineteenth Session of the Executive Committee of the Codex Alimentarius Commission' (Geneva, 3–5 July 1973); CAC, 'Alinorm 74/4: Draft Report of the Twentieth Session of the Executive Committee of the Codex Alimentarius Commission' (Rome, 28 June 1974).

[13] CAC, 'Alinorm 74/44: Report of the tenth Session of the Codex Alimentarius Commission' (Rome, 1–11 July 1974).

[14] CAC, 'Appendix III to Alinorm 74/44: Statement by GATT Representative to the 10th Session of the Joint FAO/WHO Codex Alimentarius Commission) (Rome, 1 July 1974).

[15] See CAC, 'Alinorm 79/3: Report of the Twenty-Fifth Session of the Executive Committee of the Codex Alimentarius Commission' (Geneva, WHO, 10–13 July 1979).

[16] CAC, 'Alinorm 89/3: Report of the Thirty-Fifth Session of the Executive Committee of the Codex Alimentarius Commission' (Geneva, WHO, 4–8 July 1988).

allowed GATT to seek the expert advice and assistance of international organisations in dispute situations, such as the Codex.[17]

In 1991, the above mentioned effort had already led to the 'draft agreement on sanitary and phytosanitary measures'. Key points addressed in the draft could already at this time be regarded as an encouragement for countries to use international standards, guidelines and recommendations, including Codex standards. It also promoted the recognition of the right of countries to use more stringent standards when scientifically justified, the adherence to requirements stating that sanitary measures be based on risk assessment, the recognition of the equivalency of alternative measures, the demand for provisions regarding the information and justification which countries must provide; and the incentive to make use of the GATT dispute settlement procedures.[18]

At this stage the Executive Committee expressed the concern 'that Codex would be under great pressure in the post-Uruguay Round environment to provide a greater volume of standards and other recommendations and to ensure their revision as required, so as to help facilitate international trade…'. It recommended 'that a structural long-term solution be sought by the sponsoring organisations to ensure adequate funding for JECFA and JMPR meetings…' and stressed 'that it was important to accelerate the procedure whereby standards and other recommendations would be developed, especially in response to the demands which would be placed on the Commission as a result of the completion of the Uruguay Round…'.[19] The twenty-first session of the CAC hosted a detailed discussion of the questions relating to the implementation of the Uruguay round of multilateral trade negotiations, which was in turn based on discussions and recommendations of the forty-first and forty-second sessions of the Executive Committee.[20]

With the creation of the World Trade Organisation (WTO) as the international body dealing with the rules of trade between its member nations, a multilateral framework of basic rules for the development, adoption and enforcement of measures to protect human health and to minimise the potential negative effects of such measures on trade came into force. With respect to food safety, the most important principles are laid down in the Agreement on the Application of Sanitary and

[17] CAC, 'Alinorm 89/40: Report of the Eighteenth Session of the Joint FAO/WHO Codex Alimentarius Commission' (Geneva, WHO, 3–12 July 1989).

[18] CAC, 'Alinorm 91/40: Report of the Nineteenth Session of the Joint FAO/WHO Codex Alimentarius Commission' (Rome, 1–10 July 1991).

[19] CAC, 'Alinorm 93/3: Report of the Thirty-Ninth Session of the Executive Committee of the Codex Alimentarius Commission' (30 June–3 July 1992).

[20] CAC, 'Alinorm 95/37: Report of the Twenty-First Session of the Joint FAO/WHO Codex Alimentarius Commission' (Rome, 3–8 July 1995).

Phytosanitary Measures or SPS agreement.[21] A condensed extract of selected provisions/principles with relevance for the understanding of the Codex Alimentarius work in the area of food safety and the context of world trade is given below:

— Members have the right to take all necessary measures for the protection of human health;
— Measures should be based on scientific principles and not be maintained without sufficient scientific evidence;
— Members shall base their measures on international standards (for food safety the recognised international standards include the standards recommended by the Codex Alimentarius Commission);
— Measures which conform to international standards shall be deemed to be necessary to protect human health; there is, however, no legal obligation on WTO members to apply any Codex standard;
— Members shall accept the measures of other Members as equivalent, if the exporting Member's measures achieve the importing Member's appropriate level of protection;
— Members shall ensure that their measures are based on an assessment of the risks to human health, taking into account risk assessment techniques developed by the relevant international organisations;
— In the assessment of risks, Members shall take into account available scientific evidence;
— In cases where relevant scientific evidence is insufficient, a Member may adopt measures provisionally. Under such circumstances, Members shall seek to obtain the additional information, which are necessary for a more objective assessment of risk, within a reasonable period of time.

The SPS Agreement defines risk assessment as:

> The evaluation of the likelihood of entry, establishment or spread of a pest or disease within the territory of an importing Member according to the sanitary or phytosanitary measures which might be applied, and of the associated potential biological and economic consequences; or the evaluation of the potential for adverse effects on human or animal health arising from the presence of additives, contaminants, toxins or disease-causing organisms in food, beverages or feedstuffs.

IV. FOOD SAFETY RISK ANALYSIS AND THE ROLE OF SCIENCE IN THE CODEX ALIMENTARIUS

From the outset, the CAC has taken 'health, scientific, technological, economic and administrative points of view' into account.[22] The FAO/WHO

[21] This can be downloaded from the WTO website at www.wto.org/english/docs_e/legal_e/15-sps.pdf.
[22] CAC, 'Alinorm 62/8: Report of the FAO/WHO Conference on Food Standards' (Geneva, FAO, 1–5 October 1962).

conference on food standards, chemicals in food and food trade held in March 1991 recommended—in view of the possible new international status of the Codex standards under the GATT agreements—an early review programme to examine all Codex standards for their current relevance and sound scientific basis. It was agreed that the timeliness of Codex procedures for the establishment and review of standards should be re-examined. All Codex committees and the Joint FAO/WHO Expert Committees (JECFA and JMPR) should continue to base their evaluations on scientific principles and ensure consistency in their risk assessment determinations.

The CAC discussed the issue of risk assessment procedures used by its subsidiary and advisory bodies and itself during its twentieth session.[23] Consultants had previously prepared a working document which documented that several areas of Codex activity did not conform to risk analysis principles. The Committee recognised the need for rapid progress in implementing risk analysis in Codex work. It was proposed that the Codex Committee on General Principles[24] should address the adoption of risk analysis, including the possibility of changes in the rules of procedure and in the terms of reference of relevant Codex Committees.

The twenty-first session of the CAC examined a proposal of the forty-first session of the Executive Committee to set out four statements of principle which confirmed the pre-eminent role of science in Codex decision-making processes, while allowing for other factors to be taken into account. This initial discussion in which the Commission confirmed that Codex standards and other texts should be based on the principle of sound science was followed by many debates in subsequent sessions before a final wording was adopted. However, the twenty-first session—in order to strengthen the role of science in the Codex decision-making process—asked the Secretariat to draw the attention of the Directors-General of the FAO and WHO to the Commission's desire to increase transparency in the working procedures of expert panels. They specifically referred to JECFA and JMPR procedures with regard to the selection

[23] CAC, 'Alinorm 93/40: Report of the Twentieth Session of the Joint FAO/WHO Codex Alimentarius Commission' (Geneva, 28 June–7 July 1993).

[24] CAC, *Procedural Manual* (n 2) describes the Terms of Reference of the Codex Committee on General Principles as follows: 'To deal with such procedural and general matters as are referred to it by the Codex Alimentarius Commission. Such matters have included the establishment of the General Principles which define the purpose and scope of the Codex Alimentarius, the nature of Codex standards and the forms of acceptance by countries of Codex standards; the development of Guidelines for Codex Committees; the development of a mechanism for examining any economic impact statements submitted by governments concerning possible implications for their economies of some of the individual standards or some of the provisions thereof; the establishment of a Code of Ethics for the International Trade in Food.'

and adequate geographical representation of experts, and declaration of interest. Their statement was amended during subsequent sessions.

The main recommendations on risk assessment and risk management of extensive expert consultations were incorporated into the discussion paper, 'The Application of Risk Assessment Principles in Codex'[25] submitted to the twenty-second session of the Commission. The Commission adopted a basic set of terms on an interim basis. Revised draft definitions for risk management and risk communication were proposed by the fourteenth session of the Codex Committee on General Principles[26] and were adopted at the twenty-third session of the Commission. The current CAC Procedural Manual defines risk analysis as a 'process consisting of three components: risk assessment, risk management and risk communication'.

The twenty-second session of the CAC[27] initiated an action plan for Codex-wide development and application of risk analysis principles and guidelines involving the Codex Committee on General Principles and all the other relevant Codex Committees. According to this action plan, Codex Committees involved in any aspect of risk analysis should formally describe their implementation of the Codex principles and guidelines and develop standards using these principles and guidelines as a checklist. In doing so, they would adhere closely to their documented risk assessment/risk management policies. Working principles for risk analysis for application in the Procedural Manual of the Codex Alimentarius framework were adopted by the twenty-sixth session of the CAC.[28] The principles which are currently in force are laid down in section III of the seventeenth edition of the Procedural Manual and cover all aspects of risk analysis.

The first draft prepared by a subsidiary body and adopted by the CAC was the document, 'Draft Risk Analysis Principles Applied by the Codex Committee on Food Additives and Contaminants' (CCFAC) adopted at the twenty-eighth session of the CAC.

During its twenty-first and twenty-second session respectively, the CAC took two important decisions concerning the role of science in the Codex decision-making process and the principles relating to food safety risk assessment. The final texts can currently be found in the General

[25] CAC, 'Alinorm 97/9 – Rev.1' (CAC/LIM 21).

[26] Joint FAO/WHO Food Standards Programme, Codex Alimentarius Commission, Twenty-third Session, (Rome, 28 June–3 July 1999). 'Report of the fourteenth Session of the Codex Committee on General Principles' (Paris, France, 19–23 April 1999). Alinorm 99/33A, para 11–15 and app III.

[27] CAC, 'Alinorm 97/37: Twenty-secondSession' (Report) (Geneva, 23–28 June 1997).

[28] CAC, 'Alinorm 03/41: Twenty-sixth Session' (Report) (FAO Headquarters, Rome, 30 June–7 July 2003) app IV.

Decisions appendix of the seventeenth Procedural Manual. They read as follows:[29]

Statements of Principle concerning the Role of Science in the Codex Decision-Making Process and the Extent to which other Factors are taken into Account

1. The food standards, guidelines and other recommendations of the Codex Alimentarius shall be based on the principle of sound scientific analysis and evidence, involving a thorough review of all relevant information so that the standards assure the quality and safety of the food supply.
2. When elaborating and deciding upon food standards the Codex Alimentarius will consider, where appropriate, other legitimate factors relevant for the health protection of consumers and for the promotion of fair practices in food trade.
3. In this regard it is noted that food labelling plays an important role in furthering both of these objectives.
4. When the situation arises that members of the Codex agree on the necessary level of protection of public health but hold differing views about other considerations, members may abstain from acceptance of the relevant standard without necessarily preventing decisions by the Codex.

Criteria for the Consideration of the Other Factors Referred to in the Second Statement of Principle

— when health and safety matters are concerned the *Statements of Principle Concerning the Role of Science* and the *Statements of Principle Relating to the Role of Food Safety Risk Assessment* should be followed;
— other legitimate factors relevant for health protection and fair trade practices may be identified thoughout the risk management process, and risk managers should indicate how these factors affect the selection of risk management options and the development of standards, guidelines and related texts.
— consideration of other factors should not affect the scientific basis of risk analysis; in this process, the separation between risk assessment and risk management should be respected, in order to ensure the scientific integrity of the risk assessment;
— it should be recognized that some legitimate concerns of governments are not generally applicable or relevant world-wide;
— only those factors which can be accepted on a world-wide basis, or on a regional basis in the case of regional standards and related texts, should be taken into account in the framework of Codex;

[29] http://www.codexalimentarius.net/web/procedural_manual.jsp.

— the consideration of specific other factors during the development of risk management recommendations of the Codex Alimentarius Commission and its subsidiary bodies should be clearly documented, including the rationale for their integration, on a case-by-case basis;
— the feasibility of risk management options due to the nature and particular constraints of the production or processing methods, transport and storage, especially in developing countries may be considered; concerns related to economic interests and trade issues in general should be substantiated by quantifiable data;
— the integration of other legitimate factors in risk management should not create unjustified barriers to trade; particular attention should be given to the impact on developing countries of the inclusion of such other factors.

Statements of Principles relating to the Role of Food Safety Risk Assessment

1. Health and safety aspects of Codex decisions and recommendations should be based on a risk assessment, as appropriate to the circumstances.
2. Food safety risk assessment should be soundly based on science, should incorporate the four steps of the risk assessment process, and should be documented in a transparent manner.
3. There should be a functional separation of risk assessment and risk management, while recognizing that some interactions are essential for a pragmatic approach.
4. Risk assessment should use available quantitative information to the greatest extent possible and risk characterizations should be presented in readily understandable and useful form.

V. THE ROLES OF JECFA AND JMPR IN THE ELABORATION OF CODEX STANDARDS FOR RESIDUES OF PESTICIDES AND VETERINARY DRUGS

Risk assessment, risk management and risk communication should take place within an overarching food safety management system; however, there should be a clear functional separation of risk assessment and risk management in order to ensure the scientific integrity of the risk assessment process. Therefore, JECFA and JMPR are not part of the Codex system but interact through the Secretariat with the Codex Committees. Although risk assessment is primarily based on science, it is not 100 per cent pure science because the expert committees have to take the risk assessment policies established by the risk managers into account. Such policies should be established in advance and in an interactive manner with the expert committees.

The JECFA is an ad hoc expert body giving advice on the risk assessment of food chemicals, including natural constituents, food additives, contaminants and veterinary drug residues. Members of JECFA are scientists serving in their individual capacities as experts having been selected by the two agencies on the basis of publicly transparent selection criteria and in consultation with their governments.[30] In addition to expertise, a balance of geographic representation of the global membership of the two organisations is considered essential. Before an expert is formally invited, she/he has to inform the Joint JECFA Secretariat of any personal or financial interest in any substance on the agenda. Since JECFA is an independent scientific body, it is free to develop its own evaluation policies, which have evolved over many years. The WHO group of experts within JECFA is responsible for the toxicological evaluation and establishment of an Acceptable Daily Intake (ADI) or other exposure limits. ADIs established by JECFA are upper limits of dietary intakes, which can be ingested daily over a lifetime without appreciable health risk, and are based on contemporary scientific criteria and knowledge. The FAO group of experts reviews those studies relevant for establishing Maximum Residue Limits (MRLs). The MRLs are calculated by taking into account established good practices in the use of veterinary drugs, the availability of analytical methods for enforcement and by using arbitrary conservative food consumption figures for the intake ('exposure') assessment.[31] The FAO group also reviews analytical methods suitable for the enforcement of MRLs.

The JMPR is also an independent expert ad hoc body,[32] which has evaluated pesticides over more than 35 years with the aim of estimating the maximum residue levels in food and feed which are likely to result from legally permitted uses of pesticides. The WHO Toxicological Core Assessment Group is responsible for reviewing pesticide toxicological data and estimating ADIs for humans. In addition, as data and circumstances dictate, the Group estimates acute Reference Doses (acute RfDs),

[30] The current roster of JECFA experts for residues of veterinary drugs can be found using the following links: WHO group of experts: www.who.int/ipcs/food/jecfa/en/roster.pdf. FAO group of experts (2007–2011): www.fao.org/ag/agn/agns/files/2007_09_28_FAO_Roster_Veterinary_Drugs.pdf.

[31] The workflow is strongly influenced by a definition of Codex maximum limit for residues of veterinary drugs (MRLVD developed by the CCRVFD and included in the Procedural Manual (see CAC, *Procedural Manual* (n 2) 43).

[32] The current roster of JMPR experts for pesticide residues can be found using the following links: WHO group of experts:www.who.int/ipcs/food/jmpr/en/jmpr_roster_web.pdf. FAO group of experts:www.fao.org/ag/agp/agpp/pesticid/JMPR/JMPR_Roster_07.pdf.

thus limiting single high exposure, and characterises other toxicological criteria such as non-dietary exposures. The WHO Environmental Core Assessment Group's role also consists of identifying risks to organisms in the environment. The FAO Panel, in turn, reviews use patterns resulting from already approved national uses of pesticides (Good Agricultural Practices (GAPs)) and other relevant data on which estimates of MRLs, dietary intakes, and methods of analysis can be based on. The maximum residue levels are recommended to the CCPR as being suitable for a consideration as Codex MRLs.

In terms of the risk analysis paradigm, one could summarise that whereas the hazard identification and hazard characterisation steps lay primarily in the domain of the WHO expert groups of the two committees, the exposure assessment step is primarily the domain of the FAO expert groups. The risk characterisation step should be carried out by the expert committees as a whole. With regard to the final output of the risk assessment, the two combined panels (WHO and FAO part) have joint responsibility.

The complete output of JECFA and JMPR is currently publicly available online[33] from the 'JECFA main page' at WHO[34] and the corresponding JMPR page,[35] as well as from the JECFA page at the FAO[36] and the corresponding JMPR page.[37] A database of MRLs for residues of veterinary drugs in foods is available from the Codex Alimentarius website at the FAO.[38] A similar database of MRLs of pesticides is also available on the Codex Alimentarius website at the FAO.[39]

A comparison of the output of the two expert committees with the number of substances requiring international evaluation reveals the following—hundreds of substances are currently used as active principles in health products developed for the treatment of food-producing animals. The number of substances used as pesticides is even higher and may range above 1000. However, not all of these substances fulfil the criteria for priority evaluation by the Codex system:

— The substance must be available for use as a commercial product.
— The use of the product must give rise to public health concerns due to residues in or on a food (or feed).
— Commodities moving in international trade have the potential to create problems.

33 Links last tested on 30 March 2009.
34 See www.who.int/ipcs/food/jecfa/en/index.html.
35 See www.who.int/ipcs/food/jmpr/en/index.html.
36 See www.fao.org/ag/agn/agns/jecfa_index_en.asp.
37 See www.fao.org/ag/AGP/AGPP/Pesticid/JMPR/PM_JMPR.htm.
38 See www.codexalimentarius.net/mrls/vetdrugs/jsp/vetd_q-e.jsp.
39 See www.codexalimentarius.net/mrls/pestdes/jsp/pest_q-e.jsp.

Using these criteria, the number of substances possibly requiring the establishment of international Maximum Residue Limits for Veterinary Drugs (MRLVDs) probably ranges below 200, while the number of substances requiring international Maximum Residue Limits for Pesticide Residues (MRLPs) is certainly somewhat higher. Foods containing residues of any of these substances could potentially be a hazard to the health of consumers and could consequently create problems in international trade. However, many of these substances have never been subjected to an international evaluation.

Since the introduction of contemporary methods of risk assessment, the JECFA has evaluated approximately 80 substances (by counting groups of substances that have the same ADI as one substance). The FAO/WHO Joint Meeting on Pesticide Residues, on the other hand, has evaluated (and, up to several times, re-evaluated) more than 250 substances.

VI. EXAMPLE: RISK ASSESSMENT OF RESIDUES OF VETERINARY DRUGS

As described earlier, risk assessment is a scientifically based process consisting of hazard identification, hazard characterisation, exposure assessment, and risk characterisation.

A. Hazard Identification

The process of hazard identification is similar for all 'food chemicals' (chemically defined substances of low molecular weight, such as natural constituents, additives, environmental contaminants, toxins and residues). Therefore, the basic concepts can be outlined jointly both for veterinary drugs and for other categories of chemical substances.

It is not possible to completely separate the hazard identification and hazard characterisation steps in practice. However, the usefulness of a JECFA evaluation of the active principle of a veterinary drug depends critically on the quality of the research conducted for identifying the hazard. Therefore, the information required is substantial and ranges from valid, well designed, animal-based toxicity studies conducted in accordance with internationally recognised protocols (Organisation for Economic Cooperation and Development (OECD) under conditions of Good Laboratory Practice (GLP) to validate in vitro techniques and even establish structural alerts or structure activity relationships. 'Well designed' means primarily: adequate selection of species; strain/genetic make-up; sex; stage of life; number of animals per dose group and statistical design; adequate selection and spacing of doses possibly allowing the determination of a No Observed Effect Level (NOEL); and finally, a suitable route of administration (per oral route, preferably via the diet).

For the hazard identification of substances which require international evaluation, typically, a defined set of animal tests (ideally covering the entire range of possible adverse health effects) are routinely necessary, irrespective of the expected exposure of consumers. Information on dose-dependent toxicokinetic properties of veterinary drugs, including rate and extent of absorption, distribution, pre-systemic and systemic metabolism and excretion in test animals, in the target species of animals (and, where available, in humans), is always indispensable for hazard identification, as well as for hazard characterisation and may help to design and interpret other studies. If metabolites are formed in those food-producing animals which were not observed in the laboratory, separate animal testing of those metabolites may be necessary. Additionally, other special studies may be required on a case by case basis.

JECFA has developed a special approach for antimicrobial substances to identify and characterise antimicrobial hazards which could have adverse effects on the microbial flora of the gut and also to determine an antimicrobial ADI, typically on the basis of specifically designed in vitro studies.

Often overlooked is the fact that the results of any evaluations are only strictly applicable to a specified test substance used throughout the tests. Therefore, the availability of the results of the specification of the test substance is important, in particular information on purity (or impurities) and on isomeric composition.

At the end of the hazard identification, both the effects which are considered adverse and the identity of the molecules causing these effects are known or else either the gaps of knowledge or the data, which would be required before a final evaluation can take place, are clearly defined.

B. Hazard Characterisation

During the risk assessment of veterinary drugs, this step primarily focuses on the dose-response relationship for critical adverse effects, the identification of the most sensitive species/strain for a given effect, and the extrapolation from animals to humans. Furthermore, any information elucidating the key processes involved in toxicity are important. Again, toxicokinetic data may play an important role. They may, for example, provide information on the formation of critical metabolites and on binding to cellular macromolecules, but may also give explanations for quantitative species differences and inter-individual variability.

The Expert Committee's approach to use dose-response information in hazard characterisation is based on the traditional assumption[40] that non-cancer endpoints and non-genotoxic cancer endpoints display dose thresholds. If a substance causes only threshold responses in the exposed population of test animals, the Committee determines for every critical effect the dose level at which there are no significant increases in frequency and severity of the effect between the exposed groups and the control groups. This dose level is called No Observed [Adverse] Effect Level (NO[A]EL). The lowest NO[A]EL or highest dose which does not cause any toxicity is typically, but not always, taken as the starting point for deriving the Acceptable Daily Intake (ADI). The choice is also determined by the required 'safety factors' (SF), according to which the NOEL is divided in order to take account of the small size of the test group of animals, the inter-individual and inter-species variability, the nature of the critical effects and the quality of the data. In fact, the combination of NOEL and SF resulting in the lowest intake (and thereby the largest margin of safety for all critical effects observed in the exposed animals) is finally used to allocate the ADI. The JECFA/ADIs are always presented in a range from zero to an upper limit, encouraging efforts to keep human exposure as low as 'Good Practice in the Use of Veterinary Drugs' (GPVD)[41] allows.

For effects involving non-threshold mechanisms, the NOEL/SF approach cannot be used. The expert committee has not yet developed an alternative approach to deal with substances exhibiting such effects.

At the end of the hazard characterisation step performed by JECFA, and if the database was adequate, the upper limit of the range of acceptable daily intakes of the hazardous agent is known. It is assumed that intakes over lifetime at or below this limit would not pose an appreciable risk to the health of consumers.

C. From ADI to MRL and Exposure Assessment

The development of a proposal of a Maximum Residue Level for Veterinary Drugs (MRLVD), which is the final Codex Standard, requires additional information, as follows:

— Information on established 'Good Practice in the Use of Veterinary Drugs' (GPVDs) in different countries and regions of the world (conditions

[40] The existence of a threshold cannot be proven from the data of a dose-response relationship.

[41] CAC, *Procedural Manual* (n 2) defines: Good Practice in the Use of Veterinary Drugs (GPVD) is the official recommended or authorized usage including withdrawal periods, approved by national authorities, of veterinary drugs under practical conditions.

of use of the drug including, for instance, approved formulations, target species of animal, route of administration, recommended doses and established withdrawal times).

— Comparative kinetic and metabolism evaluation in laboratory and food-producing animals.

— Residue depletion studies in target species of animals bracketing the withdrawal time and using the highest recommended dose of the authorised formulation, the recommended frequency and the route of administration. These studies should provide information on total residues of concern according to the results of the hazard identification step (major residue components including free and bound residues) and should permit selection of a 'marker residue' and 'target tissues' as a basis for setting MRLVDs and determining the ratio between marker residue and total residue of concern. The marker residue is considered representative for all types of relevant residues. The Codex' MRLVD are expressed on that basis.

— Description and performance characteristics of the analytical procedures used for the determination of residues in the above mentioned depletion studies.

— Analytical routine methods that may be used for monitoring compliance with MRLVD by regulatory authorities.

— Where applicable—studies designed to assess the impact of antimicrobial residues on food processing.

The evaluation of this information is complex and requires the application of sophisticated statistical approaches. Depending on the use of the drug JECFA proposes MRLVDs for a variable set of commodities, for instance, muscle, liver, kidney and fat if meat- producing animals are involved.

For the residues of concern, the Expert Committee carries out an intake assessment as a surrogate for a sophisticated exposure assessment, which is neither feasible under normal conditions of availability of data at the international level nor necessary, provided the approach to the intake assessment is sufficiently consumer-protective. The results of the dietary intake assessment are compared with the ADI. Standards are only proposed if the estimated long-term intake theoretically resulting from the implementation of the proposed standards ranges below the ADI. JECFA currently calculates a single intake estimate, the 'Estimated Daily Intake' (EDI), in order to predict long-term intakes. It uses the following daily intake figures (for a standard 60 kg person) in these calculations: 300 g of muscle (muscle and skin in natural proportions in the case of fish), 100 g of liver, 50 g of kidney, 50 g of tissue fat (skin and fat in the case of poultry and pigs), 100 g of egg, 1.5 l of milk, and 20 g of honey.

D. Risk Characterisation

Risk characterisation is the step in risk assessment in which the results of the hazard characterisation and exposure assessment are integrated and transformed into advice to risk managers. The final output and the complexity of the risk characterisation step depend on the mandate given to risk assessors. The desired output in the case of veterinary drugs consists primarily of a set of proposed draft MRLVDs if a substance has successfully passed the evaluation. In this case, the output is explained in a public report justifying the selection of the proposed MRLVDs on the basis of an accurate description and discussion of the results of the three steps, hazard identification, hazard characterisation and exposure assessment. If no ADI and/or MRLVDs could be recommended, this is also explained. In cases of gaps in information, the data requirements to be fulfilled before a further review takes place are defined.

Striving for the functional separation between scientific risk assessment and management of the risks the output of JECFA is further discussed and undergoes the above described[42] stepwise procedure of the CAC until it eventually becomes a Codex Standard.

Establishing a MRL represents only one of the many options risk managers have at hand and use to reduce risks, while these other available options are being used by regulatory authorities at the national level. The main reason for the selective development of MRLVDs and comparable standards at the international level is that such standards have the greatest potential to create barriers to trade, if not harmonised. It is thus important to note that MRLVDs are not the only means of consumer health protection. The Codex system only establishes such standards if safe conditions of use of the substance in veterinary drugs have been authorised at national levels.

[42] See Chapter II.

6

The Contribution of Global Administrative Law to Enhancing the Legitimacy of the Codex Alimentarius Commission

ALEXIA HERWIG*

I. INTRODUCTION

THE PURPOSE OF this chapter is to assess the contribution of administrative law concepts in addressing the legitimacy deficits of the Codex Alimentarius Commission (CAC). This Commission develops food standards that have become accepted as reference standards for World Trade Organisation (WTO) law. Several scholars have offered global administrative law as a way of enhancing the accountability of international governance, sometimes as an alternative source of legitimacy to more normative concepts like democracy or human rights (Cassesse 2005: 687–89; Esty 2006; Kingsbury et al 2005; Kingsbury, Krisch and Stewart 2005: 42–59).[1]

This issue is not only of academic interest—in 2002 the CAC carried out a review of its standard-setting procedure in order to address shortcomings (Food and Agriculture Organisation of the United Nations (FAO) and World Health Organisation (WHO) Report; Hüller and Maier 2006). Do global administrative law concepts provide an appropriate benchmark for judging the reforms proposed during the CAC review process?

* This contribution is partly based on a presentation by the author and Leo Maier at the Law and Society Conference in Berlin in 2007. The author is grateful to the participants of the Oñati conference 'Public Law beyond the State' for insightful comments and to the editors for their careful scrutiny of this contribution.

[1] See also the individual contributions to this volume and to 37 *New York University Journal of International Law and Politics* 2005 and 17 *European Journal of International Law* 2006; Möllers, Voßkuhle, and Walter 2007; Möllers 2005. For a cautionary note on transposing domestic administrative law concepts to WTO governance, see Cassese 2005b.

This chapter proceeds in three main sections. The next section provides a brief introduction to the CAC and to the status of CAC standards under WTO law. The following section presents the legitimacy deficits of the CAC, while the last section introduces administrative law models and gauges their contribution to enhancing the legitimacy of the CAC. The models' plausibility when applied to the international order and to the CAC will be assessed.

Moreover, it will be argued that the contribution of administrative law concepts to the legitimacy of international governance in general and that of the CAC in particular remains limited because the scholarship on global administrative law still lacks a normative vision of global justice.[2]

II. AN OVERVIEW OF THE CAC

A. The CAC as a Standard-Setting Body

The CAC was created under the joint auspices of the FAO and the WHO (Sander 2000: 335–38). Its legal basis is a joint resolution by the two parent organisations.[3] The CAC implements the Joint Food Standards Programme, the objective of which is to protect the health of consumers, to ensure fair practices in the food trade and to determine priorities for global or regional standards and finalise and amend such standards as appropriate.[4] These food standards are aimed at protecting consumers' health and ensuring fair practices in the food trade[5] and ensuring a sound, wholesome food for the consumer which is free from adulteration and correctly labelled and presented.[6] In spite of the dual mandate, the Working Principles for Risk affirm that health protection should be the primary objective of the CAC standards.[7] The Commission has established several specialised committees, notably commodities or vertical committees that elaborate product-specific standards, horizontal committees setting standards for, inter alia, food additives, labelling and pesticide residues, as well as cross-cutting issues such as standards for good risk analysis and regional committees.[8] In order to investigate specific issues, the Codex

[2] For similar conclusions concerning the CAC, see Pereira (2008) (Pereira does not speak of a constitutional project, yet what he mentions, parliaments and courts, describes a constitutional infrastructure) and more generally, see Harlow 2006: 187, 208.

[3] FAO and WHO 'Understanding the Codex Alimentarius Commission' 7.

[4] Statutes of the CAC in the *Procedural Manual* of the CAC: CAC (2008) 'General Principles of the Codex Alimentarius Commission': para 1.

[5] Ibid para 1.

[6] Ibid para 3.

[7] CAC (2008) 'Working Principles for Risk Analysis for Application in the Framework of the Codex Alimentarius': para 27.

[8] FAO and WHO 'Understanding the Codex Alimentarius Commission': 17–19.

has also established task forces, including the Intergovernmental Task Force on Foods Derived from Biotechnology.[9]

There is an institutional separation of risk assessment and risk management in the CAC (CAC (2008) 'Working Principles for Risk Analysis for Application in the Framework of the Codex Alimentarius': para 3).[10] The risk assessment is carried out by the Joint Expert Committee on Food Additives (JECFA), the Joint Meetings on Pesticide Residues (JMPR) and the Joint Meeting on Microbiological Risk Assessment (JEMRA), all of which operate under the auspices of the FAO and WHO.[11] The International Dairy Federation performs the risk assessment for dairy products.[12] The risk management is carried out by specialised committees and the general Commission.[13] The actual elaboration and drafting of the standards usually occurs in the former.[14] The Commission, however, is the final decision-making body. It decides on all standards, as well as all changes to procedures and the work programme of the Commission (Statutes of the CAC: art 1). Although risk assessment and risk management are kept separate institutionally, the CAC recognises that the two are necessarily intertwined for pragmatic reasons and also when a risk assessment policy is developed.[15] This is the case because risk assessment must often rely on inferences and extrapolations whose correctness cannot be proven and is largely determined by risk management considerations.

The members of the JECFA and the JMPR are independent scientists who are selected by the parent organisations without input from national governments.[16] The members of the general Commission are national

[9] Ibid.

[10] See also the contribution of Arnold in chapter five and Hüller and Maier (2006: 281–86) (arguing in favour of this analytical distinction).

[11] FAO and WHO 'Understanding the Codex Alimentarius Commission': 23–24; CAC (2008) 'Procedures for the Elaboration of the Codex Standards and Related Texts': Introduction and Part 3, 1.

[12] CAC (2008) 'Procedures for the Elaboration of the Codex Standards and Related Texts': Introduction and Part 3, 2.

[13] CAC (2008) 'Working Principles for Risk Analysis for Application in the Framework of the Codex Alimentarius: para 3.

[14] CAC (2008) 'Procedures for the Elaboration of the Codex Standards and Related Texts': Introduction and Part 3, 1.

[15] CAC (2008) Working Principles for Risk Analysis for Application in the Framework of the Codex Alimentarius': para 9, 13–16; CAC (2008) 'Statements of Principle Relating to the Role of Food Safety Risk Assessment'.

[16] CAC (2008) 'Rules of Procedure of the Codex Alimentarius Commission': Rule IV and Constitution of the Food and Agriculture Organisation art VI: '...The individuals appointed in their personal capacity shall, as regards the Organization, be designated either by the Conference, the Council, selected Member Nations or Associate Members, or by the Director-General, as decided by the Conference or Council'. FAO is responsible for selecting members to deal with the development of specifications for the identity and purity of food additives and the assessment of residue levels of veterinary drugs in food. WHO selects members to deal with the toxicological evaluations of the substances. See FAO Fact Sheet—What is JECFA?.

delegates (CAC (2008) 'General Principles of the Codex Alimentarius Commission': para 3) but there is also a strong influence of private actors in the CAC through four different avenues. First, the CAC grants to certain non-governmental organisations (NGOs) the status of observers (CAC (2008) 'Rules of Procedure of the Codex Alimentarius Commission': Rule IX.4). This implies the right to speak and make written submissions in CAC meetings but not the right to cast votes.[17] Second, governments may decide to include civil society and business representatives in their delegations to the CAC (Herwig 2004: 199, 204). Third, the industry concerned by a potential standard often submits information to the expert committees, but the experts in return are expected to conduct their own independent review (FAO Fact Sheet–What is JECFA?: 2). Fourth, governments can decide whether they want to consult private actors on draft CAC standards.[18] The specialised committees are staffed with government experts from the respective fields and representatives from industry, as well as some consumer organisations (CAC (2008) 'Rules of Procedure of the Codex Alimentarius Commission': Rule XI.4; Sander 2000: 340–45).[19]

The general Commission usually operates on a consensus basis, although decision-taking by simple majority is possible (ibid: Rules VIII.1 and VIII.2). The CAC Rules of Procedure state that: '[t]he Commission shall make every effort to reach agreement on the adoption or amendment of standards by consensus. Decisions to adopt or amend standards may be taken by voting only if such efforts to reach consensus have failed' (ibid: Rule XII.2). The consensual decision-making procedure has been strengthened during recent years as the Codex has adopted guidelines on measures to facilitate consensus (CAC (2008) 'Measures to Facilitate Consensus': 197). Meetings of the general Commission are public unless the Commission decides otherwise (CAC (2008) 'Rules of Procedure of the Codex Alimentarius Commission': Rule VI.6). The general Commission also publishes a report of the meeting, which includes minority opinions (ibid: Rule X.1). The specialised Codex Committees work under the same procedure as the Codex Commission, including the emphasis on consensual decision-making with a possibility for majority-voting (ibid: Rule XI.11). The FAO/WHO expert committees normally take decisions

[17] CAC (2008) 'Principles Concerning the Participation of International Non-Governmental Organizations in the Work of the Codex Alimentarius Commission'.

[18] In the US, a Federal Register notice mentions the standards due to be adopted at the next Codex Commission meeting, but does not provide details of the draft standards or the US position. The Trade Agreements Act of 1979, as amended, s 491 19 USC 2578 requires that the agency responsible for a particular Codex standard shall provide for public comment. See Federal Register Notice 29531 of May 31 2001.

[19] Members shall, as far as possible, be specialists in the field.

by consensus, but there is also a possibility of including minority reports (FAO Fact Sheet–What is JECFA?: 3).

The elaboration of Codex standards takes place according to an eight-step procedure with a possibility of a fast track procedure.[20] Once a committee has elaborated a draft standard, the standard is sent out to governments for comments.[21] Comments and proposed amendments are then reviewed by the specialised committee that will amend the draft if necessary.[22] The draft standard is then submitted to the Commission for approval as a draft standard with 'due consideration [given]... to any comments that may be submitted by any of its Members regarding the implication which the proposed draft standard or any provision thereof may have for their economic interests'.[23] After a second round of comments with the possibility of further amendment, the draft is submitted to the Commission to be adopted as a Codex standard.[24]

The CAC has made attempts to strengthen the participation of developing countries. The establishment of a trust fund of US $40 million in 2003 to finance the participation of developing countries and the requirement that specialised committees are co-chaired by developing countries, facilitate a more widespread participation of developing countries.[25] During the first year of financial assistance provided through the trust fund, 19 per cent of all assisted countries participated for the first time in Codex activities.[26] However, due to a lack of donor pledges, the fund had to be cut back on its activities and now only reimburses travel expenses.[27]

In recent years, both the Codex and its parent organisations have undertaken steps to ensure the scientific integrity of their risk assessments. The Codex has also adopted provisions about conflicts of interests of experts and transparency of the selection procedure.[28] It has also made efforts to codify and streamline its risk assessment procedure. The Codex has adopted texts which clearly articulate its risk assessment procedures and the role that precaution and other relevant factors play in developing food

[20] CAC (2008) 'Procedure for the Elaboration of Codex Standards and Related Texts': para 6, Part 3 and 4. For a more detailed overview over the eight-step procedure, see the contribution of Arnold in chapter five.

[21] Procedures for the Elaboration of Codex Standards and Related Texts: Steps 1, 2 and 3, para 3 and Step 4.

[22] Ibid: Step 5.

[23] Ibid: Step 8.

[24] Uniform Procedure for the Elaboration of Codex Standards: Steps 6, 7 and 8.

[25] FAO/WHO 'Project and Fund for Enhanced Participation in Codex'.

[26] Ibid.

[27] See www.who.int/foodsafety/codex/trustfund.en.

[28] CAC (2008) 'Working Principles for Risk Analysis for Application in the Framework of the Codex Alimentarius': para 18.

standards.[29] In a nutshell, these standards affirm the principle of sound science, call for quantitative data, whenever possible, for transparent and accessible documentation of the risk analysis, for an explicit consideration of uncertainty in the risk assessment and for consistency between cases and consideration of the trade-restrictiveness of standards.[30] The CAC has also sought to create a more principled way of dealing with those policy factors that influence risk regulation. In CAC terminology, these are called 'other legitimate factors' (OLFs) and refer to aspects other than human health protection and the economic interests of the CAC members, which are relevant for international food standards, such as environmental protection and animal welfare. Concerning OLFs, only those which can be accepted on a world-wide basis shall be taken into account and risk managers shall explain how the consideration of OLFs affects risk management.[31]

B. The Status of CAC Standards under WTO Law

i. The Sanitary and Phytosanitary Agreement

Prior to 1994, CAC standards were not recognised under the General Agreement on Tariffs and Trade (GATT). CAC members were free to decide whether they wanted to accept a CAC standard or not. Post 1994, CAC standards have become reference standards for national food safety measures under the Sanitary and Phytosanitary (SPS) Agreement. A member can initiate a WTO dispute settlement procedure if it considers that another member's sanitary measure lacks justification. The WTO panel will then examine whether the defending member has sufficient scientific justification for its measure. A member should base its regulation on CAC standards, but is free to depart from them if it can provide scientific

[29] Ibid; CAC (2008) 'Risk Analysis Principles Applied by the Codex Committee on Food Additives and the Codex Committee on Contaminants in Foods'; CAC (2008) 'Policy of the Codex Committee on Contaminants in Foods for Exposure Assessment of Contaminants and Toxins in Foods or Food Groups'; CAC (2008) 'Risk Analysis Principles Applied by the Codex Committee on Pesticide Residues'; CAC (2008) 'Risk Analysis Principles Applied by the Codex Committee on Residues of Veterinary Drugs in Foods'; CAC (2008) 'Statements of Principle Concerning the Role of Science in the Codex Decision-Making Process and the Extent to which other Factors are Taken into Account'; CAC (2008) 'Statements of Principle Relating to the Role of Food Safety Risk Assessment'. A more detailed account is set forth in the contribution of Arnold in chapter five.

[30] CAC (2008) 'Statements of Principle Relating to the Role of Food Safety Risk Assessment': 196; CAC (2008) 'Working Principles for Risk Analysis for Application in the Framework of the Codex Alimentarius': paras 4, 6, 10, 11, 23, 25, 31, 34.

[31] CAC (2008) 'Statements of Principle Concerning the Role of Science in the Codex Decision-Making Process and the Extent to which other Factors are taken into Account': 194.

justification. This does not make CAC standards binding but—as a result of the SPS Agreement—the right of WTO members to depart from CAC standards is conditional. Via WTO dispute settlement, the enforcement of CAC standards has therefore been strengthened.[32]

Concerning CAC standards, the SPS Agreement distinguishes between three types of situation:

(i) The national measure conforms to the CAC standard.
(ii) It is based on the CAC standard.
(iii) The national measure is neither based on—nor conforms to—the CAC standard.

If a member's standards entirely conform to the relevant Codex standard, it can benefit from a safe haven provision because the measure is then deemed to be necessary for human health protection and consistent with the GATT (SPS Agreement article 3.2). Members are also called upon to base their SPS measures on international standards, guidelines or recommendations (SPS Agreement articles 3.1 and 3.2). Article 3.1 provides that:

> To harmonize sanitary and phytosanitary measures on as wide a basis as possible, Members shall base their sanitary or phytosanitary measures on international standards, guidelines or recommendations, where they exist, except as otherwise provided for in this Agreement, and in particular in paragraph 3.

While the notion of 'conform to' suggests that members implement Codex standards verbatim, the notion of 'based on' indicates a looser connection between the SPS measure and the international standard. In *EC–Hormones*, the Appellate Body considered that a measure that only adheres to parts of an international standard could be considered as being based on that standard (WTO Appellate Body Report, EC–Hormones: para 163). It also noted that 'based on' commonly means 'stand on' or 'founded or built on' or 'supported by' (ibid: para 163). *EC-Hormones* indicates that measures which bear no relation to the risk established in the process of international standardisation will not be considered to be based on international standards.

The SPS Agreement defines international standards related to food safety as '...standards, guidelines and recommendations established by the Codex Alimentarius Commission relating to food additives, veterinary drug and pesticide residues, contaminants, methods of analysis and sampling, and codes and guidelines of hygienic practice' (SPS Agreement Annex a 2(a)).

Article 3.1 of the SPS Agreement seems to distinguish between international standards, guidelines and recommendations, but the definition in the Annex indicates that guidelines and recommendations are subsumed

[32] See also Victor 2000: 892.

under the concept of international standards. As a consequence, the same obligations apply, regardless of whether a CAC document is termed a standard, a guideline or a recommendation.

Although the SPS Agreement expresses the desire to further harmonisation, members are neither obliged to conform their SPS measures to international standards, nor to base them on international standards. Article 3.3 states:

> Members may introduce or maintain sanitary or phytosanitary measures which result in a higher level of sanitary or phytosanitary protection than would be achieved by measures based on the relevant international standards, guidelines or recommendations, if there is a scientific justification, or as a consequence of the level of sanitary or phytosanitary protection a Member determines to be appropriate in accordance with the relevant provisions of paragraphs 1 through 8 of Article 5.[33] Notwithstanding the above, all measures which result in a level of sanitary or phytosanitary protection different from that which would be achieved by measures based on international standards, guidelines or recommendations shall not be inconsistent with any other provision of this Agreement.

The Appellate Body has found that members retain the right to determine the level of protection against risk autonomously and has characterised this right as important (ibid: paras 104 and 172). The decision in *EC–Hormones* makes it clear that there is no obligation to use international standards (ibid: para 165). The Appellate Body stated that:

> [t]o read Article 3.1 as requiring Members to harmonise their SPS measures *by conforming those measures with international standards,* guidelines and recommendations, *in the here and now,* is in effect, to vest such international standards, guidelines and recommendations (which are by the terms of the Codex *recommendatory* in form and nature) with *obligatory* force and effect. The Panel's interpretation of Article 3.1 would, in other words, transform those standards, guidelines and recommendations into binding *norms.* But, as already noted, the *SPS Agreement* itself sets out no indication of any intent on the part of the Members to do so (ibid: para 165).

Article 2.1 also suggests that members can derogate from international standards because it establishes their right to take any measures necessary for the protection of human health (SPS Agreement article 2.1). The decision to adopt higher levels of protection is therefore a conditional right and not an exception to a rule of harmonisation.[34]

[33] For the purposes of para 3 of art 3, there is a scientific justification if, on the basis of an examination and evaluation of available scientific information in conformity with the relevant provisions of this Agreement, a member determines that the relevant international standards, guidelines or recommendations are not sufficient to achieve its appropriate level of sanitary or phytosanitary protection.

[34] See WTO Panel Report, EC–Hormones, WT/DS26/R/USA: para 8.86, where the panel had found otherwise.

Article 3.3 might suggest that any measures with a higher level of protection than that of international standards can no longer be considered as being based on such international standards. The Panel in *EC-Hormones* argued that for measures to be based on international standards, an identity of protection levels was required (WTO Panel Report, EC-Hormones, (US): para 8.73; WTO Panel Report EC-Hormones (Canada): para 8.76)). The Appellate Body made some disapproving references in respect of the Panel's interpretation, but did not rule on the interpretation itself. It stated that the Panel seemed to read more into the text of article 3.3 than it actually supported (WTO Appellate Body Report, EC–Hormones: 168). It should be noted that the text of article 3.1 and the notion of 'based on' do not explicitly preclude an interpretation that regards national measures with a higher level of protection as still to be based on that standard. However, even if international standards can sometimes form the basis of a national measure with a higher level of protection, the latter still needs to comply with the general obligations of the SPS Agreement enshrined in articles 2.2 and 5.1, which notably include the concepts of sufficient scientific evidence and risk assessment. In terms of the obligations relating to scientific evidence, there would therefore be no meaningful difference between measures which are not based on international standards and measures which are based on international standards but achieve a higher level of protection than the one embodied in the standard.

How difficult it is to derogate from a CAC standard also depends on the other obligations of the SPS Agreement a member has to comply with. A full discussion of those obligations is beyond the scope of this article. It suffices to note that a member has either one of two options: (i) it can show that its measure is based on a risk assessment in accordance with article 5.1; or (ii) it can show that scientific evidence (including the evidence that is the basis of the CAC standard) is insufficient and adopt a provisional measure that is based on available pertinent information in accordance with article 5.7 (SPS Agreement articles 5.1 and 5.7).[35] The concept of 'based on' has been interpreted in a way as to require a risk assessment that is specific to the substance and exposure targeted by the

[35] Article 5.1 reads: 'Members shall ensure that their sanitary or phytosanitary measures are based on an assessment, as appropriate to the circumstances, of the risks to human, animal or plant life or health, taking into account risk assessment techniques developed by the relevant international organizations.' Article 5.7 reads: 'In cases where relevant scientific evidence is insufficient, a Member may provisionally adopt sanitary or phytosanitary measures on the bases of available pertinent information, including that from the relevant international organizations as well as from sanitary or phytosanitary measures applied by other Members. In such circumstances, Members shall seek to obtain the additional information necessary for a more objective assessment of risk and review the sanitary or phytosanitary measure accordingly within a reasonable period of time.'

measure.[36] In *EC–Hormones*, studies about the harmfulness of different amounts of hormones as opposed to residue levels of such hormones at levels found in treated meat were considered as being too general to sufficiently warrant and reasonably support the EC ban on residues of such hormones in beef.[37] In addition to those obligations concerning scientific justification, the national measure may not be more trade-restrictive than required in order to fulfil its objective. Moreover, the level of risk tolerance may not deviate from levels for similar hazards or substances without justification (SPS Agreement articles 5.5 and 5.6).

In *US–Continued Suspension* and *Canada–Continued Suspension,* the Appellate Body confirmed that recourse to article 5.7 is not precluded when an international standard exists because the standard does not imply that there is sufficient scientific evidence.[38] The scientific evidence underlying the CAC standard has merely probative value for the question of whether evidence is sufficient, rather than being dispositive.[39] Moreover, the new evidence challenging the risk assessment underlying a CAC standard does not need to rise to the level of a paradigm shift.[40] The evidence underlying the CAC standard may, however, constitute available pertinent information, which a member needs to use as a basis for provisional measures.

The decisions of the Appellate Body in *US-Continued Suspension* and *Canada-Continued Suspension* suggest that CAC standards can be derogated from relatively easily if a member adopts provisional measures. The evidence that members need to provide in this case does not have to be of a fundamentally different nature or a new discovery. Rather, provisional, inconclusive evidence suggesting, for example, that safe exposure levels *could* be lower than those established in CAC risk assessment; or that exposure *could* be higher because an exposure pathway has been overlooked is probably adequate enough to demonstrate that scientific evidence is insufficient.

The ease or difficulty with which members can deviate from CAC standards is, of course, heavily fact-specific. Generally, the more robust the

[36] WTO Appellate Body Report, EC–Hormones: para 200; WTO Panel Report, EC-Hormones (US): para 8.257; WTO Panel Report, EC-Hormones (Canada): para 8.260; WTO Panel Report, Australia-Salmon: para 8.74; WTO Appellate Body Report, Japan-Apples: para 202; WTO Panel Report, Japan-Apples 8.271; Herwig 2008: 837; Sykes 2005: 189.

[37] WTO Appellate Body Report, EC–Hormones: para 200; WTO Panel Report, EC-Hormones (USA): para 8.257; WTO Panel Report, EC-Hormones (Canada): para 8.260.

[38] WTO Appellate Body Report, US–Continued Suspension: paras 694–95; WTO Appellate Body Report, Canada–Continued Suspension: paras 694–95.

[39] WTO Appellate Body Report, US–Continued Suspension: paras 696–97; WTO Appellate Body Report, Canada–Continued Suspension: paras 696–97.

[40] WTO Appellate Body Report, US–Continued Suspension: para 705; WTO Appellate Body Report, Canada–Continued Suspension: para 705.

science upon which a CAC standard is based, the more difficult it will be for this member to deviate from the standard.

ii. The Agreement on Technical Barriers to Trade

CAC food-naming and labelling standards unrelated to food safety are given an important role under the Agreement on Technical Barriers to Trade (TBT Agreement) because the Appellate Body in *EC–Sardines* decided that CAC standards are relevant international standards under article 2.4 (WTO Appellate Body Report, EC–Sardines: para 227). Article 2.4 is the key obligation of the TBT Agreement. It requires that:

> [w]here technical regulations are required and relevant international standards exist or their completion is imminent, Members shall use them, or the relevant parts of them, as a basis for their technical regulations except when such international standard or relevant parts would be an ineffective or inappropriate means for the fulfilment of the legitimate objectives pursued, for instance because of fundamental climatic or geographical factors or fundamental technological problems.

The TBT Agreement also sets forth the obligation of basing a voluntary measure of central government bodies on international standards.[41]

In *EC–Sardines*, the Panel concluded that an international standard can be regarded 'as a basis for' a technical regulation when it is used as the principal constituent or fundamental principle for the purpose of enacting this respective technical regulation (WTO Panel Report, EC–Sardines: para 7.78). The Appellate Body agreed with interpreting the TBT Agreement along the same lines as the SPS Agreement and supported the Panel's finding (ibid: para 244). It also noted '...that there must be a very strong and very close relationship between two things in order to be able to say that one is "the basis for" the other' (ibid: para 245).

However, members do not need to base their technical regulations or standards of central government bodies on an international standard if this would be an ineffective or inappropriate means for the fulfilment of legitimate objectives pursued.[42] It should be noted that the TBT Agreement recognises technical, safety and consumer protection objectives as legitimate. The following objectives are also expressly mentioned as being legitimate: national security requirements, the prevention of deceptive practices, protection of human health or safety, animal or plant life or health, or the environment (TBT Agreement article 2.2). The list of

[41] TBT Agreement, Code of Good Practice for the Preparation, Adoption and Application of Standards, together with article 4 of the TBT Agreement.

[42] TBT Agreement article 2.4, Code of Good Practice for the Adoption, Preparation and Application of Standards: para H.

objectives that are legitimate is open-ended because the expressly listed objectives are preceded by the words: '[s]uch legitimate objectives are, *inter alia*' (TBT Agreement article 2.4). The Panel in *EC–Sardines* considered market transparency, consumer protection and fair competition to be legitimate objectives under article 2.4 (WTO Panel Report, EC–Sardines: para 7, 122). What other objectives might be considered legitimate is not clear, but objectives such as fair-trade or religious consumer preferences could be deemed legitimate. If such ethical preferences became accepted as legitimate objectives, a member could invoke these under the TBT Agreement in order to derogate from CAC standards that pertain to food safety. Non-safety standards of the CAC always fall under the TBT Agreement. For CAC food safety standards, the application of the SPS or TBT Agreement hinges on the type of measure that the member takes when derogating from CAC standards. If the measures protect against health risks, the SPS Agreement applies. If the measures pursue non-health objectives such as animal welfare or consumer information objectives, the TBT Agreement applies.

If a technical regulation pursues one of the expressly listed objectives and is in accordance with the relevant international standard, the technical regulation is presumed not to create an unnecessary obstacle to international trade (TBT Agreement article 2.5). This implies two things: first, measures in accordance with international standards that pursue other objectives than the ones expressly listed do not benefit from this presumption. Second, the 'safe haven' for measures pursuing expressly listed objectives and being in accordance with international standards is only a presumption. In other words, a complaining member can rebut this presumption and thereby indirectly attack international standards, including the Codex naming and non-safety labelling standards. This also raises the question of how the words 'in accordance with' are to be interpreted. Is the term more similar to the notion of 'conform to'; in which case national technical regulations that have a looser connection to the international standard do not enjoy any special protection under the TBT Agreement? Or is it similar to the concept of 'based on', in which case the TBT Agreement would not distinguish between measures with a strong or a looser connection to international standards?

Members also have to use relevant, existing international standards as the basis for their conformity assessment procedures, unless they can justify the non-use of international standards. Article 5.4 states that:

> [m]embers shall ensure that central government bodies use them, or the relevant parts of them, as a basis for their conformity assessment procedures, except where, as duly explained upon request, such guides or recommendations or relevant parts are inappropriate for the Members concerned…

By way of example, article 5.4 then goes on to list objectives which could justify derogation of conformity assessment procedures from international standards.

Finally, with respect to private standardisation bodies, both the SPS and TBT Agreement call on members to take reasonable measures to ensure that these private bodies comply with the provisions of the two agreements. This, of course, also includes the provisions on harmonisation of national measures through international standards.

The Panel and Appellate Body reports in *EC–Sardines* provide some guidance on how the terms 'inappropriate' and 'ineffective' are to be interpreted. The Appellate Body found that the EC naming regulation for sardines was not based on the CAC standard since it contradicted it (WTO Appellate Body Report, EC–Sardines: paras 248, 249 and 257). Concerning the burden of proving the 'ineffectiveness' and 'inappropriateness' of international standards, the Appellate Body noted the conceptual similarities to articles 3.1 and 3.3 of the SPS Agreement and consequently assigned the initial burden of proof to Peru as the complaining party (ibid: paras 274, 275 and 282). In other words, the right to set higher levels of protection than those of international standards is not an exception to the rule or an obligation of using international standards as a basis, but an autonomous right. Under this allocation of the burden of proof, the complaining party has to discharge the burden of making the *prima facie* case that the relevant CAC naming standard was an effective and appropriate means to fulfill the EC's concerns with consumer deception and market transparency. The harmonisation provision of the TBT Agreement is therefore weaker than in the SPS Agreement because the complaining party initially has to show that the international standard is appropriate and effective. In the SPS Agreement, the complainant only needs to show that the defending party has failed to base its measure on a risk assessment, but not whether the CAC food safety standard is appropriate, effective or safe enough.

The Panel in *EC–Sardines* drew a distinction between the term 'inappropriate' and 'ineffective'. It considered that 'effectiveness' pertained to the results of the means which were employed, whereas 'appropriateness' pertained to the nature of the means employed and their suitability (WTO Panel Report, EC–Sardines: para 7.116). The Appellate Body agreed both with this determination (WTO Appellate Body Report, EC–Sardines: paras 285 and 289) and with the final finding of the panel that the EC had acted inconsistently with article 2.4 (ibid: para 291). The Panel then turned to the term 'legitimate objectives'. According to the Panel, the list of objectives is not a closed one (ibid: para 285; Panel Report, EC–Sardines: para 7.118). *EC–Sardines* makes it clear that it is the prerogative of panels or the Appellate Body to determine whether the objectives which the measure pursues are legitimate (WTO Appellate

Body Report, EC–Sardines: para 286; Desmedt 2001: 459). The Panel drew on the definition of 'legitimate interests' in *Canada–Pharmaceutical Patents* as encompassing a normative claim calling for protection of interests supported by relevant public policies or other social norms (WTO Panel Report, EC–Sardines: para 7.121).

Another interesting issue in *EC–Sardines* that has brought into focus the CAC's decision-making procedure was whether the CAC naming standard met the definition of an international standard in the TBT Agreement. According to the explanatory note in Annex 1 of the Agreement, '[s]tandards prepared by the international standardization community are based on consensus. This Agreement covers also documents that are not based on consensus'. The EC argued that the CAC's majority voting entailed that its naming standard did not qualify as an international standard according to the definition. The Panel, supported by the Appellate Body, did not agree with this and pointed out that the definition was explicit about the TBT Agreement also being applied to documents that were not based on consensus (ibid: paras 7.118 and 7.90; WTO Appellate Body Report, EC–Sardines: paras 222–27). In *EC–Hormones,* the EC also argued that the CAC food safety standard should be disregarded since it had been passed through majority voting. In that case, the Panel found that it only had to ascertain whether an international standard existed, regardless of the kind of standardisation organisation's decision-making procedure (WTO Panel Report, EC-Hormones (USA): para 8.69). Panels and Appellate Body will, in other words, not act as an administrative law tribunal vis-à-vis international standardisation organisations.

C. Conclusion on this Section

The CAC can be described as a system of transnational administrative committees whose standards, guidelines and recommendations contribute to a form of positive harmonisation in international trade.[43] Although CAC standards are not per se obligatory for WTO members under either the SPS or the TBT Agreement, they may nevertheless have to use them if they cannot prove that the higher level of protection they desire is warranted. This has undoubtedly strengthened the influence of CAC standards. Non-use of CAC standards without giving any reasons, as was possible prior to 1994, is no longer an option. Even where a member

[43] Under positive harmonisation, market integration takes places through common product standards developed at the international level. This is to be distinguished from negative harmonisation, in which no common standard exists. Instead, courts or tribunals vet national product requirements to ensure that they are not discriminatory or overly trade-restrictive.

uses the CAC standard with specified deviations, these deviations need to be justified according to the terms of the SPS and TBT Agreement, as applicable. Thus, the CAC exercises a kind of power which may be characterised as a power at arm's length. As with any phenomenon of power, the question of legitimation arises. It will be treated in the next section.

Finally, it should be noted that the SPS and TBT Agreement contain softly-worded provisions to facilitate the active participation of developing country WTO members in international organisations/international standard-setting bodies.[44]

III. PERCEIVED LEGITIMATION DEFICITS OF THE CAC

In the literature on the CAC, several legitimation problems have been discussed. They relate to the procedural fairness of the CAC and to the substantive rationality of outcomes. The alleged deficits concern the stages of scientific risk assessment, risk management and judicial review via the link to the WTO.

A. Risk Assessment

Concerning the stage of risk assessment, the concerns with procedural fairness relate mostly to the absence of transparency and reason-giving during expert-selection for the FAO-WHO roster and during opinion-formation when JECFA or JEMRA assess specific substances (Bevilacqua nd: 9–10; Herwig 2004: 212; Thomas 2004: 14–15). Masson-Mathee further suggests that the conflict of interest rules should define 'interest' more widely so as to include previous research as a situation of a conflict of interest (Masson-Mathee 2006).[45] There may also be a concern that the substantive rationality of the risk assessment is compromised because the expertise in question is not sufficiently plural or representative of the entire CAC membership.[46] The risk assessment policy guidance given to the expert committees has also been seen as scant or too imprecise, leaving discretion to scientists to make policy choices (Masson-Mathee 2006: 218–21).

[44] SPS Agreement art 10.4 [should encourage and facilitate the active participation], TBT Agreement art 12.5 [reasonable, available measures...which facilitates active and representative participation of relevant bodies in all Members].

[45] This may be very difficult to implement since one facet of scientific qualification is, of course, the publication record of the experts on the issue under review.

[46] The point is not one of procedural fairness, ie that all CAC members should have scientists representing them but that the health conditions of developing countries may not be sufficiently taken into account if scientists from developing countries do not participate in the risk assessment, thereby reducing the substantive rationality of CAC standards.

The outsourcing of standard-setting to private and other international bodies is seen as a potential problem both with respect to procedural legitimacy and substantive rationality for these bodies do not allow for similarly broad-based participation as the CAC and pursue different aims (Masson-Mathee 2006: 225–28, 257).[47] It is notable that the private bodies to whom the standard-setting is outsourced also produce proposals for risk regulation and that the same concerns therefore apply to risk management.

B. Risk Management

At the stage of risk management, the question of the appropriate decision-rule for the specialised committees and the general Commission has been discussed in the literature recurrently (Bevilacqua nd: 13; Herwig 2004: 212; Hüller and Maier 2006: 292–95). Decision-making by consensus allows only one country to prevent the adoption of a standard and it also favours the status quo (ibid). The slowness and opaqueness of consensus-building processes is a further disadvantage (Bevilacqua nd: 10; Hüller and Maier 2006: 295; Masson-Mathee 2006: 236, 255). The problem with decision-making through majority voting is that it is insensitive towards the intensity of preferences and does not necessarily lead to the adoption of the most reasonable position, as such a position can be outvoted (Herwig 2004: 213; Hüller and Maier 2006: 295). The shadow of the vote may also constrain preceding deliberations under consensual decision-making (Hüller and Maier 2006: 295). It has been criticised that a single Codex member can call for a vote and that there is no definition of when consensus has failed, leaving it up to the chair of the committee to call for a vote (Masson-Mathee 2006: 233–35).

There is also a complex interrelation between the CAC decision-rule and accountability to national constituencies (Bevilacqua nd: 10). It may be tempting to regard the consensus-rule as maximising accountability to national constituencies and majority-voting as minimising such accountability. However, if one considers that one country could theoretically veto the adoption of a CAC standard under the consensus rule, it becomes apparent that the consensus rule diminishes accountability to all those national constituencies in favour of a CAC standard.

The decision-making procedure has also been criticised with regard to the opportunities and abilities of developing countries and NGOs to

[47] For example, milk standards by the private International Dairy Federation are fed into the CAC elaboration process at step 2. Assuming that the drafting stage is where input is most effective, CAC members and observers are prevented from participating meaningfully in the standard-setting for milk products.

participate. On a formal level, it has been criticised that the Executive Committee lacks opportunities for participation and transparency (Hüller and Maier 2006: 297).[48] On a material level, there are important structural impediments to equal participation of developing countries in the Codex, such as lack of scientific expertise, personnel and financial means (Herwig 2004: 214; Hüller and Maier 2006: 275, 297; Livermore 2006: 783; Masson-Mathee 2006: 244–45; Pereira 2008: 1693, 1709).[49] Consumer NGOs also have fewer resources than business organisations (Herwig 2004: 214; Hüller and Maier 2006: 297; Masson-Mathee 2006: 251). Several commentators criticise the dominance of business interests at the CAC (Bevilacqua nd: 7–8; Livermore 2006: 785; Thomas 2004: 18). Bevilacqua adds that NGOs are often not representative internally and suggests that only NGOs representing the common good should be allowed to participate (Bevilacqua nd: 7–8). In a similar vein, he laments the lack of democratic guarantees of the CAC which are performed by elections or parliamentary controls (Bevilacqua nd: 12). It has also been criticised that formal opportunities for NGO involvement are not used enough due to the unwillingness of states to involve their domestic civil society and that opportunities for participation occur at the wrong place which reduces their impact (Herwig 2004: 214–15; Pereira 2008: 1693, 1708, 1709). Pereira suggested that the CAC should already involve private actors in the development of standards before the first draft of a standard is available so as to allow them greater impact.[50] Pereira also argues that because risk assessment matters so much in the CAC, the impact of participation at the stage of risk management is diminished in cases without uncertainty (Pereira 2008: 1693, 1707). Pereira leaves it unclear whether this claim refers to a lack of substantive rationality (too much science, too little policy), or to an imbalance in substantive rationality compared to procedural legitimacy (too outcome-focused, participation meaningless). Concerning the procedural fairness of the CAC towards civil society, Hüller and Maier suggested areason-giving requirement in response to the submissions made by civil society representatives at the levels of agenda-setting, strategic planning and risk management (Hüller and Maier 2006: 280). Others have cautioned that strengthening civil society participation further reduces the already limited impact of developing countries in the CAC (Masson-Mathee 2006: 249).

[48] The trade-off between having a strategic management board and broad participation could be solved by a representative membership in the Executive Committee.

[49] Hüller and Maier and Pereira argue that the Trust Fund does not foster developing country participation much since it only finances the attendance of meetings while what is needed is capacity-building in developing countries.

[50] With further references Pereira 2008: 1693, 1707.

With regards to substantive rationality, several commentators criticise that trade interests are given too much weight in the CAC (Herwig 2004: 212–13; Thomas 2004: 13, 18–19). The failure of the CAC to define 'other legitimate factors' more clearly and to give them adequate weight is also seen as a problem (Poli 2004: 625). It remains unclear what policies can be defined as OLFs and what weight OLFs should have in the decision-making process of international standards compared to human health protection and economic interests, the latter of which are expressly included in the mandate of the CAC. It has also been argued that next to the requirement to provide scientific evidence, the economic impact of CAC standards and certain OLFs need to be considered. Furthermore, the CAC should assess direct and indirect health trade-offs brought about by the economic impact of CAC standards more systematically (Hüller and Maier 2006: 289–91).[51] In the light of the role given to CAC standards under the SPS and TBT Agreement, commentators have also suggested that the CAC should find better ways of dealing with uncertainty by adopting standards, which either leave a corridor of options or have a sunset clause (Hüller and Maier 2006: 288). Due to the detailed nature of CAC standards and their role under WTO law, the lack of safeguards and flexibility in CAC standards is considered as reducing their appropriateness for local conditions (Masson-Mathee 2006: 261). It has also been argued that the CAC lacks institutional legitimacy. The reasons given by Masson-Mathee are numerous: first, it has no mandate to adopt binding standards, yet its standards can become obligatory under WTO law (Masson-Mathee 2006: 203–5). Second, the relative autonomy of the specialised committees and their unclear and overlapping relationship with each other are perceived to impede a coherent operation of the CAC (Masson-Mathee 2006: 206–17).

Finally, a procedural or substantive criticism is also that judicial review of the activities of the CAC is missing (Livermore 2006: 768, 789–91; Bevilacqua nd: 14). As a result, erroneous decisions are difficult to correct and those aggrieved by CAC activities lack a voice.

C. Conclusion on this Section

The purpose of this section has been to map the criticisms offered in respect of the CAC as linked with the WTO and nation states. Several of the criticisms are incommensurate with others. For instance, strengthening the role

[51] They would claim, for instance, that the indirect health impacts of a CAC standard have to be considered if the standard negatively affects developing countries' economic interests and through it, leads to a worsening of the health of the population.

of OLFs can reduce the scientific rationality of CAC standards because it introduces new grounds for adopting or rejecting a CAC standard. Further, one cannot realise a deliberative model of participation for the CAC and establish simple majority voting as the only or preferred decision-rule at the same time.

It is not necessary to assess the validity of each of these criticisms in detail and to resolve conflicts between them for the purposes of this contribution. It seems relatively uncontroversial that risk regulation should lead to right or rational outcomes, which are protective of our health but also of other policy objectives (Herwig 2004: 830–31, 841–42). This brings into focus the question of the definition of OLFs, the ways of dealing with them in a structured manner and the relative weight of scientific and non-scientific aspects with regard to a final decision on risk. Furthermore, it seems uncontroversial that processes of participation can help establish substantive rationality in disputed cases and revision of old decisions by allowing for exchanges of arguments and information.[52] This brings up the question of formal and material inequalities in participation and which decision-rule is best for the CAC. The contribution of global administrative law to legitimacy of the CAC should accordingly be judged at a minimum by whether they help address these problems in a *normatively plausible* manner.

IV. SOLUTIONS OFFERED BY CONCEPTS OF GLOBAL ADMINISTRATIVE LAW

The following section presents several models of administrative law that might be invoked as a foundation for a global administrative law. For each model, their internal plausibility when applied to the international order and to the CAC will be judged. Empirical conditions which favour or inhibit the transposition of administrative law concepts to the international level are also discussed, where relevant.

A. Legality Model

In liberal domestic democracies, the principle of legality requires administrative institutions to act within the bounds of their legal mandate conferred through the constitution, the democratic principals and their representatives. Their powers are thus limited by law. A 'thick' principle of legality transmits important constitutional values and the will of

[52] For such a defence of procedural standards of legitimacy in the context of the world trade order, see Herwig and Hüller 2008: 243–44.

democratically elected representatives to the administration, thus serving the ideals of *Rechtsstaatlichkeit* and democracy. A 'thin' version of the principle of legality focuses only on its function of protection against arbitrary administrative action and its promotion of legal certainty.

Some have argued that the rule of law is also operative internationally (Dyzenhaus 2005: 127; Cassesse 2005a: 690–94). According to one author:

> [a]t global level, the key requirement of the rule of law is a legal order with fixed and stable general principles, together with formal rights of access to courts for the resolution of disputes. The rule of law doctrine may also operate to lock the machinery in place through a process of constitutionalization (Harlow 2006: 195).

Even if these empirical key requirements were present, there is still the question of what is meant by an international principle of legality. At least two open questions come to mind regardless of whether one thinks of a thick or a thin international principle of legality: (i) who has the definitional authority to set the boundaries for administrative action; and (ii) who or what level of governance is to be bound? The following discussion will reveal that these questions are of a normative importance because they touch upon the existence of a constitutional *demos*, the validity of concepts of global justice and the appropriate level for exercising regulatory authority.

i. Problems with a 'Thick' Principle of Legality

The 'thick' version of the principle of legality is supposed to serve the ideals of democracy and constitutional values. Two questions come up immediately: which *demos* and constitutional values are the relevant ones? International or national ones? Should there be national *demoi* with diverse conceptions of democracy, or a cosmopolitan *demos* with a single conception of democracy? Similarly, should the principle of legality serve national constitutional values or international ones?

Depending on which constituency one favours, existing international law rules turn out to be more or less problematic. International treaties and other documents are generally negotiated by representatives of the executive with little oversight by parliaments (Benvenisti 1999: 200). Often, representatives from the developed world are able to participate more meaningfully in the negotiations than representatives from developed countries.

A model which regards the representation of national *demoi* through the executive as conferring the relevant democratic credentials to international law, encounters at least three problems:[53] first, many states are

[53] For a detailed analysis of the problems of what we call 'nation-state proceduralism', see Herwig and Hüller 2008: 239–41.

not internally democratic and thus not representative of their citizens. Second, unequal abilities of states to participate in international law-making means that citizens from some nation states are less represented. Third, the link between participation of the executive in international law-making and domestic democratically elected institutions is often remote. Apart from the members' ability to contract out of a treaty, multilateral treaties are also very difficult to change once they are in place. This process of 'hands-tying' or 'locking in' of commitments has been criticised as undemocratic because it removes the possibility of changing laws (Howse 2002b: 92–95; Howse and Nicolaïdis 2001; Howse 2002a: 106–7).

If a cosmopolitan *demos* is seen as the relevant constituency, a model of cosmopolitan democracy would require some form of direct participation or representative citizen input into international treaty-making. Global parliaments or direct citizen participation are certainly a far-flung utopia in international law-making. While the existing NGOs' participation in treaty-making processes may incorporate values derived from global public interest, it is questionable whether they are sufficiently representative of all interests (Harlow 2006: 204)[54] and whether they do not simply tilt the balance further in favour of developed countries because many developing countries lack the liberal democratic infrastructure that allows civil society to flourish.

Concerning the relevant constitutional values, one model might see the purpose of the principle of legality in serving international values. However, which one? Is *ius cogens* the normative ideal because it represents a kind of universal common ground? This lowest common denominator might be too restrictive towards our diverse conceptions of the right and the good. The norms of *ius cogens* would hardly constrain international or global administrative action in any meaningful way. For liberal democracies, such unconstrained administrative action would most likely be unacceptable. Regarding human rights as the relevant international constitutional value system might have too much of a Western flavour in order to get accepted as a normative ideal.[55] And while they look constitutional, they enjoy the same status as any other 'simple' international law as a matter of positive law. Others have suggested that auto-constitutionalisation processes occur in diverse societal law-making fora as a result of legitimation demands being placed on these fora (Teubner and Fischer-Lescano 2004; Teubner 2004). This 'societal constitutionalism' might also constitute a resource of constitutional values to be served by a principle of legality. Probably the most poignant question that can be asked of

[54] With further references.

[55] Petersmann has for a long time argued that WTO law should also protect human rights, as it seems on the dual grounds that they are universally accepted and morally desirable. See Petersmann 2006, 2003, 2002 and 2001.

'societal constitutionalism' in the present context is whether it has any notion of a constitution as being a higher set of binding norms that cannot easily be derogated from and that would turn the principle of legality into something meaningful. In the account of societal constitutionalism, nothing seems to prevent the actors from opting out of constitutionalisation by creating another set of social norms. This would make the principle of legality merely one of provisional convenience and largely emaciate it of its protective function as a fundamental constitutional value system.

Another approach for vouchsafing the principle of legality could be to require international administration to conform to the values of national constitutional law. Here, incompatibilities between the values protected by national constitutional law are a problem, particularly with respect to differences between liberal democracies and illiberal undemocratic regimes. However, even between different Western administrative law regimes such incompatibilities could arise.

ii. Problems with a 'Thin' Principle of Legality

As with a 'thick' principle of legality, a 'thin' principle can be defined internationally or locally. An internationally defined 'thin' principle of legality would simply require something like regime integrity through faithfulness to founding treaties and the prevention of international bodies straying into neighbouring regimes.[56] It is difficult to imagine a principle of legality operating in the fragmented world of international law being characterised by loosely-worded regimes with overlapping competences. Issue-overlap and relatively open-ended rules give treaty interpreters or organisations considerable discretion in how to deal with such cross-border matters.[57] Another problem results in the fact that international governance often takes place through non-binding norms that are nevertheless often complied with by states or by private parties. This makes it very difficult to pin down the exact locus of where decisions are being taken and where it is necessary to exercise controls.[58] For all these reasons, an international principle of legality is not able to curtail arbitrary action by international bodies or to promote legal certainty as effectively as in nation states.

A locally defined 'thin' principle of legality would simply require treaty negotiators to observe their domestic negotiating mandate and, presumably, thereby ensure consistency with all domestic laws (whatever

[56] Discussed in Kingsbury, Krisch and Stewart 2005: 43–45.

[57] See also Pereira 2008: 1683, 1714.

[58] Note that one may well be directed back to the domestic realm or to the decision of individual corporations as the decision-making centre when it comes to compliance with non-binding norms.

their content).[59] In practice, control of the executive in international negotiations is achieved through ex ante hands-tying as when the US Congress grants Fast Track authority for WTO negotiations but more often so through ex post ratification of treaties. Obviously, other mechanisms can be imagined likewise. This bottom-up approach encounters the practical problem of how domestic control of negotiators can be most effective. During ratifications, parliaments look at treaties as a package and are simply not able to examine each provision. Moreover, if they were to do so, international governance through multilateral treaties or bodies would most likely break down.

iii. Scope of the Principle of Legality

Another issue that needs to be addressed is the scope of application of a principle of legality. Is it directed at international institutions and global bodies to ensure that they do not act ultra vires with regard to the founding treaties or the diverse national laws, which regulate the participation of national executive officials in transnational regulatory structures? Or is it primarily directed at nation states, requiring them to observe their international law obligations? In the former case, and given the limited democratic credentials of international law-making, an international principle of legality would only make incremental contributions to promoting fundamental values and democracy. In the latter case, a principle of legality might make matters worse. Many critics rightly caution of an undesirable juridification of the political process (Harlow 2006: 187, 198).[60]

iv. Application to the CAC

One can perceive certain affinities between the legality model and the CAC. For one, use and non-use of CAC standards have become juridified through the SPS and TBT Agreement. Trade of food products is therefore increasingly structured through international legal norms. Furthermore, as chapter five by Arnold shows, there have been concerns about how the CAC conforms to self-imposed administrative law-like standards.

However, the application of the legality model to the CAC raises several open questions and reveals some problems. If one applies the principle of legality specifically to the CAC and considers WTO law and the CAC standards higher law to which national administrative decisions must conform, the objection arises that the WTO is not a perfect rule-of-law system. Its Understanding on the Settlement of Disputes still contains

[59] Discussed in Kingsbury, Krisch, and Stewart 2005: 43–45.

[60] See also the contributions in respect of the WTO by Howse 2002b: 92–95; Howse and Nicolaïdis 2001; Howse 2002a: 106–07.

important elements of diplomacy as it prefers mutually acceptable solutions in trade disputes to adjudication.[61] If one believes that the WTO already interferes too much with national autonomy, the strong rule of law values promoted by an international principle of legality would actually reduce legitimacy.

If the principle of legality is to apply to the CAC and WTO and requires, for instance, conformity with human rights, the question of judicial review of the acts and omissions of the CAC and the WTO, as well as issues of standing before such potential tribunals, arise but simply remain unresolved.[62] As pointed out earlier, WTO dispute settlement panels have so far refrained from turning themselves into a tribunal of administrative procedure vis-à-vis the CAC.

If the principle is supposed to hold the CAC to national legal standards, several concerns come up: first, the participation of national officials in CAC activities occurs within broad bounds of discretion, meaning that there is little real parliamentary or constitutional oversight. Second, requiring compliance with many national detailed legal norms would decelerate the CAC standard-setting process even further. As chapter five by Arnold stresses, there are already concerns about the slowness and lack of efficiency of the CAC standard-setting process. If one intends on designing adequate standards of legitimation for the CAC, one has to take trade-offs between promoting rule of law values and efficiency of the procedure into account as both could ultimately affect legitimacy.[63]

As the preceding discussion has shown, one cannot jump to the conclusion that the proliferation of international law and the compliance with it, installs something akin to a principle of legality, which guides international administrative governance and states' foreign policies. The principle of legality operates against the backdrop of a normative constitutional project, which is deeply contested at the international level. It also presumes an existing constitutional infrastructure which is designating powers of the legislature, executive and judicative. This is, however, certainly not the case or at least extremely difficult to replicate at an

[61] The DSU exhibits a clear preference for mutually acceptable solutions over the strict enforcement of its rules. WTO, Understanding on the Rules and Procedures Governing the Settlement of Disputes art 3.7 reads: 'A solution mutually acceptable to the parties to a dispute and consistent with the covered agreements is clearly to be preferred. In the absence of a mutually agreed solution, the first objective of the dispute settlement mechanism is usually to secure the withdrawal of the measures concerned if these are found to be inconsistent with the provisions of any of the covered agreements.'

[62] In respect of international law more generally, Esty argues that there is a lack of tribunals to examine whether international organisations have not acted ultra vires. (Esty 2006).

[63] The basic idea behind the 'thick' model of legality is that that the observance of laws supplies output and input legitimacy to the administration. Both require a decision-making procedure that is actually capable of delivering results.

international level. Because of its *'normative anaemia'*, the 'thin' principle of legality also ultimately fails to address the key legitimation problems of the CAC identified in section III.C.

B. Rationality Model

Administrative law concepts can also have the primary purpose of enhancing the rationality of administrative decisions. Standards requiring the review of the reasonableness of decisions, of the scientific evidence of regulatory decisions and conflict of interest rules, all seek to enhance the rationality of decisions. Also, the proportionality principle has to be included in this model because it represents a way of balancing conflicting objectives.

i. Problems Relating to the Definition of Substantive Rationality

Some suggest rationality criteria for international administrative risk governance. Victor argues that a judicial review of the accuracy of the scientific basis of administrative decisions is sensible and that precautionary measures should be restricted (Victor 2001: 319–21). Such a view is primarily concerned with the epistemic validity of empirical phenomena underlying administrative rule-making. One might think that the methods of science are so widely accepted that scientific conclusions enjoy universal validity.

However, while this conclusion may be valid in respect of 'research' science, it does not always persist when it comes to 'regulatory' science.[64] As argued elsewhere, hazards may also be regulated based on non-empirical, moral grounds and even accept scientific evidence that is not yet fully conclusive (Herwig 2004: 841–43; Peel 2004). This brings up the question of whether the moral objectives are valid and their infringement weighty enough to render a regulation rational.[65] Ultimately, this will again require the elaboration of some universal core values. In addition, foods have also various ethical dimensions; from animal welfare to protection of the environment and religious eating habits (Echols 2001: 3 et seq, 148 et seq). How ethical values ought to relate to rights and obligations of justice is much contested in normative domestic political theory. Given even greater diversity internationally, this issue is more difficult to resolve in relation to international governance.

[64] The distinction between 'research' science, ie laboratory science and 'regulatory' science, ie science at the basis of regulatory decisions comes from Jasanoff 1990: 77–79.

[65] For example, the interest in protecting scope for organic agriculture by regulating genetically modified organisms (GMOs) in various ways may not be acceptable to multinationals seeking to market GMOs.

With the proportionality principle and the review of the reasonableness of administrative decisions, similar questions about the acceptability of objectives and the weighting of conflicting objectives arise that can only be decided by taking a normative decision on the importance of the interests concerned.[66]

In addition, it has already been argued above that substantive criteria of rationality require adequate decision-making procedures which can generate rational outcomes in unclear, contested cases and correct erroneous decisions. A model for administrative law that fails to propose standards of administrative procedure is therefore not very convincing.

ii. Application to the CAC

The first thing that becomes apparent when applying the rationality model to the CAC and linking it both to the WTO and the nation states is how close it comes to the status quo, which emphasises sound science for CAC decision-making and contains WTO law obligations for the provision of sufficient (scientific) evidence and proportionality (least-trade-restrictive-means).[67] Some non-scientific aspects of standards are explicitly considered in Codex decision-making (fair trade practices, economic impacts), while others are merely allowed (OLFs).

As the preceding section has shown, the role of science and non-scientific factors and of trade versus non-trade concerns is much contested and there are perceptions of the CAC and the WTO being biased in favour of a technical and economic rationality. If the rationality model primarily emphasises sound scientific evidence, it misses precisely those perceived rationality deficits, which concern non-scientific and non-trade factors.

Moreover, to the extent that the weighting of those substantive interests involved is not possible to be established conclusively, strong arguments for strengthening participation and remedying persistent deficits with respect to participation in the CAC and WTO persist. Yet, they are not addressed by a model of administrative law focusing on the rationality of the decisions.

Empirically speaking, it is also highly uncertain whether the CAC, as linked to the WTO and nation states, would even constitute a governance structure in which policy-oriented rationality could articulate itself in a *legally structured* way. The TBT Agreement's notion of 'legitimate objectives' might enable WTO members to rely on non-scientific reasons for derogating from CAC standards. This could force the CAC to adopt

[66] Similarly Scott 2004: 20–29.

[67] SPS Agreement arts 2.2, 5.6; TBT Agreement arts 2.2, 2.3, 3.1, 4.1 and Annex 3. See also Arnold's contribution in chapter five.

more useful and precise guidelines for dealing with OLFs. However, it is entirely unclear whether WTO dispute settlement panels or the Appellate Body would be willing to review CAC standards as to whether they deal with non-scientific factors.

C. Due Process or Good Governance Model

Concepts of due process focus on providing ex ante and/or ex post accountability mechanisms, such as the provision of a hearing, the right to receive reasoned decisions, transparency of decisions and access to courts. Domestically, the provision of due process in administrative rule-making serves to protect individuals from arbitrary, capricious or unreasonable decisions. It is also supposed to ensure that the administration acts in accordance with the wishes of the citizens and obtains all relevant information, thus enhancing the rationality of decisions. The access to courts constitutes an ex post mechanism to protect against arbitrary, capricious or unreasonable decisions.

i. Problems with a Participatory Model

Openness, participation and transparency look like attractive values for global administrative law to foster.[68] Given the limited democratic vetting of international law-making processes by states, it might be the best way to confer procedural legitimacy on them. At first blush, a due process model of administrative law can achieve simultaneous accountability to national *demoi* and a cosmopolitan constituency. The potential for conflict between the two has already been discussed as a problem above. If one accepts the idea that processes of deliberation lead to the emergence of the best reasons, the reasoned responses to stakeholder comments furnished by international administrative governance bodies should be acceptable to the international and the various national constituencies.

However, the due process model of administrative law is overly idealistic. First, there is the public choice problem of unequal abilities to make use of due process opportunities, which arise because of differences in access to information, financial and human resources or also the specificity of the issue as has been mentioned above. Furthermore, diffuse interests, such as consumer interests, are generally more difficult to organise than concentrated interests such as those of companies. If the participatory procedures are not perfect, they can no longer guarantee

[68] For an account proposing a good governance model for international governance, see Esty 2006: 1523–34. Esty also argues for checks and balances through horizontally and vertically divided powers.

that international administrative decisions and rules are based on the best reasons and that everyone had a fair chance to participate. One could, of course, imagine several corrective mechanisms to make up for deficient procedures. In this respect, Harlow has pointed out an interesting paradox: in countries like the United States, the problem of unequal access to participatory mechanisms is at least somewhat counterbalanced, if not addressed, by the existence of a democratically elected parliament (Harlow 2006: 204). Internationally, however, it is precisely the absence of any representative democratic mechanism which makes good governance models look so attractive in the first place (Harlow 2006: 204).[69]

Second, it is unrealistic to assume that participatory administrative processes will always end in agreement on the best reasons. If this is so, a default mechanism for making decisions, such as majority voting, is required. A voting rule must inexorably define who is entitled to vote—are states, representing their people, entitled to vote, or individuals, NGOs or all of them? By necessary implication, it thereby defines the constitutive *demos* of international governance. As I have argued above, this is a fundamental normative question about the validity (or not) of a cosmopolitan or national conception of democracy.

ii. Application to the CAC

The CAC, of course, scores considerably well on transparency and publication. It allows for scrutiny by observers, publishes documents and follows an iterated procedure for elaborating CAC standards that allow CAC member states opportunities to consult with national stakeholders. At the risk management stage, a full discussion of views relating to the economic impact of standards is emphasised. Chapter five by Arnold highlights various aspects that can be seen as improving the transparency of CAC decision-making, which is functional for due process rights: CAC committees should describe their implementation of CAC standards and guidelines, the separation between risk assessment and risk management should be respected, the consideration of 'OLFs' should be documented clearly and reveal the rationale for their integration, and finally the selection of experts should be transparent, thus ensuring their independence and sufficient geographical representation (Arnold, in chapter five).

However, it has to be noted that due process rights fail to address material inequality as one of the key reasons for why due process rights favour the more resourceful. Formal due process rights will do nothing to

[69] According to Möllers, due to the absence of strong democratic controls of transnational administration due process rights at least do not run into conflict with democracy and are therefore appropriate. However, this statement is not well supported because it deducts normative consequences from facts. See Möllers 2005: 385.

remedy the persisting problems arising from inequalities of information, money and resources.

Furthermore, the problem of deciding on an acceptable decision-making rule for the CAC remains unresolved by a participatory model of administrative law. This is because the participatory models discussed by global administrative law scholars refrain from addressing the issue of who the relevant constitutive *demos* for international governance ought to be in the end.

D. Pluralistic Models

Due to the difficulties in applying a single model of administrative law to the global level, some authors have instead argued for a pluralism of models. Pluralism may also result from applying 'top-down' (international, global) and 'bottom-up' (regional, national, or local) administrative law mechanisms together (Kingsbury, Krisch and Stewart 2005: 55–58). To these vertical mechanisms, one might also add horizontal mechanisms that result from international institutions and governance mechanisms having different competences (Esty 2006: 1534). The allocation of competences in a multilevel governance framework has affinities with a system of checks and balances. What sets pluralistic accounts apart, however, is the fact that they refrain from giving any coherent and systematic account of how the principles and institutions or bodies should fit together.

i. Global Administrative Law Pluralism

Krisch argues for a pluralistic global administrative law that combines different administrative law principles, institutions and constituents to which accountability is owed (Krisch 2006: 262–74). The plurality of constituents is considered to be appropriate since there is no single model deemed correct which defines the relevant constituents (states, individuals, civil society, regions) in the international order (Krisch 2006: 262–74). The different institutions and levels of governance are characterised by overlapping or conflicting jurisdiction and contestation, as well as pragmatic accommodation rather than coherence. It is claimed that this pluralism fosters the right of participation and accountability because international organisations or bodies sharing jurisdiction with other institutions are constantly subject to challenge and no one organisation is competent to take a final, binding decision on an issue (Krisch 2006: 266–67). The alleged result is that this preserves a balance between the different interests and opens a space for contestation and radical transformation (Krisch 2006: 269–74).

a. Problems with Global Administrative Law Pluralism

One has to wonder whether the pluralism of international institutions, public-private bodies and informal global governance mechanisms does not actually lessen legitimation. First of all, this web of institutions and bodies makes it difficult for weaker, less resourceful players to maintain oversight, provide input into decision-making and control through ex post accountability mechanisms because (i) the real place, where decisions are taken is not known and (ii) these actors do not have the resources to exert influence in so many fora.[70] Some have even gone as far as describing this pluralism as a deliberative attempt of the powerful to preserve their dominant position (Pereira 2008: 1717). Furthermore, there are the concerns of de-formalisation and de-legalisation as unaccountable diplomatic elites or international officials manage overlaps and conflicts between regimes based on their regime's political bias rather than according to legal rules (Koskenniemi 2007: 6–9, 11–16; 2002: 484 et seq).

One has also put forth the argument that the rules governing a particular institution reflect the prevailing underlying chain of power and authority (Harlow 2006: 189). If this were the case, any global administrative law principles that exist would merely reaffirm the dominance of the powerful. There indeed seems to be a 'catch-22' with pluralistic models claiming pluralism as their sole justification: if the powerless and excluded, whom administrative law principles crucially protect, want to hold global and international institutions to account, they have—paradoxically—to be powerful and influential enough to organise a rivaling governance mechanism or institution in order to do so. Those not powerful enough would be left without protection.

In the final analysis, pluralism is no value in itself. What needs to be shown is that accountability mechanisms result from fragmented global governance that work to the advantage of the weak and underprivileged (Harlow 2006: 273, 276). Krisch, of course, recognises power disparities and internally undemocratic constituencies as a problem for pluralist accounts. He suggests a pre-screening of groups for their internal inclusiveness and certain procedural mechanisms such as tolerance or mutual recognition between overlapping governance mechanisms to combat power disparities. However, these procedural mechanisms are still unable to combat the exclusion of those who are unable or lack knowledge to articulate their concerns due to material or structural impediments.

[70] See also the contribution of Gupta in chapter 11.

b. Application to the CAC

How appropriate is the pluralistic global administrative law model for the CAC? The linkage of the WTO to the CAC and to outside scientific and technical expertise, prized in the SPS and TBT Agreement, has certainly fostered the accountability of the WTO and its members. For the WTO, the reliance on international standards means that its trade disciplines are simultaneously accepted as good food safety protection. At the same time, the rights of members to set higher standards of protection than those of CAC standards—if there is sufficient scientific evidence or they demonstrate that the scientific evidence underlying a CAC standard is insufficient—forces the CAC to show that its standards are based on sound science, are free from bias and reflect current scientific knowledge. According to Joerges, the concept of scientific evidence has also helped to render WTO members accountable to each other. Essentially, it requires the regulating importing member to explain its regulatory choices by reference to a criterion that can reasonably be accepted by all those concerned. As Joerges has written, '[b]y resorting to scientific expertise, legal systems subject themselves to 'external' validity criteria–and overcome their territorial parochialism precisely for this reason' (Joerges and Godt 2005: 93, 111).

WTO members can in turn hold the WTO dispute settlement panels to account by not implementing dispute settlement reports with which they disagree. Persistent non-implementation as in the *EC–Hormones* and *EC–Biotech* report certainly has a strong signalling function towards panels and the Appellate Body that their reports are perceived as illegitimate or erroneous.

At the same time, there are reasons to doubt that the potential conflicts between the WTO and its members over dispute settlement findings and the other mechanisms identified result in sufficient legitimation. For one, developing countries may find it too difficult to produce the scientific evidence needed to be able to regulate a food product. Non-implementation of WTO dispute settlement reports could also be too costly for developing countries as to be a realistic option for them.[71] Thus, in certain respects, the WTO actually reinforces the effects of exclusion of developing countries from decision-making in the CAC.[72]

[71] Note that their exports can be penalised by retaliatory tariffs if they do not implement a DSB report.

[72] However, the reverse is also true: with the WTO and its dispute settlement system, developing countries are better able to assert their interests than if they only had bilateral trade agreements. The claim here is merely that the WTO has serious deficiencies with respect to the ability of developing countries to assert their interests.

Another issue that has to be borne in mind is the informality and network character of global governance (Kingsbury, Krisch and Stewart 2005: 53; Harlow 2006: 212). Informal network governance reduces transparency and accountability.[73] For instance, private bodies like the International Dairy Foundation may not be subject to strict accountability standards because its activity is ignored or inaccessible. Consider also the example of the long-standing beef hormones dispute at the WTO. The Panel and Appellate Body had found the EC ban on beef treated with growth hormones lacking an adequate risk assessment. However, they did not decide whether the EC ban could be maintained as a provisional precautionary measure. The EC did not change its ban on growth hormones and was subject to authorised retaliatory tariffs from Canada and the United States. Until the decision in *US & Canada–Continued Suspension*, it was unclear whether the EC could maintain the same ban in substance and justify it as a provisional precautionary measure and the WTO, Canada and the United States had taken a wrong decision or whether the EC was to be condemned for trade protectionism. Such intransparency reduces the ability of other actors to hold institutions in international food safety governance to account.

In addition, the accountability on food safety is but one issue of food policy. Others are food security and rural development in developing countries, the protection of biodiversity, consumer preferences unrelated to food safety aspects, the preservation of organic agriculture and the production of green fuels. While some of these issues are dealt with in other international regimes, it is not clear whether the CAC or the TBT Agreement actually integrate these objectives.

ii. Subsidiarity Model

Carol Harlow is sceptical about the benefits linked to the emergence of a global administrative law. Instead, she argues for pluralism, subsidiarity and the preservation of spaces for democratic decision-making through less juridification of the international realm (Harlow 2006: 213–14).[74] She fears that global administrative law and its juridified institutions remove decisions from the political realm and diminish opportunities for experiment and change (Harlow 2006: 213). With others, she fears that:

> politics become the politics of procedure, a struggle for the power to define, for jurisdiction: the question is not so much whether a weighing of interest has to

[73] The network character of global governance has been discussed as an accountability problem many times over. See, for instance, Picciotto 1996–97: 1020–22, 1047–50.

[74] With further references.

take place, but rather which authority in the final analysis is empowered to do the weighing.

This is the clinching argument for pluralism: for diversity as the overarching value and for subsidiarity as the fundamental principle of global administrative law. Otherwise, the likely contribution of global administrative law will be to stifle what is democratic and legitimate what is not (Harlow 2006: 213–14). Harlow warns that the transfer of administrative law principles to other states and contexts bears aspects of colonisation. One unwelcome consequence of this can be that developing countries are burdened with the costly implementation of administrative law principles that do not benefit their (poor, uneducated) citizens, but rather multinational corporations and developed countries (Harlow 2006: 211).[75] Another unwelcome consequence can be that the legal transplants are inappropriate for the system into which they are transplanted because they are largely reflective of Anglo-Saxon administrative law (Harlow 2006: 187, 211).

a. Problems with the Subsidiarity Model

In the following paragraphs the proposal for subsidiarity will be understood as if it referred to a national definition of the administrative law principles governing international administrative-like activities and a scaling back of international administrative governance, where possible.[76] It is put forth that subsidiarity is indeed an important principle of a global constitution and global administrative law. Compared to the nation state, a global public sphere is much less developed, there are greater material inequalities, and consensus on substantive values is likely to be thinner at the international level. All these factors considerably reduce the appeal of a uniform model of global administrative law focused on strong due process rights or the promotion of substantive values.

However, it is also important to bear in mind the shortcomings of the nation state (Krisch 2006: 159, 270). With extraterritorial effects of national laws and actions, democratic processes of the nation state are unable to take account of foreign interests, which are affected by their decisions, and national substantive values may turn out to be parochial (Joerges 2005). The incapacity of the nation state to balance all affected interest calls for establishing global procedures, institutions, laws and norms that are able to perform this task.

Scaling back international governance or making it non-binding can also have adverse consequences for the interests of developing countries

[75] With further references.

[76] It is not clear whether Harlow only refers to administrative law principles, international administrative governance, or both.

because it leaves them subject to unmitigated power differences between states. If nation state governance fails to protect the interests of poor and weak states, the principle of subsidiarity would call for the adoption of international rules, and their application might well just confirm that international law and administrative-type governance are necessary and here to stay. If this is so the question of their legitimation poses itself anew.

b. Application to the CAC

Would it make sense to apply the principle of subsidiarity to define administrative law principles for the CAC? This would entail the proliferation of diverse conceptions of national administrative law throughout the development of national standpoints in the CAC and the decision-making of the CAC itself. With regard to participatory rights, it seems possible to allow each CAC member to define whether or not it wants to consult its citizenry on CAC positions. However, some CAC members might consider the outcome of consultative processes as binding while others do not. This raises the problem of how CAC decision-making is to be organised in order to respect these diverse conceptions of participation. To the extent that the administrative law of some of the members of the CAC calls for transparency and access to documents and other national administrative laws seek to maintain the secrecy of documents and deliberations, there would be an irresolvable conflict and a strong need to finally take a decision on a global rule of administrative procedure. Similar incompatibilities between CAC members can also arise concerning the substantive rationality of CAC standards.

Would it also be reasonable to use the subsidiarity principle in order to scale back international risk and trade governance? It is submitted that there are good reasons for maintaining international food safety standards and trade rules. They place developing countries in a better position to assert their preferences than if they were left at the mercy of the trade and food safety decisions of large, industrialised countries. The special status given to CAC standards in the SPS and TBT Agreement may also encourage laggard countries to adopt adequate food safety protection in order to gain access to export markets. This could lead to an overall higher level of food safety than if states were left to their own devices in regulating the influx of foreign food products into their territories.

E. Conclusion on this Section

This contribution attempted to assess whether concepts of administrative law help to solve the alleged legitimation problems of the CAC. It is clear that having administrative law-like principles will confer more legitimacy on international administrative governance than if they did not exist altogether. For instance, the requirement of taking into account scientific expertise leads to more rational regulatory decision-making about existing risks than if scientific expertise were disregarded. Enticing the experts to examine all pertinent evidence will render the CAC procedures more transparent and will foster the rationality of decisions. Furthermore, there is also the transformative power of law—because of due process rights in the CAC, especially those allowing actors active participation in the standard-setting procedure, the interests of developing countries and also non-food safety aspects will be given a more prominent place in debates at the CAC.

Each model of global administrative law looked at in isolation has significant shortcomings: stakeholders' formal and materially unequal access to international administrative governance, the problematic relationship between international administrative decisions and standards with the internal accountability of states, the informal character of international administrative governance and, finally, the unclear definition of which higher values global administrative law is supposed to serve. These shortcomings coincide to a certain extent with what has been identified as the basic legitimacy problems of the CAC, namely unequal opportunities for participation for developing countries and certain NGOs, the definition of OLFs, the decision-rule for the CAC, and the relationship between international and national levels of authority.

There is a risk that administrative law concepts could even be dysfunctional to CAC-WTO nation state governance. For instance, improved formal participation rights of civil society exacerbate the problem of access of developing countries. Tightening the conditions for derogations from CAC standards under WTO law could unduly interfere with democracy, which the nation state can still guarantee to a fuller extent.

Of course, the shortcomings of the administrative law models and of CAC-WTO nation state governance are not irremediable. A suasive attempt at doing so would, however, require facing several normative issues head-on: which conception of procedural legitimacy and standards, higher values and other standards of substantive rationality should we prefer and what can be considered the relevant *demos?* Should there be a single conception of procedural legitimacy and substantive rationality or can we imagine a diversity of principles encompassing different levels of governance, unified only by a few over-arching global principles?

I can only sketch an answer here: it is suggested that there are good reasons for promoting due process rights in CAC decision-making. Due process rights for civil society organisations and even interested individuals can increase the amount of information available to a CAC standard and favour the correction of erroneous decisions. If they are coupled with an adequate decision-rule, they can also supply substantive values which will serve as a guide for decisions in concrete cases (for a full justification, see Herwig and Hüller 2006: 131). This brings into focus two further questions: which decision-rule should the CAC follow and how should the injustice arising from the inability of developing countries and their populations be addressed?

The CAC needs to define decision-making rules that generate reasonable outcomes and valorise participation while still being effective and respecting the national democratic procedures. It is suggested that the consensus decision-rule combined with deliberative procedures that allow for reasoned argumentation and structured exchanges of information is capable of generating reasonable outcomes. Also, it will minimise interference with national democratic procedures which again should privilege some form of deliberation. However, in order to preserve the efficiency of CAC decision-making, it is necessary to either introduce qualified consensus procedures (consensus with specified deviations), standards with sunset-clauses or qualified or super-qualified majority voting provisions.

As due process rights structurally benefit industrialised countries and their civil society representatives, substantive principles are necessary to protect those who are excluded from participation due to being materially disadvantaged (for a full justification, see Herwig and Hüller 2006: 131). In other words, the CAC-WTO needs to find ways of dealing with the developmental impact of CAC standards. The CAC Trust Fund for developing country participation in the CAC is a starting point, but more is needed in order to offset the structural deficits being endured by developing countries and some societal interests, which prevent their efficient participation. Mandatory capacity-building, technical assistance for the adaptation of high standards and developmental-impact assessments of draft CAC standards can all be ways to combat the injustice arising from the exclusion of developing countries from the CAC. Guidelines for how to deal with adverse developmental impacts of CAC standards may need to be developed, which would lead to an understanding about developmental objectives and human health protection. CAC standards could even have direct effects on the wellbeing of citizens of developing countries. In the former case, the interests in poverty alleviation are as weighty as the interest in human health protection, because of which justice would require some countervailing development-assistance. Where the developmental impacts of CAC standards are less severe, the interest in human health protection should prevail but the development-interest might, for instance, be taken into account when choosing between equally effective risk management options.

Human health protection objectives and severe poverty alleviation should therefore be accepted as core substantive standards of CAC decision-making and WTO law must respect safety measures when dealing with food issues.

Finally, decisions also need to be taken on how to integrate other, non-core, non-scientific factors such as environmental protection or animal welfare and how to rank them with regard to the economic-developmental impacts of CAC standards. It is suggested that while serious environmental concerns with CAC standards should be able to trump moderate concerns related to economic and trade impacts, they should not do away with health protection concerns related to CAC standards. To the extent that substantive concerns are not universally shared (eg concerns with animal welfare or special consumer preferences), it makes sense to allow for national autonomy in the SPS and TBT Agreements, subject to the constraint of these regulations meeting real concerns, not unduly burdening developing countries, protecting human health and employing means that are least restrictive of trade.

The reforms of the CAC-WTO nation state food safety governance structure suggested above take a normative position on the appropriate *demos*, higher global values (health protection, poverty alleviation, development) and the allocation of regulatory authority across levels of governance. It is against such a backdrop of a global justice conception that questions on the design of global administrative law-like principles and their contribution to legitimacy can be answered.

V. MAIN CONCLUSION

It is suggested that projects proposing global administrative law as a new way of infusing international administrative governance with legitimacy fail to demonstrate that global administrative law can in fact lead to beneficial results. This is because they are under-ambitious. As a matter of fact these projects put forth administrative law in place of a normative vision of global justice—yet it is exactly such a normative project which is required. By showing which administrative law principles should be applied and how they cohere, one would be able to address and show the most challenging legitimation deficits of the CAC. Put differently, it has to be shown that principles of administrative law drawn from the nation state actually do promote justice and procedural fairness in a global context. This, first and foremost, requires a convincing account of what global justice and procedural fairness would require, on which—as far as I can tell—the jury has only just started deliberating.

REFERENCES

Benvenisti, E (1999) 'Exit and Voice in the Age of Globalization' 98 *Michigan Law Review* 167, 200.

Bevilacqua, D (nd) 'The Codex Alimentarius Commission: Increasing Accountability through Transparency', paper presented at the second Viterbo global administrative law seminar www.irpa.eu/index.asp?idA=169.

Cassesse, S (2005a) 'Administrative Law without the State: The Challenge of Global Regulation' 37 *New York University Journal of International Law and Politics* 663–87.

—— (2005b) 'Global Standards for National Administrative Procedure'68 *Law and Contemporary Problems* 109.

CAC (2008) 'General Principles of the Codex Alimentarius Commission' in *Procedural Manual*, 18th edn (Rome, WHO/FAO) 16.

—— (2008) 'Measures to Facilitate Consensus' in Procedural Manual, 18th edn (Rome WHO/FAO) 174.

—— (2008) 'Policy of the Codex Committee on Contaminants in Food for Exposure Assessment of Contaminants and Toxins in Foods or Food Groups' in *Procedural Manual*, 18th edn (Rome, WHO/FAO) 86.

—— (2008) 'Principles Concerning the Participation of International Non-governmental Organizations in the Work of the Codex Alimentarius Commission' in *Procedural Manual*, 18th edn (Rome, WHO/FAO) 23.

—— (2008) 'Procedures for the Elaboration of Codex Standards and Related Texts' in *Procedural Manual*, 18th edn (Rome, WHO/FAO) 29.

—— (2008) 'Risk Analysis Principles Applied by the Codex Committee on Food Additives and the Codex Committee on Contaminants in Foods' in *Procedural Manual*, 18th edn (Rome, WHO/FAO) 76.

—— (2008) 'Risk Analysis Principles Applied by the Codex Committee on Pesticide Residues' in *Procedural Manual*, 18th edn (Rome, WHO/FAO) 97.

—— (2008) 'Risk Analysis Principles Applied by the Codex Committee on Residues of Veterinary Drugs in Foods' in *Procedural Manual*, 18th edn (Rome, WHO/FAO) 89.

—— (2008) 'Rules of Procedure of the Codex Alimentarius Commission' in *Procedural Manual*, 18th edn (Rome, WHO/FAO) 6.

—— (2008) 'Statements of Principle Concerning the Role of Science in the Codex Decision-Making Process and the Extent to which other Factors are taken into Account' in *Procedural Manual*, 18th edn (Rome, WHO/FAO) 171.

—— (2008) 'Statements of Principle Relating to the Role of Food Safety Risk Assessment' in *Procedural Manual*, 18th edn (Rome, WHO/FAO) 173.

—— (2008) 'Statutes of the Codex Alimentarius Commission' in *Procedural Manual*, 18th edn (Rome, WHO/FAO) 4.

—— (2008) 'Procedures for the Elaboration of Codex Standards and Related Texts' in *Procedural Manual*, 18th edn (Rome, WHO/FAO) 29.

—— (2008) 'Working Principles for Risk Analysis for Application in the Framework of the Codex Alimentarius' in *Procedural Manual*, 18th edn(Rome, WHO/FAO) 68.

Desmedt, A (2001) 'Proportionality in WTO Law' 4 *Journal of International Economic Law* 44–459.

Dyzenhaus, D (2005) 'The Rule of (Administrative) Law in International Law' 68 *Law and Contemporary Problems* 127.
Echols, M (2001) *Food Safety and the WTO: The Interplay of Culture, Science and Technology* (New York, Kluwer Law International).
Esty, DC (2006) 'Good Governance at the Supranational Scale: Globalizing Administrative Law' 115 *Yale Law Journal* 1490.
FAO Constitution of the Food and Agriculture Organization www.fao.org/docrep/010/k1713e/k1713e00.htm.
FAO Fact Sheet—What is JECFA? www.fao.org/es/ESN/jecfa/files/what-e.pdf.
FAO/WHO Project and Fund for Enhanced Participation in Codex, SDE/FOS/CodexTF/1 www.who.int/foodsafety/codex/en/gen_inf.pdf.
FAO/WHO Project and Fund for Enhanced Participation in Codex CAC/27INF.9 www.who.int/foodsafety/codex/trustfund.en.
FAO/WHO (2002) 'Report of the Evaluation of the Codex Alimentarius and Other FAO and WHO Food Standards Work' www.who.int/entity/foodsafety/codex/en/codex_eval_report_en.pdf.
FAO/WHO 'Understanding the Codex Alimentarius Commission'
≤ftp://ftp.fao.org/docrep/fao/008/y7867e/y7867e00.pdf.
Harlow, C (2006) 'Global Administrative Law: The Quest for Principles and Values' 17 *European Journal of International Law* 187–88.
Herwig, A (2004) 'Transnational Governance Regimes for Foods Derived from Bio-Technology and their Legitimacy' in C Joerges, IJ Sand and G Teubner (eds), *Transnational Governance and Constitutionalism* (Oxford, Hart Publishing) 199–204.
Herwig, A (2008) 'Whither Science in WTO Dispute Settlement?' 21 *Leiden Journal of International Law* 823–37.
Herwig, A and Hüller, T (2006) 'Towards Normative Legitimacy of the World Trade Order' in C Joerges and PF Kjaer (eds), *Transnational Standards of Social Protection. Contrasting European and International Governance* (Oslo, RECON Report No 4) 223–54.
Howse, R (2002) 'From Politics to Technocracy—and Back Again: The Fate of the Multilateral Trading Regime' 1 *American Journal of International Law* 94–106.
—— (2002) 'How to Begin to Think About the Democratic Deficit at the WTO' in S Griller (ed), *International Economic Governance and Non-Economic Concerns: New Challenges for the International Legal Order* (Wien, Springer) 79–101.
Howse , R and Nicolaïdis, K (2001) 'Legitimacy and Global Governance: Why Constitutionalizing the WTO Is a Step Too Far' in RB Porter, P Sauve, A Subramanian and B Zampetti (eds), *Efficiency, Equity, Legitimacy: The Multilateral Trading System at the Millennium* (Washington DC, Brookings/Harvard University Press, 2002) 227–52.
Hüller, T and Maier, ML (2006) 'Fixing the Codex? Global Food Safety Governance under Review' in C Joerges and EU Petersmann (eds), *Constitutionalism, Multilevel Trade Governance and Social Regulation* (Oxford, Hart Publishing) 267–99.
Jasanoff, S (1990) *The Fifth Branch/ Science Advisers as Policymakers?* (Cambridge Mass, Harvard University Press).
Joerges, C (2005b) 'Juridification Patters for Social Regulation and the WTO: A Theoretical Framework' (Bremen, *Transtate Working Paper* No 17).

Joerges, C and Godt, C (2005) 'Free Trade: The Erosion of National and Birth of Transnational Governance' in M Zürn and S Leibfried (eds), *Transformations of the State* (Cambridge, CUP) 93–117.

Kingsbury B, Krisch, N, and Stewart RB (2005) 'Foreword: Global Governance as Administration—National and Transnational Approaches to Global Administrative Law' 68 *Law and Contemporary Problems* 1.

—— (2005) 'The Emergence of Global Administrative Law' 68 *Law and Contemporary Problems* 15–61.

Kingsbury B and Krisch N (eds) (2006) 'Symposium: Global Governance and Global Administrative Law in the International Legal Order' 17 *European Journal of International Law* 1–13.

Koskenniemi, M (2002) *The Gentle Civilizer of Nations: The Rise and Fall of International Law, 1870-1960* (Cambridge, CUP).

—— (2007) 'The Fate of Public International Law: Between Technique and Politics' 70 *Modern Law Review* 1–11.

Krisch, N (2006) 'The Pluralism of Global Administrative Law' 17 *European Journal of International Law* 247–88.

Livermore, MA (2006) 'Authority and Legitimacy in Global Governance: Deliberation, Institutional Differentiation, and the Codex Alimentarius' 81 *NYU Law Review* 766–83.

Masson-Matthee, MD (2006) *The Codex Alimentarius Commission and its Standards* (The Hague, TMC Asser Press).

Möllers, C (2005) 'Transnationale Behördenkooperation: Verfassungs- und völkerrechtliche Probleme transnationaler administrativer Standardsetzung' 65 *Zeitschrift für Ausländisches Öffentliches Recht* 351–84.

Möllers, C, Voßkuhle, A, and Walter, C (eds) (2007) *Internationales Verwaltungsrecht: Eine Analyse anhand von Referenzgebieten* (Tübingen, Mohr Siebeck).

New York University Journal of International Law and Politics Symposium (2005) 37 *New York University Journal of International Law and Politics*.

Office of the Federal Register, National Archives and Records Administration, Federal Register Notice 29531 of 31 May 2001 www.gpoaccess.gov/fr/.

Peel, J (2004) *Risk Regulation under the WTO/SPS Agreement: Science as an International Normative Yardstick* (New York, NYU School of Law, Jean Monnet Working Paper 02/04).

Pereira, RA (2008) 'Why Would International Administrative Activity Be Any Less Legitimate?—A Study of the Codex Alimentarius Commission' 9 *German Law Journal* 1693–717.

Petersmann, EU (2001) 'European and International Constitutional Law: Time for Promoting, Cosmopolitan Democracy in the WTO' in Gd Búrca and J Scott (eds), *The EU and the WTO: Legal and Constitutional Issues* (Oxford, Hart Publishing) 81–110.

—— (2002) 'Constitutionalism and WTO Law: From a State-Centered Approach Towards a Human Rights Approach in International Economic Law' in DL Kennedy and JD Southwick (eds), *The Political Economy of International Trade Law/ Essays in Honor of Robert E. Hudec* (Cambridge, CUP) 32–67.

—— (2003) 'Constitutional Primacy and Indivisibility of Human Rights in International Law? The Unfinished Human Rights Revolution and the Emerging

Global Integration Law' in S Griller (ed), *International Governance and Non-Economic Concerns: New Challenges for the International Legal Order* (Wien, New York, Springer) 211–66.
—— (2006) 'Multilevel Governance Requires Multilevel Constitutionalism' in C Joerges and EU Petersmann (eds), *Constitutionalism, Multilevel Trade Governance and Social Regulation* (Oxford, Hart Publishing) 5–58.
Piciotto, S (1996/1997) 'Networks in International Economic Integration: Fragmented States and the Dilemmas of Neo-liberalism' 17 *Northwestern Journal of International Law and Business* 1014–47.
Poli, S (2004) 'The European Community and the Adoption of International Food Standards Within the Codex Alimentarius Commission' 10 *European Law Journal* 613–25.
Sander, G (2000) 'Gesundheitsschutz in der WTO—eine neue Bedeutung der Codex Alimentarius Commission im Lebensmittelrecht?' 3 *Zeitschrift für Europarechtliche Studien* 335–75.
Scott, J (2004) *European Regulation of GMOs: Thinking About Judicial Review in the WTO* (New York, Jean Monnet Working Paper 04/04).
Shapiro, M (2004) *'Deliberative', 'Independent' Technocracy v. Democratic Politics: Will the Globe Echo the EU?* (New York, NYU School of Law Institute for International Law and Justice Working Paper No 5).
Sykes, AO (2005) 'Domestic Regulation, Sovereignty, and Scientific Evidence Requirements: A Pessimistic View' in AO Sykes and PC Mavroidis (eds), *The WTO and International Trade Law/Dispute Settlement?* (Cheltenham, UK; Northhampton, MA, Edward Elgar) 178–89.
Teubner, G (2004) 'Societal Constitutionalism' in C Joerges, IJ Sand and G Teubner (eds), *Transnational Governance and Constututionalism* (Oxford, Hart Publishing) 37.
Teubner, G and Fischer Lescano, A (2004) 'Regime-Collisions: The Vain Search for Legal Unity, in the Fragmentation of Global Law' 25 *Michigan Journal of International Law* 999.
Thomas, UP (2004) 'The Codex Alimentarius and Environment-Related Food Safety: the Functioning of the Global Standards' 1 *Economic Policy and Law* 14.
Victor, DG (2000) 'The Sanitary and Phytosanitary Agreement of the WTO: An Assessment After Five Years' 32 *New York University Journal of Law and Politics* 865–92.
Victor, M (2001) 'Precaution or Protectionism? The Precautionary Principle, Genetically Modified Organisms and Allowing Unfounded Fears to Undermine Free Trade' *Transnational Lawyer* 295–19.
WTO Agreement on the Application of Sanitary and Phytosanitary Measures [SPS Agreement].
—— Agreement on Technical Barriers to Trade [TBT Agreement].
—— Agreement on Technical Barriers to Trade, Code of Good Practice for the Preparation, Adoption and Application of Standards.
—— Appellate Body Report, Canada-Continued Suspension of Obligations in the EC-Hormones Dispute, WT/DS321/AB/R, adopted 14 November 2008 [Canada-Continued Suspension].

—— Appellate Body Report, European Communities—Measures Concerning Meat and Meat Products (Hormones), WT/DS26/AB/R, WT/DS48/AB/R, adopted 13 February 1998 [EC-Hormones].
—— Appellate Body Report, European Communities—Trade Description of Sardines, WT/DS231/1B/R, adopted 23 October 2002 [EC-Sardines].
—— Appellate Body Report, Japan—Measures Affecting the Importation of Apples, WT/DS245/AB/R, adopted 10 December 2003 [Japan-Apples].
—— Appellate Body Report, United States-Continued Suspension of Obligations in the EC-Hormones Dispute, WT/DS320/AB/R, adopted 14 November 2008 [US-Continued Suspension].
—— Panel Report, Australia–Measures Affecting Importation of Salmon, WT/DS18/R, adopted 20 October 1998 [Australia–Salmon].
—— Panel Report, European Communities- Measures Affecting Meat and Meat Products (Hormones) (Canada), WT/DS48/R, adopted 13 February 1998 [EC-Hormones (Canada)].
—— Panel Report, European Communities—Measures Affecting Meat and Meat Products (Hormones) (United States), WT/DS40/R, adopted 13 February 1998 [EC-Hormones (US)].
—— Panel Report, European Communities—Trade Description of Sardines, WT/DS231/R, adopted 23 October 2002 [EC-Sardines].

Part IV

Institutional Dynamics and Member State Control

7

Autonomy or Adaptability? Environmental Integration in the World Bank

ALEXANDRA LINDENTHAL[1]

I. INTRODUCTION

INTERNATIONAL ORGANISATIONS ARE important actors in international relations. They fulfil diverse functions for the nation states that have founded them in order to tackle problems that reach beyond their boundaries (like global environmental pollution) and/or that exceed the problem-solving capacities of single nation states (for example development shortfalls in less developed countries). Generally, international organisations are provided with an administrative structure. To ensure an effective operation of international organisations, it is inevitable that international administrations are endowed with a certain degree of room for manoeuvre by their Member States. However, if an international administration uses this unavoidable room for manoeuvre to follow its own agenda without taking the interests of the organisation's Member States seriously into account, this administrative autonomy (Hasenclever and Mayer 2007: 24–8; Koch 2008: 14–20) may make it difficult for the Member States to regain control and to adapt an international organisation to new external requirements (March 1994) that were unforeseen at the time of its establishment.

Even though (or precisely because) an international administration can reach some degree of autonomy, it is possible that the international organisation fulfills its functions. The World Health Organisation's (WHO) management of the SARS outbreak illustrates that the autonomy

[1] I would like to thank the editors of this volume, as well as Martin Koch for their critical comments on an earlier version of this chapter and Lea Schönfeld for language corrections.

of its 'administrative element' did safeguard the organisation's ability to solve a global health crisis (Cortell and Peterson 2006). In this case, the WHO's staff engaged in slack[2] to avoid the international spread of the disease (ibid: 263–67). According to Cortell and Peterson, the 'professional staff of medical and public health advocates sought to do what was necessary to stem the epidemics of infectious disease, not to follow the political dictates of its principals' (ibid: 271).

Considering this, I do not want to imply that the autonomy of international administrations principally and necessarily results in negative consequences, like the loss of problem-solving capacities of international organisations, and therefore needs to be avoided. However, I argue that the autonomy of the administrative arm can endanger the problem-solving capacity and hence the legitimacy (*cf* ibid: 270) of an international organisation as a whole with regard to new and unforeseen demands stemming from the administration's external environment. Here, 'external' either refers to a demand arising from the Member States of the international organisation, or from the broader international society in which the international organisation—and thus its administration—is embedded. Thus, I agree with Barnett and Finnemore who criticise 'an uncritical optimism about IO behavior' and point out that 'bureaucracies can also be inefficient, ineffective, repressive, and unaccountable' (Barnett and Finnemore 1999: 726).

This chapter starts with the assumption that it may prove difficult for Member States to adjust an international organisation to new demands and to redesign it in accordance with their (changed) interests if an international bureaucracy has become an autonomous actor. To exemplify that adapting an international organisation to new requirements turns out to be challenging if an organisation has gained some degree of autonomy from its Member States, I will refer to the World Bank's efforts to integrate environmental protection into its activities. Moreover, this chapter asks which factors explain the autonomy of the World Bank's administration that has hindered environmental integration. Usually, students of international relations theory either prefer the rationalist principal-agent theory like Hawkins et al (2006a) or a constructivist approach rooted in sociological institutionalism like Barnett and Finnemore (Barnett and Finnemore 1999; Finnemore 1996) to analyse and explain the behaviour of international organisations. Rather, I will demonstrate that both theoretical perspectives are suited to explaining the autonomy of the World Bank's administration that has hindered the integration of environmental concerns and endangered its legitimacy (defined as its (perceived) right to rule).

[2] Cortell and Peterson define *slack* as an 'independent action undesired by the principal' (Cortell and Peterson 2006: 256); see also section II of this chapter.

Even though international administrations are important actors in global governance, they are mostly treated as black boxes by political scientists (Benner et al 2009: 206). Also, the interplay between international administrations and intergovernmental bodies within international organisations is still insufficiently explored in political sciences (Liese and Weinlich 2006: 492). This is even more surprising as the structure of this relationship is important for the legitimacy of an international organisation as an entity. This chapter hence wants to contribute to the starting theoretical and empirical debate on this relationship. Thus, it is structured as follows.

First, I will briefly present two theoretical perspectives that are appropriate when analysing the autonomy of international organisations—the rationalist principal-agent theory on the one hand and a constructive approach, with a focus on organisational culture(s), on the other hand. Principal-agent theory admits that international organisations are not only arenas through which states, as the main actors of the international system, pursue their interests, but actors with their own rights that follow their own interests. In their seminal article on power and pathologies of international organisations, Barnett and Finnemore (1999) introduced a sociological perspective to explain the power of international organisations and their potential for dysfunctional behaviour. Relating to their assumptions on organisational dysfunction, I will show that the organisational culture of the World Bank is an important source for its deviant behaviour. While these authors, however, regard an international organisation to a large extent as an organisational entity, called bureaucracy, I will differentiate between the administrative arm and the intergovernmental bodies of an international organisation.

Second, I will describe the attempts of the World Bank to integrate environmental concerns into its activities. Thereby, I will focus on the interaction between the World Bank's administrative arm (the Secretariat) and the Member States (Executive Board). The overview of the World Bank's environmental integration efforts is divided into three periods. It starts with the 1970s when the World Bank formally began to address environmental issues. Then, after some external critique, the World Bank enhanced its efforts to integrate environmental aspects into its activities. During the third period, beginning in the early 1990s, internal World Bank reports that were made publicly available shed light on the difficulties in integrating environmental aspects in the past. Even though the internal critique led to some further institutional reforms, the desired outcomes did not occur. As there already is some instructive literature, such as empirical studies or publications of the World Bank, which is dealing explicitly or implicitly with the World Bank's environment policy (Gehring and Kerler 2007; Gutner 2005; Marschinski and Behrle 2007; Nielson and Tierney 2003; Park 2007), I will refer to these throughout this chapter.

Third, it will be shown that both perspectives offer convincing theoretical reasons for the autonomy of the World Bank's bureaucracy which hindered environmental integration. Furthermore, it will shortly be described how far this autonomisation influenced the World Bank's legitimacy. According to my findings and those of previous studies I will finally suggest combining the principal-agent model with a sociological perspective to explain the autonomy of international bureaucracies.

II. RATIONALIST AND SOCIOLOGICAL APPROACHES TO ADMINISTRATIVE AUTONOMY

The principal-agent theory as well as a constructive approach to organisational behaviour, are promising theoretical perspectives explaining the autonomy of international administrations. A short overview of the assumptions of the rationalist and the sociological strand is given below. As (neo-)realism neglects the role of international administrations in world politics and traditional institutionalism is rather focused on intergovernmental institutions, those well-known theories of international relations are not suitable for analysing international bureaucracies.

Principal-agent theorists start from the premise that states (principals) as rational actors choose to delegate authority to international organisations (agents) if they are able to fulfill specific functions for them. This delegation is based on the assumption that the benefits of delegation are higher than the costs expected by agency losses. According to Hawkins et al, delegation is 'a conditional grant of authority from a principal to an agent that empowers the latter to act on behalf of the former' (Hawkins et al 2006b: 7). For example, by delegating, states reap gains from specialisation if the agent possesses information, expertise, or other resources to perform a task. Just as their principals, international organisations strategically pursue their interests. Thereby, it is supposed that the strategic behaviour of international organisations conflicts with the expectations of their creators. In addition, this interaction is characterised by uncertainty as the principal is lacking the necessary information to assess whether the agent actually serves his interests. The principal-agent theory assumes that states employ mechanisms of control not only to ensure that their interests are served by international organisations, but also to avoid agency slack (Gilardi and Braun 2002; Hawkins et al 2006b; Pollack 1997; 2006).[3] To maintain an international organisation's legitimacy, it is necessary that the principal establishes

[3] For the problem of administrative autonomy at the international level from a jurisprudential perspective, see Bernstorff 2008; Friedrich 2008; and Zacharias 2008.

procedures that ensure the transparency of decision-making processes, as well as accountability structures within the organisation. Hence, an international organisation is considered legitimate as long as it serves the principals' interests.

In this context, Pollack differentiates between administrative procedures that 'define *ex ante* the scope of agency activity' and oversight procedures which, on the other hand, allow principals ex post to monitor agency behaviour and to influence it through the application of sanctions (Pollack 1997: 108). The former comprises contractual rules that may be less or more restrictive. Oversight procedures encompass direct monitoring of agents by principals ('police patrols') and a less direct monitoring that relies on third parties ('fire alarm') (ibid: 110 et seq).[4] Autonomy can consequently be described as 'the range of maneuver available to agents after the principal has selected screening, monitoring and sanctioning mechanisms intended to constrain their behavior' (Hawkins et al 2006b: 8). While autonomy denotes the 'range of independent action that is available to an agent and can be used to benefit or undermine the principal', agency slack means 'actual behavior that is undesired' (ibid). Thus, organisational autonomy depends on the efficiency of the control mechanisms. In addition, agents can take advantage of a constellation of collective principals with heterogeneous preferences to enhance their independence (Pollack 1997: 112). Applying the principal-agent model, authors at times offer interesting empirical insights into the internal structure of international organisations and the relationship between its administrative elements and the intergovernmental bodies (Broz and Hawes 2006; Cortell and Peterson 2006; Nielson and Tierney 2003). Nonetheless, the attributes of agents often attract less interest than the principals because it is supposed that the latter design or select 'optimal' agents corresponding with their preferences (Hawkins et al 2006b: 36).

It is also instructive to view international organisations through sociological lenses like Barnett and Finnemore (1999) do in their seminal article on power and pathologies of international organisations. Regarding several assumptions, their 'sociological approach' agrees with the principal-agent theory. Like the authors from rationalist theory, they conceptualise international organisations as powerful (amongst others because of their control over information and expertise) and autonomous actors operating against the background of structural constraints (ibid: 707). Similar to the principal-agent model, this theoretical strand wants to know why 'organizations that are not efficient or effective servants of member

[4] Hawkins et al (2006b: 26–31) offer a detailed description of a principal's mechanism of control.

interests might exist' (ibid: 703).[5] As this approach is interested in the dysfunctional behaviour of international organisations that 'undermines the stated goals of the organization' (ibid: 702), this perspective sheds light on the reasons of administrative autonomy.

While the principal-agent theory focuses on states as creators of international organisations, this approach places the organisation itself in the centre of research without ignoring the role of its environments. Even though it is admitted that demands from states may override internal cultural dynamics, cultural forces are seen as an important source for deviant behaviour (Barnett and Finnemore 1999: 702; Koch 2008: 216). While its culture (defined as rules, routines, beliefs, etc)[6] on the one hand makes an international organisation effective, the (sub-)organisational culture may on the other hand cause dysfunctional autonomy (Barnett and Finnemore 1999: 719 et seq; Egeberg 1998: 3). For example, an international administration that strictly acts according to formalised internal rules and has established its own routines may tend to ignore external demands (from states, non-governmental organisations, etc) or internal demands (from the steering committee or other organisational units) that are inconsistent with its own rules and routines. Likewise, while expertise and specialisation are important features of international organisations (March and Olsen 1989), professionalism that is linked to a particular logic of appropriate behaviour may implicate a limited 'field of vision' of bureaucrats and result in an insulation of the organisation which will finally result in dysfunction. Professional training may reinforce this effect (Barnett and Finnemore 1999: 723; *cf* DiMaggio and Powell 1991: 70–4). Moreover, the fact that organisational subunits have their own norms, world views, interests, professions, etc may result in different ways of perceiving the organisation's environment and in diverse interpretations of the organisation's mission and goals. This may finally also lead to an autonomous behaviour of international organisations.

The sociological neo-institutionalism regards legitimacy as a relationship between an organisation and its environment. From this perspective, legitimacy can be defined as a 'perception or assumption that the actions of an entity are desirable, proper, or appropriate within some socially constructed system of norms, values, beliefs, and definitions' (Suchman 1995: 574). Legitimacy is necessary for the persistence of an organisation which may use different strategies to gain and maintain legitimacy (ibid: 585–97). How an organisation acts towards its environment may have

[5] As regards principal-agent theory, it is criticised from a sociological perspective that the interests of principal and agent are given a priori. In contrast, approaches from organisational sociology are based on the premise that actors are embedded and that interests are endogenous to interaction.

[6] See also Sackmann 1993; Meyerson and Martin 1994.

consequences for its legitimacy. For instance, ignoring societal demands may result in a loss of legitimacy and hence challenge the organisation's persistence. This is based on the assumption of Meyer and Rowan (1977: 341) that an organisation's formal structure and its 'day-to-day work activities' are only loosely coupled. In search for legitimacy, an organisation adapts its formal structures according to external demands while its actual work practices remain unchanged. Thereby, an organisation buffers its internal activities from external demands (ibid). Hence, if an organisation does not perceive external changes or ignores them as a consequence of its autonomisation, it may eventually lose its legitimacy.

III. ENVIRONMENTAL INTEGRATION IN THE WORLD BANK

The World Bank[7] was established in 1944 to stabilise the international economic system. After the conclusion of the reconstruction in Europe, its field of activities shifted towards the financing of development aid. The granting of loans to the World Bank's Member States is project-oriented and the Bank supports the recipient countries in the planning and implementation phase of the financed projects (Rittberger and Zangl 1995: 53-5). The Member States are represented in the Bank's Board of Governors and the Executive Board. The Board of Governors, the plenary organ of the World Bank, is composed of representatives of all 186 Member States. The member governments delegated decision-making authority for all decisions over operations and policies to the Bank's Board of Executive Directors (Nielson and Tierney 2003: 254; *cf* Möllers 2008: 241). The Executive Board consists of the President and 24 executive directors acting as a unit. The five largest shareholders (France, Germany, Japan, the United Kingdom and the United States) each appoint an executive director, while the other member countries are represented by the remaining 19 executive directors. The Executive Board oversees the Bank's business, including the approval of loans and the supervision of financial decisions. The decisions of the Executive Board are prepared by the Secretariat (Gehring and Kerler 2007: 228). The President of the World Bank, who is responsible for the overall management of the Bank, chairs the meetings of the Executive Board.

The requirement to consider environmental issues throughout its activities can be regarded as a new and, at the time of its establishment,

[7] The World Bank (officially the International Bank for Reconstruction and Development (IBRD)) is part of the World Bank Group. In addition to the IBRD, the World Bank Group is composed of the International Development Association (IDA), the International Finance Corporation (IFC), the Multilateral Investment Guarantee Agency (MIGA), and the International Centre for Settlement of Investment Disputes (ICSID).

unforeseen demand for the World Bank. The World Bank's efforts to integrate environmental concerns into its activities can be divided into three phases. The first phase runs from the 1970s until the beginning of the 1980s. At that time, the World Bank—more precisely its Secretariat—became active as regards environment protection. The second period, running from the mid 1980s until the beginning of the 1990s, starts with an external critique on the World Bank's environmental performance followed by some first institutional reforms. It ends with internal Bank reports detecting significant difficulties with the integration of environmental concerns. The last stage covers the period from the early 1990s to the beginning of this century and is characterised by the Bank's intensified efforts to improve environmental mainstreaming.

In the 1970s and 1980s the environment became an issue and also development policy turned towards environmental concerns (Gehring and Kerler 2007: 230). In 1970, the World Bank established an office responsible for environmental issues. Because it turned towards environment protection early on, the World Bank was initially regarded as a pioneer. Nevertheless, it was lacking a consistent environmental strategy (Park 2007: 539). In 1975, the Secretariat adopted some environmental guidelines, but these non-binding recommendations were often ignored. Until 1983, the environment office only had three environmental specialists on its staff which were integrated into the project-approval process of the World Bank at a later stage, which however, merely made environmental recommendations only occasionally (Gehring and Kerler 2007: 230; Nielson and Tierney 2003: 253).

During the second period, integration of environmental concerns[8] also turned out to be challenging for the World Bank. In view of the criticism of non-governmental organisations (NGOs) and some Member States, institutional environment reforms were introduced under the new President of the World Bank.

In the early 1980s, the World Bank was blamed for having financed projects that led to environmental disasters in Brazil and Indonesia (Nielson and Tierney 2003: 241). Environmental NGOs protested against the World Bank's methods and demanded a change in lending practices. Because direct appeals to the Bank failed, critics called on Member States' governments—especially on the United States as the most important shareholder of the Bank—to put pressure on the World Bank (Gehring and Kerler 2007: 230 et seq; Nielson and Tierney 2003: 256 et seq). In 1986, the United States indeed exerted pressure on the World Bank as it rejected a project due to environmental reasons and threatened not to accept the planned capital

[8] For the World Bank (2001: 11), environmental integration means to 'ensure that environmental concerns are fully internalized—mainstreamed—into all Bank's activities'.

increase of the Bank unless it modified its behaviour (Gehring and Kerler 2007: 231). Because the World Bank only complied in part (see below), the US Congress in 1994 again threatened to withhold future funds from the Bank unless it changed its practices (Nielson and Tierney 2003: 241). Also, some Member States' representatives on the Executive Board sought to ensure that the changes the World Bank had promised would be implemented. The Bank reacted with institutional reforms and altered its lending portfolio by increasing environmental lending and decreasing projects which caused environmental harm (ibid).

Until the first environment-related reforms of 1987, the granting of projects was running in two phases (Gehring and Kerler 2007: 228–29). In the first phase, the Secretariat prepared the projects. In the second phase, the Executive Board decided on financing. The World Bank was committed by its founding treaties to decide exclusively on economic criteria. It was expected that the delegation of project planning and reporting evaluation to the Secretariat would result in economically and technically sound drafts uninfluenced by political considerations. The apolitical stance of the Secretariat was brought forward by the fact that the staff was employed directly by the Secretariat, not by the Member States. Even though projects only came into effect with the approval of the Executive Board that could veto the Secretariat's proposals, the decision-making process was mainly formed by the Secretariat (ibid).

In 1987, the new President of the World Bank, Barber Conable, announced some institutional reforms concerning environment protection and the World Bank began to mainstream environmental criteria into its operations (Park 2007: 539).[9] Binding environmental safeguards were introduced in the same year. This meant that decisions on granting projects were bound to obligatory environmental (and social) guidelines defining a minimum standard of protection for projects financed by the World Bank. Specialised units were established to ensure compliance with the safeguards; in the case of controversial projects, the executive directors became involved in the decision-making process at an earlier stage. Additionally, environmental impact assessments of projects became mandatory (Gehring and Kerler 2007: 234, 247; Marschinski and Behrle 2007: 11). Furthermore, the World Bank's office of environmental and scientific affairs was reorganised into a separate environment department which could operate with more personnel; the number of employees of the environmental unit grew from six to 30. In addition, the new President

[9] Also in the 1980s, the European Commission of the European Union began to push environmental integration. To integrate environmental considerations into Community policies, the Directorate-General for the Environment played an important role (Kopp-Malek et al 2009: 122–39).

promised a new category of free-standing environmental loans (Nielson and Tierney 2003: 258).

During the third period, criticism did not stop and internal World Bank reports also detected some major problems with environmental mainstreaming. For the first time, the World Bank started developing environmental strategies. These strategies—the second strategy paper is expected to be completed at the end of 2010—take the feedback of the Bank's Independent Evaluation Group (IEG) into consideration.

Despite the institutional reforms, internal World Bank reports in the early 1990s detected that over a third of World Bank projects proved unsatisfactory as regards meeting the Bank's own environmental standards (Marschinski and Behrle 2007: 1). Nielson and Tierney stated that the 1987 reforms 'failed to alter core Bank practice' (Nielson and Tierney 2003: 259). Even though the reforms were a small step in the right direction, they neither satisfied external critics or the Executive Board. The World Bank reacted by improving its monitoring and evaluation procedures (Marschinski and Behrle 2007: 1; Nielson and Tierney 2003: 260).

To control the Secretariat, currently more than 10,000 employees from over 160 countries, the Executive Board established an independent inspection panel in 1993 to hear complaints from groups that were directly affected by World Bank projects (Gehring and Kerler 2007: 233–37; Nielson and Tierney 2003: 262). Also further on, the Secretariat started to initiate, plan and evaluate the projects, which the Executive Board then decides on. In addition, external actors may use the inspection procedure to verify whether a project is consistent with the binding safeguards of the World Bank. Since persons concerned with World Bank decisions have the opportunity to file a complaint against these, the Bank becomes accountable to civil society (Gehring and Kerler 2007: 235). The inspection panel has a further effect—because external actors bring 'outside information to the inspection panel and thus the executive board [...], board members found it much easier to get information about the likely impacts of Bank projects before the projects were implemented' (Nielson and Tierney 2003: 263). Like the binding environmental safeguards, the inspection panel—a quasi-administrative control procedure—was initiated to restrain the Secretariat's room for manoeuvre (Gehring and Kerler 2007: 233).[10]

[10] Gehring and Kerler (2007: 239–41) quote an example for the effectiveness of the binding environmental safeguards in connection with the inspection panel. According to the authors, the conflict concerning the environmental compatibility of the Chad-Cameroon-Pipeline (start of construction was in 1999) shows that the Secretariat rejected the documents presented by the applicants and insisted on a revision of the original plans in accordance with the environmental safeguards. The revised survey report finally complied with the Secretariat's requirements.

Furthermore, the loan approval process was modified in 1993–94. After the changes, board members were involved in the planning phases of Bank projects at an earlier stage, and 'they began to exercise their option to question or suggest changes to projects long before they reached the decision phase' (Nielson and Tierney 2003: 263). Also, the number of personnel employed as environmental staff increased dramatically and the type of staff hired by the World Bank changed insofar as more environmental economists and engineers, as well as biologists, were employed. Hence, the Executive Board could be more certain that the Bank staff had the ability to analyse the environmental impacts of projects. This also went in line with a 1994 decision, since which each World Bank project with a potential environmental impact has been assigned an environmental project manager who assesses the environmental impact and sends an evaluation report to the Executive Board (ibid). Since then, the board members 'have received better and more timely information about the environmental impact of Bank projects' (ibid: 264). Also, loan disbursements for projects categorised as environmentally sensitive cannot commence until the environmental impact assessment is completed and documents are submitted to the Executive Board (ibid).

Regarding the Wolfensohn Presidency from 1995–05, Marschinski and Behrle observe an often-stated 'discrepancy between the World Bank's green rhetoric and its mixed environmental performance on the ground' (Marschinski and Behrle 2007: 22). Among other factors, this increased rationalisation has indirectly weakened the implementation of environmental objectives. In 1996, against the background of Wolfensohn's restructure of the World Bank, decision-power was transferred to country directors who were given 'considerable latitude and powers' (ibid). As a result, environmental safeguards 'have been applied with varying vigor across World Bank operations and it depends on the regional team in how far the environmental impacts of World Bank projects are monitored' (ibid; *cf* Gutner 2005: 779; Park 2007: 540). Not all staff members insisted on strict compliance with the safeguard policies; according to an investigation of the inspection panel some regarded them simply as 'idealized policy statements' (Marschinski and Behrle 2007: 23).

In 1973, the IEG, an independent unit within the World Bank that reports directly to the Executive Board, was founded. The IEG started as an 'experimental program' and presently considers itself 'a major department with a record of accomplishment and influence within the Bank and beyond.' The IEG 'assesses what works, and what does not'.[11] Hence, the evaluation group also reviewed the Bank's record in the environmental area. Its feedback poured into the first environmental strategy

[11] See the IEG's website at http://web.worldbank.org/ last visited 29 March 2010.

of the World Bank (2001) and consequently, the strategy addresses some significant problems the World Bank had with environmental mainstreaming.

First of all, the strategy paper emphasises 'the importance of integrating environment into country development programs, sector strategies, and investments' (ibid: 3). It criticises that the environment had only been 'the concern of a small, specialized group' (ibid). In this context, the paper condemns that Bank professionals often see environmental issues as a 'self-standing agenda and not as an element of their core tasks of supporting development and poverty reduction' (ibid: 11 et seq). Moreover, it is stated that the design and performance of both sectoral projects, as well as environmentally-dedicated projects, needs to be improved with regard to environmental requirements. The World Bank's safeguard system is seen as an essential tool for integrating environmental concerns into development policies, programmes and projects. Therefore, the quality and consistency of the application of safeguard policies should be improved. To enhance its record on environmental integration some further institutional changes are seen as essential, like establishing clear lines of responsibility and incentives throughout the institution. In this context, the training of environmental as well as non-environmental staff has been announced and 'Green Awards' are being promised as incentives for non-environmental specialists in order to mainstream environment into their operations and programmes. To address the objectives of the proposed strategy, an increase of the Bank's budget funding until 2006 is deemed necessary (ibid: 23–30).

Also in the following years, the evaluation department was sceptical on environmental integration in the World Bank. In 2002, it reiterated its critique that environmental concerns were not integrated into the Bank's core objectives and country strategies (Park 2007: 542). Again in a World Bank publication of 2004, the Bank's performance in regards to environmental integration was seen as critical (ibid: 543). In 2008, the environmental performance of the World Bank was evaluated by the IEG. The group noted that the World Bank 'has made progress since 1990 as an advocate for the environment' (World Bank 2009: 1). However, the IEG identified 'external and internal constraints to the treatment of environmental issues in many country programs' of the World Bank. To increase its effectiveness with regard to environmental issues, the IEG suggested amongst others to 'provide greater attention to environmental sustainability in the World Bank Group' and to 'move to more cross-sectoral and spatially-oriented approaches and strengthen staff skills' (ibid). The findings of the IEG were incorporated into the concept note of the new environment strategy, which is expected to be completed by December 2010 under the lead of the environment department (ibid).

IV. EXPLAINING THE WORLD BANK'S AUTONOMY

Integrating environmental concerns into the World Bank's activities proved difficult because of the autonomy it attained vis-à-vis its Member States. In the following, it will be demonstrated that both the principal-agent theory and sociological approaches to organisational behaviour offer theoretical reasons that explain this organisational autonomy which has hindered the integration of environmental concerns. From both perspectives, the process of autonomisation can be seen as resulting in a loss of different forms of legitimacy since the mid-1980s. Officially, the World Bank has tried to regain its legitimacy, especially with establishing monitoring procedures.

During the first phase from the 1970s until the beginning of the 1980s, the World Bank was acting independently from its Member States (Nielson and Tierney 2003: 242; *cf* Biermann and Siebenhüner 2007: 20). Because the donor countries were of the perception that the World Bank performed its tasks and was 'not engaged in activities that fundamentally conflicted' with their interests, the World Bank was left to its own devices (Nielson and Tierney 2003: 253). This was not without consequences for environmental issues. Even though there were some environmental guidelines, the World Bank's 'task manager and project officers did just about as they pleased' (ibid).

According to the principal-agent theory, this autonomy results from the 'broad discretion' that the Member States granted the World Bank (Hawkins et al 2006b: 27). It is assumable that the Member States did not show much interest in environmental issues because the environmental staff of the World Bank was 'without budget or authority within the organization' and hence could 'neither monitor nor enforce compliance with the organization's environmental guidelines' (Nielson and Tierney 2003: 253 et seq). Furthermore, the Executive Board was unable to evaluate and control the Bank's projects as regards environmental requirements due to a lack of human resources and expertise (Gehring and Kerler 2007: 230). Hence, this situation is a result of organisational autonomy, not of agency slack.

From a sociological perspective, the World Bank's behaviour can be explained with its lack of serious external demands to pay attention to environment protection, combined with the fact that the Secretariat followed its own rules and routines and tended to ignore new concerns. In this phase, the World Bank was perceived as producing the expected outcomes by its Member States since they rather focused on output legitimacy. Thus, further legitimacy deficits were not detected.

In the second period (from the mid 1980s to the beginning of the 1990s), the World Bank's behaviour came close to agency slack as the Bank only partly complied with the requirements of the Member States concerning environmental protection. The institutional reforms described above satisfied neither external critics nor the Executive Board. That reforms took place at all can be explained with the principal-agent theory assuming that the room for manoeuvre of the agent depends on the convergence of interests of the collective principal (Nielson and Tierney 2003: 258). In the mid 1980s, the interests of the powerful Member States represented on the Executive Board started converging. The Member States wanted to regain control over the Secretariat and were willing to sanction the undesired behaviour. This constellation of interests finally resulted in personal and administrative changes at the Bank (Betz 2007: 339; Gehring and Kerler 2007: 231; Nielson and Tierney 2003: 265).

As principal-agent theory would have predicted it, the Executive Board designed new rules and institutions to constrain the agent more tightly (Hawkins et al 2006b: 27). As the theory supposes, the 'fire alarm' of the NGOs had been crucial in detecting the undesired behaviour of the World Bank and to enable the Member States to react against it (Nielson and Tierney 2003: 254; for the role of NGOs as regards compliance control, see also Oeter in chapter eight).

That the World Bank had not directly responded to the NGOs' criticism can be explained with sociological approaches to organisational behaviour. The World Bank regarded compliance with the demands of these civil society actors not as important for its legitimacy and persistence. While the principal-agent theory thus offers a convincing explanation for the constricted autonomy of the World Bank (as a result of the reforms of 1987), the sociological perspective sheds light on why the World Bank did not entirely change its behaviour regardless of the demands of the Member States. Even though the World Bank is constrained by its Member States, an 'independent culture and agendas for action' can be identified (Barnett and Finnemore 1999: 705). Thus, the undesired behaviour can be explained with the Bank's manifested professional culture that was dominated by neoclassically-trained economists. This economically trained staff had developed its own logic of an appropriate behaviour which was, however, counter-productive towards environmental mainstreaming (Biermann and Siebenhüner 2007: 23; Weaver 2007: 495). As regards legitimacy, the World Bank suffered from a lack of procedural legitimacy. The Member States—as the Bank's principal—reacted by establishing monitoring procedures and further institutional and structural reforms to regain control and hence legitimacy.

The behaviour of the World Bank in the third phase, starting in the early 1990s, can also be explained with combining principal-agent theory and insights from sociological approaches. According to the principal-agent theory, the strengthened monitoring procedures—like the inspection panel and the activities of the evaluation group—should have restricted the undesired autonomous behaviour of the World Bank and hence resulted in a better integration of environmental concerns. Although the inspection panel had successfully restricted the Secretariat's room for manoeuvre and indirectly increased the information available to the Executive Board (and thereby reduced its dependence on the World Bank's staff), internal evaluation showed that environmental mainstreaming at the World Bank was rather disappointing until today. While the World Bank was active in trying to 'green' its image, changes in the 'real operational practices of the Bank' were less visible (Weaver 2007: 504).

From a sociological perspective, this can be explained with the intention of the World Bank to buffer its internal activities from external influences while, for reasons of legitimacy, the Bank symbolically adapted its formal structures to the external demands. This effect was strengthened by the World Bank's economic organisational culture and the routinised behaviour of its foremost economic staff (Marschinski and Behrle 2007: 28).[12] This can be exemplified by the fact that environmental safeguard procedures were not always 'implemented wholeheartedly by [...] project staff' as the operations evaluation department criticised (ibid: 11). Even under the presidency of Wolfensohn, who tried to push environmental reforms forward, environmental integration did not improve in essence. Consequently, not even strong personal leadership[13] was able to alter 'deep-rooted habits and procedures' within the large World Bank's bureaucracy (Marschinski and Behrle 2007: 27; *cf* Gutner 2005: 773; Weaver 2007: 540). Thus, the manifestations of organisational culture led to persistence, inertia and finally to a resistance to change (Meyerson and Martin 1994: 112; Sackmann 1983: 404; Zucker 1977).

While principal-agent theory emphasises the value of external expertise (as this would reduce the dependence of the Executive Board on the Secretariat), a sociological perspective would argue for a well-informed staff in terms of environmental concerns who seem to be needed throughout the World Bank's bureaucracy to ensure that environmental mainstreaming captures the whole organisation (Marschinski and Behrle 2007: 28). Instead, the World Bank relied on consultants and got criticised for using external expertise as this resulted in an inconsistent quality of its environmental assessment reports (ibid: 21). Finally, the failure of environmental mainstreaming shows that the World Bank lacks outcome legitimacy at least in this regard. To keep up its organisational performance, the World Bank modified its operational strategies without calling into question the organisational values. Further research seems to be necessary to analyse the attitudes of the World Bank's Member

[12] Likewise, environmental integration in the European Commission's directorates-general, responsible for enterprise, energy and transport policies, occasionally proved difficult because of their professional cultures (Kopp-Malek et al 2009: 69–122).

[13] See Meyerson and Martin 1994; March, 1994 for the role of personal leadership as a trigger for organisational change.

States towards environmental mainstreaming, to find out if the collective principal is really interested in environmental progress or willing to tolerate this form of legitimacy deficit as the outcome is consistent with its hidden agenda.

V. CONCLUSION

Even though they are aware of the benefits of the principal-agent theory, some authors rightly criticise that this theory alone cannot satisfactorily explain an agent's actual behaviour (Gould 2006: 207; Gutner 2005: 281). Thus, they take principal-agent theory as a starting point and then make use of different perspectives to look into the agent's black box. For example, Cortell and Peterson (2006) examine the characteristics of the agent and focus on cultural variables like professional ethics and common values of the international staff of, for example, the WHO or the World Trade Organisation, to explain their behaviour vis-à-vis their Member States.

In the same vein, Weaver (2007) emphasises the importance of the internal character and dynamics of international organisations if one wants to understand how autonomous bureaucratic behaviour occurs. Similarly, Hawkins and Jacoby (2006) use insights from sociological neo-institutionalism to make assumptions on the strategic behaviour of the European Human Rights Commission and Court.

Likewise, I argue that integrating insights from sociological approaches to organisational behaviour into the principal-agent model is fruitful for understanding the behaviour of international organisations. Above, it has been shown that the autonomy of the World Bank's bureaucracy hindered environmental integration and that these theoretical strands offer complementary explanations for this independence. To avoid undesired behaviour of international organisations, it is essential to know the reasons behind administrative autonomy.

While the rationalist theory can explain why and under what conditions mechanisms of control were introduced and strengthened, sociological approaches offer feasible reasons why and how the World Bank nonetheless engaged in an undesired behaviour as regards environmental integration. By integrating sociological approaches, it may, for instance, become possible to identify strategies an agent uses to bypass the principal's control mechanisms. Hence, empirically these theoretical approaches seem to be powerful complements (*cf* Hawkins and Jacoby 2006: 213; Venzke 2008: 1417 et seq; Weaver 2007: 498).

Finally, I want to stress the fact that organisational culture(s) can certainly be a source of 'good' behaviour (Barnett and Finnemore 1999: 719) as the above cited example of the WHO has shown. However, if an international administration insulates itself from its external environments (ibid: 722), including the interests and ideas embedded in them, and hence develops an internal culture that avoids conforming to external expectations, this may result in dysfunctional behaviour and hence endanger the legitimacy and survival of the international organisation. If this is the case, a change in the organisational culture is necessary (*cf* Sackmann 1983: 403). With an independent and influential evaluation department within the World Bank, which also monitors its environmental performance, the Bank is possibly on its way to change its organisational cultures and promote environmental integration. On the basis of a literature review, I offered some (albeit incomplete) insights into the environmental activities of the World Bank. Further analysis is needed in order to demonstrate whether the environmental performance of the World Bank conforms to appropriate standards defined by independent experts outside the organisation. Only then will it be possible to draw more detailed conclusions on the Bank's legitimacy.

REFERENCES

Barnett, MN and Finnemore, M (1999) 'The Politics, Power, and Pathologies of International Organizations' 53 *International Organization* 699.

Benner, T, Mergenthaler, S and Rotmann, P (2009) 'Internationale Bürokratien und Organisationslernen' 16 *Zeitschrift für Internationale Beziehungen* 203.

Bernstorff, J von (2008) 'Procedures of Decision-Making and the Role of Law in International Organizations' 9 *German Law Journal* 1939.

Betz, J (2007) 'Macht und Ohnmacht der internationalen Finanzinstitutionen—IWF und Weltbank' in A Hasenclever, KD Wolf and M Zürn (eds), *Macht und Ohnmacht internationaler Institutionen* (Frankfurt/New York, Campus).

Biermann, F and Siebenhüner, B (2007) *Managers of Global Change. Core Findings from the MANUS Project* (Amsterdam, Global Governance Working Paper No 25).

Broz, JL and Hawes, MB (2006) 'US Domestic Politics and International Monetary Fund Policy' in DG Hawkins, DA Lake, DL Nielson and MJ Tierney (eds), *Delegation and Agency in International Organizations* (Cambridge, Cambridge University Press).

Cortell, AP and Peterson, S (2006) 'Dutiful Agents, rouge Actors, or both? Staffing, Voting Rules, and Slack in the WHO and WTO' in DG Hawkins, DA Lake, DL Nielson and MJ Tierney (eds), *Delegation and Agency in International Organizations* (Cambridge, Cambridge University Press).

DiMaggio, PJ and Powell, WW (1991) 'The Iron Cage Revisited: Institutional Isomorphism and Collective Rationality in Organizational Fields' in PJ DiMaggio and WW Powell (eds), *The New Institutionalism in Organizational Analysis* (Chicago, University of Chicago Press).

Ecker-Ehrhardt, M and Zürn, M (2007) 'Die Politisierung internationaler Institutionen' 20-21 *Aus Politik und Zeitgeschichte* 24.

Egeberg, M (1998) 'Causes of Bureaucratic Autonomy: The Impact of Organizational and Cultural Factors' (Oslo, Arena Working Papers No 15).

Finnemore, M (1996) 'Norms, Culture, and World Politics: Insights from Sociology's Institutionalism' 50 *International Organization* 325.
Friedrich, J (2008) 'Legal Challenges of Nonbinding Instruments: The Case of the FAO Code of Conduct for Responsible Fisheries' 9 *German Law Journal* 1539.
Gehring, T and Kerler, MA (2007) 'Neue Entscheidungsverfahren in der Weltbank. Wie institutionelle Strukturen zu gutem Regieren führen' 14 *Zeitschrift für Internationale Beziehungen* 217.
Gilardi, F and Braun, D (2002) 'Delegation aus Sicht der Prinzipal-Agent-Theorie' 43 *Politische Vierteljahresschrift* 147.
Gould, ER (2006) 'Delegating IMF Conditionality: Understanding Variations in Control and Conformity' in DG Hawkins, DA Lake, DL Nielson and MJ Tierney (eds), *Delegation and Agency in International Organizations* (Cambridge, Cambridge University Press).
Gutner, T (2005) 'World Bank Environmental Reform: Revisiting Lessons from Agency Theory' 59 *International Organization* 773.
Hasenclever, A and Mayer, P (2007) 'Macht und Ohnmacht internationaler Organisationen' in A Hasenclever, KD Wolf and M Zürn (eds), *Macht und Ohnmacht internationaler Institutionen* (Frankfurt/New York, Campus).
Hawkins, DG and Jacoby, W (2006) 'How Agents Matter' in DG Hawkins, DA Lake, DL Nielson and MJ Tierney (eds), *Delegation and Agency in International Organizations* (Cambridge, Cambridge University Press).
Hawkins, DG, Lake, DA, Nielson, DL and Tierney, MJ (eds) (2006a) *Delegation and Agency in International Organizations* (Cambridge, Cambridge University Press).
—— (2006b) 'Delegation under Anarchy: States, International Organization and Principal-Agent Theory' in DG Hawkins, DA Lake, DL Nielson and MJ Tierney (eds), *Delegation and Agency in International Organizations* (Cambridge, Cambridge University Press).
Koch, M (2008) *Verselbständigungsprozesse internationaler Organisationen* (Wiesbaden, VS Verlag).
Kopp-Malek, T, Koch, M and Lindenthal, A (2009) *Die Europäische Kommission als lernende Organisation? Die Umsetzung des umweltpolitischen Integrationsprinzips in ausgewählten Generaldirektionen der Europäischen Kommission* (Wiesbaden, VS Verlag).
Liese, A and Weinlich, S (2006) 'Die Rolle von Verwaltungsstäben internationaler Organisationen. Lücken, Tücken und Konturen eines (neuen) Forschungsfelds' 37 *Politische Vierteljahresschrift-Sonderheft* 491.
March, JG (1994) 'How We Talk and How We Act: Administrative Theory and Administrative Life' in H Tsoukas (ed), *New Thinking in Organizational Behaviour. From Social Engineering to Reflective Action* (Oxford et al, Butterworth-Heinemann).
March, JG and Olsen, JP (1989) *Rediscovering Institutions. The Organizational Basis of Politics* (New York, Free Press).
Marschinski, R and Behrle, S (2007) *The World Bank: Making the Business Case for the Environment* (Amsterdam, Global Governance Working Paper No 21).
Meyer, JW and Rowan, B (1977) 'Institutionalized Organizations: Formal Structure as Myth and Ceremony' 83 *American Journal of Sociology* 340.

Meyerson, D and Martin, J (1994) 'Cultural Change: An Integration of Three Different Views' in H Tsoukas (ed), *New Thinking in Organizational Behaviour. From Social Engineering to Reflective Action* (Oxford et al, Butterworth-Heinemann).
Möllers, C (2008) 'Die Governance-Konstellation: Transnationale Beobachtung durch öffentliches Recht' 41 *Politische Vierteljahresschrift-Sonderheft* 238.
Nielson, DL and Tierney, MJ (2003) 'Delegation to International Organizations: Agency Theory and World Bank Environmental Reform' 57 *International Organization* 241.
Park, S (2007) 'The World Bank Group: Championing Sustainable Development Norms?' 13 *Global Governance* 535.
Pollack, MA (1997) 'Delegation, Agency, and Agenda Setting in the European Community' 55 *International Organization* 99.
—— (2006) 'Delegation and Discretion in the European Union' in DG Hawkins, DA Lake, DL Nielson and MJ Tierney (eds), *Delegation and Agency in International Organizations* (Cambridge, Cambridge University Press).
Rittberger, V and Zangl, B (1995) *Internationale Organisationen. Politik und Geschichte* (Opladen, Leske + Budrich).
Sackmann, S (1983) 'Organisationskultur: Die unsichtbare Einflussgröße' 14 *Gruppendynamik* 393.
Suchman, MC (1995) 'Managing Legitimacy: Strategic and Institutional Approaches' 20 *Academy of Management Review* 571.
Venzke, I (2008) 'International Bureaucracies from a Political Science Perspective — Agency, Authority and International Institutional Law' 9 *German Law Journal* 1401.
Weaver, C (2007) 'The World's Bank and the Bank's World' 13 *Global Governance* 493.
World Bank (2001) *Making Sustainable Commitments. An Environment Strategy for the World Bank* (Washington).
—— (2009) 'The World Bank Group Environment Strategy. Concept Note' (http://siteresources.worldbank.org/; 29 March 2010)
Zacharias, D (2008) 'The UNESCO Regime for the Protection of World Heritage as Prototype of an Autonomy-Gaining International Institution' 9 *German Law Journal* 1833.
Zucker, LG (1977) 'The Role of Institutionalization in Culture Persistence' 42 *American Sociologic Review* 726.

8

The Openness of International Organisations for Transnational Public Rule-Making

STEFAN OETER

I. INTRODUCTION: PUBLIC RULE-MAKING AS A PREROGATIVE OF STATE INSTITUTIONS

PUBLIC RULE-MAKING HAS traditionally been a prerogative of the state. The prototype of such public rule-making is statutory legislation enacted by Parliament. As a complementary mode, executive rule-making in the form of decrees and ordinances enacted by the Government as collegiate-body (or by individual ministries) has shaped our image of public rule-making. Such legislation by public bodies may, in certain cases, refer to products of private rule-making, such as technical standards drafted by private standardisation organisations or professional codes of ethics drawn up by associations of professionals of a certain field (Bernstorff 2003: 511–26). Indirectly, via techniques of reference, such private rule-making may become part of public legislation. Perhaps an even more important development is the 'de-centering' of the state. Our traditional construction of public rule-making, at least as far as public law specialists are concerned, was shaped by a strong degree of centralisation of authority. Competent bodies for public rule-making were the parliament, the government and (with a more or less limited role) the head of state. To a certain degree this has changed dramatically, since the authority of setting binding rules as a 'public' body has trickled down to agencies and autonomous or semi-autonomous administrative bodies (Trute 2006: 307 paras 60–88). The result of such process in international relations is the famous phenomenon of 'disaggregating the state', as it was evoked by Anne-Marie Slaughter in her magisterial book *A New World Order* (Slaughter 2004: 12–35). The phenomenon as such is nearly indisputable—the complexity of modern governance requires more and more specialised expertise that cannot be organised in traditional ministerial structures, but requires organisation in more or less autonomous specialised agencies. There exists a wide variation of institutional set-ups in this regard, with famous examples such as the US-type 'regulatory agencies', autonomous central banks, semi-autonomous competition authorities, but also—in the German case—autonomous entities of public law such as churches, public broadcasters, universities, bar associations and other professional associations of the liberal professions organised as public law bodies with (albeit limited) competences of self-regulation (Trute 2006: 307 paras 82–88). Public rule-making thus goes much beyond classical parliamentary legislation and executive rule-making by governments, comprises a wide array of rule-making by administrative agencies and other public bodies.

II. THE ROLE OF INTERNATIONAL ORGANISATIONS IN PUBLIC RULE-MAKING

Such a process of 'disaggregating the state' goes along with simultaneous processes of 'internationalisation' of governance structures. Growing interdependency at a regional and global level has forced states to engage in exercises of rule-making 'beyond the nation-state'. A prototypical form of such rule-making at the international level is the classical international treaty—a body of codified rules negotiated by governmental experts and diplomats at inter-governmental conferences, signed by members of government, then presented to national parliaments for consent and finally ratified by the head of state (eg Tomuschat 2001: 308–24). Such international treaties are the mirroring form of statutory legislation at the international level. Testing out in which fields such treaties might be necessary and which content they might have is usually 'outsourced' to international organisations. As well as the task of producing a first draft of such treaties, international organisations are not 'legislators' in the traditional sense of national legal orders (Schemers and Blokker 2003: 790–821), but they play an important role in international rule-making by shaping the drafting work, by providing the infrastructure for inter-governmental negotiations and—last but not least—by administering the treaty networks, servicing the bodies formed under such treaties and monitoring the implementation of treaty obligations (ibid: 874–900). Such a role entrusted to international organisations should not be underestimated, although in a strict sense it is not 'rule-making'.

The last decades, from 1945 onwards, have seen an exponential growth of international organisations in number but also in the quality of the tasks and functions entrusted to them (eg Tomuschat 2001: 124). Such organisations started as a kind of service tool for international cooperation in specialised fields, offering secretarial services for meetings of governmental experts and for conferences, administering institutionalised networks of experts and specialised authorities, drafting 'soft law' standards and procedures, monitoring the ways and means of how states are adapting to such joint policy programmes and standards (Bindschedler 1983: 123–28, 133–34). Later on, states also started to pool the prerogative of international rule-making in a genuine sense, although limited to specific sectorial fields, in international organisations by entrusting them with the task of preparing and drafting treaties on recurring issues of international affairs. States still have a decisive say in such rule-making, since treaties need signature (and in more important cases also ratification) by states' organs. Public rule-making in these organisations is a very formalised affair and usually needs a specific form, the form of international treaties, in order to become legally binding.

Admittedly, we can observe a widespread phenomenon called the 'setting of treaties on wheels' (Schemers and Blokker 2003: 722–48; Franck 1995: 30–35). The founding treaties of international organisations provide for some programmatic objectives and create an institutional arrangement which is then mandated to operationalise the abstract and general programme into concrete, operational rules. Such 'operationalisation', however, is usually not done in the traditional form of (additional) treaty-making, but is done in the facilitated procedure of organ decision in the framework of the relevant international organisation (Schemers and Blokker 2003: 765–832). Such 'operationalisation' by internal procedures and decisions inside international organisations often will not lead to formally binding rules. In some technical organisations, it is provided that the central decision-making organs may adopt binding decisions on issues of technical detail as provided for in the founding treaties, but in most cases the relevant organ decision will be a mere resolution or recommendation of a (formally) non-binding character (ibid: 765–79). However, such seemingly 'non-binding' decisions can have far-reaching legal significance, in particular as 'subsequent state practice in applying the treaty' in the sense of article 31 paragraph 3 lit (b) of the Vienna Convention on the Law of Treaties.

Dominant actors in the organs of international organisations are still the representatives of Member States, but it is the specialist expert from the executive branch that usually represents the state in the technical bodies of specialised organisations. The decision is usually taken by such experts in a procedure of consensus, sometimes even in majority voting, and not in the usual procedure of amending treaties, handled by the diplomatic apparatus that negotiates an amendment to the treaty and then submits it to parliament for ratification. In such a procedure of consensus-building under specialised experts, inside an expert 'epistemic community', it is—according to all experience—much easier to find a result than by agreeing on a new, more specific rule via treaty-making (Hass 1992: 1–35; Bernstorff 2008: 1947–49).

In a number of cases, these procedures of 'operationalisation' of abstract programmes down to operational rules lead, as has already been mentioned, to legally binding obligations under international law (Schemers and Blokker 2003: 822–32). This is, however, only the case if the representatives of national executives were explicitly entrusted with setting binding sector-specific rules (mostly of a technical nature). Most often this kind of binding 'secondary law' inside international organisations is subject to stringent procedural requirements. Contrary to European Union law, simple majority voting is a rare exception. If voting is provided for at all, it usually requires a relatively high threshold of majority. Often, states prefer requirements of consensus in order to secure national veto positions (ibid: 534–49). Such a veto position may lead to organisational paralysis, may force states into complex package deals—but states are rather reluctant to submit themselves to majority decisions at the international level. Even if majority of voting is provided for in principle, real decision-making usually follows consensual patterns—although the 'shadow of majority voting' may play an important role in such cases, since it forces persistent objectors into willingness to seek compromises.

To sum up: traditional international rule-making, in the form of treaty-making, is cumbersome because negotiations are not only complex and protracted, but the final procedures of making treaties legally binding require the consent of all the governments of states that shall be bound, as well as (at least with treaties requiring ratification) the consent of national parliaments. Collecting all the declarations of consent may cost a lot of time, several years, sometimes even decades, and makes the whole procedure—to a certain degree—hostage to internal politics of Member States. If—in the intermediate time—a national government changes, the achieved consent may break down because the new government might declare that it does not like to be bound by the proposed treaty any more. Important treaties, like the Law of the Sea Convention or the 1977 Additional Protocols to the Geneva Conventions, have experienced such fate with the transition of the Carter administration to the Reagan administration, to give only some telling examples.

Treaty-making is also relatively inefficient in its results since it often leads to bodies of rules that stick to the 'lowest common denominator', thus codifying rules that are obviously insufficient to cope with the challenges which were the reason for entering into negotiations in the first place. Sometimes, treaty-making ends up in a 'pyrrhic victory' if seen under a policy perspective—the results, be they completely insufficient, are often carved in stone for a long time since all political energy has been absorbed by protracted negotiations and the results fixed in the treaty are difficult to change anyway. International treaties, at least if being multilateral treaties organising a large network of Member States, are difficult (if not impossible) to change afterwards. Treaties like the World

Trade Organisation (WTO) Agreement, the *International Covenant on Civil and Political Rights* (ICCPR) or the Geneva Conventions would need the consent of all the existing Member States, ie 130, 150 or 190 states, in order to be changed, a 'mission impossible'. This leads to a troublesome phenomenon—if states have once, with widespread participation, agreed on a multilateral treaty, it becomes nearly impossible to modify its rules, to adapt them to changing circumstances.

III. THE DRIVE TOWARDS INFORMALITY

As a consequence, international organisations, as well as states organised in such organisations, have begun to form parallel transnational administrative networks clustered around international organisations. Such networks have proven to be quite useful, since one can develop rules and standards inside such (informal) networks in a much more informal setting (and following much more informal procedures), with the objective of creating modes of rule-making that are quicker in achieving results, that are more efficient in terms of problem-solving, that are more flexible, and that may easily be adapted to changing circumstances (Bernstorff 2008: 1946–47). However, there is a price to be paid for such flexibility: the rules resulting from such informal procedures are usually not formally binding in legal terms, but will constitute mere standards of 'soft law'.[1] This does not mean that such rules are useless. A consensus achieved in a specific 'epistemic community' of experts may provide a strong guidance for future policy-making. If every expert feels attached to the 'common standard' and thinks that this is the way to go, national administrations (run by such experts) will usually abide by the agreed rules and standards. There are inherent limitations—such informal rule-making does not work in arenas where several 'epistemic communities' are involved, or where the issue becomes a topic of general political discussion. Its potential is limited to 'technical' issues usually dealt with by a relatively close expert community.

Such 'transnational' rule-making has usually been delegated to special bodies that incorporate special expertise not available in the usual fora of decision-making in international organisations, the council or assembly of the organisation. The model seems to have been rather successful. During the last decades we have seen an enormous growth of such specialised bodies either within the framework of international organisations or annexed to international organisations that are involved in the business of rule-making (eg Bogdandy and Dann 2008: 2013–39). Transnational

[1] As to the concept of 'soft law', see Tomuschat (2001: 349–55).

administrative networks (TANs) are not identical to international organisations and its organs, but often coexist in a close, even symbiotic relationship with the relevant international organisation. The membership of certain specialised transnational administrative networks will often converge more or less with the membership in a specialised organ of the sectorially relevant international organisation. Sometimes, the international organisation is the product of a successful transnational administrative network, sometimes an international organisation will develop its own sideline of transnational administrative networks in order to be able to shift problematic dossiers to the informal world of such networks, whilst the network may finally use the formal procedures of the international organisation in order to formalise certain results of informal negotiations. All in all, it is difficult to generalise the relationship between transnational administrative networks and international organisations.

Parts of these transnational administrative networks, but also (parallel or competing) technical bodies within international organisations are staffed with members of specialised bureaucracies beyond the club of usual actors of international diplomacy (Bernstorff 2009: 277–302). Some of them even include experts from industry and Non-Governmental Organisations (NGOs). The advantage of such bodies is, first, the possibility to widen the knowledge-base of decision-making, thus trying to escape the epistemological limitations of public rule-making, and second, the informality that allows to have an open discourse and develop rules beyond the usual mechanisms of public scrutiny (Bernstorff 2009: 279–81). Shifting rule-making to specialised expert bodies or networks has a definite advantage insofar as the discussions in such bodies are to a certain degree much less 'political', more oriented towards standards of professionalism in a certain technical field, and less dominated by ideological and/or political cleavages. Such 'depoliticisation', going along with entrusting rule-making to expert bodies and networks, helps in finding a consensus on substance. Under a professional ethic of 'expertise', it is usually much easier to formulate an agreed standard than under the perceived dictates of 'national interest' (Bernstorff 2008: 1946–47). Discussions in such bodies and networks resembles much more the ideal of a 'deliberation' than this might ever be achieved in the processes of political bargaining which are typical for the formal, 'political' bodies of international organisations.

The following remarks will endeavour to reconstruct the organisational evolution leading to such new forms of public rule-making, and will then—from an institutionalist perspective—try to grasp the rationale behind such development and will attempt to develop a taxonomy of forms of transnational public rule-making in the context of international organisations. A concluding analysis of the problems linked to such modes of rule-making will be undertaken to sketch the inherent limits that the development towards a more informal public rule-making of a transnational nature has to cope with. Transparency and legitimacy of public rule-making may suffer, thus reminding us that a complete 'informalisation' of public rule-making would erode the basis of public authority in modern constitutionalism (Somek 2009: 323–49; Bernstorff 2009: 288–99).

IV. THE EVOLUTION OF TRANSNATIONAL RULE-MAKING IN THE CONTEXT OF INTERNATIONAL ORGANISATIONS

Transnational administrative networks are not at all a new phenomenon, as Christian Tietje reminds us in chapter one on the history of transnational administrative networks. What is clearly new, however, at least from a historical perspective, is the role that international organisations play in bringing together and organising such networks. International organisations were rare phenomena in the international system of the nineteenth and early twentieth century (Bindschedler 1983: 123). The flowering of international organisations is mostly a phenomenon of the second half of the twentieth century. They are either creations of the direct post-World War II order or have developed in the succeeding decades.[2] The purpose and function of such organisations have usually been twofold: they were created in order to assist states in international legal rule-making, as an administrative infrastructure for preparing and servicing inter-governmental negotiations, and often they were also intended as a catalyst for a transnational administrative network in a specific field. Usually, such a first-run transnational administrative network has a coordination function: bringing administrations together to discuss common issues, to exchange information on how they deal with cases and problems that transcend national borders, and to develop common strategies on how to cope with common problems (Bogdandy and Dann 2008: 2020–33). As a result of such discussions, national administrations will learn how their partner administrations in other states perceive a certain problem, how they approach it, and what the political and administrative strategies are in coping with such problems.

This does not exclude activities specifically directed at standard-setting and/or rule-making, however. Rule-making, with the instrument of 'recommendations', is an old characteristic of international organisations. Such recommendations do not enjoy the same legal status as treaty law, but they may nevertheless become legally binding in a formal sense.

[2] Ibid: 123.

Even if they don't, they exercise a strong influence upon administrative practice in Member States since they express a professional consensus of experts. Ignoring such a consensus may make a member of an epistemic community open to strong peer group pressure; after all, they do not want to become an outsider (Bernstorff 2008: 1946–48). The actor concerned will avoid attacking the rule frontally; the actor will prefer denying the applicability of the rule in the individual case or will open a dispute on the interpretation and construction of the unwanted rule. Accordingly, at least on the surface, such formally 'non-binding' rules may operate in a very comparable manner as formally binding sets of rules.

V. THE RATIONALE OF TRANSNATIONAL RULE-MAKING IN THE CONTEXT OF INTERNATIONAL ORGANISATIONS

A question arises from this finding—what is the rationale of transnational rule-making in the context of international organisations? International organisations usually serve as the catalyst, the organisational core of the expert community that tries to develop rules beyond traditional treaty-making—norms that are flexible in their making and are relatively easy to adapt to changed circumstances later on. The institutional structure of an international organisation gives an element of institutional stability and permanency that an expert network driven purely by state administrations would have difficulty developing (Slaughter 2004: 152–61). Networks of specialised administrative bodies often lack the organisational infrastructure that is needed if one wants to systematically coordinate activities on a transnational plane. In these cases, one national administration will usually have to serve as coordinating agency, administering the contacts of the bodies and entities involved, organising meetings and monitoring what is happening in the aftermath of genuine rule-making, in terms of implementation of the rules set. National administrative bodies are easily overburdened with such tasks of a coordinator; in principle, international organisations are much better suited to serve that purpose. International organisations profit from a professional staff composed of technical experts socialised in a multicultural setting, a staff that is much better suited to handle the organisation and daily operation of such professional networks than national administrations. The international organisation has a clear mandate to take care of international contacts, to bring members of expert communities together at one table and to try to develop a consensus under experts on what should be an undisputed rule and/or standard.

The secretariat of international organisations often also has more leeway in political terms than national administrations. The secretariat of an international organisation is not representing the political agenda of one

Member State and its Government, but constitutes a separate international actor that is partly and deliberately made autonomous from national politics (Zacharias 2008: 1933–64). This means that a network secretariat staffed by an international organisation has more freedom to develop proposals for rule-making going against declared interests of individual Member States. Not that there is no political pressure in the secretariat of an international organisation, but that type of political pressure is of a more general nature. It is not linked to specific issues that have been given a high political profile in individual states' self-definition of their 'national interest'. International organisations can—in drafting new rules and standards—ignore such vested interests to a certain degree. Admittedly, there is a limit to such autonomy. Also, international organisations have to bear in mind strongly entrenched 'vested interests' at a national level, in order to calculate which kind of newly-formulated rule might find acceptance afterwards. However, this does not necessarily inhibit drafting work—drafting work that will often be oriented towards professional standards of technical proficiency and towards the perceived adequacy in meeting an underlying political challenge.

However, this does not completely explain why specialised bureaucracies tend to evade into the network-type of arrangements of informal rule-making. Several arguments might speak in favour of informal modes of rule-making. One is the tendency towards 'mission-creep', extending the mandate given to an international organisation to its outer limits, or even going beyond that mandate (Bernstorff 2008: 1945–46). In formal institutions, such 'mission-creep' would all too easily come to its limits. However, if actors shift their activities to an informal setting, formal mandates do not count anymore. An additional aspect is the argument of effectiveness which has already been mentioned above. Traditional modes of rule-making in the form of international treaties are extremely cumbersome, time-consuming and produce enormous transaction costs. Informal rule-making in transnational administrative networks offers a much leaner procedure and much more flexible arrangements of rule-making. Further arguments of effectiveness might also exist. Formal treaty-making might, in a lot of cases, tend towards substantial results that might be described as 'lowest common denominator'; the formal veto positions of players forces actors to enter into compromise packages that endanger the whole enterprise of rule-making. Limiting formal rule-making to certain abstract, programmatic rules and leaving the operationalisation of such rules to expert bodies helps in achieving sensible results (Bogdandy and Dann 2008: 2024–25).

Another 'comparative advantage' of rule-making inside bodies of international organisations or in transnational administrative networks linked to such international organisations can be observed when looking at issues of implementation and compliance control. States are more willing to entrust the task of compliance control, ie monitoring the ways and means of how international rules and standards are implemented, and the results of such implementation to international organisations than to administrative bodies of other states. The result is that compliance control nearly always lies in the hands of international organisations (Oeter 1997: 101–69). Reporting procedures, peer-group review, but also on-site inspections undertaken on the initiative of international organisations are regular instruments in the tool box of institutionalised compliance control.[3] It is easier to accept such intrusive mechanisms when a neutral third, like an international organisation, is entrusted with the relevant functions than if foreign administrations act as supervisors.

In the field of compliance control, in particular, we find a routine of taking on board civil society actors, mostly NGOs, as partners (Bernstorff 2009: 279–80). Often, it is nearly impossible to extract all the information needed for systematic compliance control from state sources—state organs and administrative bodies do not always know what is really going on in certain sectors of society. Often, some participation of NGOs is needed in order to secure a reliable informational basis for compliance control. Any practitioner involved in systems based on state reports knows this phenomenon well: without additional bits and pieces of information coming from civil society, at its best in the form of so-called 'shadow reports', it would often be close to impossible to gain a clear picture of what the record of implementation looks like in a certain country (Liese 2006: 51–69). Even in systems using technical means of collecting data, like quantitative measuring of certain physical or chemical factors, the support of NGOs will often be needed.

VI. THE VARIOUS FORMS OF TRANSNATIONAL RULE-MAKING IN THE CONTEXT OF INTERNATIONAL ORGANISATIONS

If we look at the spectre of different forms that transnational rule-making might take, we find a broad range of possible solutions. These solutions range from very traditional forms of international treaty-making to civil society-based standard-setting enterprises that are either mandated in advance by international organisations, or are afterwards validated by international organisations. As the most current form in-between these two poles, the various kinds of 'soft law' standards, usually adopted as 'resolutions' or 'recommendations', play a particularly important role.[4] These standards adopted by the organs of an international organisation

[3] See the survey of such mechanisms given by Schermers/Blokker 2003: 880–900.
[4] See also Goldmann 2008: 1865–1908.

without any further procedure of ratification are normally not legally binding. Only rarely, in very exceptional cases, such standards adopted by a mere decision of an organ of an international organisation become binding in a formal sense. We can find these exceptional cases in some organisations of regional integration, like the European Union, the African Union, *North American Free Trade Agreement* (NAFTA), Mercosur, but also in some technical organisations such as the *International Civil Aviation Organization* (ICAO) or the International Telecommunication Union (Schermers/Blokker 2003: 824–32; Goldmann 2008: 1893–1900). In some very limited areas, the WTO is also familiar with such binding decisions adopted by the organs of the WTO—most prominently in the case of the granting of waivers.[5]

In general, however, we find a strict separation between binding forms of rule-making that usually have to take on the format of classical international law's formal treaty-making, and informal kinds of rule-making, generally described in international legal doctrine as forms of 'soft law'. The second category is qualified as 'soft' by international lawyers because the rules and standards adopted in the form of resolutions or recommendations usually lack the quality of being legally binding. This does not say anything on their practical impact. So-called 'soft law' standards may in practice be much more efficient than formally legally binding rules of treaty law relegated by states to more or less symbolic devices—a fate that not seldom happens to treaty obligations. National administrations quite often tend to perceive international legal obligations as some kind of 'incomplete rules' of dubious legal quality that should not be taken too seriously. Due to the cumbersome procedures of consensus-building in treaty negotiations, the resulting rules will often constitute a kind of 'formula compromise', a very general norm at a high level of abstraction that needs further operationalisation.

If one bears this in mind, the (seemingly deficient) quality of not being formally-binding proves not to be such a problem. It is rather the binding character of international legal obligations in daily administrative practice that is often somewhat doubtful. In contrast to formal obligations, the lack of a binding nature often tends to be a strategic advantage of 'informal' ways of rule-making. Because such standards are—at least formally—not binding, they can be adopted in a much more lean and flexible procedure than standards in legally binding form. You do not need a cumbersome procedure of treaty-making with participation (and formal consent) of national parliaments, nor a consultation or coordination between different ministries. This spares a lot of time and political energy. Accordingly, specialised administrations show a strong bias towards such 'informal'

[5] As to this instrument see Hilf and Oeter 2005: 195.

means of rule-making. Here, the specialists of a certain sector can deal with each other without interference from the outside and can agree on a result that they consider to be politically sensible without having to fear intervention from general politics. In this way 'epistemic communities' of professional experts tend to set their own sector-specific standards—a rule-making that has the charm of some 'clinical isolation' from general politics and the usual formalities of international law.

The flexibility opened up in this way can also be used to incorporate representatives of business and civil society into the work of rule-making. There is a clear tendency towards the development of 'hybrid' forms of networks (Bernstorff 2009: 279–83). Such 'hybrid' networks might form at the outset of a certain rule-making effort, in particular if 'advocacy networks' succeed in convincing states to adopt a certain set of rules. The task of operationalising and administering the set of rules fixed in the treaty regime will usually be given to an intergovernmental international organisation. There may be good reasons, however, to include civil society actors in the network from the beginning. The structure of the Red Cross movement is a perfect example for such an arrangement (Haug and Gasser 1993). Humanitarian law was the result of a societal movement—of an 'advocacy network'—to phrase it in modern terminology. The Red Cross founded by Henri Dunant, clearly a private organisation, soon convinced governments to take up the issue in international legal treaties. The auxiliary societies that were needed to make the whole system operational, however, were again civil society organisations. In order to develop the system further, the relevant state bureaucracies from the defence sector and foreign affairs ministries linked up with the corresponding civil society sector and formed a joint network of public and private actors. The regular conferences of states parties, the so-called 'Red Cross Conferences', are not classical inter-state conferences but include, alongside the government delegates, representatives of the national Red Cross movements.[6] Both types of actors together are entrusted with the task of operationalising the Geneva Convention system by further rules of an operational, secondary nature—and both types of actors enter into so-called 'pledges', unilateral promises presented to the other parties.

For epistemological reasons, this might quite often make sense. The circles of business and civil society that will afterwards be immediately confronted with the consequences of the proposed standards and rules often have much better information on the potential repercussions on the societal sectors to be regulated than the administrations formally responsible for the sector in the internal governmental systems. To give these circles or their representatives a direct saying in the formulation of

6 See also International Committee of the Red Cross 1994.

standards might help a lot in avoiding mistakes and counterproductive effects. The formal settings of traditional international negotiations and conferences, however, are to a certain degree hostile towards such civil society involvement. In informal procedures it is much easier to bring about the participation and involvement of those societal sectors concerned than in formalised settings of traditional inter-state negotiations. Overarching networks comprising important civil society organisations might also help to overcome internal political resistance from other segments of bureaucracy (Bernstorff 2009: 283–88).

An even more radical form of civil society involvement is the 'outsourcing' of material standard-setting to private organisations, institutionalised networks of private actors. The 'outsourced' processes of standard-setting may still remain part of public rule-making, as long as the international/transnational rules agreed on between states and the respective administrative bodies incorporate the results of such private rule-making (Schuler 2008: 1753–77). In relatively technical sectors of transnational administrative law we have quite a series of examples for such linkage between transnational public rule-making and private standard-setting. However, even under more traditional international legal arrangements, as for example in the context of the WTO, we find such incorporation of private-rule making into public rule-making—think of the reference of the Agreement on Technical Barriers to Trade (TBT) to private sectors' endeavours in the setting-up of technical standards (Hoekman and Kostecki 2001: 185–95).

We can find similar phenomena in the stage of rule interpretation and compliance control. In a lot of treaty regimes, be it in human rights, in environmental law, in international economic law, etc states are not willing to entrust executive bodies with the task of formal rule-making in the sense of 'secondary law'. The task to operationalise the vague and by far too general, largely programmatic standards of treaty law is then left to procedures of treaty interpretation and of monitoring compliance with the treaty. Monitoring states' activities in the implementation of complex international agreements, however, may be practically impossible for inter-state institutions in their traditional composition. Even bodies of governmental experts might not be able to gain a complete picture of what is going on under a specific treaty. Accordingly, for monitoring compliance in sectors where high technical expertise is needed or where very complex arrangements have to be observed in order to give a reliable assessment of the degree of implementation, the involvement of private actors may be necessary. The institutional structures of international organisations have long ago started to take that into consideration (Deisenroth 2000). Even formal mechanisms of compliance control provided for in international treaties more and more often provide for the incorporation of information delivered by civil society actors. This has become a regular part of state reporting procedures, where state reports are regularly balanced by NGO 'shadow reports'. Some treaty bodies instituted by international treaties have now even become formally authorised to interact with NGOs and to take into consideration the information delivered by such civil society actors.[7] The treaty bodies under the two Council of Europe treaties on the protection of national and linguistic minorities, for example, deal directly with NGOs representing minority communities, in addition to state reports and further information delivered by state bureaucracies (Oeter 2004: 131–57). Through their practice of 'on-the-spot visits' in countries under evaluation, they formally discuss issues with civil society representatives and later confront state representatives with the information gained in that way. As a result, a discursive triangle between state administrations, the relevant expert bodies of international organisations and NGOs is created that leads to a qualitatively different kind of discourse than the one that has traditionally been used in inter-state institutions.

However, not all institutional environments are open to such 'hybrid' arrangements. In the WTO, for example, there persisted a long-standing dispute on the role that NGOs should play in the institutional setting (Hilf and Oerter 2005: 152). Most states, in particular the majority of third world states, have shown extreme reluctance to allow a formalised role for NGOs—mostly out of fear of 'regulatory capture', because they are afraid (not without reason) that the organisationally strong NGOs of the North might capture the attention and leave a decisive footprint in the internal decision-making of the organisation, ending up strengthening the concerns and interests of industrialised societies—interests that are overrepresented in the context of the WTO system anyway (Oeter 2004: 361–69).

VII. THE INHERENT LIMITS OF TRANSNATIONAL RULE-MAKING IN THE CONTEXT OF INTERNATIONAL ORGANISATIONS

Transnational rule-making in the context of international organisations has its limits, however. First, there are simple functional limits to such modes of rule-making. In essence it works only where we have clearly defined 'epistemic communities' of administrative experts that can use the advantage of getting rid of the formalities of classical international treaty-making in order to achieve a facilitated mode of rule-making. Such new, transnational modes of rule-making will only be advantageous, however, if the experts can more easily agree on standards than diplomats

[7] See eg art 16 para 2 of the European Charter of Regional or Minority Languages of 1992, ETS No 148.

and politicians would do in the formal procedure of treaty-making. From a functional perspective, such a facilitated mode already becomes problematic when the interests of several 'epistemic communities' of experts overlap and the various communities of specialists cannot easily agree on a common standard.[8] In that situation a kind of arbiter is necessary anyway—and that arbiter will be found either in governmental hierarchy or in political coordination mechanisms at an inter-agency level or even at cabinet level.

There may also emerge collateral damages of facilitated 'transnational' rule-making by administrative bodies. Transparency may suffer. From the outside it may often be difficult to get an idea about what is going on in such highly specialised expert networks and how certain results were eventually achieved. Contrary to formal international negotiations that often take place under a certain public scrutiny and under close monitoring by various administrative agencies/entities, public rule-making at a transnational, inter-administrative level will often happen below the horizon of public attention (Bernstorff 2009: 288–99). As a result, such transnational rule-making may be perceived as rule-making 'by stealth'. Suddenly there exists a standard, and no outsider, ie any person not belonging to the relevant expert community, has an idea how such a standard came about.

In constitutional terms, the trend towards 'informality' of public rule-making threatens to erode the basis of public authority in a modern constitutional system. Public rule-making, at least as far as it has serious repercussions for the life of the population and for business transactions and civil society activities, needs an underlying control by public discourse. Such discourse, however, needs a basic degree of transparency and of public attention, and—at least in the case of rule-making of major political importance—the symbolic debate of the parliament that makes it visible to the public audience that an important decision is being taken. If public rule-making completely fades away from traditional treaty-making with its formalised role of parliaments in the adoption of rules, these arrangements securing some degree of public discourse—and some degree of democratic legitimacy—do no longer work (Deitelhoff 2009: 303–21). Rule-making becomes a purely technocratic exercise. In a lot of highly technical fields, this may make sense. For such technical issues one might solely rely on so-called 'output legitimacy'. However, we should be aware that the shift from formal procedures to 'informal' means of transnational rule making has its political price—a price that must be taken seriously. Accordingly, there is a need to intensively police the boundary line between different kinds of rule-making that

[8] As to this problem, see in particular Fischer-Lescano and Teubner 2006: 72–98, 127–57.

might be sensibly done in a 'transnational' way, and the more political issues of rule-making that require public scrutiny and the symbolic discourse of parliamentarism (Bast 2009: 185–94). Rule-making in its very essence is a political enterprise, not a purely technocratic endeavour that could be left more or less completely to bureaucratic experts. Thus, in many contexts rule-making will need some kind of 'input legitimation' (Lübbe-Wolff 2009: 127–42). This is even true for informal types of rule-making—formal law-making, in the way of a kind of secondary legislation, will always be coupled to the realm of institutionalised 'executive' law-making. The traditional perception that informal rule-making is not really problematic since it does not create any legally binding effects has proven to be overtly naïve—even 'soft law' creates de facto kinds of 'binding effects'. As has been analysed in the course of this contribution, transnational administrative networks creep into the realm of political decision-making exactly because they are often more effective in creating coordinated actions of state organs than formal law-making by treaties. Informal rule-making, however, has to cope with certain inherent problems: it produces external effects that might be described as 'legal externalities', and it might in particular affect non-participants, actors that were not involved in the network developing the rule. Accordingly, in such cases procedural safeguards will be needed—safeguards that in rule-making give a voice to stakeholders which might be affected, safeguards that guarantee that specific interests and concerns of the common good, irrespective of their different capabilities to organise, are balanced in a transparent way. Any suspicion of 'regulatory capture' must be avoided.

VIII. CONCLUSIONS

We have seen that the distinction between the making of legally binding and legally non-binding rules is not completely irrelevant in practice, since it has severe procedural consequences. Formal rule-making that leads to legally binding rules will always be institutionalised in a stringent set of procedural and institutional requirements. Non-binding standards, however, were traditionally neglected in the writings of international legal scholars. However, more recent studies on transnational administrative networks demonstrate that even informal networks engaged in the formulation of seemingly ‹non-binding', soft law standards may produce results with a far-reaching importance (Pereira 2008: 1693–718). Accordingly, the quest for a much more advanced proceduralisation comes up concerning such rule-making networks. Critical issues of legitimacy are at stake, and without serious attempts at developing some basic standards of ‹input legitimacy' of procedural minimum standards, such efforts at informal rule-making will soon get stuck in a quagmire of legitimacy disputes. Of particular concern in this regard are non-participant stakeholders that are affected by the rules set, the problem of 'regulatory capture' and the concern about how issues of the 'public good' may find an adequate representation in such kinds of informal rule-making (Venzke 2008: 1401–428). These are not insurmountable obstacles, but the practice of transnational administrative networks and of international organisations will have to travel a long way until they fulfil such requirements. The inclusion of civil society actors, and the ensuing development of 'hybrid' types of networks, might help here to a certain degree—although such 'hybrid networks' do not solve all the problems and might themselves give rise to new problems.

REFERENCES

Bast, J (2009) 'Das Demokratiedefizit fragmentierter Internationalisierung' in H Brunkhorst (ed), *Demokratie in der Weltgesellschaft* (Baden-Baden, Nomos) 185–94.

Bernstorff, J von (2003) 'Democratic Global Internet Regulation? Governance Networks, International Law and the Shadow of Hegemony' 9 *European Law Journal* 511–26.

—— (2008) 'Procedures of Decision-Making and the Role of Law in International Organizations' 9 *German Law Journal* 1947–49.

—— (2009) 'Zivilgesellschaftliche Partizipation in Internationalen Organisationen: Form globaler Demokratie oder Baustein westlicher Expertenherrschaft?' in H Brunkhorst (ed), *Demokratie in der Weltgesellschaft* (Baden-Baden, Nomos) 277–302.

Bindschedler, RL (1983) 'International Organizations, General Aspects' in R Bernhardt (ed), *Encyclopedia of Public International Law*, Inst 5 (Amsterdam, North-Holland) 119–140.

Bogdandy, A von and Dann, P (2008) 'International Composite Administration: Conceptualizing Multi-Level and Network Aspects of the Exercise of International Public Authority' 9 *German Law Journal* 2013–39.

Deisenroth, D (2000) 'Societal Verification: Wave of the Future?' in T Findlay (ed), *Verification Yearbook 2000* (London, VERTIC) 265–68.

Deitelhoff, N (2009) 'Fairness oder Demokratie? Zu den Chancen deliberativer Verfahren im internationalen Regieren' in H Brunkhorst (ed), *Demokratie in der Weltgesellschaft* (Baden-Baden, Nomos) 303–21.

Fischer-Lescano, A and Teubner, G (2006) 'Regime-Kollisionen. Zur Fragmentierung des globalen Rechts' (Frankfurt aM, Suhrkamp).

Franck, TM (1995) *Fairness in International Law and Institutions* (Oxford, Clarendon) 30–34.

Goldmann, M (2008) 'Inside Relative Normativity: From Sources to Standard Instruments for the Exercise of International Public Authority' 9 *German Law Journal* 1865–908.

Haas, PM (1992) 'Introduction: Epistemic Communities and International Policy Coordination' 46 *International Organization* 1–35.
Haug, H and Gasser, HP (1993) (eds) *Humanity for All. The International Red Cross and Red Crescent Movement* (Bern, Haupt).
Hilf, M and Oeter, S (2005) *WTO-Recht* (Baden-Baden, Nomos).
Hoekman, BM and Kostecki, MM (2001) *The Political Economy of the World Trading System* (Oxford, OUP).
International Committee of the Red Cross (ed) (1994) *Handbook of the Red Cross and Red Crescent Movement* (Geneva, ICRC).
Liese, A (2006) Epistula (non) 'Erubescit. Das Staatenberichtsverfahren als Instrument internationaler Rechtsdurchsetzung' 81 *Die Friedens-Warte*, 51–69.
Lübbe-Wolff, G (2009) 'Die Internationalisierung der Politik und der Machtverlust der Parlamente' in H Brunkhorst (ed), *Demokratie in der Weltgesellschaft* (Baden-Baden, Nomos) 127–42.
Oeter, S (1997) 'Inspection in International Law–Monitoring Compliance and the Problem of Implementation in International Law' 28 *Netherlands Yearbook of International Law* 101–69.
—— (2004) 'The European Charter of Regional or Minority Languages' in ECMI/ Council of Europe (ed), *Mechanisms for the Implementation of Minority Rights* (Strasbourg, Council of Europe Publishing) 131–57.
—— (2004) 'Comment: Globalization, Welfare, and the Democratization of the WTO' in E Benvenisti and G Nolte (eds), *The Welfare State, Globalization, and International Law* (Berlin, Springer) 361–69.
Pereira, RA (2008) 'Why Would International Administrative Activity Be Any less Legitimate?—A Study of the Codex Alimentarius Commission' in 9 *German Law Journal* 1693–718.
Schermers, HG and Blokker, NM (2003) *International Institutional Law*, 4th edn (Leiden, Nijhoff) 790–821.
Schuler, G (2008) 'Effective Governance through Decentralized Soft Implementation: The OECD Guidelines for Multinational Enterprises' 9 *German Law Journal* 1753–77.
Slaughter, AM (2004) *A New World Order* (Princeton, Princeton University Press) 12–35.
Somek, A (2009) 'Demokratie als Verwaltung: Wider die deliberativ halbierte Demokratie' in H Brunkhorst (ed), *Demokratie in der Weltgesellschaft* (Baden-Baden, Nomos) 323–49.
Tomuschat, C (2001) 'International Law: Ensuring the Survival of Mankind on the Eve of a New Century, in Hague Academy of International Law' (ed) 281 *Recueil des Cours* (The Hague, Nijhoff) 9–438, 308–24.
Trute, HH (2006) 'Die demokratische Legitimation der Verwaltung' in W Hoffmann-Riem, E Schmidt-Assmann and A Vosskuhle (eds), *Grundlagen des Verwaltungsrechts Vol.1: Methoden, Maßstäbe, Aufgaben, Organisation* (München, CH Beck) 307–90.
Venzke, I (2008) 'International Bureaucracies from a Political Science Perspective–Agency, Authority and International institutional Law' 9 *German Law Journal* 1401–28.
Zacharias, D (2008) 'The UNESCO Regime for the Protection of World Heritage as Prototype of an Autonomy-Gaining International Institution' 9 *German Law Journal* 1833–64.

Part V

Regional Representation and Participation of Civil Society

9

Towards 'Open' Transnational Administrative Networks: Emerging Structural Features

KARSTEN NOWROT

I. INTRODUCTION

THE TRANSBOUNDARY COOPERATION of national bureaucracies on an informal or even institutionalised basis is not a recent phenomenon. Rather, the roots of these developments date well back into the nineteenth century. Furthermore, these transgovernmental relations have received attention by scholars, who published on this topic as early as from the 1840s onwards. However, from the early twentieth century until the 1990s, this phenomenon received little attention from the majority of academics (see generally thereto Tietje 2010).

In spite of its longstanding tradition, there are a number of aspects frequently connected with this form of internationalisation of administrative relations, which are of relatively recent origin. In general, these relations have increasing importance in state practice (see eg Slaughter 2004: 44 et seq). Corresponding to this fact, legal scholars and social scientists have also shown renewed interest in this research topic. In particular, two issues rank prominently among the body of literature that address what is now frequently characterised as 'transnational administrative networks'. First,—with very few exceptions and proportional to the awareness of their rising practical importance—it has only been in the previous decade that these cooperative relations have been viewed as having 'produced their own *legal problems*' (Schmidt-Aßmann 2006: 258). This includes various challenges with regard to, inter alia, aspects of participation, transparency, acceptance, accountability, orientation towards the common good, and, from a broader perspective, the increasingly important issue of legitimacy.[1] Second, in recent years there has been a notable change in the descriptive and analytical approaches to conceptualising the international cooperation of national administrative units, including the possible involvement of their counterparts from international organisations in this regard. In the past, individual scholars classified this phenomenon as 'technical internationalism',[2] 'multibureaucratic decisionmaking' (Kaiser 1971: 708) and 'transgovernmental relations' (Keohane and Nye 1974: 41 et seq). By contrast, more recently, scholars have taken up the term and concept of 'networks', which is mirrored in descriptions such as 'transnational administrative networks', 'transgovernmental networks' or 'transnational bureaucracy networks'.[3] This reinforces the prominent position occupied by the notion of 'networkism' in many other academic disciplines (Nickel 2006: 167 et seq)—a perception which even gave rise to the stipulation of a new and interdisciplinary scientific paradigm of network analysis (see eg Schweizer 2003: 152 et seq).

Networks are commonly understood as polycentric and relatively stable structures, lying in the borderland between hierarchical organisations and purely market-oriented mechanisms.[4] Applying this concept to transnational administrative relations leads from an analytical perspective to the conclusion that this phenomenon joins the class of a variety of private and intermediate global governance regimes of more recent origin, such as the United Nations Global Compact, the Global Reporting Initiative (GRI), the Forest Stewardship Council (FSC) or the Marine Stewardship Council (MSC). The potential of these and numerous other network-structured initiatives as steering subjects in the international realm is also receiving increasing attention. Consequently, the notion of 'transnational administrative networks' also provides an analytical basis for comparing the cooperative structures of bureaucrats with other steering mechanisms of an intermediate or private character.

Against this background, the present contribution is aimed at evaluating the emergence of a number of organisational features in private and intermediate global governance regimes in light of their potential significance for the structural configuration of transnational administrative networks. Thereby, particular emphasis will be placed on processes of regionalisation and the formation of representative organs. In addition, the contribution also addresses the underlying reasons

[1] For a few examples of contributions that address these issues, see Picciotto 1996/1997: 1045 et seq; Hamann and Ruiz Fabri 2008; Möllers 2005: 378 et seq; also, as early as at the beginning of the 1970s, see Kaiser 1971; Keohane and Nye 1974: 60.

[2] See Tietje 2010, with additional references.

[3] See eg Slaughter 2004: 36 et seq; Raustiala 2002; Warning 2006.

[4] On these characteristics of network structures, see eg, Peters 2001: 217 et seq.

for these structural developments within steering networks, as well as their role when facing the abovementioned challenges and concerns arising from the internationalisation of administrative relations. It will be argued that—in addition to developing and implementing overarching normative guiding principles—further attention should be given to the organisational perspective when assessing potential approaches to make this type of transnational public governance more effective. Furthermore, the analysis will reveal that processes of regionalisation and the emergence of representative bodies in network structures can considerably contribute in enhancing the often-disputed legitimacy of these steering mechanisms. The structural features developed in the realm of private and intermediate steering regimes have thus the notable potential to play a significant part in the development of a model of the 'open administrative network' as a necessary new paradigm for today's transgovernmental relations.

The chapter is divided into three parts. The first part (II.) starts by providing a brief overview of the functions and limits of the network concept. The discussion will furthermore focus on two organisational characteristics of intermediate and private steering networks, as well as their visibility in the realm of transnational administrative networks. The second part (III.) evaluates the underlying motives for these organisational developments and the extent of their applicability to transgovernmental cooperative regimes. Finally, the third part (IV.) addresses the legitimacy challenges arising from network governance. This final section outlines the need for a partial reconceptualisation of transgovernmental relations on the basis of a model of the 'open' transnational administrative network that takes into account the potential of the structural features developed primarily by their intermediate and private counterparts.

Finally, it appears important to emphasise that the findings developed and expressed in this contribution are not based on anything close to a comprehensive analysis of all existing transnational administrative networks. Rather, its empirical basis is limited to research on institutional developments in a number of well-known bureaucracy steering regimes that have already received considerable attention in the literature. Among these are the International Organization of Securities Commissions (IOSCO), the Codex Alimentarius Commission (CAC), the Intergovernmental Forum on Chemical Safety (IFCS), the Inter-Organization Programme for the Sound Management of Chemicals (IOMC), and the Basel Committee on Banking Supervision. This narrower empirical scope certainly does not foreclose the possibility that the conclusions drawn in this contribution are of general application in the realm of transnational administrative networks. However, a respective confirmation is subject to further in-depth analysis of this field in the future.

II. REDISCOVERING TRADITIONAL ORGANISATIONAL CHARACTERISTICS IN NETWORK STRUCTURES

A. Functions and Limits of the Network Model—an Overview

In light of its popularity in a growing number of academic disciplines, the term 'network' has sometimes been issued the 'mixed blessing' of being no more than a 'buzzword' (see thereto Nohria 1992: 3; Börzel 1998: 253). However, recourse to this concept in connection with the steering phenomenon of administrative as well as private and intermediate regimes should not merely be regarded as mirroring a popular trend. Instead, it constitutes a, in principle, legitimate approach to describe and categorise a variety of steering mechanisms. Although they are not all of recent origin, such mechanisms are of increasing practical importance in the international system and cannot—at least in their entirety—be captured by traditional categories (see eg Schuppert 2006: 1058 et seq; Vesting 2004a: 64).

Nevertheless, applying the term and idea of networks is no substitute for—and thus does not release from—an analysis of the organisational structures of these steering phenomena. It is frequently emphasised that the strength of the network model lies in its value as a descriptive category. Consequently, at least at first sight, its utility as a methodological approach for the conceptualisation of the cooperative regimes is rather limited (Kenis and Schneider 1991: 44; Möllers 2005: 382). Therefore, it is not sufficient to merely take recourse to this concept when trying to clarify the 'in its openness from a legal perspective rather irritating term "network"' (Franzius 2006: 197). Rather, there is a clear need to move beyond a descriptive network model in order to provide the necessary theoretical basis for its conceptualisation and normative evaluation. This task requires first and foremost the identification of a suitable approach for the analytical penetration of the organisational structures and legitimacy challenges arising from these steering networks (see eg Ziller 2004: 280 et seq).

From a legal perspective, recourse can be taken in this regard to some ideas currently discussed in connection with the conceptualisation of the European Union's normative order, as well as the normative structure of the international system as a whole. The views expressed in this connection are in principle also applicable to the dogmatic analysis of networks. Based on their methodological approaches, it is possible to identify two main lines of argument in the literature: the '*sui generis* approach' and the '*transfer* approach' (Nowrot 2007: 124 et seq). The *sui generis* approach is based on the assumption that the novel phenomenon does not only require a new descriptive categorisation. Rather, also the respective conceptualisation cannot take recourse to traditional state-centred models. Therefore, precisely in order to overcome the 'perseverance of the "touch of stateness"', the development of equally unprecedented analytical concepts is necessary (Shaw and Wiener 2000: 65 et seq; Schmitter 1996: 132 et seq).

This line of reasoning is also sometimes advanced in scholarly writings on networks, eg by qualifying networks as 'legal institutions *sui generis*' (Teubner 2003: 46) or where doubts are expressed as to whether these phenomena can be conceptualised on the basis of familiar categories (Schuppert 2006: 1059; Vesting 2004a: 64 et seq). Nevertheless, the core of this approach—the call for the application of models *sui generis*—has certain dogmatic flaws, at least if taken as the analytical starting point. The classification of a phenomenon as *sui generis* itself may—as already emphasised in the literature—reflect a degree of classificatory incompetence and mirroring awkwardness (MacCormick 1999: 142; Dann 2006: 55). However, it is even more difficult to reconcile the underlying assumption of the need for a 'conceptual *tabula rasa*' with the commonly shared perception that the legal analysis requires the adoption of a comparative approach oriented towards the identification of similarities with existing categories and concepts.[5]

In light of these findings, the present evaluation of certain organisational features developed in steering networks will primarily be based on the 'transfer approach'. This approach revolves around an assessment of the applicability of traditional state-centred concepts—by way of a deliberate transfer and, thus if necessary, with adjustments—to new normative phenomena (generally eg von Bogdandy 2006: 9 et seq). While having already for quite some time been taken recourse to with regard to the European Union and the international legal system, so far it has largely been neglected in recent discussions on the conceptualisation of the organisational structures developed by transnational administrative, intermediate and private networks.

B. Emerging Structural Features in Private and Intermediate Governance Networks

As yet, no consensus has emerged on the constitutive elements of networks. Nevertheless, an overview of the literature reveals that networks are often characterised as informal, 'loosely-structured' dialogue-, learning- and standard-setting fora with a 'horizontal form of organization' (see eg,

[5] See eg, von Bogdandy 2006: 10 ('Yet this demand clashes with the very nature of legal thinking, which, at its heart, is comparative and dependent on the repertoire of established doctrines of viable institutions.').

Raustiala 2002: 5; Vesting 2004b: 259 et seq; Khagram 2006: 100). According to this perception, these characteristics distinguish networks from traditional, predominantly hierarchically-organised regulatory mechanisms operating at the domestic level. In addition, they also differentiate networks from international governmental organisations, with their often quite elaborate institutional structures and membership only being open to certain categories of actors, in particular states and in some cases other international organisations (Witte, Reinicke and Brenner 2000: 179, 184).

This general characterisation of networks most certainly continues to apply to many, probably even the majority of these steering regimes. Nevertheless, more recently an increasing number of intermediate and private governance networks have not only acquired a remarkable degree of organisational consolidation (Möllers 2005: 371; Warning 2006: 322 et seq), they are also increasingly displaying structural features that can be captured and systemised by taking recourse to state-based concepts. In order to illustrate this proposition, the following section will look at two tendencies—regionalisation and the creation of representative organs—as processes that might eventually result in the emergence of federalised and parliamentarised network structures.

i. Vertical Dimension: The Case of Regionalised Network Structures

Despite their still primarily horizontal form of organisation, a number of private and intermediate networks have established—again in the form of networks—regional sub-units which enjoy considerable autonomy in the exercise of their functions.

A first, practical, example of this type of 'association of networks' or 'network of networks' (Thérien and Pouliot 2006: 56) is the structural design of the FSC. This steering regime has already attracted considerable attention in the literature.[6] Frequently characterised in the literature as a transnational network, the institution was founded in 1993 and is aimed at the promotion of responsible forest management on the basis of a certification scheme.[7] As of April 2010, it consisted of 828 members, among them corporations, Non-Governmental Organisations (NGOs), business associations, trade unions and individuals.[8] Originally, the FSC had displayed a quite centralised, horizontal structure. However, in 2002,

[6] See the observation by Vogel 2008: 275 ('more research has been published on the FSC and forestry codes than on all other codes combined').

[7] Generally on the FSC see www.fsc.org; as well as, for example, Nowrot 2009a, with numerous further references.

[8] Forest Stewardship Council Membership List of 1 April 2010 at www.fsc.org/fileadmin/web-data/public/document_center/membership_documents/FSC_Membership_List_2010_04_01.pdf.

it started to develop 'a comprehensive strategy to decentralize its global network' aimed at increasing the effectiveness of its steering regime by paying closer attention to regional distinctions. As a consequence of this process, as of April 2010, more than 50 'national initiatives' enjoy a considerable degree of independence in terms of their organisational structure, and have already developed more than 30 national forest management standards. The FSC now regards these initiatives as 'the foundation of [its] global network' and ' [its] gateway to the members and stakeholders' (see Nowrot 2009a: 881 et seq).

The institutional structure of the equally well-known United Nations Global Compact constitutes another notable example in this regard. Initiated by the former UN Secretary-General Kofi Annan in 1999, the Global Compact dialogue forum and learning network is perhaps the most important initiative for promoting corporate social responsibility at the global level.[9] Previously quite centrally organised, the reorganisation of the Global Compact was carried out mainly on the basis of its 'New Governance Structure', which was published in September 2005 by the Global Compact Office.[10] The Global Compact recognised that its 65 'Local Networks'[11] 'play increasingly important roles in rooting the Global Compact within different national, cultural and language contexts, and also in helping to manage the organizational consequences of rapid expansion'.[12] As a consequence, the steering functions of these sub-networks within the initiative as a whole were strengthened, and their status and self-governing character clarified (Nowrot 2005: 21 et seq). The continued 'critical' significance of these entities within the Global Compact as a whole has also, for example, more recently found its expression in the discussions in the Global Compact Board on 'The Strategic Direction of the UN Global Compact, 2008-2009'.[13]

These examples show the tendency among private and intermediate governance networks to create a more complex institutional framework by developing decentralised, vertical structures. Such regionalisation processes are even more significant given that the networks in question

[9] Generally on the United Nations Global Compact see www.unglobalcompact.org; see also Braun and Pies 2009; Nowrot 2005, which contain numerous additional references.

[10] See 'The Global Compact's Next Phase' of 6 September 2005 at www.unglobalcompact.org/docs/about_the_gc/2.3/gc_gov_framew.pdf.

[11] This represents the number of local networks as of April 2010.

[12] 'The Global Compact's Next Phase' of 6 September 2005 para 3.11 (n 10).

[13] See Final Report on the Meeting of the Global Compact Board at the United Nations Headquarters in New York on 1 May 2008, 6 at www.unglobalcompact.org/docs/news_events/9.1_news_archives/2008_05_21/GCBoardreport_May2008_final.pdf; see also generally the 2007 United Nations Global Compact Network Report—Deepening the Engagement of Participants at the Local Level at www.unglobalcompact.org/docs/news_events/8.1/LNReport_FINAL.pdf.

increasingly display organisational features which create a structural kind of 'unity in diversity'—a characteristic commonly associated at the domestic level with the principle of federalism (see eg, Korioth 2006: 599). Thereby, it hardly needs to be emphasised that the application of the concept of federalism to steering regimes (eg, governance networks in the international system) differs considerably from the state-centred understanding of this principle at the national level. However, as already pointed out, the 'transfer approach' does not involve exporting state-centred concepts 'lock, stock and barrel' to governance regimes at the supra- and international level (see eg, von Bogdandy 2006: 10). Rather, it focuses on a deliberate transfer that takes into account the differences between states and more recent forms of governance regimes. This represents a sectoral reformulation of federalism, which results in a more functional and de-territorialised understanding of the concept that is equally applicable to respective structures in the supra- and international realms.[14] These developments result from processes that are related to a type of 'top-down federalisation' (generally thereto eg, Maier 1990: 228) and have the potential to produce some type of federalised network structure (see also Meidinger 2006: 66 et seq; Kern 2003: 289).

ii. Horizontal Dimension: Creation of Representative Organs

Turning to the horizontal dimension, it is noteworthy that an increasing number of intermediate and private steering networks possess at least one institutionalised 'executive organ', such as the Board of Directors of the GRI and the FSC or the Global Compact Office. Even more significant is that they have also created formalised bodies made up of representatives from all of the network members, such as the 'Global Compact Leaders Summit' or the FSC General Assembly. In principle, these formal bodies resemble the plenary organs of traditional international organisations. However, some of these plenary bodies have made remarkable modifications relative to the organs of their classical counterparts. The most well known example is probably the FSC General Assembly, which consists of a social, environmental and economic chamber. Voting power is equally divided among the three chambers, with the aim 'to maintain the balance of voting power between different interests without having to limit the number of members'.[15] Moreover, in order to 'achieve a balance between

[14] On the increasing support in the literature of this proposition see eg, Delbrück 2004; Peters 2001: 183 et seq; Oeter 2006; Nowrot 2006: 664 et seq, each with additional references.

[15] See para 12 of the By-Laws of the Forest Stewardship Council of September 1994, last revised in June 2006 at www.fsc.org/fileadmin/web-data/public/document_center/institutional_documents/1_1_FSC_By_Laws_2006.pdf.

Northern and Southern perspectives within each chamber', these bodies are further divided into a Northern and a Southern 'sub-chamber', both of which hold 50 per cent of the voting power of the respective chamber.[16]

Already, these innovative organisational structures—a division of its General Assembly into a producer, a trade and industry, as well as a civil society chamber with equal voting powers has also for instance been adopted by the Common Code for the Coffee Community (4C Association)[17]—are quite notable (see eg, Kern 2003: 302 et seq; Meidinger 2006: 53; Dingwerth 2008). However, this also applies in particular to governing bodies created by private and intermediate networks that consist of a limited number of individuals being elected by the network members, often in separate ballots within each category of participating actors. A vivid example is the 'Global Compact Board' established by the UN Global Compact on the basis of its 'New Governance Structure' in September 2005 (Nowrot 2005: 18 et seq). It is comprised of 20 members representing four 'constituency groups': the United Nations, business, civil society and labour. These members act in a 'personal capacity' and have the task of providing 'ongoing strategic and policy advice for the initiative as a whole'.[18] While its current members were appointed by the UN Secretary-General in April 2006 following 'a comprehensive consultation process involving all Global Compact stakeholders, including the Local Networks',[19] it is envisioned that subsequent representatives 'will be determined by elections (within groupings) to three-year terms, with one-third of the seats being up for election every year'. There is also the possibility for one additional term by re-election.[20]

Another example in this regard is the revised governance structure of the GRI—a network aimed at developing and improving universally applicable sustainability reporting guidelines[21]—which included the creation of the 'GRI Stakeholder Council'. It consists of 60 members from five geographic regions, which represent the four constituent categories: business, mediating institutions, civil society and labour. Twenty members of the Stakeholder Council are rotated annually. From this group, 12 members are elected by their respective stakeholder constituency and eight are

[16] Ibid paras 13 and 14; see also Nowrot 2009a: 872 et seq.

[17] See § 12 of the Statutes of the Common Code for the Coffee Community Association of 2007 at www.sustainable-coffee.net/download/2007/4C_004_Statutes_v1.0_en.pdf.

[18] See para 4.5 of the document 'The Global Compact's Next Phase' of 6 September 2005 at www.unglobalcompact.org/docs/about_the_gc/2.3/gc_gov_framew.pdf.

[19] See www.unglobalcompact.org/.

[20] Paragraph 4.7 of the document 'The Global Compact's Next Phase' of 6 September 2005 at www.unglobalcompact.org/docs/about_the_gc/2.3/gc_gov_framew.pdf.

[21] Generally, on the GRI, see www.globalreporting.org/Home; see also eg, Nowrot 2009b, with additional references.

appointed by the Stakeholder Council itself.[22] Furthermore, the Council of the 4C Association is worth mentioning: it is made up of 17 members elected by the three chambers of the General Assembly, and functions as the network's 'representative decision making body'.[23] Finally, to mention one further example, attention can be drawn to the MSC, an institution that works towards environmentally responsible fisheries management and practices on the basis of a labelling scheme.[24] The MSC's Stakeholder Council 'act[s] as a point of reference, participation, liaison and representation' and is comprised of up to 40 representatives, who are nominated by the three constituencies: the public interest, commercial and socio-economic categories, as well as the recently created developing world category (Nowrot 2009c: 713 et seq).

These types of 'network organs' cannot merely be regarded as another (aside from the secretariats) executive body of the steering network, a perception that is, for example, frequently applied to the UN Security Council in the realm of the traditional international organisations (see eg, Delbrück 2002: para 1). Such a characterisation is already precluded by the self-conception of the networks, which regularly emphasise the representative function of these stakeholder councils[25] as a reference to a central element of parliamentarianism. The GRI, for instance, even regards this body as 'similar to a parliament'.[26] This representative function is also demonstrated by the fact that the members of these stakeholder councils are neither bound by the instructions nor exchangeable representatives of the network members. This is not the case with regard to state representatives in the respective organs of international organisations (see eg, Schermers and Blokker 2003: §§ 412, 418). Since the representatives are elected in their individual capacity, and thus do not serve as 'representatives of their professional organizations or associations', they are holders of an independent mandate. Although they are 'expected to represent broadly their stakeholder constituency

[22] See paragraphs 2.1 et seq of the Rules and Procedures for the GRI Stakeholder Council, approved by the GRI Board of Directors on 1 June 2007 at www.globalreporting.org/NR/rdonlyres/7C983DFA-ED76-46EC-8096-C0C7B16DB6DB/0/SakeholderCouncilRandP.pdf; see also Nowrot 2009b: 122 et seq.

[23] See the By-Laws for the Council of the Common Code for the Coffee Community Association at www.sustainable-coffee.net/download/2007/4C_008_Bylaws_Council_v1.0_en.pdf; as well as § 13 of the Statutes of the Common Code for the Coffee Community Association of 2007 at www.sustainable-coffee.net/download/2007/4C_004_Statutes_v1.0_en.pdf.

[24] On the MSC, see the information provided at www.msc.org; see also, eg, Nowrot 2009c, with additional references.

[25] See eg, the By-Laws for the Council of the Common Code for the Coffee Community Association at www.sustainable-coffee.net/download/2007/4C_008_Bylaws_Council_v1.0_en.pdf.

[26] See www.globalreporting.org/AboutGRI/WhoWeAre/StakeholderCouncil.

and region from which they were elected',[27] their primary function is to provide 'ongoing strategic and policy advice for the initiative as a whole'.[28]

These institutional developments that have led to the creation of representative organs must be evaluated in light of the intense debate on the need for and possibilities of parliamentarising governance structures beyond the reach of the nation state, an issue that up until now has primarily been discussed with regard to the organisational structure of traditional international organisations. Admittedly, the proposals brought forward in this regard have remained theoretical and are unlikely to be implemented on a practical level any time soon (see eg, Delbrück 2003: 37). Nevertheless, due to their innovative character, the current organisational tendencies in private and intermediate governance networks, as well as the experience to be gathered from their functioning in the future clearly have the potential to contribute to the evolution of parliamentarianism in the institutional structures at the transnational level—an issue that has already been qualified as 'one of the most important contemporary challenges' (von Bogdandy 2005: 464).

C. ... and Transnational Administrative Networks?

From a comparative perspective, the question arises whether and to what extent these organisational characteristics are also identifiable in the realm of transnational bureaucracy networks. In the same way as private and intermediate governance regimes, an increasing number of these forms of international administrative cooperation no longer mirror the still conventional perception of networks as exclusively loosely structured fora. Rather, some of them have developed a remarkable degree of institutionalisation which is clearly comparable to the organisational structures of traditional international organisations (Möllers 2005: 371; Warning 2006: 322 et seq). Significant examples in this regard are the institutional settings of the IOSCO,[29] the CAC (Herwig 2010), the IFCS, the IOMC (on the latter two institutions see eg, Warning 2006; Warning 2009),

[27] Paragraph 2.2.3 of the Rules and Procedures for the GRI Stakeholder Council, approved by the GRI Board of Directors on 1 June 2007, see www.globalreporting.org/NR/rdonlyres/7C983DFA-ED76-46EC-8096-C0C7B16DB6DB/0/SakeholderCouncilRandP.pdf.

[28] Paragraph 4.5 of the document 'The Global Compact's Next Phase' of 6 September 2005, see www.unglobalcompact.org/docs/about_the_gc/2.3/gc_gov_framew.pdf; see also eg, Marine Stewardship Council Terms of Reference of July 2002 at www.msc.org/assets/docs/Governance/TORofStC.doc.

[29] On IOSCO in general, as well as its institutional structure see www.iosco.org; see also eg, Alexander 2009.

and the (primarily intermediate) governance network constituted by the International Organization for Standardization (ISO) (Tamm Hallström and Higgins 2009). Furthermore, even the Basel Committee on Banking Supervision—probably one of the most well-known administrative regulatory networks, often perceived as a 'small, homogeneous, and insular' club of bankers as well as bureaucrats and thus regularly subject to criticism as to its legitimacy (see eg, Barr and Miller 2006: 17 et seq; De Meester 2008: 108)—displays an organisational structure consisting of four main sub-committees as well as various sub-groups and working groups.[30]

Despite these general similarities, at least the empirical basis of the present analysis[31] does not support the conclusion that transnational administrative networks have currently developed regionalised or representative organisational structures to the same extent as their pendants in the realm of private and intermediate governance regimes. Thereby, one has to acknowledge the emergence of certain decentralisation tendencies within the institutional structure of some of these bureaucracy networks. IOSCO, for instance, has four 'Regional Standing Committees': the Africa/Middle East, Asia-Pacific, European and Interamerican Committee. According to the description provided by this association, these committees are to 'meet to discuss specific regional problems of the members of IOSCO' and elect one member each of the IOSCO Executive Committee.[32] Among the committees and task forces of the CAC are also six regional committees: the Food and Agriculture Organisation of the United Nations (FAO)/World Health Organization (WHO) Coordinating Committees for Africa, Asia, Europe, Latin America and Caribbean, the Near East, as well as North America and South West Pacific.[33] An additional example is the IFCS, which in accordance with its 'Terms of Reference' also aims at providing 'policy guidance with particular emphasis on regional and subregional cooperation'.[34] It has established five 'Regional Groups' covering Africa, Asia and Pacific, Central and Eastern Europe, Latin America and the Caribbean as well as 'Western Europe and Others'.

However, in comparison to the abovementioned bodies in private and intermediate governance networks, these regional groups and committees do not presently enjoy a similar position and degree of autonomy within the network as a whole. Aside from their role in electing the members of executive bodies, they also do not exercise any substantial

[30] For further details see www.bis.org/bcbs/organigram.pdf.

[31] See above (I.).

[32] See IOSCO Annual Report 2007 www.iosco.org/annual_reports/annual_report_2007/# at 34.

[33] See www.codexalimentarius.net/web/committees.jsp.

[34] IFCS Guidelines and Procedures of November 2006 www.who.int/ifcs/documents/ifcs_guidelines.pdf at 13.

direct steering functions within the overall framework of the respective transnational administrative network. This generally more passive and thus less significant status (relative to the network as a whole) distinguishes them, for example, from the 'National Initiatives' of the FSC, which occupy an essential role in the 'multilevel system of standard setting' through the development of national forest management standards (Dingwerth 2008). The same applies to the 'Local Networks' of the United Nations Global Compact, which, for instance, 'play an important role in support of the communications on progress and integrity measures'[35] at the implementation level, such as the, by now, more formalised complaint procedure.[36] Although the institutional structure of some transnational administrative networks displays tendencies of decentralisation, these trends cannot be equated so far with the regionalisation processes emerging in the realm of private and intermediate networks, which could potentially lead to the emergence of some type of federalised network structures.[37]

Similar conclusions can be drawn with regard to processes for creating representative bodies in the organisational structures of transnational administrative networks. Some of the members, such as the Executive Committee of IOSCO and the Forum Standing Committee of IFCS, are designated via elections by the participating entities.[38] However, these selection processes cannot be equated with the emergence of the above-mentioned forms of 'stakeholder councils' in private and intermediate governance regimes. Rather, these bear a closer resemblance to the operating procedures of the executive organs of traditional international organisations, a view that is supported by the clear executive character and functions of these committees.

III. EVALUATING THE STRUCTURAL TRENDS: INTENDED INFORMALITY VERSUS OPTIMISED STEERING CAPACITIES

These findings support the frequently shared perception of the structural diversity of governance networks (see eg, Schuppert 2000: 386). Apparently,

[35] Paragraph 4.3 of the document 'The Global Compact's Next Phase' of 6 September 2005 at www.unglobalcompact.org/docs/about_the_gc/2.3/gc_gov_framew.pdf.

[36] See thereto Global Compact Note on Integrity Measures, at No 4, last updated on 26 November 2007 at www.unglobalcompact.org/docs/about_the_gc/Integrity_measures/Integrity_Measure_Note_Eng_Dec07.pdf.

[37] Generally, on the distinction between decentralisation and federalisation at the domestic level see eg, Maier 1990: 228.

[38] See IOSCO Annual Report 2007 www.iosco.org/annual_reports/annual_report_2007/# at 34; and para 7.2 of the Terms of References of the IFCS Guidelines and Procedures of November 2006 at www.who.int/ifcs/documents/ifcs_guidelines.pdf.

processes of regionalisation and the emergence of representative bodies—at least on the basis of the empirical scope of this analysis[39]—are not manifested to the same extent in the institutional design of cooperative steering regimes, such as the transnational administrative networks whose members do predominantly belong to only one specific category of actors and often intentionally strive for more flexible, informal arrangements (see eg, Zaring 1998: 301 et seq, 329). Although this does not foreclose the emergence of organisational structures altogether, it is in fact presumably precisely the importance attached to the informality of their relationships and the corresponding reserved attitude towards an institutionalised and specified allocation and delegation of 'competences', which prevents transnational bureaucracy regimes from developing the structural features that are increasingly displayed by intermediate and private networks in the transnational realm.

In addition, albeit speculative, it might not be too far-fetched to assume that the cooperating administrative units do not intend to draw attention to the increasingly prominent role in the steering structures of the international system by modelling these arrangements after traditional international organisations or basing them on state-centred concepts. It should be noted that the creation of transnational administrative networks after all finds one of its primary motivations and justifications in the fact that these regimes differ from traditional international organisations (see also Möllers 2008: 221), which are perceived to be considerably more formalised and institutionalised, but also more or less unsuitable and unnecessary for the respective purposes pursued. These findings might also serve as a possible explanation for the fact that, although the participating administrative bodies are most certainly in their respective domestic setting quite accustomed to parliamentary and federal (sub-)structures, they do not generally utilise these same institutional approaches when forming bureaucracy steering regimes at the transnational level.

To the contrary, processes of regionalisation and the establishment of new representative bodies are increasingly visible in the organisational structures of governance networks that have already reached a certain size in terms of the number of participants (regarding this, see Kern 2003: 289) and whose members include a variety of different categories of supra-, sub- and, in particular, non-state actors such as NGOs, corporations, business associations, trade unions and individuals. Often, the informal nature of their cooperative relationships does not particularly matter to these members. They do not intentionally strive for the 'culture of informality' resulting from the network character of their arrangements.

[39] See above (I.).

Instead, structural reasons have caused these actors to develop other institutional frameworks in order to consolidate their governance regimes. Prominently among these reasons is the fact that it is under current public international law, in the same way as with regard to administrative units, impossible for them to create an international organisation in the classical sense (see eg, Zaring 1998: 305 et seq, 327 et seq; Möllers 2005: 370 et seq). While the respective consolidation processes sometimes result in the emergence of new, innovative organisational forms, the members of these networks also make use of concepts that are common to international organisations or which have their roots in domestic approaches.

Another point worth exploring in connection with the potential applicability of these organisational developments to transnational administrative networks is an evaluation of the underlying motives that lead to the emergence of these structures. A first aspect contributing to the development of regionalised structures in the organisation of governance networks might already be identified in the decentralised character of the international system as a whole. At the domestic level, it is frequently observed that the public and private institutions of federal states typically also take the form of federal organisational arrangements (see eg, Korioth 2006: 599). Aside from this specific factor, the considerations generally connected with the establishment of federal structures are manifold and disputed. Nevertheless, there is almost general agreement that the ordering concept of federalism intends to create—by way of political and legal decentralisation—conditions for subject- and citizen-oriented decision-making processes that take into account regional particularities. In this way, federal structures help to stabilise and integrate the regime as a whole by means of effective and—from the perspective of its members and other affected persons and entities—accepted steering mechanisms (see eg, Jestaedt 2004: 795 et seq).

In principle, these underlying considerations are also applicable to the respective institutional developments in private and intermediate networks. This is a further indication that these organisational tendencies might eventually lead to the emergence of federalised network structures. Already the examples of the FSC and the Global Compact show that the creation of regionalised structures is also aimed at, inter alia, the observance of regional particularities by 'rooting the Global Compact within different national, cultural and language contexts',[40] the multiplication of opportunities for participation by network members and other

[40] See para 3.11 of the document 'The Global Compact's Next Phase' of 6 September 2005 at www.unglobalcompact.org/docs/about_the_gc/2.3/gc_gov_framew.pdf.

interested actors,[41] and enhancing the effectiveness of the network's steering functions.[42]

Similar considerations form the underlying basis of structural developments in a growing number of private and intermediate governance networks that have resulted in the emergence of representative organs. Reflecting one of the essential purposes pursued by the modern idea of representation, they are also aimed at creating preconditions for the effective steering capacity of larger networks by mitigating the negative effects of a possible 'cacophony of unstructured participation' (Chesterman 2008: 49) on the basis of boards and councils whose members represent the respective regime as a whole. Due to the fact that they were elected by the participants, such bodies can base their decisions generally on the acceptance of the network members.[43]

In sum, it is not merely a kind of 'institutional mimicry' which forms the underlying motive for the emergence of regionalised and representative institutional structures in larger regimes consisting of a variety of different categories of actors. Rather, the respective organisational features can be explained on the basis of considerations of framing the decision-making processes within governance networks in a more effective way, as well as at the same time increasing the acceptance of the respective results and thus—with effectiveness and acceptance mutually reinforcing each other—ultimately optimising the steering capacities of these networks.

IV. LEGITIMACY PROLIFERATED: TOWARDS A PARADIGM OF THE 'OPEN ADMINISTRATIVE NETWORK'

The process of regionalisation of network structures and the emergence of representative bodies do not only serve to optimise the steering capacities of the transnational regimes in question. Depending on one's understanding of this concept, they also have the potential to contribute to the legitimacy of the governance functions exercised by these arrangements. The legitimatory challenges that arise from the steering activities of administrative, intermediate and private networks in the transnational realm

[41] See eg, FSC Social Strategy: Building and Implementing a Social Agenda, Version 2.1 of 17 February 2003 at www.fsc.org/keepout/en/content_areas/77/32/files/FSC_Social_Strategy_version_2_1.pdf Appendix VI: The Challenge of Decentralization at 50 ('FSC's decentralization process [...] has the potential to better involve members and stakeholders in the FSC system and to encourage participation in discussions on systems and policy').

[42] Ibid ('Decentralization is seen as a tool to improve the efficiency and effectiveness of FSC's delivery of its mission').

[43] Generally, on the notion that representation aims at creating effective governance structures for larger political units, while at the same time providing for participatory rights of the members, see Madison 1982: 63 et seq; Mill 1861: 69.

have already been qualified as 'emerging as one of the central questions—perhaps *the* central question—in contemporary world politics' (Moravcsik 2005: 212). Taking into account the complexity of these issues—which are in addition intrinsically tied to the controversy about the legitimacy of the changing regulatory structures at the domestic level as well as in the international system as a whole—it hardly needs to be emphasised that it will neither be feasible to, nor is this contribution aimed at elaborating on all the manifold implications of the possible existence of and potential remedies for the 'chronic lack of legitimacy' (Picciotto 1996/1997: 1047; see also eg, Möllers 2008: 220 et seq) of these types of network governance in a comprehensive way.[44] Since this contribution is primarily aimed at evaluating the applicability of state-centred concepts to network structures, this final part largely confines itself to explore—on the basis of the currently intensive and controversial discussions as to the legitimacy of steering networks as well as respective developments in practice—the emergence of the 'open administrative network' model as a new paradigm for transgovernmental relations.

In light of the fact that the diversity and complexity of regulatory mechanisms in the international realm don't, in general, allow for the establishment of comparable allocative structures, it becomes more and more recognised also among legal scholars that traditional concepts of legitimacy developed under the conditions of the territorial nation state such as, in particular, the one requiring 'unbroken' and preferably rather short 'chains of legitimacy' (see eg, Böckenförde 2004: 438 et seq) constitute an increasingly inadequate approach for legitimising the respective steering regimes.[45] The distinction between 'input-oriented' and 'output-oriented' models developed by Fritz Scharpf (Scharpf 1972, 21 et seq; see also Peters 2001: 517 et seq) is useful for identifying three main lines of argument in the literature regarding the resulting need for a conceptual change of legitimacy. Some scholars have exclusively relied on 'input-oriented' legitimising strategies by developing transnational concepts of democracy. David Held's model of a 'cosmopolitan democracy' (see eg, Held 1995: 221 et seq) falls within this category, even though its implementation appears quite unrealistic at this time (Zürn and Leibfried 2005: 22). On the other end of the spectrum are those academics that argue for an entirely 'output-oriented' model of legitimacy (see eg, Peters 2001: 580 et seq).

The majority of legal scholars, however, who are sympathetic towards a conceptual change of the understanding of legitimacy, favour more

[44] For a more comprehensive assessment, see eg, Slaughter 2004: 217 et seq; Delbrück 2003; Möllers 2005: 278 et seq; Nowrot 2006: 601 et seq, each with further references.

[45] See eg, Tietje 2003: 1094 et seq; Kingsbury, Krisch and Stewart 2005: 48 et seq; Hoffmann-Riem 1999: 375.

complex approaches comprising of input- and output-oriented elements.[46] According to these pluralistic models, it is necessary to determine for each individual regulatory regime whether a sufficient number of legitimising factors exist that substitute or mutually reinforce each other (see eg, Hoffmann-Riem 1999: 377; Schliesky 2004: 719). Although there is no *numerus clausus* to limit the potential aspects to be taken into account (Schliesky 2004: 719), it is nevertheless possible to identify a number of factors that are regarded as important. From an output-oriented perspective, the effective realisation of the common good is generally viewed as one of the most important legitimising factors for such regulatory structures.[47] In order to facilitate this optimal orientation towards the realisation of the common good, a prominent position is—in the realm of 'input-oriented' factors—occupied by the requirement of transparency in the decision- and rule-making processes. Furthermore, transparency also constitutes one of the central preconditions for providing effective opportunities for participation by interested and affected actors.[48]

When applying these pluralistic approaches to transnational governance networks, it is first important to emphasise the potential that regionalisation processes and the emergence of representative bodies have to contribute to the legitimacy of these steering mechanisms. The purpose of these institutional structures is to enhance the effectiveness and acceptance of member-oriented decision-making processes that take into account regional particularities. These aims are generally recognised as important legitimising factors (Hoffmann-Riem 1999: 377; Schliesky 2004: 718 et seq).

By requiring that steering regimes work towards the realisation of the common good on the basis of transparent, as well as participatory and thus inclusive decision-making processes, it can—from a broader perspective—furthermore be concluded that the respective pluralistic understanding is, with regard to the necessary prerequisites for achieving an adequate level of legitimacy, in principle oriented towards the role model of what can be characterised as an open, cooperative and thereby inclusive transnational governance network. Indeed, a number of developments in practice indicate that the model of an open transnational steering network is beginning to emerge as an overarching paradigm, or normative 'guiding vision' (see Voßkuhle 2007: 137 et seq), for private, intermediate as well as bureaucracy networks. Steering regimes in the intermediate and private sectors have in general always—albeit to a varying degree—striven to

[46] See eg, Krisch 2006; Schliesky 2004: 588 et seq, each with numerous further references.
[47] See eg, Hoffmann-Riem 1999: 377; Schliesky 2004: 691.
[48] On the importance of these two legitimising factors see eg, Hoffmann-Riem 1999: 377; Cassese 2005: 688 et seq.

promote transparent and inclusive decision-making procedures. This is for example also indicated by the respective processes of regionalisation and parliamentarisation. However, transnational administrative networks have also more recently started to display—on the basis of various techniques—a more open attitude towards providing other categories of actors with opportunities for participation.

From an institutional perspective, a quite ambitious approach to enhance participatory options is the possibility of membership without voting rights granted by some transnational administrative networks to certain categories of non-state actors. For example, in 1999 the International Association of Insurance Supervisors (IAIS) introduced a new membership category called 'observership' for insurance companies, insurance brokers or accounting firms. Membership in this category entitles the (currently more than 120) observer members to be involved in all consultation procedures.[49] Further examples are provided by the 'affiliate membership' of IOSCO,[50] the possibility of participation without the right to vote given to intergovernmental organisations as well as NGOs by the IFCS,[51] and the opportunity for 'international industry, labour and public interest non-governmental organizations that have significant activities in the area of focus' to participate as members in the 'Technical Coordinating Groups' of IOMC.[52] Finally, the CAC also offers a number of options for private actors to participate in its standard-setting activities. Although membership in the CAC is limited to states in accordance with article 2 of the Statutes of the CAC,[53] international NGOs, including business associations, can obtain an 'observer status' on the basis of the 'Principles concerning the Participation of International Non-Governmental Organizations in the Work of the Codex Alimentarius Commission'. This status includes, inter alia, the right to submit written statements and to take part in the discussions upon invitation by the respective chairpersons.[54] CAC members also have the opportunity to, and frequently do, include representatives from the business sector and NGOs in their national delegations (see eg, Herwig 2010; Nowrot 2006: 309 et seq).

[49] See www.iaisweb.org/; as well as eg, Baker and Mathews 2009: 378.

[50] See www.iosco.org/about/index.cfm?section=categories.

[51] See paras 3.2 and 3.3 of the Terms of References of the IFCS Guidelines and Procedures of November 2006 at www.who.int/ifcs/documents/ifcs_guidelines.pdf; as well as Warning 2009.

[52] See www.who.int/iomc/groups/standard_operating_procedures.pdf; see also eg, Warning 2009.

[53] Statutes of the CAC, reprinted in: Codex Alimentarius Commission 2010. ftp://ftp.fao.org/codex/Publications/ProcManuals/Manual_19e.pdf.

[54] See para 5.1 of the Principles concerning the Participation of International Non-Governmental Organizations in the Work of the Codex Alimentarius Commission, reprinted in ibid.

A number of transnational administrative networks have also created an institutionalised cooperative structure, which promotes an opening up towards other networks of the same category. For example, the 'Joint Forum' was established in 1996 under the aegis of the Basel Committee on Banking Supervision, the IOSCO and IAIS in order 'to deal with issues common to the banking, securities and insurance sectors, including the regulation of financial conglomerates'.[55] In addition, these steering regimes have more recently also developed a number of other more informal approaches to improve their transparency and inclusiveness. To mention but one example in this connection, the Basel Committee on Banking Supervision—despite being characterised as 'relatively robust in the face of external [legitimacy] challenges' (Marcussen 2006: 203)—has, in the process of revising its Capital Accord of 1988, which is commonly referred to as 'Basel I', considerably enhanced its efforts to provide for transparency and public consultation. Whereas the negotiations leading to the adoption of Basel I were 'conducted more or less exclusively within the circles of supervisory experts with some input from academics' (Speyer 2006: 113; see also eg, Barr and Miller 2006: 24), the development of the revised Capital Adequacy Framework (Basel II) between 1999 and 2004 was accompanied by the publication of drafts authored by the Basel Committee and influenced by various consultation processes.[56]

V. OUTLOOK

In light of these developments in the transgovernmental realm, it should, finally, also be stated that the categorisation of this currently emerging paradigm of an open, cooperative transnational governance network certainly borrows from the model of 'open statehood'. According to this concept, the increasing international interdependence and permeability of states has not only led to profound changes in the international system and its legal order, but ultimately also affects our understanding of statehood itself (see eg, Hobe 1997; Hobe and Nowrot 2007: 274 et seq). The previously prevailing perception of 'closed statehood', a term reminiscent of Johann Gottlieb Fichte's *Der geschloßne Handelsstaat* published in 1800, characterised by the sovereign state acting as a unitary entity in international relations and being 'based on the notions of self-assertion, self-reliance, and self-sufficiency' (Delbrück 2001: 5), gave way to an understanding of the state opening up to international cooperation. This was achieved by states creating and participating in formal and informal

[55] See the information at www.bis.org/bcbs/jointforum.htm.

[56] See eg, Barr and Miller 2006: 24 et seq; Tsingou 2008; Speyer 2006: 109 et seq; De Meester 2008: 108 et seq.

cooperative mechanisms not only at the interstate level, but in particular also with increasingly influential non-state actors in order to provide an effective regulatory scheme for the political, economic, ecological and social processes which they are, to a growing extent, unable to control while acting on their own. The necessarily reconceptualised perception of the sovereignty of these 'open states' was famously expressed by Abram Chayes and Antonia Handler Chayes in their outstanding work 'The New Sovereignty':

> It is that, for all but a few self-isolated nations, sovereignty no longer consists in the freedom of states to act independently, in their perceived self-interest, but in membership in reasonably good standing in the regimes that make up the substance of international life' (Chayes and Handler Chayes 1995: 27).

In light of the conceptual content of the model of 'open statehood', the application of this term and concept to the realm of transnational administrative networks appears to be appropriate for at least two reasons. On the one hand, the internationalisation of administrative relations is not only generally challenging the 'state-centralized theory on public law that placed the state to the centre of any consideration' (Schmidt-Aßmann 2006: 251). Rather, it has also frequently been perceived as contributing to the need for a changing understanding of statehood and thus to the emergence of the notion of the 'open state' (see eg, Hobe 1997; Hobe and Nowrot 2007: 274 et seq). On the other hand, the paradigm of open transnational administrative networks rightly conveys the need—in order to prevent, in this realm, the continuation or resurrection of the notion of closed statehood by other means—for the underlying conceptual ideas of open stateness to also become widely accepted with regard to these increasingly important bureaucracy steering regimes.

REFERENCES

Alexander, K (2009) 'International Organization of Securities Commissions' in C Tietje and A Brouder (eds), *Handbook of Transnational Economic Governance Regimes* (Leiden/Boston, Martinus Nijhoff) 439–47.

Baker, T and Mathews, E (2009) 'International Association of Insurance Supervisors' in C Tietje and A Brouder (eds), *Handbook of Transnational Economic Governance Regimes* (Leiden/Boston, Martinus Nijhoff) 377–84.

Barr, MS and Miller, GP (2006) 'Global Administrative Law: The View from Basel' 17 *European Journal of International Law* 15–46.

Böckenförde, W (2004) 'Demokratie als Verfassungsprinzip' in J Isensee and P Kirchhof (eds), *Handbuch des Staatsrechts der Bundesrepublik Deutschland,* 3rd edn (Heidelberg, CF Müller) vol II, 429–96.

Börzel, TA (1998) 'Organizing Babylon—On the Different Conceptions of Policy Networks' 76 *Public Administration* 253–73.

von Bogdandy, A (2005) 'Parlamentarismus in Europa: Eine Verfalls- oder Erfolgsgeschichte?' 130 *Archiv des öffentlichen Rechts* 445–64.
—— (2006) 'Constitutional Principles' in A von Bogdandy and J Bast (eds), *Principles of European Constitutional Law* (Oxford and Portland, Hart Publishing) 3–52.
Braun, J and Pies, I (2009) 'United Nations Global Compact' in C Tietje and A Brouder (eds), *Handbook of Transnational Economic Governance Regimes* (Leiden/Boston, Martinus Nijhoff) 253–65.
Cassese, A (2005) 'Administrative Law Without the State? The Challenge of Global Regulation' 37 *New York University Journal of International Law & Politics* 663–94.
Chayes, A and Handler Chayes, A (1995) *The New Sovereignty—Compliance with International Regulatory Regimes* (Cambridge et al, Harvard University Press).
Chesterman, S (2008) 'Globalization Rules: Accountability, Power, and the Prospects for Global Administrative Law' 14 *Global Governance* 39–52.
Codex Alimentarius Commission (CAC) (2010) *Procedural Manual*, 9th edn (CAC).
Dann, P (2006) 'Thoughts on a Methodology of European Constitutional Law' in P Dann and M Rynkowski (eds), *The Unity of the European Constitution* (Berlin et al, Springer) 37–59.
De Meester, B (2008) 'Multilevel Banking Regulation: An Assessment of the Role of the EC in the Light of Coherence and Democratic Legitimacy' in A Follesdal, RA Wessel, and J Wouters (eds), *Multilevel Regulation and the EU—The Interplay between Global, European and National Normative Processes* (Leiden/Boston, Martinus Nijhoff) 101–43.
Delbrück, J (2001) 'Structural Changes in the International System and its Legal Order' 11 *Schweizerische Zeitschrift für Internationales und Europäisches Recht* 1–36.
—— (2002) Article 24 in B Simma (ed), *The Charter of the United Nations—A Commentary*, 2nd edn (Oxford, Oxford University Press) vol I, 442–52.
—— (2003) 'Exercising Public Authority Beyond the State: Transnational Democracy and/or Alternative Legitimation Strategies?' 10 *Indiana Journal of Global Legal Studies* 29–43.
—— (2004) 'Transnational Federalism: Problems and Prospects of Allocating Public Authority Beyond the State' 11 *Indiana Journal of Global Legal Studies* 31–55.
Dingwerth, K (2008) 'North-South Parity in Global Governance: The Affirmative Procedures of the Forest Stewardship Council' 14 *Global Governance* 53–71.
Franzius, C (2006) 'Governance und Regelungsstrukturen' 97 *Verwaltungs-Archiv* 186–219.
Hamann, A and Ruiz Fabri, H (2008) 'Transnational Networks and Constitutionalism' 6 *International Journal of Constitutional Law* 481–508.
Held, D (1995) *Democracy and the Global Order—From the Modern State to Cosmopolitan Governance* (Cambridge, Polity Press).
Hobe, S (1997) 'Statehood at the End of the 20th Century—The Model of the Open State: A German Perspective' 2 *Austrian Review of International and European Law* 127–54.
Hobe, S and Nowrot, K (2007) 'Whither the Sovereign State?' 50 *German Yearbook of International Law* 243–302.

Hoffmann-Riem, W (1999) 'Strukturen des Europäischen Verwaltungsrechts—Perspektiven der Systembildung' in E Schmidt-Aßmann and W Hoffmann-Riem (eds), *Strukturen des Europäischen Verwaltungsrechts* (Baden-Baden, Nomos) 317–82.

Jestaedt, M (2004) 'Bundesstaat als Verfassungsprinzip' in J Isensee and P Kirchhof (eds), *Handbuch des Staatsrechts der Bundesrepublik Deutschland*, 3rd edn (Heidelberg, CF Müller) vol II, 785–841.

Kaiser, K (1971) 'Transnational Relations as a Threat to the Democratic Process' 25 *International Organization* 706–20.

Kenis, P and Schneider, V (1991) 'Policy Networks and Policy Analysis: Scrutinizing a New Analytical Toolbox' in B Marin and R Mayntz (eds), *Policy Networks—Empirical Evidence and Theoretical Considerations* (Frankfurt aM, Campus) 25–59.

Keohane, RO and Nye, JS (1974) 'Transgovernmental Relations and International Organizations' 27 *World Politics* 39–62.

Kern, K (2003) 'Globale Governance durch transnationale Netzwerkorganisationen—Möglichkeiten und Grenzen zivilgesellschaftlicher Selbstorganisation' in D Gosewinkel et al (eds), *Zivilgesellschaft—national und transnational* (Berlin, Sigma) 285–307.

Khagram, S (2006) 'Possible Future Architectures of Global Governance: A Transnational Perspective/Prospective' 12 *Global Governance* 97–117.

Kingsbury, B, Krisch, N and Stewart RB (2005) 'The Emergence of Global Administrative Law' 68 *Law and Contemporary Problems* 15–61.

Korioth, S (2006) 'Föderalismus' in W Heun, M Honecker, M Morlok and J Wieland (eds), *Evangelisches Staatslexikon* (Stuttgart, Kohlhammer) 596–600.

Krisch, N (2006) 'The Pluralism of Global Administrative Law' in 17 *European Journal of International Law* 247–78.

MacCormick, N (1999) *Questioning Sovereignty—Law, State, and Nation in the European Commonwealth* (Oxford, Oxford University Press).

Madison, J (1982) 'The Federalist No. 14, November 30, 1787' in A Hamilton, J Madison and J Jay, *The Federalist Papers* (with an Introduction and Commentary by G Wills, New York et al, Bantam) 62–67.

Maier, H (1990) 'Der Föderalismus—Ursprünge und Wandlungen' 115 *Archiv des öffentlichen Rechts* 213–30.

Marcussen, M (2006) 'The Transnational Governance Network of Central Bankers' in M-L Djelic and K Sahlin-Andersson (eds), *Transnational Governance—Institutional Dynamics of Regulation* (Cambridge, Cambridge University Press) 180–204.

Meidinger, E (2006) 'The Administrative Law of Global Private-Public Regulation: The Case of Forestry' 17 *European Journal of International Law* 47–87.

Mill, JS (1861) *Considerations on Representative Government*, 2nd edn (London, Parker & Bourn).

Möllers, C (2005) 'Transnationale Behördenkooperation' 65 *Zeitschrift für ausländisches öffentliches Recht und Völkerrecht* 351–89.

—— (2008) *Die drei Gewalten—Legitimation der Gewaltengliederung in Verfassungsstaat, Europäischer Integration und Internationalisierung* (Weilerswist, Velbrück Wissenschaft).

Moravcsik, A (2005) 'Is there a Democratic Deficit in World Politics? A Framework for Analysis' in D Held and M Koenig-Archibugi (eds), *Global Governance and Public Accountability* (Malden et al, Blackwell) 212–39.
Nickel, R (2006) 'Participatory Transnational Governance' in C Joerges and E-U Petersmann (eds), *Constitutionalism, Multilevel Trade Governance and Social Regulation* (Oxford/Portland, Hart Publishing) 157–95.
Nohria, N (1992) 'Is a Network Perspective a Useful Way of Studying Organizations?' in N Nohria and RG Eccles (eds), *Networks and Organizations: Structure, Form, and Action* (Boston, Harvard Business School Press) 1–22.
Nowrot, K (2005) *The New Governance Structure of the Global Compact* (Halle/Saale, Beiträge zum Transnationalen Wirtschaftsrecht No 47).
—— (2006) *Normative Ordnungsstruktur und private Wirkungsmacht* (Berlin, Berliner Wissenschafts-Verlag).
—— (2007) 'On the Unifying Self-Conception of a Republican European Union' in N Neuwahl and S Haack (eds), *Unresolved Issues of the Constitution for Europe—Rethinking the Crisis* (Montréal, Les Éditions Thémis) 107–32.
—— (2009a) 'Forest Stewardship Council' in C Tietje and A Brouder (eds), *Handbook of Transnational Economic Governance Regimes* (Leiden/Boston, Martinus Nijhoff) 865–87.
—— (2009b) 'Global Reporting Initiative' in C Tietje and A Brouder (eds), *Handbook of Transnational Economic Governance Regimes* (Leiden/Boston, Martinus Nijhoff) 117–32.
—— (2009c) 'Marine Stewardship Council' in C Tietje and A Brouder (eds), *Handbook of Transnational Economic Governance Regimes* (Leiden/Boston, Martinus Nijhoff) 705–29.
Oeter, S (2006) 'Federalism and Democracy' in A von Bogdandy and J Bast (eds), *Principles of European Constitutional Law* (Oxford and Portland, Hart Publishing) 53–93.
Peters, A (2001) *Elemente einer Theorie der Verfassung Europas* (Berlin, Duncker & Humblot).
Picciotto, S (1996/1997) 'Networks in International Economic Integration: Fragmented States and the Dilemmas of Neo-Liberalism' 17 *Northwestern Journal of International Law & Business* 1014–56.
Raustiala, K (2002) 'The Architecture of International Cooperation: Transgovernmental Networks and the Future of International Law' 43 *Virginia Journal of International Law* 1–92.
Scharpf, F (1972) *Demokratietheorie zwischen Utopie und Anpassung*, 2nd edn (Konstanz, Universitäts-Verlag).
Schermers, HG and Blokker, NM (2003) *International Institutional Law*, 4th edn (Boston et al, Martinus Nijhoff).
Schliesky, U (2004) *Souveränität und Legitimation von Herrschaftsgewalt* (Tübingen, Mohr Siebeck).
Schmidt-Aßmann, E (2006) 'Internationalisation of Administrative Law: Actors, Fields and Techniques of Internationalisation—Impact of International Law on National Administrative Law' 18 *Revue européenne de droit public* 249–68.
Schmitter, PC (1996) 'Imagining the Future of the Euro-Polity with the Help of New Concepts' in G Marks, FW Scharpf, PC Schmitter and W Streeck (eds), *Governance in the European Union* (London et al, SAGE) 121–50.

Schuppert, GF (2000) *Verwaltungswissenschaft* (Baden-Baden, Nomos).
—— (2006) 'Verwaltungsorganisation und Verwaltungsorganisationsrecht als Steuerungsfaktoren' in W Hoffmann-Riem, E Schmidt-Aßmann and A Voßkuhle (eds), *Grundlagen des Verwaltungsrechts* (Munich, CH Beck) vol I, 995–1081.
Schweizer, S (2003) *Politische Steuerung selbstorganisierter Netzwerke* (Baden-Baden, Nomos).
Shaw, J and Wiener, A (2000) 'The Paradox of the European Polity' in MG Cowles and M Smith (eds), *The State of the European Union* (Oxford, Oxford University Press) vol 5, 64–88.
Slaughter, A-M (2004) *A New World Order* (Princeton/Oxford, Princeton University Press).
Speyer, B (2006) 'Governing Global Financial Markets—Basel I and II: The Role of Non-State Actors' in GF Schuppert (ed), *Global Governance and the Role of Non-State Actors* (Baden-Baden, Nomos) 101–16.
Tamm Hallström, K and Higgins, W (2009) 'International Organization for Standardization' in C Tietje and A Brouder (eds), *Handbook of Transnational Economic Governance Regimes* (Leiden/Boston, Martinus Nijhoff) 201–11.
Teubner, G (2003) 'Die Perspektive soziologischer Jurisprudenz: Das Recht der Netzwerke' in S Machura and S Ulbrich (eds), *Recht-Gesellschaft-Kommunikation: Festschrift für Klaus F. Röhl* (Baden-Baden, Nomos) 40–50.
Thérien, J-P and Pouliot, V (2006) 'The Global Compact: Shifting the Politics of International Development?' in 12 *Global Governance* 55–75.
Tietje, C (2003) 'Die Staatsrechtslehre und die Veränderung ihres Gegenstandes: Konsequenzen von Europäisierung und Internationalisierung' in 118 *Deutsches Verwaltungsblatt* 1081–96.
—— (2010) 'History of Transnational Administrative Networks' in chapter one of this volume.
Tsingou, E (2008) 'Transnational Private Governance and the Basel Process—Banking Regulation and Supervision, Private Interests and Basel II' in J-C Graz and A Nölke (eds), *Transnational Private Governance and its Limits* (London et al, Routledge) 58–68.
Vesting, T (2004a) 'Die Staatsrechtslehre und die Veränderung ihres Gegenstandes: Konsequenzen von Europäisierung und Internationalisierung' 63 *Veröffentlichungen der Vereinigung der Deutschen Staatsrechtslehrer* 41–70.
—— (2004b) 'The Network Economy as a Challenge to Create New Public Law (beyond the State)' in K-H Ladeur (ed), *Public Governance in the Age of Globalization* (Aldershot/Burlington, Ashgate) 247–87.
Vogel, D (2008) 'Private Global Business Regulation' 11 *Annual Review of Political Science* 261–82.
Voßkuhle, A (2007) 'The Reform Approach in the German Science of Administrative Law: The Neue Verwaltungsrechtswissenschaft' in M Ruffert (ed), *The Transformation of Administrative Law in Europe* (Munich, Sellier) 89–141.
Warning, M (2006) 'Transnational Bureaucracy Networks: A Resource of Global Environmental Governance? The Case of Chemical Safety' in G Winter (ed), *Multilevel Governance of Global Environmental Change* (Cambridge, Cambridge University Press) 305–29.
—— (2009) *Transnational Public Governance* (Basingstoke, Palgrave Macmillan).

Witte, JM, Reinicke, WH and Brenner, T (2000) 'Beyond Multilateralism: Global Public Policy Networks' *Internationale Politik und Gesellschaft* 176–88.

Zaring, D (1998) 'International Law by Other Means: The Twilight Existence of International Financial Regulatory Organizations' 33 *Texas International Law Journal* 281–330.

Ziller, J (2004) 'Public Administration, Networks and Law' in A Benz, H Siedentopf and K-P Sommermann (eds), *Institutionenwandel in Regierung und Verwaltung—Festschrift für Klaus König zum 70. Geburtstag* (Berlin, Duncker & Humblot) 279–84.

Zürn, M and Leibfried, S (2005) 'Reconfiguring the National Constellation' in S Leibfried and M Zürn (eds), *Transformations of the State?* (Cambridge, Cambridge University Press) 1–36.

10

Transnational Governance Networks and Democracy: What Are the Standards?

JENS STEFFEK AND MARIANA GOMES PEREIRA

I. DEMOCRACY AND INTER/TRANSNATIONAL GOVERNANCE: THE RISE OF A DEBATE

IS TRANSNATIONAL GOVERNANCE through networks a serious threat to democracy or can it help adapt it to the global interdependencies of the twenty-first century? Scholarly assessments are mixed. Optimists often point to the potential for more participation and enhanced quality of policy-making through governance networks. Sceptics respond by highlighting problems of inequality, exclusion, and lack of accountability. In this chapter we seek to bring a bit more theoretical and conceptual rigor to this debate and suggest an agenda for empirical research. We distinguish two key dimensions for assessing the democratic quality of governance networks. First, there is the 'internal perspective', focusing on the composition of governance networks and their mode of operation. Here, we would need to study which societal interests are represented in the governance network, and how deliberative equality is protected against power asymmetries. Second, there is the 'external perspective', focusing on the relations between networks and their wider societal environment. One key problem in this respect is the linking of debates that take place within networks to wider public discourses; a second major issue is the ability of citizens or groups to effectively contest the decisions or recommendations made by a network. We conclude that if transnational governance networks are representative, if their deliberations are shielded against capture by powerful interest groups, if they are responsive to public criticism, and if their decisions can be contested there is no need to worry about their impact on democracy.

Concerns about the legitimacy and accountability of international and transnational governance[1] are a relatively recent phenomenon. Elementary forms of international governance date back at least to the multilateral conference diplomacy of the eighteenth and nineteenth century (see also Tietje in chapter one). Its key function was the preservation of peace and the establishment of some rudimentary form of international order (*cf* Coplin 1964). It was supplemented in the course of the nineteenth century by forms of functional, issue-specific cooperation among states to tackle problems arising from increasing mobility, economic interdependence, and the advent of new technologies. Typical problems regulated by such early forms of functional governance concerned transboundary traffic rules,[2] transboundary postal services,[3] telecommunications,[4] and intellectual property rights (*cf* Paris Convention 1883; Berne Convention 1886).

Over the course of the twentieth century, international governance intensified enormously. The foundation of new organisations and more informal governance regimes did not occur as a linear development, but came in waves of internationalisation—waves that were particularly pronounced after the two world wars (Kennedy 1987). The dual core of international peace diplomacy and functional regulation of interdependencies merged into the idea of 'international organisation' (Kratochwil and Ruggie 1986), explicitly linked by the assumption that continuous functional cooperation would promote peace. For most of its history,

[1] International governance is understood here very generically as cooperation among states in order to solve political or social problems with a transboundary dimension. Transnational governance means cooperation among states and private actors, or exclusively among private actors, in order to solve political or social problems with a transboundary dimension. For a delineation of the two, see the classic discussion of transnational relations in Keohane and Nye (1971).

[2] The oldest existing functional international organisation is the Central Commission for Navigation on the Rhine. In 1815, the Final Act of the Congress of Vienna established the principle of freedom of navigation on international waterways. Concerning the river Rhine, it called for the creation of a Central Commission 'in order to ensure a precise control of the enforcement of common rules as well as to provide an authority used as a means of communication between riparian States with regard to all aspects of navigation' (annex to the Final Act of the Congress of Vienna, cit exact). The first meeting of the Commission was held in 1816 and, on 31 March 1831, the Convention of Mainz was signed, which provided a set of statutory provisions concerning navigation on the Rhine. The regime was amended in 1868 and is concerned with the freedom of navigation, equal treatment of all boatsmen and fleets, simplification of customs clearance, obligation of Member States to maintain the waterway, uniform regulations for the safety of vessels, etc.

[3] The Universal Postal Union (UPU), established in 1874, sets rules for international mail exchange.

[4] In 1865 the first International Telegraph Convention was signed and the International Telegraph Union (ITU) was established to facilitate subsequent amendments to this initial agreement. The International Telecommunication Union, as it is called today, expanded its regulation with the pace of technical progress to areas such as telephone and radio regulation.

international governance has not been regarded as a problem but rather as a necessity and an achievement. In the field of security, international organisation and international organisations in the plural were regarded as a cure against war, the scourge of humanity. In various functional policy areas they were often framed as the only possible solution to coordination problems arising from international interdependence. To most observers, the crucial question was if, or under what specific conditions, the institutions of governance worked, and not whether they impinged upon national autonomy and democratic self-governance.

A broad academic debate about international governance as a threat to democracy did not start until the 1990s, although the issue had been raised earlier (*cf* Kaiser 1971). This re-framing was built upon two other major changes in perception (*cf* Steffek 2007: 180). First, the notion emerged that international governance was a relationship of domination, rather than a mere effort at coordination. We should recall that until the 1980s many international relations scholars saw international organisations and regimes as handmaidens of hegemonic states (*cf* Krasner 1983). Their debate over international governance centered on the question over whether these institutions were really independent structures of political authority. Only the emergent consensus that international governance institutions had some independent authority and political influence paved the way for diagnosing problems of an international regime's legitimacy and democratic quality.[5]

Along with the acknowledgement that international organisations or regimes had some independent political power came a second reconceptualisation. International governance was not perceived any more as a purely intergovernmental affair but as establishing a direct relationship of authority and subjugation between international organisations and citizens. Citizens, not states, became increasingly regarded as the real addressees of norms and rules negotiated at the international level. This reframing has had repercussions on the question of legitimacy and democracy. If states are both creators and addressees of international rules and regulation, we may speak of a form of self-governance in which legitimacy problems do not really arise. If, however, citizens are affected by rules in whose creation they have not been involved in any meaningful sense, the democratic deficit becomes obvious. This, we should emphasise, is not a question of legal doctrine but a question of popular perception. Over the last 15 years or so much scholarly energy has been invested into a debate over the legitimation of international organisations, such as the

[5] For early statements on legitimacy, see Hurrell 1993; on democracy Held 1995 and Bohman 1999.

European Union, the United Nations or the World Trade Organisation.[6] The focus of that debate was on public international organisations, their constitutions, their institutional set-up, their policy-making procedures, in other words, their organisational shell and bones.

What became somewhat neglected were networks, both intergovernmental and transnational,[7] that often involve many different actors, some public and some private, and may span many different levels of policy-making, from national to global. Network governance tends to escape direct state control that (at least in theory) still exists in 'member-driven' international organisations (see also Oeter in chapter eight). As a consequence, the legitimation argument that international governance is self-governance by a number of national governments and directly accountable to parliaments, does not hold any more. In this chapter we take issue with the complex relationship between transnational network governance and democracy. The goal is not to spell out a comprehensive theoretical account of what a democratic form of network governance would look like. Our aim is much more modest. We seek to highlight the crucial dimensions of governance networks that one would need to study in order to arrive at such a normative vision and, on the basis of that analysis, seek to determine some minimum standards.

This chapter is organised as follows. The next section clarifies our notion of network governance and transnational governance networks. We also specify what we mean by the term 'democracy' and how we apply it to the phenomenon of transnational governance networks. Section C takes issue with the internal functioning of governance networks and discusses the crucial issues of representation and their mode of operation. In section D we turn to the external dimension and discuss the relationship between governance networks and their social environment. In particular, we focus on the external transparency and visibility of networks and the possibilities for citizens to challenge policy choices made by the network. In section E we draw some conclusions regarding minimum standards for governance networks.

II. NETWORK GOVERNANCE AND GOVERNANCE NETWORKS

The suggestion that politics takes place in networks is almost a truism. All political decisions are prepared and formulated in some sort of social network. Even under conventional forms of government, office holders

[6] For an overview of the debate on the EU, see Føllesdal 2006; for global governance Patomäki and Teivainen 2004.

[7] Transnational relations, as opposed to international or intergovernmental relations, are defined as involving at least one non-state actor, see Keohane and Nye 1971.

consult with colleagues, bureaucrats, experts, lobbyists, journalists, spouses, etc. Some of this activity is taking place within the formal structures of government, such as parliament and its committees, but much is informal and invisible to outsiders. The phenomenon of such social networks of policy-making has been described, for instance, in Robert Dahl's celebrated book *Who Governs* (Dahl 1961). However, this is not exactly what is meant by the term governance network today.

The term 'governance network' is an adaptation of the term 'policy network' which has been widely used since the 1970s. The debate about policy networks initially developed in the field of public policy analysis and public administration, but spread into the literature on inter- and transnational governance, especially in the European context.[8] What exactly is a policy network? There are various definitions of the term and also distinct national perspectives on this issue. Börzel identified a common definitional core among them, defining a policy network as

> a set of relatively stable relationships which are of non-hierarchical and interdependent nature linking a variety of actors, who share common interests with regard to a policy and who exchange resources to pursue these shared interests acknowledging that co-operation is the best way to achieve common goals (Börzel 1998: 254).

This definition already illustrates that it is a short way from network to governance: we have a variety of actors with different resources situated in a non-hierarchical relationship and committed to cooperation in support of a common interest. Many definitions of the term 'governance', be it local or global, would also include these elements (Dingwerth and Pattberg 2006). Conceptually speaking, networks and governance are natural friends.[9] While governance is an activity or a bundle of distinct activities, networks are the concrete social structures in which these activities take place.

With regard to the situation beyond the nation state we can distinguish between different types of governance and respective networks. They are distinguished mainly by the status and official affiliation of the actors involved. The traditional form of political decision-making beyond the state was intergovernmental and may be called 'executive multilateralism' (Keohane and Nye 2000: 26). It is 'executive' because it is dominated by national governments and only remotely controlled by parliaments. It is 'multilateral' as many states participate in it on the basis of formal equality and reciprocity (Ruggie 1992). When decisions are taken under this form of governance it happens in a purely intergovernmental way, that is, voting rights are reserved for state representatives and the influence

[8] For an overview see Börzel 1998.
[9] This point is made in exemplary fashion by Rhodes 1996.

of non-state actors is limited to informal lobbying of national delegations. Due to its emphasis on the executive and the fact that it is shielded against parliamentary control and public scrutiny, this form of governance is often described as having a massive legitimacy deficit. Although the term 'executive multilateralism' may evoke images of global conference diplomacy, policy networks exist here and are usually called government networks (Slaughter 2004). In fact, the arguably most influential networks of governance beyond the state are intergovernmental in character, composed of national politicians, bureaucrats, judges and experts (Drezner 2007; Slaughter 2004). Such intergovernmental networks exist alongside or within inter- and supranational organisations.

The second type of governance beyond the state may be called 'participatory multilateralism'.[10] This form of political decision-making retains many of the core features of executive multilateralism. In particular, the 'intergovernmental core' of decision-making remains untouched as voting rights are reserved for state representatives (Kissling and Steffek 2008). Where non-state actors, such as advocacy non-governmental organisations (NGOs) and business associations, are becoming involved here, it is mainly in an advisory role. Their capacity to substantially influence decisions made by governments through these consultative mechanisms is limited, or at least hard to document properly (Friedrich 2008; Dany 2006). However, governance networks that exist under this type typically include non-state actors in a more official and formalised role than in a traditional lobbying scenario.

The third type of governance network may be labelled public-private partnership (PPP). PPPs are a form of joint venture that includes public and private actors. Although most PPPs are mainly geared towards implementing relatively well-specified projects or policies, authoritative decision-making often occurs in that process and non-state actors also have a say in the decision-making process.[11] Thus, private actors can be regarded as true partners in governance, not as lobbyists or advocates. PPPs exist at all levels of politics but have become particularly popular as global partnerships or compacts between public and private bodies (Ruggie 2003). Transnational governance networks of the PPP type are heavily populated by private actors, in particular businesses, and state representatives have lost their dominant status.

A fourth type of governance to be distinguished here is purely private in character and may also be described as transnationalism, or societal self-governance. This term refers to issue areas in which the state has

[10] The term 'complex multilateralism', to denote the same type of governance arrangements, is used in O'Brien et al 2000.

[11] For an overview of transnational PPPs, see Schäferhoff, Campe and Kaan 2007.

never been active or in which it has ceded competencies to private institutions. Under this form of governance, sometimes called the 'new transnationalism' (Dingwerth 2007), private actors replace state representatives as decision-makers. Some organisations beyond the state fall into this category, such as the Forest Stewardship Council or the World Commission on Dams. The political importance of this new transnationalism should probably not be overstated. Nevertheless, private transnationalism represents a new type of governance in that private actors negotiate and implement rules in issue areas that states prefer not to tackle. The four types of governance discussed here are displayed in Table 1 below.

Governance networks exist under all four types of governance shown in Table 1. In the following we will argue that they should be measured to the same standards and criteria, despite the differences in formal status. Generally speaking, the relationship of governance networks with democracy is an uneasy one, no matter if these networks are local, national or global in scope. There are in fact quite contradictory opinions as to whether governance networks constitute a threat to democracy or rather the perfect way of adapting it to complexities of the post-Westphalian age.[12] However, at least in the policy and public administration literature, 'policy networks are usually seen to have enriched democracy in a sophisticated polity' (Greenway, Salter and Hart 2007: 718). On closer inspection we find a number of different reasons given for such a positive assessment. First, the turn from government to governance is often interpreted

Table 1: Four Types of Governance 'Beyond the State'

Type	Decision-making	Image of non-state actors
Executive multilateralism	Intergovernmental	Lobbyists
Participatory multilateralism	Intergovernmental	Advisers
Public-private partnership	Joint	Partners
Private governance	Private	Decision-makers

[12] For an outline of the respective positions, see Klijn and Skelcher 2007; Sørensen and Torfing 2006.

as a move away from command and control to *less hierarchical* forms of decision-making (Kettl 2002: 128).[13] This may open up new spaces for deliberation and cooperation. Second, it is also argued that governance networks are *broader in scope* than traditional legislative and executive bodies and can strengthen participation of citizens and/or stakeholders, that is, those affected by the decisions (Benner, Reinicke and Witte 2004). Due to this broad participation, governance networks can tap into *more bodies of knowledge* and expertise and therefore are able to deliver better solutions to complex problems (Haas 1992). Last but not least, it is argued that governance networks are geared towards *consensus* and therefore feature a deliberative mode of interaction, in which adversarial bargaining is replaced with arguing and attempts at persuasion, fostering trust among participants (Borras and Conzelmann 2007).[14]

In this chapter we seek to systematise this wide array of arguments by distinguishing several features that any analysis of the democratic quality of governance networks would need to look at. How do we identify those dimensions? We are not emanating from any particular institutional model of democracy and we do not argue a priori that the representative or parliamentary institutional form is the best or only way to realise democracy. Nor do we develop criteria with a view to network governance in one particular institutional setting, such as the European Union. Our theoretical point of departure is more abstract. We start from the axiomatic assumption that democracy means to realise the political self-determination of citizens on the basis of equality among individuals. We insist that any assessment of the democratic quality of whatever form of government or governance must relate back to this fundamental idea and hence would need to adopt the citizens' perspective. In principle, this applies also to international and transnational modes of governance. The institutional features of governance networks that we need to study and assess hence would be those that are most directly related to the self-governance requirement and the equality requirement.

The process of democratic governance has two major aspects, which may be labelled input and control. With regard to input, citizens should have a realistic opportunity to make their interests, concerns and values heard and impact the policy process. It is obvious that not every single citizen may be able to directly intervene in global governance. Therefore, some organisation and aggregation of citizens' concerns seems to be indispensable in practice. As democratic equality requires that the

[13] Kettl cautions, however, that many horizontal relationships of governance have not really supplanted the vertical ones, but rather have been added to them.

[14] For a discussion of potential trade-offs between different benefits resulting from participation, see Steffek and Ferretti 2009.

political process is shielded effectively against asymmetries in wealth and power, it must be avoided that one particular social group comes to dominate the process, as we will explain below. The second dimension is about controlling the conduct of persons in power and monitoring the responsiveness of the political institutions to the input made. If we take the combination of self-governance and equality to be the core standard for any form of democratic government or governance, the features of networks to be studied in a critical inquiry would be fourfold:

1. Composition of the network.
2. Quality of deliberation in the network.
3. Accountability of the network to the public.
4. Possibility to contest decisions made in the network.

These four features of governance networks will be discussed in the remainder of this article. While the first two relate to the internal characteristics of a network, the latter refer to the relationship between the network and its environment. The literature on governance networks and democracy has put great emphasis on the first, internal dimension. The external relations of governance networks are not so well studied, especially with regard to networks' accountability to individual citizens rather than states or parliaments.

III. DEMOCRATIC QUALITY OF GOVERNANCE NETWORKS: THE INTERNAL DIMENSION

A. Composition of the Network

The first feature to study when approaching a transnational governance network is its composition. What national and/or sectorial interests are represented in the network? What voices are present during discussions? With regard to membership, governance networks may be usefully divided along the lines of the typology outlined in the previous section. Intergovernmental networks,[15] the type prevalent under *executive multilateralism*, are only populated by members of governments and/or public administration. 'Government networks are largely composed of national government officials, interacting either with each other, or, less frequently, with their supranational counterparts. Those national officials

[15] Intergovernmental networks have been at times distinguished from 'transgovernmental networks', ie those in which members of ministries or national executive agencies are collaborating over extended periods of time. They are often removed from direct supervision by ministers or the diplomatic service. For the distinction and its implications see Risse-Kappen 1995.

are responsible to national constituencies for their domestic and [...] their transgovernmental activities' (Slaughter 2004: 218). In such 'transgovernmental' networks, representation follows national, rather than functional, lines. From a citizens' perspective, a chain of representation via elected members of parliament, who define national interests in the respective issue area, through to the diplomats and experts from public administration who implement them, is assumed. In reality, however, transgovernmental networks easily escape such democratic control mechanisms. As a study on the ratification of the Marrakech Agreement establishing the World Trade Organisation has shown, most national parliaments do not scrutinise even the most important international treaties (Bellmann and Gerster 1996). Why should we assume that they routinely supervise what is going on in transgovernmental networks working on issues of much less salience?

Under *participatory multilateralism*, non-state actors are involved more systematically in the policy process. In the respective governance networks, we therefore find a mix of interested private parties and state representatives, of territorial and functional representation. With regard to the functional side of representation, it is thus crucial that all concerned societal groups are present in such an extended policy network. If, for instance, regulation of hazardous chemicals is at stake in a network, we would expect that not only industry is represented, but also organised labour and groups that promote health and environmental concerns.

In practice, what groups can be present will at least to some degree depend on the rules of access. It has been suggested in this context that '[r]egarding the right to participate, persons/organizations should be entitled to participate depending on their possession of some quality or resource relevant to the substance of the problem that has to be solved' (Gbikpi and Grote 2002: 21). The burden of proof, therefore, is often on the applicant. Many international organisations that consult with stakeholders regulate interest group or NGO access precisely along these lines. In the accreditation procedure, interested groups are required to demonstrate any contributions they could potentially offer. Where membership is selected by gatekeepers, there is always a certain threat of exclusion from governance networks. Societal asymmetries in resource availability, political expertise and capacities of effective self-organisation of private parties become paramount (Schattschneider 1960). As membership often requires previous efforts at societal self-organisation to be demonstrated, there may be biases in who is actually represented in those networks, with particular difficulties affecting diffuse interests, which are harder to organise in society than heavily affected sectoral interests (Olson 1965). In a similar vein, public-private governance networks may exclude the marginalised and the less educated, perhaps even more so than representative political systems, in which the mechanism of 'one citizen one vote' provides incentives for the formation of protest parties. In practice, participatory governance networks may be less hierarchical than government, but just as elite-driven.

This participation problem also seems to apply to stronger forms of private party involvement, such as public-private partnerships, or purely private modes of governance. Enhanced private participation in governance cannot guarantee, and might even pose a threat to, democratic equality. Why should governance networks that aim to include private expertise or resources reach out to disadvantaged societal groups that possess neither? Empirical studies report that representation of developing countries is low in private transnational governance networks, particularly so when participation requires expertise (Dingwerth 2008). The difficulties of public-private or purely private governance networks that rely on voluntary participation to include the unorganised, less educated and materially deprived, is a problem relevant to the democratic quality of governance schemes. Therefore, networks may need to employ specific mechanisms of empowerment for disadvantaged groups in order to become more inclusive.

B. Quality of Deliberation in the Network

The second issue to be studied in any empirical investigation of the democratic quality of governance networks is their internal mode of operation. Our initial normative postulation, widely shared in the literature (*cf* Dingwerth 2007: 31; Borras and Conzelmann 2007; Steffek and Nanz 2008; Gerstenberg and Sabel 2001), is that governance networks ought to function deliberatively. A discussion qualifies as deliberative when it is consensus-oriented and it can be expected that the better argument will win out, irrespective of the social standing and material resources of the speakers involved.[16] Deliberative policy-making can be conceptualised as a cooperative search for the 'best solution', and works on the assumption that this 'best solution' will be discovered only through the communication process. It is often claimed that governance through networks is particularly conducive to deliberative decision-making, or 'arguing'.[17] Governance networks are said to operate more deliberatively because majority decisions are often unavailable (or inappropriate) and consensus is the default goal (Schmitter 2002). In addition, prolonged cooperation in a small group helps to build trust conducive to deliberative policy-making. Where only the better argument counts (and not an

[16] Such a mode of collective decision-making is outlined by Habermas 1984.
[17] For the concept of arguing, see Risse 2000.

actor's resources or threat potential), not only may decisions be of better quality, but deliberative policy-making also functions to protect equality, a key requirement of democracy, as identified above.

However, creating an optimal deliberative process is not an easy task, especially because systematic distortion by power asymmetries poses a challenge to deliberative equality. Even formally inclusive deliberative processes may enact structural biases in which more powerful and socially advantaged actors are able to dominate the processes with their interests and perspectives (Young 2001: 677). In the real world of politics, structural inequality favours agents with greater resources, knowledge, or connections. They can influence deliberation in many ways. Most subtly, agenda-setting or promoting a 'leading discourse' constrains the alternatives that political actors consider in their deliberations. In such cases, a false consensus—or in Habermasian terms, a 'systematically distorted communication' (Habermas 1970: 205)—results, in which deliberation actually masks the reproduction of power and injustice. As Buckinx notices, even inside deliberative forums, 'more attention may be paid, or more credit attributed, to the contribution and opinion of an expert member from a hegemonic power, than to a representative of a Third World state' (Bucknix 2006: 1).

Whether or not discussions in governance networks qualify as deliberation is hence an open, and essentially empirical, question. Studies of the deliberative quality of political discourse have focused either on parliamentary debate (Steiner et al 2004), which can be observed and is well-recorded, or on participatory exercises at the local level (Holzinger 2001: 414). From first studies of intergovernmental and European-level negotiation, we know that arguing and deliberation, at least in the emphatic sense used in political theory, is empirically an exception rather than the rule (Deitelhoff and Müller 2005).[18] In addition, there is good evidence to document the abundance of strategic bargaining and pressuring in global intergovernmental networks (Drezner 2007).

IV. DEMOCRATIC QUALITY OF GOVERNANCE NETWORKS: THE EXTERNAL DIMENSION

A. Accountability of the Network to the Wider Public

Aside from the *internal* characteristics of networks discussed so far, there is another important dimension of the democratic quality of governance networks: the *external* accountability of the network towards the

[18] On the EU, see Yoichiro Usui 2007.

wider public. Numerous scholars have advanced the argument that all transnational governance structures should be monitored and supervised to prevent abuses of power and negative externalities.[19] The problem is embedding governance networks into the wider political architecture, securing control of their proceedings, and making their workings transparent and comprehensible to citizens. 'Networks are based on flexible and functional peer relationships. Their very informality and clubishness, however, invite exclusion and make monitoring and participation by non-state actors and other government officials often difficult' (Raustiala 2002: 24). For lay people at least, the operation of multidimensional policy networks is rather hard to comprehend. Along with geographical distance and language barriers, the emergence of governance networks has blurred the citizens' picture of who is doing what in politics beyond the state. Therefore, '[n]etwork governance obscures the process of and accountability for public policy formulation, decision making, and execution' (Mathur and Skelcher 2007: 235).

In particular, the question of how governance networks are embedded into the wider polity has been critically discussed. In that discussion, however, there is a tendency to frame the public accountability problem as a problem of linkage to hierarchical control by elected politicians (Torfing 2007: 20). The underlying assumption is that supervision by elected bodies is missing most prominently, and that the solution is to restore accountability to parliaments. However, even if such parliamentary supervision could be achieved, it remains questionable whether this would resolve the 'stealth problematique'. If democratic governance is essentially self-governance of the people by the people, then citizens should have the opportunity to be informed and to formulate or revise their opinion on network actions. This is, we submit, the real challenge and conundrum—how to relate governance, especially transnational governance, to processes of public communication that can reach citizens. No matter what version of democracy we subscribe to, whether it is a republican, pluralist or deliberative ideal, self-governance will always and necessarily require reliably informed citizens.

Public accountability, when understood as accountability to the wider public,[20] is central to the functioning of any democratic political system. 'Public accountability is understood as a more informal but direct accountability to the public, interested community groups and individuals' (Sinclair 1995: 225). Hence, public accountability is the accountability of power-holders towards critical questions and commentary arising from

[19] On the EU, see Curtin 1996; Heritier 2003; on the global setting, see Grant and Keohane 2005.

[20] On this point see Steffek 2010.

the public sphere (*cf* Papadopoulus 2007: 477). The democratic rationale behind it is that those who are responsible for decisions can be identified, their contribution to decisions can be clarified, and their conduct effectively monitored by citizens (Benz 2006: 107). Public accountability in this sense is not equal to democratic accountability, which is the more encompassing concept. It should be instead regarded as a necessary element enabling other accountability mechanisms, most importantly elections or judicial review, to function smoothly. It is not an umbrella term, but rather denotes a specific type of accountability relationship that functions through critical debate in the public sphere and that contributes to the broader task of democratic accountability.

How can such a model of democratic accountability, which owes a lot to the national setting, be applied to transnational governance networks? Quite obviously, in the transnational sphere we do not have elections that would provide a solid mechanism of political accountability. Some authors even doubt whether there is something like a transnational public sphere. This issue is so crucial that it needs some discussion. The public sphere is conceived here, with Jürgen Habermas, as 'a realm of our social life in which something approaching public opinion can be formed' (Habermas 1974: 51). It 'can best be described as a network for communicating information and points of view' (Habermas 1996: 360). To understand its role in the democratic political system, it is useful to recall a distinction made by Habermas between the centre of the political system and the periphery. Situated at the centre are the sites of democratic decision-making and judicial review, such as parliaments, governments and the court system. The periphery consists of processes of public communication that surround and 'besiege' the formal institutions of democratic decision-making. This communicative space, in which opinions on governance are formed and demands articulated, develops in civil society, beyond the state and the economy (Bohman 1998). The existence of a non-governmental and not-for-profit realm is therefore essential for the functioning of a democracy. It is here that new issues and concerns arise, and it is here that political routines are challenged (Habermas 1974: 367).[21]

The emphasis on a public sphere is not specific to deliberative theories of democracy, such as Habermas's. Rather, it has a systematic place in many variants of democratic theory.

> There is a close link between theories of the public sphere and democratic theory more generally. Democratic theory focuses on accountability and responsiveness in the decision-making process; theories of the public sphere focus on the role of communication in facilitating or hindering this process (Ferree et al 2002: 289).

[21] See also Peters 1993.

The existence of national public spheres is rather uncontroversial and usually taken for granted. However, a public sphere conceived as a communicative space is not a priori defined by national boundaries but by the boundaries of communication flows. Those can, in theory, transcend national borders, although in practice they may do so only to a limited extent (*cf* Castells 2008: 78; Fraser 2007).

Does a transnational public sphere already exist and can it provide for the critical monitoring and review of governance? Some authors, such as Bohman (Bohman 1998), Eckersley (Eckersley 2007: 329), Germain (Germain 2004: 68) and Payne and Samhat (Payne and Samhat 2004) already see such communicative arenas at work in international politics. It is beyond doubt that important challenges to international governance have arisen from transnational communications. Since the 'battle in Seattle' in 1999, many international organisations such as the World Bank, the World Trade Organisation (WTO) and the International Monetary Fund (IMF) have become subject to critical public review (Kaldor 2000; Steffek 2003; Woods 2000). Public campaigns at least contributed to the failure of the negotiations of the Multilateral Agreement on Investments (MAI) in 1998. In addition, public pressure has been evidently brought to bear in cases of maladministration and abuse of power by officials in international organisations. The resignations of the Santer Commission in the European Union in 1999 and of Paul Wolfowitz as President of the World Bank in 2007 have shown that mechanisms of scandalisation that are part and parcel of public accountability can function on the transnational level. Indeed, the Santer case, which is well researched, has shown that alleged nepotism and corruption in the Santer Commission was debated in the media throughout Europe in very similar terms (Meyer 1999; Trenz 2000). Similar phenomena have been observed in the European discussion about the participation of Jörg Haider's party in the Austrian Government (Van de Steeg 2006: 609). Public media may still be segmented along national and functional lines, but in critical cases transnational mobilisation seems to work. International governance can be exposed to public scrutiny and hence public accountability does exist, at least as ex post review of office holders' conduct.

Another insight that needs to be stressed in this context is that public spheres, whether national or transnational, come in the plural. Habermas introduced the idea of a network of various public spheres as overlapping discursive arenas that, taken together, constitute the public sphere of modern societies (Habermas 1974: 373). An emergent transnational sphere may hence not amount to a unified, or general, public sphere, but rather a segmented patchwork of sectoral publics that are interwoven (Eriksen 2005; Nanz and Steffek 2004). Sectoral publics converge around issues of interest to certain constituencies, and to the extent that these issues are tackled by international governance arrangements, may become genuinely transnational in character.

Thus, it would not be absurd to argue that transnational governance networks should be linked to the emergent global public sphere. They should be transparent, make their documentation available to everyone interested and provide explanation for the choices they make. At the same time we also need to stress that a functioning media infrastructure cannot be provided by the networks themselves. They are dependent upon certain conditions created by organised civil society. The work of civil society, especially of NGOs and transnational social movements, is crucial for the emergence of a public sphere in global politics. The empirical evidence suggests that non-governmental actors play a key role in triggering transnational public debates on global governance, thus rendering international governance more transparent and accountable (Scholte 2004).

Nevertheless, to put such a mechanism of accountability in motion, civil society still faces great challenges. There are, for example, many difficulties in drawing the necessary resources to sustain intensive transnational activism. Non-governmental actors must make use not only of material resources, such as adequate funds, staff, premises, equipment and supplies, but also of political power, substantiated in their relationships with ruling authorities and in their capacity to draw extensive coverage from the mass media, if their initiatives of accountability promotion will indeed reach significant results. When calling for effective transparency, for example, they must either draw on such powers of pressure or hope for benevolent governance network officials so that meaningful information can be disclosed. There is then still a lot of room left for unsympathetic authorities to ignore, belittle or obstruct civil society's efforts to hold governance networks more accountable (Scholte 2004).

These problems reveal a second major issue when considering the suitability of the envisioned mechanism for holding governance networks publicly accountable. As an instrument of accountability, it must not overlook the relationship of power asymmetry (Keohane 2006) between the transnational power-holders and citizens—albeit organised in civil society groups—that it addresses. This is a sensitive issue, for example, when it comes to demanding more transparency from governance networks: one must not forget that networks deploy information as power, and therefore might not be inclined to disclose it freely.

B. Possibility of Contesting Decisions Made in the Network

One of the key characteristics of the democratic mode of governance is the reversibility of political decisions. Within the state, institutionalised avenues for contestation and revision of decisions exist, both political and juridical. In the transnational setting, the question of contestation and reversibility is much more problematic. As consensus is hard to achieve, few actors are willing to reopen negotiations after an agreement has already been reached. What is more, it cannot be taken for granted in the international context that it is possible for citizens or groups to challenge a decision. The empowerment of individuals and groups with *formal means* to trigger the process of public accountability is thus indispensable, especially if transnational governance ought to work on behalf of global common interests, as it is democratically desirable.

In political philosophy, Philip Pettit stresses this point when he argues that in order for public decision-making to track the common interests of those it affects, 'the people individually and collectively must enjoy a permanent possibility of contesting what government decides' (Pettit 1997: 185). His model of contestatory democracy is based on a commitment to the ideal of freedom as non-domination, and envisions a system equipped with means of resilient and stable protection against the exercise of arbitrary power. In this model, a 'critical test of modern democracy is the extent to which opposition is not allowed but nurtured within institutions' (Agnew 2002: 67).

With such concerns in mind, Pettit argues that the touchstone for governance structured as non-domination should be its orientation towards the satisfaction of citizens' common, recognisable interests, and that is the only goal that it ought to pursue; it is the single factor that ought to be allowed to shape the formation and implementation of policies. Therefore, he advises:

> what democratic institutions have to do is, first, to establish an authorial dimension of control for searching out and generating a rich supply of presumptive common-interest policies; and second, to establish an editorial dimension of control for rigorous scrutinizing and eliminating those candidate policies and those modes of policy implementation that do not advance common, recognizable interests (Pettit 2000: 116).

But why should democratic control require both aspects? Its first dimension guards against the risk that attractive policy options to the recognisable common interest go unnoticed and unexplored. However, its second dimension is also indispensable because it guards against, what Pettit calls, false positives (the pursuit of private interests in the realm of policy-making) due to problems such as maladministration (eg neglect, inattention, delay, arbitrariness), bureaucratic corruption and the tyranny of the majority. Contestatory democracy stresses that

> the elimination of domination would require, not just that the people considered collectively cannot be ignored by government, but also that people considered severally or distributively cannot be ignored either. Otherwise put, it would

> require not just that the majority are heard in determining what common, perceived interests ought to be pursued by government, but also that relevant minorities also get a hearing: their politically avowable, perceived interests are not just ignored and flouted (Pettit 1999: 178).

For that reason, editorial control must also be available to subject policies to a rigorous testing and filtering procedure. It must also be exercised by individuals or groups at a non-collective level in order to identify false positives. The benefit of such structure is that it would rule out the factional system of governance that favours special groups, though still allowing for policies that might advance the interests of some with costs to the interests of others.

The implications of the contestatory model to the democratisation of governance networks are manifold. As Pettit explains,

> 'if democracy is a purely authorial and therefore electoral ideal, then democrats are bound to look with a cold, even implacable eye at the growth of international institutions of government. But this conclusion need not be cause for despair. For international institutions need not look so irredeemably anti-democratic under the alternative, two dimensional picture of democracy (Pettit 2005: 15).

Some of the options for contestation at the international level would be to create 'channels of appeal' available to citizens or groups that, *institutionally empowered*, could act against domination. Also, power can be increased dramatically as a climate of public opinion becomes established that can help to keep governance networks in check (see above).

Indeed, contestatory democracy presents some compelling insights for new mechanisms of democratisation of governance networks. However, most importantly, it highlights the necessity of a powerful institutional instrument of review available to the wider public (that is, non-exclusionary) and exercised by individuals or groups at a non-collective level (thus, of an editorial nature) as a crucial condition for guaranteeing democratic legitimacy of governance. Such considerations are particularly pertinent with regard to enriching the mechanism of public accountability by pointing to possible institutional foundations of an empowering 'procedure that forces decision-makers to respond to stakeholders and to publicly justify their actions, similar to parliamentary question times' (Nanz and Steffek 2004: 330). One final issue, when assessing the democratic quality of governance networks is then to investigate to what extent citizens or groups can effectively contest the decisions or recommendations made by them.

V. CONCLUSION

In this chapter we have taken issue with the democratic quality of transnational governance networks. Our aim was not to present a comprehensive model of democratic governance beyond the state, but to identify the crucial dimensions of governance and to highlight the key issues. Our starting point was not any political ideal or tradition, but rather an abstract notion of democracy as a mode of self-governance on the basis of equality. Unlike much of the existing literature on the subject, we adopted a citizen's perspective. We were also careful not to a priori privilege forms of network governance that are formally public over those that are formally private. Starting from this premise, we first distinguished two major dimensions of analysis that are of equal importance. First, there is the internal perspective that focuses on the composition and mode of operation of the network. Second, there is an external perspective, focusing on the accountability of the network to the societal environment and ultimately to citizens.

We then discussed four particular issues that are salient with regard to the democratic quality of network governance: the composition of the network; its mode of operation; its accountability towards the wider public; and the possibility to contest its choices and decisions. First, the composition of the network determines whose voices are heard and whose interests are taken into account. Problems in this respect may include the exclusion of relevant societal groups, or asymmetries in power, resources, or information among participants. With regard to the mode of operation of networks, it is often insinuated that networks are prone to deliberation rather than bargaining, and to cooperative problem-solving rather than adversarial polarisation. This is desirable from the normative point of view. There is, however, little empirical evidence beyond anecdotes that supports this particular advantage of transnational governance networks. Yet, there is hope that with appropriate institutional engineering, and in particular the empowerment of marginalised groups, network governance might be able to approach reasonable standards of inclusiveness and deliberative (e)quality.

The external accountability of governance networks, in contrast, is a real conundrum. Even if networks are inclusive and operate on the basis of deliberation, they cannot qualify as democratic unless they are accountable to the transnational public. This is not the same as being formally accountable to some elected political body at the end of a chain of delegation. Public accountability relates instead to a public sphere of communication in which opinions can be formed, and governance evaluated, by citizens. It demands a public process of communication, transnational in scope, in which governance is exposed to citizens' scrutiny. The conundrum is that the preconditions for public scrutiny can only be partially created by the governance institutions themselves. While institutions of governance can foster transparency and dissemination of information, they are unable to guarantee public debate. In a similar vein, the question of contestation and revision of choices made by networks is a pressing and so far unresolved issue. Many settings of transnational governance seem to have an inbuilt bias towards upholding a consensus that was reached. In addition, there are very few ways for affected citizens or groups to initiate a process of review that would lead, potentially, to a re-thinking and reversal of choices made.

REFERENCES

Agnew, J (2002) 'The Limits of Federalism in Transnational Democracy' in J Anderson (ed), *Transnational Democracy: Political Spaces and Border Crossings* (London, Routledge) 56–72.

Bellmann, C and Gerster, R (1996) 'Accountability in the World Trade Organization' 30 *Journal of World Trade* 31–74.

Benner, T, Reinicke, WH and Witte, JM (2004) 'Multisectoral Networks in Global Governance: Towards a Pluralistic System of Accountability' 39 *Government and Opposition* 191–210.

Benz, A (2006) 'Policy-making and Accountability in EU Multilevel Governance' in A Benz and Y Papadopoulos (eds), *Governance and Democracy—Comparing National, European and Transnational Experiences* (London, Routledge) 99–114.

Berne Convention for the Protection of Literary and Artistic Works (1886).

Börzel, T (1998) 'Organising Babylon. On the Different Conceptions of Policy Networks' 76 *Public Administration* 253–73.

Bohman, J (1998) 'The Globalization of the Public Sphere. Cosmopolitan Publicity and the Problem of Cultural Pluralism' 24 *Philosophy and Social Criticism* 199–216.

—— (1999) 'International Regimes and Democratic Governance: Political Equality and Influence in Global Institutions' 75 *International Affairs* 499–513.

Borras, S and Conzelmann, T (2007) 'Democracy, Legitimacy and Soft Modes of Governance in the EU: The Empirical Turn' 29 *Journal of European Integration* 531–48.

Buckinx, B (2006) 'Global Networks and Global Administrative Law: Ethical Concerns. Paper presented at the annual meeting of the International Studies Association, San Diego, California, USA, March 22, 2006 http://www.allacademic.com/meta/p98079_index.html, 1.

Castells, M (2008) 'The New Public Sphere: Global Civil Society, Communication Networks, and Global Governance' 616 *Annals of the American Academy of Political and Social Science* 78–93.

Coplin, CW (1964) 'International Law and Assumptions about the State System' 17 *World Politics* 615–35.

Curtin, DM (1996) 'Betwixt and Between: Democracy and Transparency in the Governance of the European Union' in J Winter et al (eds), *Reforming the Treaty on European Union—The Legal Debate* (The Hague, Kluwer) 95–121.

Dahl, RA (1961) *Who Governs? Democracy and Power in the American City* (New Haven, Yale University Press).

Dany, C (2006) *The Impact of Participation: How Civil Society Organisations Contribute to the Democratic Quality of the UN World Summit on the Information Society* (Universität Bremen, TranState Working Papers No 43).

Deitelhoff, N and Müller, H (2005) 'Theoretical Paradise—Empirically Lost? Arguing with Habermas' *31 Review of International Studies* 167–79.

Dingwerth, K (2007) *The New Transnationalism: Transnational Governance and Democratic Legitimacy* (Basingstoke: Palgrave Macmillan).

—— (2008) 'Private Transnational Governance and the Developing World: A Comparative Perspective' 52 *International Studies Quarterly* 607–34.

Dingwerth, K and Pattberg, P (2006) 'Global Governance as a Perspective on World Politics' 12 *Global Governance* 185–203.

Drezner, DW (2007) *All Politics is Global: Explaining International Regulatory Regimes* (Princeton: Princeton University Press).

Eckersley, R (2007) 'A Green Public Sphere in the WTO?: The Amicus Curiae Interventions in the Transatlantic Biotech Dispute' 13 *European Journal of International Relations* 329–56.

Eriksen, EO (2005) 'An Emerging European Public Sphere' 8 *European Journal of Social Theory* 341–63.

Ferree, MM, Gamson, WA Gerhards and Rucht, D (2002) 'Four Models of the Public Sphere in Modern Democracies' 31 *Theory and Society* 289–324.

Føllesdal, A (2006) 'The Legitimacy Deficits of the European Union' 14 *Journal of Political Philosophy* 441–68.

Fraser, N (2007) 'Transnationalizing the Public Sphere: On the Legitimacy and Efficacy of Public Opinion in a Post-Westphalian World' 24 *Theory, Culture & Society* 7–30.

Friedrich, D (2008) 'Democratic Aspiration Meets Political Reality: Participation of Organized Civil Society in Selected European Policy Processes' in J Steffek, C Kissling and P Nanz (eds), *Civil Society Participation in European and Global Governance: A Cure for the Democratic Deficit?* (Basingstoke, Palgrave Macmillan) 140–61.

Gbikpi, B and Grote, J (2002) 'From Democratic Government to Participatory Governance' in J Grote and B Gbikpi (eds), *Participatory Governance. Societal and Political Implications* (Opladen, Leske & Budrich) 17–34.

Germain, RD (2004) 'Financial Governance and the Public Sphere: Towards a Global Modality of Governance?' 24 *Policy & Society* 68–90.

Gerstenberg, O and Sabel, C (2001) 'Directly Deliberative Polyarchy: An Institutional Ideal for Europe?' in R Dehousse and C Joerges (eds), *Good Governance and Administration in Europe's Integrated Market* (Oxford, Oxford University Press) 289–342.

Grant, R and Keohane, RO (2005) 'Accountability and Abuses of Power in World Politics' 99 *American Political Science Review* 29–43.

Greenaway, J, Salter, B and Hart, S (2007) 'How Policy Networks Can Damage Democratic Health: A Case Study in the Government of Governance' 85 *Public Administration* 717–38.

Haas, PM (1992) 'Introduction: Epistemic Communities and International Policy Coordination' 46 *International Organization* 1–35.

Habermas, J (1970) 'On Systematically Distorted Communication' 13 *Inquiry* 205–18.

—— (1974) 'The Public Sphere' 3 *New German Critique* 49–55.

—— (1984) *The Theory of Communicative Action*, 2 vols (Boston: Beacon Press).

—— (1996) *Between Facts and Norms: Contributions to a Discourse Theory of Law and Democracy* (Cambridge/MA, MIT Press).
Held, D (1995) *Democracy and the Global Order. From the Modern State to Cosmopolitan Governance* (Cambridge, Polity Press).
Heritier, A (2003) 'Composite Democracy in Europe: the Role of Transparency and Access to Information' 10 *Journal of European Public Policy* 814–33.
Holzinger, K (2001) 'Verhandeln statt Argumentatieren oder Verhandeln durch Argumentieren? Eine empirische Analyse auf der Basis der Sprechakttheorie' 42 *Politische Vierteljahresschrift* 414–46.
Hurrell, A (1993) 'International Society and the Study of Regimes' in V Rittberger (ed), *Regime Theory and International Relations* (Oxford, Clarendon Press) 49–72.
Kaiser, K (1971) 'Transnational Relations as a Threat to the Democratic Process' 25 *International Organization* 706–20.
Kaldor, M (2000) 'Civilising Globalisation? The Implications of the Battle in Seattle' 29 *Millennium* 105–14.
Kennedy, D (1987) 'The Move to Institutions' 8 *Cardozo Law Review* 841–988.
Keohane, RO and Nye, J (1971) *Transnational Relations and World Politics* (Cambridge/MA, Harvard University Press).
—— (2000) 'Introduction' in J Nye and JD Donahue (eds), *Governance in a Globalizing World* (Washington/DC, Brookings Institution) 1–44.
Keohane, RO (2006) 'Accountability in World Politics' 29 *Scandinavian Political Studies* 75–87.
Kettl, DF (2002) *The Transformation of Governance: Public Administration for Twenty-first Century America* (Baltimore, Johns Hopkins University Press).
Kissling, C and Steffek, J (2008) 'CSOs and the Democratization of International Governance: Prospects and Problems' in J Steffek, C Kissling and PN Houndmills (eds), *Civil Society Participation in European and Global Governance: a Cure for the Democratic Deficit?* (Basingstoke, Palgrave Macmillan) 208–16.
Klijn, EH and Skelcher, C (2007) 'Democracy and Governance Networks: Compatible or Not?' 85 *Public Administration* 587–608.
Krasner, S (ed) (1983) *International Regimes* (Ithaca, Cornell University Press).
Kratochwil, F and Ruggie, JG (1986) 'International Organization: a State of the Art on an Art of the State' 40 *International Organization* 753–76.
Mathur, N and Skelcher, C (2007) 'Evaluating Democratic Performance: Methodolgies for Assessing the Relationship between Network Governance and Citizens' 67 *Public Administration Review* 228–37.
Meyer, C (1999) 'Political Legitimacy and the Invisibility of Politics: Exploring the European Union's Communication Deficit' 37 *Journal of Common Market Studies* 617–39.
Nanz, P and Steffek, J (2004) 'Global Governance, Participation, and the Public Sphere' 39 *Government and Opposition* 314–35.
O'Brien, R, Goetz, AM, Scholte, JA and Williams, M (2000) *Contesting Global Governance: Multilateral Economic Institutions and Global Social Movements* (Cambridge, Cambridge University Press).
Olson, M (1965) *The Logic of Collective Action: Public Goods and the Theory of Groups* (Cambridge/MA, Harvard University Press).

Papadopoulos, CY (2007) 'Problems of Democratic Accountability in Network and Multilevel Governance' 13 *European Law Journal* 469–86.

Paris Convention for the Protection of Industrial Property (1883).

Patomäki, H and Teivainen, T (2004) *A Possible World: Democratic Transformation of Global Institutions* (London, Zed Books).

Payne, RA and Samhat, N (2004) *Democratizing Global Politics: Discourse, Norms, International Regimes, and Political Community* (Albany, State University of New York Press).

Peters, B (1993) *Die Integration moderner Gesellschaften* (Frankfurt aM, Suhrkamp).

Pettit, P (1997) *Republicanism: A Theory of Freedom and Government* (Oxford, Oxford University Press).

—— (1999) 'Republican Liberty, Contestatory Democracy' in C Hacker-Cordon and I Shapiro (eds), *Democracy's Value* (Cambridge, Cambridge University Press) 163–90.

—— (2000) 'Democracy, Electoral and Contestatory' in I Shapiro and S Macedo (eds), *Designing Democratic Institutions* (New York, New York University Press) 105–46.

—— (2005) *Two-Dimensional Democracy, National and International History and Theory of International Law Series* (IILJ Working Paper 2005/8).

Raustiala, K (2002) 'The Architecture of International Cooperation: Transgovernmental Networks and the Future of International Law' 43 *Virginia Journal of International Law* 1–92.

Rhodes, RA (1996) 'The New Governance: Governing without Government' 44 *Political Studies* 652–67.

Risse, T (2000) 'Let's Argue! Communicative Action in World Politics' 54 *International Organization* 1–39.

Risse-Kappen, T (1995) 'Bringing Transnational Relations Back In' in T Risse-Kappen (ed), *Bringing Transnational Relations Back In. Non-State Actors, Domestic Structures and International Institutions* (Cambridge, Cambridge University Press) 3–36.

Ruggie, JG (1992) 'Multilateralism: The Anatomy of an Institution' 46 *International Organization* 561–98.

—— (2003) 'Taking Embedded Liberalism Global: the Corporate Connection' in D Held and M Koenig-Archibugi (eds), *Taming Globalization: Frontiers of Governance* (Cambridge, Polity Press) 93–129.

Schäferhoff, M, Campe, S and Kaan, C (2007) *Transnational Public-Private Partnerships in International Relations* (Berlin, SFB-Governance Working Paper Series).

Schattschneider, EE (1960) *The Semisovereign People: A Realist's View of Democracy in America* (New York: Holt, Rinehart).

Schmitter, PC (2002) 'Participation in Governance Arrangements: Is There Any Reason to Expect It Will Achieve Sustainable an Innovative Policies in a Multi-level Context?' in JR Grote and B Gbikpi (eds), *Participatory Governance: Political and Societal Implications* (Opladen, Leske & Budrich) 51–70.

Scholte, JA (2004) 'Civil Society and Democratically Accountable Global Governance' 39 *Government and Opposition* 211–33.

Sinclair, A (1995) 'The Chameleon of Accountability: Forms and Discourses' 20 *Accounting, Organizations and Society* 219–37.

Slaughter, AM (2004) *A New World Order* (Princeton, Princeton University Press).
Sørensen, E and Torfing, J (2006) 'Theoretical Approaches to Democratic Network Governance' in E Sørensen and J Torfing (eds), *Theories of Democratic Network Governance* (Basingstoke, Palgrave Macmillan) 233–46.
Steffek, J (2003) 'The Legitimation of International Governance: A Discourse Approach' 9 *European Journal of International Relations* 249–75.
—— (2007) 'Legitimacy in International Relations: from State Compliance to Citizen Consensus' in A Hurrelmann, S Schneider and J Steffek (eds), *Legitimacy in an Age of Global Politics* (Basingstoke, Palgrave Macmillan) 175–92.
—— (2010) 'Public Accountability and the Public Sphere of International Governance' 24 *Ethics & International Affairs* 45–68.
Steffek, J and Ferretti, MP (2009) 'Accountability or "Good Decisions?" The Rival Goals of Civil Society Participation in International Governance' 23 *Global Society* 37–57.
Steffek, J and Nanz, P (2008) 'Emergent Patterns of Civil Society Participation in Global and European Governance' in J Steffek, C Kissling and P Nanz (eds), *Civil Society Participation in European and Global Governance: A Cure for the Democratic Deficit?* (Basingstoke, Palgrave Macmillan) 1–29.
Steiner, J, Bächtiger, A, Spörndli, M and Steenbergen, MR (2004) *Deliberative Politics in Action: Analyzing Parliamentary Discourse* (Cambridge, Cambridge University Press).
Torfing, J (2007) 'Introduction: Democratic Network Governance' in M Marcussen and J Torfing (eds), *Democratic Network Governance in Europe* (Basingstoke, Palgrave Macmillan) 1–22.
Trenz, HJ (2000) 'Korruption und politischer Skandal in der EU. Auf dem Weg zu einer europäischen politischen Öffentlichkeit?' in M Bach (ed), *Die Europäisierung nationaler Gesellschaften, Sonderheft 40 der Kölner Zeitschrift für Soziologie und Sozialpsychologie* (Opladen, Westdeutscher Verlag) 332–59.
Usui, Y (2007) 'The Democratic Quality of Soft Governance in the EU Sustainable Development Strategy: A Deliberative Deficit' 29 *Journal of European Integration* 619–33.
Van de Steeg, M (2006) 'Does a Public Sphere Exist in the European Union? An Analysis of the Content of the Debate on the Haider Case' 45 *European Journal of Political Research* 609–34.
Woods, N (2000) 'The Challenge of Good Governance for the IMF and the World Bank Themselves' 28 *World Development* 823–41.
Young, IM (2001) 'Activist Challenges to Democracy' 29 *Political Theory* 670–90.

11

Developing Countries: Trapped in the Web of Sustainable Development Governance[1]

JOYEETA GUPTA

I. INTRODUCTION

INTER-STATE, CONSENT BASED treaty negotiations, as a means to bind states to international commitments, is fast becoming a very small subset of the growing governance networks and informal rules that criss-cross modern society. The rules of the game of governance are rapidly changing with shifts in the sites, actors and modes of governance. We are moving towards a global society with a multi-interpretable notion of common but differentiated responsibilities and respective capabilities of countries. These responsibilities are decided at the international and/or national level by governmental and/or non-governmental actors at different sites of governance. These responsibilities may have to be implemented in countries at different levels of development.

These changing rules of the global developmental and environmental governance game have differential impacts on countries within the context of a divided world. This chapter examines in particular how these changing procedures affect the ability of the developing world to engage in governance processes. Its key theme is that procedural equity is challenged by these changing rules and may disenfranchise developing countries.

[1] The author has worked on this chapter as part the Netherlands Organisation of Scientific Research VIDI project on International and Private Environmental Governance: 'Sustainable Development, Good Governance and the Rule of Law' (contract number: 452-02-031). The author thanks the participants at the workshop on Public Law beyond the State: Public Governance Networks and Organizations in the Transnational Sphere (Oñati, 19–20 June 2008) for their comments and, in particular, Dr Gerd Winter for his inspirational suggestions.

Before going ahead, it may be relevant to briefly reflect on the concept of a divided world. There has been and there continues to be a significant gap between the developing and developed world in terms of historical circumstances, natural, social, economic and political resources. This ever-widening gap is likely to be the central theme of international politics in the twenty-first century and will pose the single greatest threat to peace and progress in the world (Roy 1999; Gupta 2002: 130–31) and will be an enduring question for international law and politics (Odumosu 2008; Fakhri 2008). Another feature of this changing world includes the evolving role of and relationships between countries. The post Second World War period was characterised by three blocs—the first, second and third worlds with major ideological dividing lines. Following the demise of communism and the gradual incorporation of east and central Europe into the capitalist enterprise, global attention shifted from security issues to an ostensible commitment to the ideals of environment and development but within the context of an increasingly unipolar world where power relations became gradually skewed.[2] After the September 11 attacks, we have a world divided on religious lines and affiliations, where weak states have become a special focus of global attention. Over the last few years we have witnessed the rise of a multi-polar world (Mansfield 1993),[3] but with a difference. The new rising powers, China, India and Brazil, not only have increasing national income, but also immense poverty and major environmental and social governance challenges within them. They embody in themselves a major 'north-south challenge'. Furthermore, in a post 2008 world, there will probably be major changes in the group of rich countries—some may not emerge unscathed from the aftermath of the current financial crisis. It is easy to hope that this crisis will be a minor hiccup, but the fallout may be devastating for many years to come. This chapter does not, however, focus on the financial crises but will return to this point in the conclusion.

This chapter zooms in on the challenges facing developing countries in general. However, for historical and cultural-religious reasons, the developing world for the purpose of environmental negotiations includes countries that are quite wealthy, such as Singapore, Qatar and the United Arab Emirates. It includes countries that do not belong to the developed world but also do not fit well in the developing world, such as Israel and Brunei (Gupta 2008). In the last few years, Brazil, China and India have been developing rapidly and often form coalitions and negotiate either

[2] The Prime Minister of India in 1994 claimed that some countries were trying to 'create a two-track world, in which a handful of affluent countries will monopolise access to technology and sophisticated weaponry, while the rest of the world is hemmed in by all manner of restrictive regimes and conditionalities' (Rao 1994: 399).

[3] Haass (2008) refers to it as the age of non-polarity.

with Russia as BRIC (Brazil, Russia, India, China) countries or with South Africa as BASIC (Brazil, South Africa, India, China) countries. Although these countries have formed the core of the Group of 77 and China, they are increasingly becoming outliers within the developing country group. This chapter does not address these exceptions to the developing world. It focuses instead on the general governance gap between the rich and poor (countries and people) in the context of a multi-polar world.

Environmental and resource-related challenges are perhaps the single most important substantive issue that bind the countries of the earth together. They present the limits to our exploitation in an effort to enhance our economic welfare. After all, we share one earth. Development processes that do not integrate and internalise environmental costs are likely to have major spillover effects beyond this generation and beyond the state. Such integration and internalisation must also go well beyond a symbolic interpretation to be truly sustainable. While issues like global terrorism come and go on the international agenda, environmental degradation has been rapidly increasing since the industrial revolution and will continue to be on the agenda for centuries to come even if we are able to control or limit the extent to which we pollute. For example, the average sea level is likely to continue to rise for many centuries, and when biodiversity is lost, it is lost forever! The environmental and resource challenge to development will be an enduring challenge for this century.

The globally shared sustainable development agenda is the challenge of environmental degradation to development. The question is whether there is a common agenda. Developing countries are disproportionately affected by environmental problems (UN ESC 2001) and unlike the richer north these environmental problems further exacerbate existing domestic challenges such as high levels of poverty, hunger and disease, as well as rapid population growth. These factors pose enormous challenges to the already poorly endowed governance systems in the average developing country.

This economic disparity between northern and southern countries is coupled with an institutionalised bias in international relations towards northern concerns (Green and Chambers 2006; Gupta 2000 and 2001). Developing countries do not have access to the same quantity and quality of experts and experienced diplomats to help them negotiate at the international level. Furthermore, the majority of the non-governmental organisations (NGOs) and scientific communities that are involved in global governance are based in northern countries, and are perceived as pursuing a northern agenda (Biermann 2002: 297; Gupta 1997 and 2003). These realities negatively affect the ability of developing nations to participate effectively in existing treaty negotiations. In addition to these existing challenges, the global community is now facing changing rules of the governance game.

Given this background, this chapter focuses on the challenges of the changing rules of the governance game, both formal and informal, for developing countries. It addresses the question—how is the changing global legal order affecting the ability of developing countries to participate effectively in the governance of global challenges? It first discusses three key elements of the changing global legal order in five key areas of environmental and developmental cooperation. It presents three characteristics of these elements. It then discusses how these elements and characteristics serve to further disenfranchise developing country states in global governance, while still catching them in the sticky web of governance. This web of governance is inspired by the 'mobius web' discussed by Rosenau as 'rooted in the impetus to employ rules based systems that steer issues through both hierarchical and networked interactions across levels of aggregation that may encompass all the diverse collectivities and individuals who participate in the process of governance' (Rosenau 2003: 396–97). Although this book focuses more on the informal systems of governance, this chapter examines how the combination of formal and informal systems together disenfranchises developing countries.

II. CHANGING RULES OF GOVERNANCE: THE GOVERNANCE WEB

A. Introduction

This section looks at three different types of changes in the rules of global governance that society is witnessing today. It examines the evolution of state consent to administrative regulation; the evolution from single to pluralist sites (including the evolution to multi-level systems of governance) and actors of governance in the context of globalisation; and the evolution to complex hybrid public-private international law systems. Many authors see these changes as part of an integrated shift from government to governance, but I have disaggregated these into three elements in order to be able to identify the impacts of each individually on developing countries. Each of the following sub sections first elaborates briefly on the theoretical reflections in the field, and then discusses empirical developments in different fields of governance. As an example of administrative law, this chapter discusses the climate change regime; as examples of fragmentation/pluralism, this chapter discusses the water, food and pesticide regimes; and as an example of hybrid mergers between public and private legal systems, this chapter looks at the privatisation of environmental resources and the growing merger between public environmental and resource law with investment and commercial law.

B. Evolution to Administrative Regulation

Administrative regulation does not emerge from legislative or judicial sources but from the executive (Kingsbury, Krisch and Stewart 2005). While administrative regulation is an important field in domestic governance and has existed to a large extent at international level through executive decisions of the various UN agencies, the degree to which it has developed in recent years is the focus of substantial attention. Although some see administrative regulation as the sum total of many changes in the sites and decisions of governance (Krisch and Kingsbury 2006), I limit the analysis here to inter-state negotiations or organisations that are rapidly contributing to the development of rules not requiring state consent.

On the one hand, the growth of administrative regulation is both inevitable and necessary. As societies become complex and have dynamic relationships with each other, there is need for regulatory approaches to govern such behaviour and these cannot wait for state approval or consent. Professional and bureaucratic diligence pushes these systems further and further at international level. On the other hand, these systems often lack legitimacy and accountability and that has been the subject of considerable attention in recent years.

An area in which administrative regulation is most developed today is climate change law. Climate change law has an epicentre within the multilateral UN system—the negotiation and implementation bodies set up by the United Nations Framework Convention on Climate Change of 1992.[4] The Convention was adopted in 1992 soon after the negotiating process was launched in 1990. The Kyoto Protocol was adopted in 1997. These two documents are subject to formal state approval. At the same time, several far-reaching decisions are taken by the annual Conference of the Parties to the Climate Convention and the Meeting of the Parties to the Kyoto Protocol. Furthermore, the subsidiary bodies established under the regime, such as the Subsidiary Body on Science and Technological Advice, the Subsidiary Body on Implementation, the Executive Board of the Clean Development Mechanism and several other such bodies, are continuously administering the implementation of the climate change agreements through the development of definitions, elaboration of concepts and subsidiary rules. This continuous process of policy-making has been the subject of considerable legal interest.

[4] However, there are a number of other sites for legal regulation. These sites include unilaterally steered international agreements such as the Asia Pacific Partnership on Clean Development (Karlsson-Vinkhuyzen and van Asselt 2009) and Climate and the International Partnership on the Hydrogen Economy (Sindico and Gupta 2004).

This is referred to by Brunnée as interactional law-making which is supposed to reflect the continuous process of making a network of rules and regulations by subsidiary bodies that are not subject to formal state consent (Brunnée 2002). Hey refers to the process as akin to administrative regulation since '[t]hese new systemic rules have more in common with rules of national systems of public or administrative law than with traditional rules of international law' (Hey 2000). Churchill and Ulfstein find the process a sort of autonomous institutional development (Churchill and Ulfstein 2000). Thus, for example, the most controversial and politically challenging issue is the adoption of targets and timetables for participating nations—and this is subject to inter-state negotiation and state consent. However, in fact, the rules on baselines, methodologies and non-compliance mechanisms are often subject to such administrative processes. These processes may be more significant in the long run than the actual negotiations on the targets.

Thus, the international community is moving away from a system of explicit state consent to a system of implicit state consent in relation to the growing mass of administrative rules. This consent is not an ex post acceptance of what has been decided in national parliaments and their equivalent bodies, but an ex ante implicit delegation of authority to executing agencies. This is likely to be a critical problem for negotiators from the developing countries unless they quickly realise how important such implicit changes discussed in the literature, as well as occurring in fact, are for their countries and how significant it is to send well informed delegates to all relevant meetings and forums. Staying capacity is a key feature of a good negotiation strategy; but is a major shortcoming for most developing country negotiating teams.

C. Evolution to Pluralist Sites and Actors of Governance

Another key shift in global regulation is the shift from multilateralism to pluralist sites of governance with different actors. Within the context of the state, governance is no longer seen as something that is centralised and hierarchical but as resulting from a multi-level system of governance. This can be seen to imply the spread of authority between different distinct jurisdictions that leads to coherent policy or as the dispersion of authority and responsibilities to different jurisdictions and actors that may lead to competing and overlapping policy processes undertaken by different actors. Such authority need not be delegated, but may come into existence as different bodies assume responsibilities in different fields. The literature discusses this trend generally in positive terms. However, this section examines the concept of multi-level governance in relation to the inconsistencies between global policy and national policy;

and the overlapping jurisdictions of different actors at different levels of governance and focuses on the extra-territorial impacts of such multi-level governance processes arguing that domestic actors may use multiple mechanisms to shape the behaviour of extra-national actors to suit their own interests. For example, food policies made within a multi-level governance context has impacts on those who would like to export food.

Governance is also no longer seen as the exclusive activity of state actors, but is the 'the sum of the many ways individuals and institutions, public and private, manage their common affairs. It is a continuing process through which conflicting or diverse interests may be accommodated and cooperative action may be taken' (The Commission on Global Governance 1995: 2). Krahmann's seven-part analytical framework (geography, function, resources, interest, norms, decision-making, and policy implementation) analyses the various shifts in governance (Krahmann 2003). Functional fragmentation is observed in the increasing transfer of capacities to 'functionally specific agents' that were previously reserved for highly centralised agencies. The fragmentation of resources is most evident in their increasing privatisation. Interest fragmentation, Krahmann suggests, has led to a change in the perception of interests at the national level through the abandonment of the notion of the public interest, in favour of policies based on individualism and the market. Krahmann also sees fragmentation in each of the main norms associated with government: there has been a devaluation of the norm of sovereignty and an increased scepticism towards political institutions resulting in a new emphasis on the rule of law and the role of the courts; command and control is no longer seen as efficient or effective and there is a shift towards self-government; and the norm of redistribution has declined and been replaced by the idea that market mechanisms can provide more efficient and effective management. Shifts in implementation can also be seen in the growing popularity of self-enforcement mechanisms and voluntary agreements at the national, regional, and global levels (Kersbergen and Waarden 2001). It is 'law and politics blended together in a new institutional practice of management' (Kennedy 2007: 333–38). Pluralism accommodates different sources and sites of governance without any notion of hierarchy. Some authors see aspects of legal pluralism to be part of global administrative law (Krisch 2006: 247; Krisch and Kingsbury 2006).

Pluralism is seen generally in positive terms as reflecting the shift from government to governance. The more negative side of pluralism is possibly fragmentation—the notion that governance is scattered and fragmented through the system.

Within the multilateral environmental arena, the role of non-state actors has evolved over the last 50 years from actors to be consulted, through elite observers and behind the stage managers; to protected, empowered and engaged partners; to a situation in which they take the law into their own hands (Gupta 2003). The numbers of NGOs and civil society networks have grown at an astonishing rate, with 90 per cent of them emerging only in the last 30 years (Edwards 1999 and 2000). More than 40,000 international NGOs are currently active, along with an additional 20,000 transnational civil society networks. Furthermore, 51 of the world's largest economies are corporations and not states; and the 200 largest corporations have almost twice the economic clout of the poorest four fifths of humanity (Whitman 2002: 45–53). International organisations have also proliferated. It is not clear how these actors will be expected to behave at the international level, how they will be allowed to participate in global governance, what rules they will be expected to follow, who they will be accountable to, or how they will be held to account. Quite often, these bodies make their own rules regarding their role in global governance. There is already evidence of competition among NGOs to exclude other NGOs from international processes (Gupta 2003). The current global financial crisis also shows that the self-governance in the banking world, based on the notion of the 'enlightened self interest' of owners and managers, has led to a spiralling systemic failure in the financial system (Greenspan 2008: 9).

Water governance is an area of pluralism both in international *and* national law. Global water governance is diffuse. UN agencies (eg Food and Agriculture Organisation of the United Nations (FAO), World Health Organization (WHO)), funds (eg Global Environment Facility) and programmes (eg United Nations Development Programme (UNDP), *United Nations Environment Programme* (UNEP)) deal with water. More than 25 UN bodies deal with water; and although coordinated at present by UN Water, the coordination is light. UN water law originated with the request of the United Nations General Assembly (UNGA) to the International Law Commission (ILC) to develop water law. In the meantime, the International Law Association, an academic NGO, developed the Helsinki Rules on the Uses of the Waters of International Rivers in 1966. About three decades later, the UN Convention on the Law of the Non-Navigable Uses of International Watercourses (1997) was adopted (UN Convention 1997). However, this Convention has still to enter into force. Although reflecting the state of water law at the time, it ignored the parallel political development in relation to the relevant environmental, human rights and financial issues (Dellapenna and Gupta 2008). In another forum, the human right to water was adopted in the 2002 General Comment on the Right to Water by 140 countries to the Covenant on Economic, Social and Cultural Rights (General Comment No 15 2002); and the UN Human Rights Council was mandated in 2008 to appoint a special rapporteur for three years on the right to water and sanitation and in July 2010, the UN General Assembly has adopted a Resolution on the Right to Water and Sanitation. These global legal processes complement the existing

400 or so international water agreements between states (Oregon State University 2002), and those adopted under the aegis of the UN Economic Commission for Europe. In addition, there are separate policy processes within UN meetings (at Stockholm 1972; Mar Del Plata 1977; Rio 1992; Johannesburg 2002). However, the most 'noise' if not 'impact' (Gleick and Lane 2005) is being made by the non-UN, state and multi-stakeholder gatherings (at Dublin 1992; at Marrakech 1997; at the Hague 2000; at Kyoto 2003; at Oxacaca 2006 and Istanbul 2009) and expert commissions (eg The World Commission on Dams). Each of these bodies comes up with its own policy statements. These policy processes have often run parallel to the legal processes but have not in any sense obviously fed into them, unlike in other fields of governance. Furthermore, at national level, water governance is highly pluralistic in nature, especially in the developing world with multiple historic influences coexisting in these countries (Gupta and Dellapenna 2009). These multiple processes of governance promote different ideals of governance and create new forms of confusion for developing countries which do not know which forums deserve their undivided attention and which do not.[5]

Observers of the global governance processes on water see that it is a multi-faceted web of interactions (Pahl-Wostl, Gupta, and Petry 2008). This web may be the result of the perceived vacuum in global governance in these fields (Dellapenna and Gupta 2009). The divergence in terms of the issues highlighted in the different fora (equitable utilisation in water law; human right to water in human rights law, water as an economic good through the hybrid organisations) shows that the framing of the issues are very different in each forum. While the water law sphere promotes equitable sharing of water resources between countries, the human rights sphere penetrates within states to promote the right to water and sanitation—a right that increases the level of obligations on states especially with respect to those with low purchasing power. In contrast, the hybrid organisations promote the reduction of state engagement in water management and private sector participation and the profit motive in

[5] Another area of diffuse global governance is energy. Only one UN agency has an exclusive focus on energy (*International Atomic Energy Agency* (IAEA) while at least 16 others work on energy issues every day. One non-UN agency (International Energy Agency (IEA)) also has an exclusive focus on energy and works primarily in the developed world. While there is no global treaty on energy, there is one *United Nations Economic Commission for Europe* (UNECE) treaty on energy and more than 1500 agreements between countries on energy and each of the UN agencies pushes its own agenda. Energy is mostly an issue of national security and countries are unwilling to relinquish control to the international level. At the same time, different energy agencies promote or lobby against large hydro, fossil energy and/or nuclear energy creating no clear message for the developing world. Further, with the rampant promotion of liberalisation in the energy sector, national energy policy is becoming a function of the pressure put on governments by investment agencies and energy multinationals. See also Gupta and Ivanova (2009).

water management. There is evidence of forum shopping by non-state and state actors in order to promote their own specific goals and aid agencies and development banks are often used as vehicles for exporting ideals and ideologies to the developing world (eg Scheumann, Neubert and Kipping (eds) 2008).

Global food governance is another area of pluralist, multi-level and transnational systems of governance. It covers, inter alia, issues ranging from hunger, trade, fish, commodity prices, intellectual property rights and pesticides. It has moved through several stages starting from pre-world war systems that combined mercantilism, colonialism and the idea of comparative advantages. Later, the focus was on state intervention to promote food security in the core countries. In the subsequent period, agriculture was industrialised, food aid was dominant and crops and genetic information were seen as part of the global commons (Pistorius and Wijk 1999: 24; Pistorius 1997). Three decades ago, 'free' trade was marketed. Two decades ago, global commons knowledge was and continues to be privatised. Post 1995, bilateral agreements (north-south and south-south) have provided access to fish in the South; climate change has led to shifts from agricultural land use to bio-fuel production through market mechanisms and consequently food prices are on the rise (Gupta 2004). There is hunger not just in the developing world, but increasingly people in the United States have been queuing up for food aid during the economic recession. Global food governance is dealt with by UN agencies (FAO; WHO; UNDP); trade agencies (World Trade Organisation (WTO); *United Nations Conference on Trade and Development* (UNCTAD)) and World Food Summits; by international treaties (eg International Treaty on Plant Genetic Resources for Food and Agriculture; the Convention on Biological Diversity); by policy decisions (eg FAO's Freedom from Hunger Campaign, 1960, through the World Food Summits and the Millennium Development Goals to the current 2008 summit Declaration in Rome), by food multinationals and retailers.

The visions of each of these relevant agencies and actors are different and the ideological underpinnings often clash. While UN agencies focus on human needs, bank and investment regimes focus on financial stability (eg Structural Adjustment Programmes), trade regimes focus on protecting neo-liberal market ideals, countries on supranational (eg EU Common Agricultural Policy) and bilateral agreements (eg the fisheries agreements), while multinationals and retailers are developing their own policies—all of which create new challenges for the South. Thus, while free trade is promoted by the WTO, the Common Agricultural Policy of the European Union affects the ability of developing countries to market their produce to Europe, despite agreements made at Doha. The bilateral fishing treaties have colonised the fish of the poor for other richer countries in both the North and South. While the Convention on Biological Diversity focuses on ensuring access to genetic resources and guaranteeing benefit sharing, national intellectual property rights regimes are being used to patent seeds and genetic information from the South. The growing privatisation of seeds and genetic information makes it more difficult for developing countries to grow their own food as US companies (have tried to) patent basmati rice, parts of the neem *Azadirachta indica* tree, *karela*, *jamun* and eggplant for specific cures, wheat flour for making chapattis, nans and rotis, even though these have been part of Indian life for centuries (Shiva 2001). Finally, markets in the food sector are not competitive but are increasingly part of a vertically integrated system run by large companies, where most of the world grain trade is run by six companies, coffee by eight companies, coffee and banana by four companies each and these regulate, de facto, food rules in countries.

Pluralism and multi-level governance is also evident in the case of pesticide regulation. At the global level there are different regulations, including the FAO International Code of Conduct on the Distribution and Use of Pesticides, The Rotterdam Convention on the Prior Informed Consent Procedure for Certain Hazardous Chemicals and Pesticides in International Trade and the Stockholm Convention on Persistent Organic Pollutants. At the European Union level, there is a directive regulating the marketing of plant protection products, regulation on pesticide residues and a directive on a framework for Community action to achieve sustainable use of pesticides. In addition, there are activities at the non-state actor level which include the transnational approaches such as the international certification programme of the International Federation of Organic Agriculture Movements (IFOAM) for organic products and of Global Good Agricultural Practice (GAP) for fruits and vegetables. Within countries there are standards for food products adopted by different actors.

Grijp (2008) argues that pesticide regulation consists of:

- — hierarchy-based imposed law within the public law system enforced by public sanctions;
- — negotiation within the market based system leading to civil law rights and obligations and imposed by civil law rights and private sanctions; and
- — consensus-based deliberative rule-making processes leading to voluntary commitments which are enforced by social sanctions.

However, these pluralistic, transnational and multi-level governance processes can have a negative impact on the export potential of the farmers in the developing world. While the larger producers in the developing world may be able to develop the knowledge and capacity to access markets within the European Union, the smaller producers may be unable to cope with the changing forums and levels of rule-making. While states can negotiate within the WTO, they are not able to cope with the evolving transnational systems, as well as the unilateral and voluntary standards adopted within country contexts. Coping with these rules is difficult since each country has its own system of rules; each label has its own requirements and the administrative requirements bring heavy costs.

D. Evolution to Hybrid Public-Private International Law Systems

The evolution to hybrid public-private systems of governance can be seen in how contract and investment law intersects with resource and environmental law. Private international law seeks to provide legal protection for contracts, and investment law seeks to protect investors and their rights in foreign countries.

Environmental and resource governance is increasingly influenced by neo-liberal views which, inter alia, promote private sector participation in dealing with the challenges raised in the different regimes. In the mining and food arenas the private sector has been quite strong for decades. Since 1990, the banks and international declarations have pushed liberalisation in the water and energy sectors and this was also endorsed by the World Summit on Sustainable Development of 2002. In the climate change field, the adoption of the flexibility mechanisms in 1997—joint implementation and the clean development mechanism—have opened the doors for private sector participation and contract negotiation. Recently, the Netherlands has agreed with Latvia to purchase CO_2 emission rights from the latter and this has been undertaken as part of a confidential contract.

Commercial law has always been a separate field of private international law and was generally protected through domestic adjudication processes that were recognised in the contracts. However, past negative experiences with nationalisation and civil unrest in developing countries led companies to push for the protection of the rights of foreign investors in host developing countries. This led to the negotiations on the Multilateral Agreement on Investments within the Organisation for Economic Co-operation and Development (OECD) framework. However, this agreement never materialised into treaty form as a result of protests from specific developed country governments and non-state actors (Werksmann and Santoro 1998). Since then there has been rapid growth of bilateral investment treaties (about 3000) involving more than 150 countries. These are in addition to the 1965 Convention on the Settlement of Investment Disputes between States and Nationals of Other States (ICSID Convention) and provisions in the 1992 North American Free Trade Agreement (NAFTA), the 1995 Energy Charter Treaty, and the 1994 Treaty on Free Trade between Colombia, Mexico and Venezuela. Agencies such as the World Bank, UNCTAD and the Permanent Court of Arbitration are engaged in these in one way or other. These agreements specify the rights of the investors (eg national treatment; most-favoured nation treatment; fair and equitable treatment of foreign investors; compensation for expropriation; dispute settlement mechanisms).

International investment law has come under considerable critique from Southern experts (Sornarajah 2006) and Northern ones who argue that this is perceived as lacking public accountability (Sourgens 2007). When environmental/resource regimes and investment regimes come together, a number of different situations occur. First, public goods become subject to private rules. For example, when a government decides to liberalise the water sector, trade rules imply that it may not discriminate against a potential foreign investor and if the latter gets a contract, the relationship will fall under the rules of private international law, the ICSID agreement and/or the bilateral investment treaties between countries (Gupta 2004). Since these contracts are subject to confidentiality rules, there can be no open social debate about the content of these contracts. Recent examination of several contracts for the Clean Development Mechanism confirms this (Klijn et al 2009). Tecco shows that many water contracts are breaking in the developing world as water prices soar out of the reach of locals (Tecco 2008) and Schouten and Schwartz (2006) argue that this is because water is not an 'economic good' but a 'political good'—a basic necessity and governments can rise or fall on such issues. Tienhaara argues that as countries feel the need to develop new laws on environmental issues which impact on these contracts, they run into trouble as contractors argue that any change in domestic rules amounts to an expropriation of their interests and they must be compensated (Tienhaara 2009). This takes place within confidential arbitration processes or through the threat of arbitration. Developing countries have never really been in favour of investment agreements in general (Sornarajah 2006), but the situation is particularly sensitive where public goods become subject to confidentiality rules in private law contracts.

E. Inferences: The Three Characteristics of the Web of Governance

This section has argued that:

(a) Global governance is changing in a number of resource and environmental issue areas. The dynamics of governance in each issue area is different. What is clear is that there is no neat, circumscribed field of policy-making, but that the core has exploded into multiple initiatives by multiple actors, each claiming legitimacy and authority by virtue of some specific characteristic.

(b) These shifts—the shift towards administrative law; towards pluralism and multi-level governance and towards a merger of public and private international law can be characterised as the web of global governance whose silk threads are often invisible ('unnoticed'—Kingsbury, Krisch and Stewart 2005/2006) but are very strong and very sticky. When one thread breaks, it is easy to make a new thread in any permutation or combination that is seen fit by the more powerful actors in the global governance network.

(c) These changes are not the result of an explicit consensus on the need to change the rules of the game; but are autonomous changes that reflect an implicit neo-liberal, post Fukuyama perception of the core that dominates through the multiple forces of globalisation.

All these factors have an impact on the average developing country that is involuntarily trapped in this web of governance and this is the subject of the following section.

III. DIFFERENTIATED IMPACTS ON DEVELOPING COUNTRIES: THE FLIES IN THE WEB

A. Introduction

Let us then move to an exploration of how developing countries are influenced by the implicit changes in the rules of the game. This section explores the specific features of developing countries in international environmental negotiations; extrapolates the features of developing countries to deal with the different regulatory dimensions; and finally draws some conclusions.

B. The Specific Features of Developing Countries in International Climate Negotiations

Detailed empirical investigations into the behaviour of developing countries within the relatively centralised climate change regime reveal a number of challenges that the current evolution in international law poses to developing countries.

First, there is a growing frustration regarding the right to development, which the developing countries pushed in the debate on the new economic order and which was adopted as a UN declaration in 1986, which has again reared its head in the climate change discussions. Although initially the right to develop was recognised in the climate change treaty, recent literature (Weisslitz 2005; Adams 2003) and the reluctant behaviour of the developed countries to adopt far-reaching emission reduction targets to make room for the emissions of the developing countries appears to question this.

Second, in the 20 years or so since climate change appeared on the legal agenda, the knowledge of developing countries has increased but has not kept pace with the exponential developments in the North. Most of the 150 developing country negotiators (excluding the Organisation of the Petroleum Exporting Countries (OPEC) and Alliance of Small Island States AOSIS) still have a hollow negotiating mandate (Gupta 1997), which is the combined result of ideological dilemmas such as structural imbalance in knowledge between North and South (Kandlikar and Sagar 1999; Chambers 2006), poor knowledge on national costs and benefits of participation, outdated information regarding emissions as evident, for example from the 130 National Communications of developing countries on climate policy; poor pre-negotiation and intra-negotiation preparation (eg Netherlands with 15 million people has 2000 employees in the Ministry of Foreign Affairs; India with 1.2 billion people has 680 employees), and ideological and historical stances rather than a substantive position on issues such as climate change.

Third, this combines into a defensive strategy where negotiators are forced to ad lib and stick to general statements or editorial tinkering of the texts provided to them. This defensive strategy tries to be legitimate by being based on proxy indicators of legitimacy. In other words negotiators make references to precedents established in other fields or in previous meetings in order to create consistency with the national position in other issue areas.

Fourth, although the developing countries negotiate under the umbrella of the G77, the joint resources they can dedicate to climate change related issues is low and poor communication technology and inadequate social capital in many parts of the developing world has implied that they have handicapped coalition-making power. In recent years, the G77 has been chaired by OPEC countries a number of times and this has also hampered the ability of the 138 non-OPEC countries to shape the position of these countries. Together, they tend to have a brittle defensive strategy that is very vulnerable to divide and rule tactics—through word games (eg the use of 'voluntary'); side payments; issue linkages and subtle threats of retaliation (Gupta 2002). All this amounts to a handicapped negotiating power in the multilateral sessions, especially when faced with a well prepared monotheistic US delegation or highly formalised position of the supranational authority of the European Union. This is not just in terms of substantive positions, but mostly in terms of procedural and practical issues (eg numerous side events; multiple negotiating sessions with often only English as the language; round-the-clock sessions; few negotiators and so on). There is thus a structural imbalance in the bargaining process and this is not conducive to problem solving.

Finally, as the 2009 negotiations in Copenhagen demonstrate, the deep distrust of the developing countries about the willingness of the developed countries to lead in reducing their own emissions of greenhouse gases and in providing financial assistance to them was ultimately manifested in the reluctance of these countries to accept the Copenhagen Accord which was only 'noted' by the participants. Furthermore, the changing dynamics of development in the South has meant that some developed countries isolate a few large rapidly developing countries and try to develop agreements with them, further marginalising the remainder of the poorer developing countries.

C. Extrapolation from Climate Negotiations to other Areas: The Impact of Web Governance on Developing Countries

The previous section argued that developing countries are heavily disadvantaged in one single multilateral fora on the complex issue of climate change. This section extrapolates from the empirical evidence in the climate change regime to argue about the possible impacts of a complex web of governance on developing countries; these can be seen as hypotheses that need to be further tested through empirical evidence.

Administrative law and developing countries—the growth of administrative law is evident not just in the climate change field but in a number of different issue areas—for example in the Convention on Biological Diversity and the Convention on Desertification—and this affects developing countries in the following ways. First, the number of subsidiary meetings taking place in a number of different fora makes effective participation difficult for poorer countries because they have fewer human and economic resources, and dedicated research institutes that feed into the policy-making process. Negotiators who reserve their energy only for the Conference of the Parties to different treaties will find it practically impossible to undo months of sequential steps taken in the preparatory sessions. Thus, the legitimacy of the participation process is questionable. Second, the rules that emerge may thus not reflect developing country interests or knowledge. A focus, for example, on best practices and technologies is highly inappropriate for developing countries. What works best in the most sophisticated countries in the world may not work well in developing countries. Reconstructing developing countries in the image of the North without having the basic comparative wherewithal is a major problem. It is not just in the climate field that there is a knowledge imbalance. Bibliometric analysis also shows that key southern challenges in the water area are not necessarily the focus of scientific publications (Zaag, Gupta and Darvis 2009; Gupta and Zaag 2009). Third, these rules nevertheless apply to developing countries and, since they are not based on experiences and knowledge from the developing countries, they may further aggravate domestic problems.

Pluralism and developing countries—the idea of different levels of governance with authority to make decisions may affect developing countries in two ways. First, domestic rules made at different levels of governance and consumer choices influenced by such rules will have extra-territorial impacts in that sellers, and especially small sellers in developing countries, may not be able to meet the different criteria/ rules that apply at different levels of governance and thus may not get access to big markets. Second, the idea of multi-level governance, the virtues of decentralisation and subsidiarity principles are marketed to developing countries as part of the concepts of good governance and liberalisation through aid agencies and development banks. While in theory this is a good idea, in practice there is a strong tendency to suggest 'general solutions' that are not based on an understanding of how countries have actually organised their own systems of governance and what their actual weaknesses are.

The idea of multiple sites and actors of governance affects developing countries in two ways—first it is difficult to concentrate resources in any one forum because other forums may become more important and this implies that developing countries have to spread their limited resources between many forums in order to be able to have some influence on the process. In recent years, the expansion of pluralist legal forums at global level has meant that there are multiple forums dealing with specific issues and forums come and go. For example, intellectual property rights discussions have moved from the World Intellectual Property Organisation (WIPO) to the WTO. Second, some forums may be legal forums that are governed by the Law of Treaties; others may be more ad hoc fora where no specific rules of procedure are applied. This implies that while in some forums the process is to some extent predictable; in others it may not be so predictable; complicating the burden on developing countries. Third, since these are autonomous developments, there may be no question of cascading processes of meetings leading to consensus decisions, but instead there may be declarations that reflect the view of some. The World Commission on Dams is one such body whose legitimacy is highly contested and hence its recommendations are also seen as suspect (Dingwerth 2004). The different bodies that develop have their own, if at all, systems of accountability and whether they actually conform to any notion of good governance is quite questionable. The legality and legitimacy of many of these decision-making processes may be questionable; but they may nevertheless have impact. The legitimacy of the multilateral process gives way to the marketplace of ideas and the law of the market holds; there are buyers and sellers and the most powerful buyers and sellers influence the process. Fourth, ideas and concepts are often marketed by aid agencies and development banks based on their own conviction of what is perhaps a useful solution to another country's problems. Thus, instead of a consensus decision leading to a focus of resources in a particular area, the vision of aid agencies is marketed and supported by their financial resources in the developing world. Apart from China and India that are becoming powerful buyers and sellers, most developing countries will be seriously disadvantaged by this very non-transparent process of governance.

Public-private law merger and developing countries—there are three ways in which this trend will influence developing countries. First, such a merger will make public, political goods subject to private control and hence subject to rules of secrecy and confidentiality, focused on profit-making rather than meeting social goals. This is undertaken through the encouragement of rules that allow for increasing involvement of the private sector in the management of these issue areas following the adoption of liberalisation policy. This can be seen in the water, food and energy arenas and in all three areas litigation is increasingly visible. Second, the most pernicious side effect is that such state investor contracts may lead to policy-freezing in developing countries since the evolution of environmental law tends to create new restrictions on investors and reduce the profitability of their original proposals. Such new policies can be seen as expropriating the property of the investor and the fear of arbitration may push countries to make exceptions that are not in their interest (Tienhaara 2008). Such procedural changes have had substantive impacts as such mergers open up national resources for international exploitation. Years of struggle within the United Nations on the permanent sovereignty over natural resources have lost out to the new wave of neo-liberal capitalism which argues for clear property rights as a means to counter environmental degradation and resource mismanagement. Furthermore, such mergers make national issues subject to international arbitration under private/commercial international law with the entry of foreign investors into domestic markets at high costs. Third, public and commercial international law is becoming more integrated as public international law agreements increasingly call on the private sector to participate in its implementation. Thus, the Climate Change treaties invite private parties to participate in contracts to reduce greenhouse gas emissions. These contracts are mostly governed by investment treaties and are subject to the confidentiality rules of private contracts, as well as refer to (expensive) international arbitration as a way to address disputes arising from such contracts. These can potentially give rise to a range of new problems (Klijn et al 2009).

D. Inferences: Changing Rules and Sovereignty

As the rules of governance change, they affect the relatively newly achieved sovereignty of the average developing country. Following the end of colonialism, developing countries finally gained sovereignty and, as a member of the UN club, received one vote each. However, as systems of governance change to systems that do not require the use of the vote, these countries become increasingly disenfranchised. While international administrative law serves to create law that binds countries even in the absence of explicit state consent, pluralism serves to create confusion. While multi-level governance systems show how national and supra-national policies have spill-over effects in other parts of the world, the merger of public and private international law serve to demonstrate how intrusive governance systems have become as companies can sue states in international arbitration courts.

While sovereignty may be seen as a relic of the past for many post-modern scholars, the fact is all states elect their own governments based on the principle of sovereignty. States have their own fiscal systems and governments are accountable to their citizens. Where neo-liberalism has implied that the state must become smaller and only set the stage for industry to function and while this may function effectively in the context of the richer, administratively more advanced countries, this is unlikely to be the case in the poorer countries. Most developing countries have weak states and the combination of neo-liberalism and the new rules of governance only serve to further disenfranchise them.

These trends have different dynamics in different issue areas, are invisible but sticky and are the result not of a negotiated consensus but of an autonomous marketing of neo-liberal views. Developing countries have been involuntarily trapped in this web. The interests of the developing countries tend to fall in the cracks of global regulation (regulatory gaps); while the interests of the developed countries and dominant global actors tend to fall into the category of regulatory overlaps.

IV. CONCLUSIONS

This chapter set out to understand how the changing rules of the governance game affect developing countries in terms of procedure. It reached the following conclusions.

The web of governance today has three features—the development of administrative law; the development of legal pluralism and multi-level governance (merging international with municipal law), as well as legal approaches developed by non-state actors; and the merger of public and private law. The changes in these rules are not the result of negotiations and open discussions between all concerned, taking into account the perspectives of all parties, but the result of autonomous processes in a marketplace of ideas about governance where the most powerful ideas and actors push their way to the front line of decision-making.

Each resource/ environmental issue area displays different permutations and combinations of each of these changes. While climate change governance is a classic case demonstrating the development of administrative law, water, food and pesticide governance display characteristics of legal pluralism/ fragmentation. These thematic areas are increasingly subject to liberalisation and while sometimes diffuse systems of governance have led to private sector participation (eg in water and energy development), in other cases centralised systems within multilateral negotiations have led to the merger of public and private law.

Even within the classic case of interstate negotiation governed by the law of treaties, we can see that developing countries are struggling to participate effectively. In previous papers, I have highlighted how complicated the formal negotiations have become in subject areas where a variety of disciplinary sciences are relevant, and where multiple meetings held simultaneously, supplement or even displace decision-making within formal plenary sessions, have tended to disenfranchise developing countries (Gupta 2006). The relatively new changing rules of governance come over and above the existing complications in negotiation processes and have resulted in multiple negative effects on poorer countries as shown in the following table.

Developing countries are getting increasingly disenfranchised as a result of the global systems of governance (Green and Chambers 2006). While neo-liberalism allows a greater role for corporations, the UN Global Compact does not really enforce compliance, and corporate social responsibility is left to the companies in the absence of momentum on international agreements on controlling these corporations (Usui 2006). Woodward argues:

> If the main players continue changing the game, subverting the rules or simply ignoring them to maximize their own self-interest whilst augmenting harm to the majority 'other' and the human environment, the Western-extolled 'rule of law' will become meaningless, and all humanity will be imperiled (Woodward 2006).

However, the growth of administrative law, pluralistic governance, and the merger of public-private law are a necessary consequence of addressing the expanding nature of global problems and is consistent with neo-liberal ideologies and a polycentric polity possibly calls for pluralism. However, reconceptualising global law

> could face political challenges: an international order based on individual and economic rights may be too close to Western, liberal conceptions to be universally acceptable. Emphasizing the organizing role of state sovereignty may prove superior in coping with the challenge of diversity (Kingsbury, Krisch and Stewart 2005: 51).

Although Kennedy argues that there is nothing new about the changing rules of governance, that such changes have occurred many times during

Table 1: Impacts of Different Features of Governance on Developing Countries

Feature of governance	Characteristics	Impact on procedural aspects
• Administrative law.	Neither legislative, nor judicial.	Legitimacy and application of rules of procedure are questionable.
		'Consensus' rules may not reflect DC contexts.
		'Consensus' rules may aggravate domestic problems.
• Legal pluralism.	In terms of multiple levels of governance within government bodies.	Domestic rules have extra-territorial impacts on DCs.
		The export of multi-level governance, small government, decentralisation and subsidiarity through aid agencies and development banks pierces the veil of sovereignty to suggest how countries should manage their systems without first understanding them.
	In terms of multiplicity of actors and sites of governance.	Multiple forums make it difficult for developing countries to concentrate their limited resources on any one fora; forum shopping possible by more powerful countries.
		No minimum rules/law of treaties apply in many fora. Legality questionable.
		No rules of consensus; market of ideas.
		Accountability, legitimacy, legality, transparency, effectiveness, efficiency, equity questionable.
		Ideas marketed by aid agencies and banks; not always supported by global political consensus.
• Public-private law merger.	Strengthening public law or privatising public law.	Public, political goods are transformed into private, economic goods subject to private control (including secrecy, confidentiality and profit motives; eg in water).
		State policy may be frozen through the threat of arbitration (eg in mining issues).
		In implementing obligations under a public international law, countries and local actors may be inadvertently and involuntarily sucked into contracts governed by international commercial law (eg in climate change).

the last century, and that while some Europeans focus on constitutionalism, Americans on administrative regulation and pluralism and developing countries on third world approaches to international law, he agrees that the fundamental questions which drive Third World Approaches to International Law (TWAIL) are still legitimate ones, namely, how is domination and inequality—whether economic, cultural or political—reproduced in the world and how does this affect law and how might a legal intellectual in the peripheral situation respond to this (Kennedy 2007)? This chapter hopes to have made a modest contribution to that debate.

Finally, although the theme of this chapter has been that developing countries are increasingly caught in a sticky web of governance with no easy exit in sight; developed countries too are getting 'stuck'. French realisation of the potential impact of the Multilateral Agreement on Investment (MAI) on French policy helped them to successfully pull the plug out of the MAI negotiations. US realisation on the impacts of liberalisation on the steel sector led the United States to re-engage in steel protectionism. But increasingly, these countries are getting caught in the web and are unable to effectively limit, for example, the outsourcing of work to other parts of the world. While in areas like food and water governance, it may be possible to ignore the poor most of the time, in climate change governance ignoring the poor will backfire on the North. Neo-liberal approaches if not effectively balanced by state control and non-compliance mechanisms will lead to a laissez faire approach in which we may all drown.

However, there is a silver lining. The current economic crisis which involves the most powerful banks and companies, where self-regulation was increasingly the order of the day, is now subject to new rules. Tim Gaitner, US Treasury Secretary, recently said 'our system failed in basic fundamental ways' and what is needed is not 'modest repairs at the margin but new rules of the game' (Braithwaite 2009: 2). If the global community is in a mood to appreciate the need to revamp the stronghold of global power (its banks, investment and financial rules), there may be a window of opportunity to revisit the procedural inequities that developing countries are facing as a result of the new global sustainable development governance system.

REFERENCES

Adams, TB (2003) 'Is there a Legal Future for Sustainable Development in Global Warming? Justice, Economics and Protecting the Environment' 16 *George Town International Environmental Law Review* 77.

Biermann, F (2002) 'Strengthening Green Global Governance in a Disparate World Society: Would a World Environment Organization Benefit the South?' 2 *International Environmental Agreements: Politics, Law and Economics* 297.

Braithwaite, T (2009) 'Geuthner Flags 'New Rules to the Game' *Financial Times* 27 March.

Brunnée, J (2002) 'COPing with Consent: Law-Making Under Multilateral Environmental Agreements' 15 *Leiden Journal of International Law* 1.
Burght, NMJ (2010) *The Contribution of International Fisheries Law to Human Development* (Amsterdam, Vrije Universiteit thesis).
Chambers, WB (2006) 'Developing Country Scientists and Decisionmaking: An Institutional Perspective of Issues and Barriers' in JF Green and WB Chambers (eds), *The Politics of Participation in Sustainable Development Governance* (Tokyo, United Nations University Press).
Churchill, RR and Ulfstein, G (2000) 'Autonomous Institutional Arrangements in Multilateral Environmental Agreements: A Little Noticed Phenomenon in International Law' 94 *The American Journal of International Law* 623.
Committee on Climate Change (CLIM) IP/A/CLIM/IC/2007-111, Institute for European Environmental Policy (IEEP) and Ecologic, Briefing number 631-715.
Dellapenna, J and Gupta, J (2008) 'Toward Global Law on Water' 14 *Global Governance* 437.
—— (eds) (2009) *The Evolution of the Law and Politics of Water* (Dordrecht, Springer Verlag).
Dingwerth, K (2004) 'The Democratic Legitimacy of Public Private Rule Making: What Can We Learn from the World Commission on Dams?' 11 *Global Governance* 65.
Edwards, M (1999) *Future Positive: International Cooperation in the 21st Century* (London, Earthscan).
—— (2000) *NGO Rights and Responsibilities: A New Deal for Global Governance* (London, Foreign Policy Centre).
Fakhri, M (2008) 'Law as the Interplay of Ideas, Institutions, and Interests: Using Polanyi (and Foucault) to ask TWAIL Questions' 10 *International Community Law Review* 455.
General Comment No 15 (2002) 'The Right to Water, Substantive Issues Arising in the Implementation of the International Covenant on Economic, Social and Cultural Rights UN Economic and Social Council' UN Doc E/C.12/2000/11 (26 November).
Gleick, PH and J Lane (2005) 'Large International Water Meetings: Time for a Reappraisal 30 *Water International* 410.
Green, JF and Chambers, WB (eds) (2006) *The Politics of Participation in Sustainable Development Governance* (Tokyo, United Nations University Press).
Greenspan, A (2008) 'We Need a Better Cushion against Risk' *Financial Times* 27 March.
Grijp, Nvd (2008) *Regulating Pesticide Risk Reduction: The Practice and Dynamics of Legal Pluralism* (Amsterdam: Vrije Universiteit Thesis).
Gupta, J (1997) *The Climate Change Convention and Developing Countries—From Conflict to Consensus?* (Dordrecht, Kluwer Academic Publishers).
—— (2004) *(Inter)national Water Law and Governance: Paradigm Lost or Gained?* (Delft, UNESCO-IHE Institute for Water Education).
—— (2008) *Engaging Developing Countries in Climate Change Negotiations* (Brussels, European Parliament, Study for the European Parliament Study for the European Parliament's Temporary).
—— (2001) 'Legitimacy in the Real World: A Case Study of the Developing Countries, Non-Governmental Organisations and Climate Change' in

JM Coicaud and V Heiskanen (eds), *The Legitimacy of International Organizations* (Tokyo, United Nations University Press).
—— (2002) 'The Climate Convention: Can A Divided World Unite?' in J Briden and TE Downing (eds), *Managing the Earth: The Eleventh Linacre Lectures* (Oxford, Oxford University Press).
—— (2006) 'Increasing Disenfranchisement of Developing Country Actors in a Multi-Speed World' in JF Green and WB Chambers (eds), *The Politics of Participation in Sustainable Development Governance* (Tokyo, United Nations University Press).
—— (2000) 'North-South Aspects of the Climate Change Issue: Towards a Negotiating Theory and Strategy for Developing Countries' 3 *International Journal of Sustainable Development* 115.
—— (2003) 'The Role of Non-State Actors in International Environmental Affairs' 63 *Heidelberg Journal of International Law* 459.
—— (2004a) 'Global Sustainable Food Governance and Hunger: Traps and Tragedies' 5 *British Food Journal* 406.
Gupta, J and Dellapenna J (2009) 'The Challenges for the Twenty First Century: A Critical Approach' in J Dellapenna and J Gupta (eds), *The Evolution of the Law and Politics of Water* (Dordrecht, Springer Verlag).
Gupta, J and Ivanova, A (2009) 'The Challenge of Global Energy Governance' 2 *Energy Efficiency* 339 (published online).
Gupta, J and Zaag, Pvd (2009) 'The Politics of Water Science: Unresolved Water Problems and Biased Research Agendas' 9 *Global Environmental Politics* 14.
Haass, RN (2008). 'The Age of Non-Polarity: What will follow U.S. dominance' *Foreign Affairs* May/June.
Hey, E (2000) 'The Climate Change Regime Sustainable Development and International Administrative Law in the Making' 1 *INEA* 75.
Karlsson-Vinkhuyzen, SI and van Asselt, H (2009) 'Introduction: Exploring and Explaining the Asia-Pacific Partnership on Clean Development and Climate' 9 *INEA* 195.
Kandlikar, M and A Sagar (1999) 'Climate Change Research and Analysis in India: An Integrated Assessment of a North-South Divide' 9 *Global Environmental Change* 119.
Kennedy, D (2007) 'The TWAIL Conference: Keynote Address' 9 *ICLR* 333, 338.
Kersbergen, K and Waarden, F (eds) (2001) *Shifts in Governance: Problems of Legitimacy and Accountability* (The Hague, Netherlands Organization for Scientific Research).
Klijn, A-M, Gupta, J and Nijboer, A (2009) 'Privatising Environmental Resources: The Need for Supervision' 18 *Review of European Community and International Environmental Law* 172–84.
Kingsbury, B, Krisch, N and Stewart, RB (2005) 'The Emergence of Global Administrative Law' 68 *Law and Contemporary Problems* 15.
Krisch, N (2006) 'The Pluralism of Global Administrative Law' 17 *European Journal of International Law* 1.
Krisch, N and Kingsbury, B (2006) 'Introduction: Global Governance and Global Administrative Law in the International Legal Order' 17 *European Journal of International Law* 1.

Mansfield, ED (1993) 'Concentration, Polarity, and the Distribution of Power' 37 *International Studies Quarterly* 105–28.

Odumosu, IT (2008) 'Challenges for the (Present/) Future of Third World Approaches to International Law' 10 *International Community Law Review* 467.

Oregon State University (2002) *Atlas of International Freshwater Agreements* (Nairobi, UNEP).

Pahl-Wostl, C, Gupta, J and Petry, D (2008) 'Governance and the Global Water System: A Theoretical Exploration' 14 *Global Governance* 419.

Pistorius, R (1997) *Scientists, Plants and Politics: A History of the Plant Genetic Resources Movement* (Rome, International Plant Genetic Resources Institute).

Pistorius, R and Wijk, J van (eds) (1999) *The Exploitation of Plant Genetic Information: Political Strategies in Crop Development* PhD Dissertation (Amsterdam, University of Amsterdam).

Rao, PVN (1994) *Selected Speeches* (New Delhi, Government of India Publications Division) vol II.

Rosenau, JN (2003) *Dynamic Proximities: Dynamics beyond Globalization* (Princeton, Princeton University Press).

Roy, AN (1999) *The Third World in the Age of Globalization: Requiem or New Agenda* (Delhi, Madhyam Books).

Scheumann, W, Neubert, S and Kipping, M (eds) (2008) *Water Politics and Development Cooperation: Local Power Plays and Global Governance* (Dordrecht, Springer Verlag).

Schouten, M and Schwartz, K (2006) 'Water as a Political Good: Implications for Investments' 6 *INEA* 407.

Shiva, V (2001) *Protect or Plunder? Understanding Intellectual Property Rights* (London, Zed Books).

Sindico, F and Gupta, J (2004) 'Moving the Climate Change Regime Further Through a Hydrogen Protocol' 13 *Review of European Community and International Environmental Law* 175.

Sornarajah M (2006) 'A Law for Need or a Law for Greed' 6 *INEA* 329.

Sourgens, FG (2007) 'ICSID Arbitration and the Importance of Public Accountability of a Private Judicature—A Roman Law Perspective' 9 *ICLR* 59.

Tecco, N (2008) 'Financially Sustainable Investments in Developing Countries Water Sectors: What Conditions could Promote Private Sector Involvement?' 8 *INEA* 129.

The Commission on Global Governance (1995) *Our Global Neighbourhood* (Oxford, Oxford University Press).

Tienhaara, K (2009) *The Expropriation of Environmental Governance: Protecting Foreign Investors at the Expense of Public Policy* (Cambridge, Cambridge University Press).

UN Convention on the Law of the Non-Navigational Uses of International Watercourses (IWC) (1997) UN Doc A/51/869; 37 ILM 719.

UN ESC (2001) *Combating Poverty: Report of the Secretary General* E/CN.17/2001/PC/.5.

Usui, M (2006) 'Business-Society Interaction towards Sustainable Development—Corporate Social Responsibility: The Road Ahead' in JF Green and WB Chambers (eds), *The Politics of Participation in Sustainable Development Governance* (Tokyo, United Nations University Press).

Weisslitz, M (2005) 'Rethinking the Equitable Principle of Common but Differentiates Responsibility: Differential Versus Absolute Norms of Compliance and Contribution in the Global Climate Change Context' 13 *Foreign Affairs Colorado Journal of International Environmental Law and Policy* 473.
Werksman, J and Santoro, C (1998) 'Investing in Sustainable Development: The Potential Interaction between the Kyoto Protocol and the Multilateral Agreement on Investment' in WB Chambers (ed), *Global Climate Governance: Inter-linkages between the Kyoto Protocol and other Multilateral Regimes* (Tokyo, Global Environmental Information Centre).
Whitman, J (2002) 'Global Governance as the Friendly Face of Unaccountable Power' 33 *Security Dialogue* 1.
Woodward, BK (2006) 'Global Civil Society and International Law in Global Governance' 9 *ICLR* 247, 355.
Zaag, Pvd, Gupta, J and Darvis, P (2009) 'Urgent Water Problems are not Sufficiently Researched' 6 *Hydrology and Earth System Sciences* 1411.

Index

Printed by Libri Plureos GmbH in Hamburg,
Germany

9 781841 132228